Rock Music in American Culture

Rock Music in American Culture
The Sounds of Revolution
SECOND EDITION

ROBERT G. PIELKE

McFarland & Company, Inc., Publishers
Jefferson, North Carolina, and London

LIBRARY OF CONGRESS CATALOGUING-IN-PUBLICATION DATA

Pielke, Robert G., 1942–
Rock music in American culture : the sounds of revolution / Robert G. Pielke. — 2nd ed.
     p.   cm.
Includes bibliographical references and index.

ISBN 978-0-7864-4865-4
softcover : acid free paper ∞

1. Rock music — United States — History and criticism.
2. Rock music — Social aspects — United States — History.
I. Title.
ML3534.P53 2012   781.660973 — dc23   2011045870

BRITISH LIBRARY CATALOGUING DATA ARE AVAILABLE

© 2012 Robert G. Pielke. All rights reserved

No part of this book may be reproduced or transmitted in any form or by any means, electronic or mechanical, including photocopying or recording, or by any information storage and retrieval system, without permission in writing from the publisher.

Front cover images © 2011 Shutterstock

Manufactured in the United States of America

McFarland & Company, Inc., Publishers
Box 611, Jefferson, North Carolina 28640
www.mcfarlandpub.com

For Jan, who still believes in magic;
for Karen, who still imagines;
and for Emily, the girl with the faraway eyes

Table of Contents

Acknowledgments ix
Preface 1
Introduction: America's Cultural Revolution 5

Part One. Music and Culture — 9
1. Rock Music and Contemporary American Culture — 11
2. What Is Rock Music? — 15
3. A Suggested Typology — 23

Part Two. Medium and Message — 63
4. Radio: The Creation of a New Community — 67
5. Records: The Newest Testament — 80
6. Film: A Creative Tension — 92
7. Television: Bringing It All Back Home — 105
8. The Internet: You Say You Want a Web-o-lution — 120

Part Three. Revolution and Revelation — 135
9. Elvis and the Negation of the Fifties — 142
10. The Beatles and the Affirmation of the Sixties — 155
11. Dormancy and the Re-creation of the Interim — 174
12. The Counter-Reaction and Defense — 193
13. The Re-actualization and Rebirth — 223

Epilogue: The Shape of Things to Come 232
Chapter Notes 243
Bibliography 246
Index 249

Acknowledgments

"All Shook Up." Words and music by Otis Blackwell and Elvis Presley. Copyright © 1957; renewed 1985 Elvis Presley Music (BMI). All rights for Elvis Presley Music administered by Cherry River Music Co. International copyright secured. All rights reserved. Reprinted by permission of Hal Leonard Corporation.

"All You Need Is Love." © 1967 Sony/ATV Music Publishing LLC. All rights administered by Sony/ATV Music Publishing LLC, 8 Music Square West, Nashville, TN 37203. All rights reserved. Used by permission.

"Baby, Let's Play House." Written by Arthur Gunter. Copyright © 1954 (renewed) by Embassy Music Corporation (BMI), Excellorec Music, a division of AVI Music Publishing Group, Inc. Administered worldwide by Embassy Music Corporation. All rights for LPGV Music administered by Bug Music. International copyright secured. All rights reserved. Reprinted by permission of Hal Leonard Corporation.

"Ballad of a Thin Man." Written by Bob Dylan. Copyright © 1965 by Warner Bros. Inc.; renewed 1993 by Special Rider Music. All rights reserved. International copyright secured. Reprinted by permission.

"The Boxer." Copyright © 1968 Paul Simon. Used by permission of the publisher, Paul Simon Music.

"Do You Remember Rock 'n' Roll Radio?" Words and music by Douglas Colvin, Jeffrey Hyman and John Cummings. © 1980 WB Music Corp. and Taco Tunes, Inc. All rights on behalf of Taco Tunes, Inc. administered by WB Music Corp. All rights reserved. Used by permission of Alfred Music Publishing Co., Inc.

"English Boys." Words and music by Deborah Harry and Chris Stein. Copyright © 1982 Chrysalis Music and Monster Island Music. All rights administered by Chrysalis Music. All rights reserved. Reprinted by permission of Hal Leonard Corporation.

"God." © 1978 Lennon Music. All rights administered by Sony/ATV Music Publishing LLC, 8 Music Square West, Nashville, TN 37203. All rights reserved. Used by permission.

"Honest Lullaby." Words and music by Joan Baez, published by Gabriel Earl Music. Used by permission.

"I Dig Rock and Roll Music." Words and music by Paul Stookey, James Mason and Dave Dixon. © 1967 (renewed) Neworld Media Music Publishers. All rights administered by WB Music Corp. All rights reserved. Used by permission of Alfred Music Publishing Co., Inc.

"Johnny Soul'd Out" by Brian E. O'Neal. © 1980 WB Music Corp. and Maitre D'Music. All rights reserved. Used by permission of Alfred Music Publishing Co., Inc.

"Johnny Soul'd Out" © 1980 Maitre d Music Publishing, Warner/Chappell Music. All rights on behalf of Maitre d Music Publishing, Warner/Chappell Music, administered by Maitre d Music Publishing, Studio City, CA 91604. All rights reserved. Used by permission.

"New Day Woman." Words and music by Alastair McKenzie, Suzi Quatro and Leonard Tuckey. Copyright © 1975 Finchley Music Corp. Copyright renewed. Administered by Music & Media International. International copyright secured. All rights reserved. Reprinted by permission of Hal Leonard Corporation.

"No Guilt." Written by Chris Butler. Copyright © Merovingian Music. All rights for Merovingian Music controlled and administered by Spirit One Music (BMI). International copyright secured. All rights reserved. Used by permission.

Acknowledgments

"Post World War Two Blues." Words and music by Alistair Stewart. Copyright © 1973 Gwnyeth Music Ltd. Copyright renewed. All rights controlled and administered by Universal-Polygram International Publishing, Inc. All rights reserved. Used by permission. Reprinted by permission of Hal Leonard Corporation.

"Respect" by Kevin O'Neal. © 1980 WB Music Corp. and Garcon-Music. All rights administered by WB Music Corp. All rights reserved. Used by permission of Alfred Music Publishing Co., Inc.

"Revolution." © 1968 Sony/ATV Music Publishing LLC. All rights administered by Sony/ATV Music Publishing LLC, 8 Music Square West, Nashville, TN 37203. All rights reserved. Used by permission.

"Sgt. Pepper's Band." Words and music by Joan Baez, published by Gabriel Earl Music. Used by permission.

"Sweet Survivor." © 1978 Sony/ATV Music Publishing LLC, Mann and Weil Songs Inc., Silver Dawn. All rights on behalf of Sony/ATV Music Publishing LLC and Mann and Weil Songs Inc. administered by Sony/ATV Music Publishing LLC, 8 Music Square West, Nashville, TN 37203. All rights reserved. Used by permission.

"Sweet Survivor." Words and music by Peter Yarrow, Barry Mann and Cynthia Weil. © 1978 (renewed) Silver Dawn Music (ASCAP) and Sony/ATV Songs LLC (BMI). All rights reserved. Used by permission.

"Twelve Thirty (Young Girls Are Coming to the Canyon)." Words and music by John Phillips. Copyright © 1967 Universal Music Corp. Copyright renewed. All rights reserved. Used by permission. Reprinted by permission of Hal Leonard Corporation.

"Up Against the Wall Redneck Mother." Words and Music by Ray Wyle Hubbard. © 1974 (renewed 2002) Tennessee Swamp Fox Music Co. All rights controlled and administered by EMI Blackwood Music Inc. All rights reserved. International copyright secured. Used by permission. Reprinted by permission of Hal Leonard Corporation.

"Wasted on the Way." © 1982 Nash Notes. All rights administered by Sony/ATV Music Publishing LLC, 8 Music Square West, Nashville, TN 37203. All rights reserved. Used by permission.

"Willie, Waylon and Me." Written by Deborah Coe. © 1993 Showfor Music (BMI) 100%. Administered by Bluewater Music Services Corp. Used by permission.

"Won't Get Fooled Again." Words and Music by Peter Townshend. Copyright © 1971 Towser Tunes, Inc., Fabulous Music Ltd. and ABKCO Music, Inc. Copyright renewed. All rights for Towser Tunes, Inc. administered by Universal Music Publishing International MGB Ltd. All rights for Universal Music Publishing International MGB Ltd. in the U.S. administered by Universal Music—Careers. International copyright secured. All rights reserved. Reprinted by permission of Hal Leonard Corporation.

Preface

In the years following World War II, something vital and original was born in the restive caldron of American culture. Its mother was the diverse population of descendants of former slaves struggling to survive in a hostile social and political atmosphere. Its father was the equally diverse and primarily rural underclass of dispossessed Whites striving to avoid poverty. Its infant voice came from the fields of the old south and the hills of Appalachia. It was a plaintive voice yet it yearned for something better, often only a better hereafter. As it matured and sought its own future in the towns and cities further up the Mississippi and in the rapidly industrializing megalopolis of the east coast, it found new ways of expressing its voice. It also found a way to harmonize the uneasy juxtaposition of attitudes and feelings of it parents. At that moment the voice of this vital and original something came fully into its own. It was insistent, loud and bawdy and it finally had a name. It was rock and roll.

There have been numerous, worthy accounts written about the history and character of this music, but little if anything has been done to understand it as a phenomenon. Such an understanding requires certain conceptual tools in order to avoid merely blathering off the top of one's head. And there are many tools available. The ones I've used are those I encountered throughout the various stages of my academic career. And I think they work exceptionally well. The result is an analysis from — for better or worse — a varied philosophical perspective. Not everyone will agree that the tools I've used are appropriate, and not everyone will agree with my overall assessment. That is to be expected and even encouraged. My goal is not to convince anyone of the absolute truth of my analysis — there is no such thing. My goal to provide a clear and coherent understanding of *how* I see this phenomenon as well as *what* I see. So it is a subjective appraisal, as all such appraisals are, whether or not they are acknowledged as such. It's how *I* see the phenomenon of rock music in American culture, and I see it as the varied sounds of revolution.

One advantage I have is the fact that I was there at the beginning — not the absolute beginning, of course — but at certain symbolic beginning points. And I noticed what was happening. Years later, when I set about to put it all down in writing, I recalled these junctures. And at that point I had acquired the tools to make sense of what I remembered ... and what I was continuing to experience.

That first remembrance took the form of the book *You Say You Want a Revolution: Rock Music in American Culture*, published by Nelson-Hall in 1986, while I was teaching courses in philosophy and religious studies at George Mason University. While at the time it was considered somewhat out of the mainstream for academic scholarship, nevertheless, even its most ardent detractors have long since recognized the significance of rock music as a cultural phenomenon. Still, to this day, there have been few, if any, sustained, consistent, and holistic philosophical appraisals. Yet, clearly, something is still happening, and we won't know what it is without an ongoing fundamental analysis.

The first version of this phenomenological account owed a lot to the following: Jan Pielke, whose editorial work, financial support, commitment to the project, and willingness to endure the various revolutions in our respective careers provided all the necessary conditions for the manuscript's completion; Karen Pielke, who kept me in touch with a generation to whom the torch has been passed; Debra Bergoffen-Lanman, without whom there would have been neither the courage nor the self-confidence to pursue my philosophical interests in popular culture in general and rock music in particular; Larry Houlgate and Dan Rothbart, whose collegiality was both personally and professionally invaluable; the many students at George Mason University who accepted me as a fellow human being in the classroom, the cafeteria, and the Rathskeller; those folks I came to know in Shipping and Receiving at the Huntley Bookstore of the Claremont Colleges in California; Geri Thomson, whose typing of Part One was not entirely in accordance with university policy; and copyeditor David J. Deal, who also designed the first book.

The rock and roll phenomenon did not cease after the publication of that first book, of course. It is an on-going, living phenomenon and a new, updated version is long past due. Inspiration for writing *Rock Music in American Culture: The Sounds of Revolution* came primarily from two sources: my daughter Karen (who for years has pointed to elements in the book that she found alive and well in the music of her generation) and my brother Roger (who for years has noted how many libraries had my book in their collections). Both stressed that America — nay, Western civilization itself — needed the first book to be updated. Then, when a hiatus appeared between the publication of the first book in my science fiction/alternate history/time travel trilogy and its first sequel, I decided that doing an updated version was a fairly decent way of keeping me off the streets at night.

As you can imagine, it was a major undertaking, in essence, to add twenty-four years into the mix, and do so in a way that preserved the essential thesis and point of view of the original. Momentous events have occurred in our culture in the interim — computerization, the Internet, 9/11, several controversial wars, financial crises, the election of the first African-American president, a financial meltdown, the "Tea Party" movement, the "Occupy Wall Street" protests — and all of this against the musical backdrop we call rock and roll.

Aside from adding significantly to most of the chapters throughout, especially the chronology in Chapter 3, I created a completely new chapter devoted to the Internet and have a revised ending. I hope that all of this will be sufficient to reintroduce the book to classrooms in popular culture and music history where it once had a very happy home. I hope as well that it pleases those who enjoyed the first book outside of the academic setting. The book was, and continues to be, intended for everyone.

Two reviewers on the opposite ends of the spectrum deserve special "shout-outs" of appreciation. First, Richard Koenigsberg, Ph.D., in his review of the first book noted, "This is one of the most accurate and significant books ever written describing the impact of rock 'n' roll as a cultural form that worked to transform American culture."[1] With a comment like that, I could do no less than yield to the call for an update. Second, I should also give credit to one of my reviewers who was not terribly pleased with the first edition.[2] After all, were it not for his (I think) profound misunderstanding of my thesis and approach to the subject of rock music in American culture, I may have rested my case and travelled, without looking back, wistfully into writing quirky satires and alternate history/science fiction/time travel trilogies.

Americans have a need to take a critical look at themselves — where we are, where we have been and where we are going as a culture. I, of course, remain convinced that we have been, and still are, proceeding into the future in the midst of a cultural revolution.

Introduction: America's Cultural Revolution

> I hold it that a little rebellion, now and then, is a good thing.
> — Thomas Jefferson

> You say you want a revolution
> Well you know
> We all want to change the world
> You tell me that it's evolution
> Well you know
> We all want to change the world
> But when you talk about destruction
> Don't you know that you can count me out ... in
> Don't you know it's gonna be alright
> — The Beatles

As I was passing as unconsciously as possible through one of humanity's most insidious institutions, junior high school, something dramatic yet subtle was taking place in my teenage consciousness. I didn't recognize it for what it was at the time. Nobody did. But it was happening to all of us just the same. It didn't take long for the adult world to tell us what it was, however, and they weren't very happy. They called it primitive, African, the work of the devil, communistic, filthy, smutty, and obscene. We called it rock and roll. We were both right.

Today, with almost sixty years of hindsight available, the whole thing seems relatively clear, and, if possible, even more provocative than at its inception. What my fellow sufferers and I were experiencing was the beginnings of America's first genuine cultural revolution. This statement may seem exaggerated for two seemingly contradictory reasons. First, we've always been taught that America's war of independence from England was a true revolution, something of an exaggeration in itself. Second, and more important, we're reluctant to give up the American myth of a slow and steady (but inevitable) progress toward an earthly perfection. Americans have always tolerated many more disagreements over the nature of their goals than over how they could be achieved. The process was expected to be rational, well ordered, and continuous, though some small conflicts were probably inevitable. So even to suggest the possibility of a cultural revolution in America must appear not only factually absurd, but blasphemous as well. Revolution is as heretical a doctrine in America as abolishing the monarchy would be in England.

Nevertheless, despite the overwhelmingly conservative assumptions of most Americans, we are in fact in the throes of a genuine and dramatic revolution in our culture, and it behooves us to understand it before passing judgment. Others have tried, but, for one reason or another, have failed. Although still provocative, the optimistic retrospectives of Theodore Roszak and Charles Reich lacked the perspective to appreciate fully the magnitude of the period. Like all instant analyses, theirs found an equally instant oblivion as events overtook them. They were too anxious, too optimistic, too certain, and, without a doubt, too doctrinaire to make their case. Instead of providing an insightful and relatively unbiased overview, *The Making of a Counter Culture* (1968) and *The Greening of America* (1970) themselves quickly became artifacts of the period — interesting curiosities but not the kind of assessments from which we could learn something. Learning only takes place when it's possible to confront unpleasant as well as pleasant facts. Their impatience to celebrate a victory for the counterculture, I think, blinded them to the realities of historical change. Impatience rarely gets the job done.

Studies that were more recent failed for different reasons, and Morris Dickstein's *Gates of Eden: American Culture in the Sixties* is a case in point. Although seemingly able to muster up an adequate historical perspective (published in 1977), he apparently was seduced by the temptations of facile "decadization." In some of his more perceptive moments, he does recognize that history does not align its movements with the tens digit. Yet with no fully developed theory of historical change at his disposal (unlike Roszak and Reich, both of whom adopted a quasi–Hegelian-Marxian dialectic), he produced little more than a documentation of the period. He thus lacked the capacity to see the Sixties in their overall context. He did, however, employ a provocative methodological procedure — namely, the notion that history can be understood most profitably through its cultural manifestations. He opted for literature, and in so doing I think he was fundamentally mistaken. The most revealing cultural artifacts change as technology and human whims change, a fact of considerable significance, which he seemingly ignored. It is not literature but music which opens up our recent past (and hence our present and future). His single chapter on contemporary music is so severely circumscribed in its timeframe as to be worthless if not seriously misleading. Literature held sway during the first half of the twentieth century, but since the mid–Fifties, it's been nothing less than rock and roll.

Harris Wofford's massive study *Of Kennedys and Kings: Making Sense of the Sixties* was similarly flawed, but even more so. He lacked Dickstein's cultural perspective, for one thing, preferring to see history through the actions of "great men." Further, he too saw the Sixties as a virtually isolated unit, as though chunks of time existed independently of our designating them as such. However, most distressing was his omission of the music of this period. There was only one reference to The Beatles, for example, and this came only in conjunction with references to Bob Dylan, Jimi Hendrix, and Janis Joplin.

A more accurate understanding of what's happening must take into account the phenomenon of rock music as a fundamental ingredient of contemporary American culture. Moreover, if the claim that we are in the throes of a cultural revolution is to make sense, we first have to examine the nature of such upheavals. Identifying their common features may be tricky, but it should help us to recognize a cultural revolution if one should happen to show up. In the summer of 1954, in a little recording studio in Memphis, Tennessee, one showed up — and America hasn't been the same since.

There are at least six characteristics shared by all cultural revolutions. It should become obvious how they are exemplified in contemporary American culture — and exemplified, more than anything else, by rock and roll. First, they embody a fundamental challenge to the prevailing values. I don't mean by this that all existing values are rejected. As far as I know, this has never happened nor is it likely to. I'm referring to the ultimate values on which all other values are based and from which they derive their justification. Just as important, the way these values are known and justified is also placed under attack. Revolutionaries not only put forward conflicting values, they also replace the epistemological scheme.

When Billy Ward and the Dominoes sang "Sixty Minute Man," established beliefs about race, sex, and the entire puritan work ethic were attacked. When Little Richard sang anything, we were introduced to an entirely new way of experiencing life. And when John Lennon sang "Imagine," we were introduced to uncomfortable new ideas about nations, war and religion.

A second common feature, obvious but not usually recognized for its true significance, is the fact that cultural revolutions are never rapid. They take many years to develop, come to fruition, and have effect. Generally, their true beginnings are recognized as such only after several significant and highly visible events have occurred. In other words, cultural revolutions may be discernible only because of hindsight. Be this as it may, they certainly involve considerable complexities, and their workings are obviously a central concern of this book.

Closely tied to this is a third feature, that cultural revolutions inevitably produce strong Counter-Reactions. Often misunderstood as entirely new movements, they are actually revitalized, renewed, and strengthened manifestations of the established order. As such, they are an intrinsic part of the revolutionary process as a whole, and they provide the revolution with its greatest threat. With the election of Ronald Reagan as president in 1980, the Counter-Reaction in America began. It continues to this day.

A fourth feature is implicit, but it needs to be specified in order to correct a common misconception. Cultural revolutions are not merely political. Governmental institutions are altered to a greater or lesser extent, but only as a result of more fundamental changes. Thus, a revolution that aims only at political changes (as did the one in eighteenth-century America) is not a cultural revolution. Actually, the "disturbance" in America during the 1860s came much closer. Only years after its inception did we see anything hinting at rock's political implications. Unlike the folk protest movement of the early 1960s, rock's target was more basic.

An even more serious misconception is the belief that revolutions are necessarily and/or inevitably violent. Hence, the fifth observation is simply that violence is not an intrinsic component of cultural revolutions. This is not to say that violence is lacking. Some violence is always present, of course, but so too is violence present in non–revolutionary periods. As will become evident later, it was precisely the nonviolent element in rock that was most effective in purveying the new set of values.

The sixth and final characteristic is more substantive and certainly more controversial: Cultural revolutions, as such, always tend toward an expansion of individual freedom. How this idea is expressed will obviously differ, depending largely on the ways in which the status quo is understood to inhibit freedom. Yet no matter what its particular historical formulation, a revolutionary ideology will always express more confidence in the individual's capacity for self-regulation and governance than does the established order. This, in turn, is based on a conflict between two primal assumptions regarding humanity, one confident and the other pessimistic. The relatively pessimistic ideology of the established order is confronted by the relatively optimistic ideology of the revolutionaries, and this in turn is eventually confronted by a rejuvenated version of the pessimistic one. To put it another way, opposites are intrinsically related; in every affirmation, there is an implicit negation. So a cultural revolution is necessarily predicated on that which it so fervently rejects.

In the Fifties, rock and roll seemed clearly anarchistic to its detractors, a fact confirmed in the Sixties and reconfirmed today. Advocates have never disputed this. Rather, disagreements have concerned the value of this degree of freedom. As a goal in progress, perhaps only to be approximated in reality, anarchy has always been an essential component of rock and of America's cultural revolution. Yet without the established order to begin with, this anarchistic ideal would have had no context in which to thrive. Moreover, without the resulting conflict, our two *Voyagers,* launched in 1977, would not now be carrying with them into the vast emptiness of the galaxy the voice of Chuck Berry singing "Johnny B. Goode, Johnny B. Goode tonight."

In the 1980s, the advocates of traditional values were embodied in the presidency of Ronald Reagan and given a voice by the apostles of the religious right. Beginning in 1979 with the Rev. Jerry Falwell's Moral Majority and continuing with Pat Robertson's Christian Coalition in 1987, these and similar organizations provided ample opposition to the reassessment of fundamental values — a reassessment intrinsic to rock music.

Pat Buchanan took up the mantle in the 1990s with a vengeance. Although now happily ensconced, it seems, as a political commentator for MSNBC, he has not lost his fervor for warning against threats to traditional values. His speech in 1992 to the Republican Convention, wherein he gives prominence to the term "Culture War," is considered a landmark in the battle to preserve the old order. (Wikipedia has a copy and it is readily available and republished in many forms virtually everywhere.) He warned his audience that enemies are afoot in America today wanting to make radical changes. He has frequently amplified his comments on his websites, the American Cause and Right from the Beginning. Here's a taste:

> But it is not the kind of change America wants. It is not the kind of change America needs. And it is not the kind of change we can tolerate in a nation that we still call God's country.... There is a religious war going on in our country for the soul of America. It is a cultural war, as critical to the kind of nation we will one day be as was the Cold War itself ... we must take back our cities, and take back our culture, and take back our country.[1]

Buchanan's portents of disaster for America continued well into the 2000s, with his arguments in various speeches and publications that some Americans inhabit a moral universe different from his and his followers. Another organization voice, Peter Beinhart, writing in 2009 for the Council on Foreign Relations, warned against the seductive lure of Barack Obama's crusade for change. He feared that Obama might actually bring about an end to the culture war and hence capitulate to the enemy. Also in 2009, Bill Donohue's *Secular Sabotage: How Liberals Are Destroying Religion and Culture in America* brought conservative Catholics and evangelical Protestants into the fray.

The cultural revolution, in other words, is as real today as it ever was. On this point, if no other, Pat Buchanan and I fully agree. He and the other defenders of traditional values might also agree that a cultural war is the appropriate conceptual context for an understanding of that phenomenon we've come to call rock music. No wonder many parents of the 1950's "flipped their lids" when their teenagers brought those first forty-fives into their respectable, middle-class homes. Although neither those teenagers nor the adult world knew it at that time, they were being incited to rebellion. It wouldn't be the last time. But today, those downloading and listening to music on their iPods or programming Pandora radio on their computers are no longer in the dark. They are aware of what's going on. They know that they are "foot soldiers" in America's ongoing culture war.

Part One
MUSIC AND CULTURE

> Our age does offer many horrible proofs of the daemonic power with which music may lay hold upon an individual, and this individual, in turn ... may ... grip and capture a multitude, especially women ... by means of the all-disturbing power of voluptuousness.
>
> — Søren Kierkegaard

> Well bless my soul, what's wrong with me?
> I'm itchin' like a man on a fuzzy tree.
> My friends say I'm actin' wild as a bug.
> I'm in love — I'm all shook up.
> — Elvis Presley

It is hardly necessary to argue for a relationship between music and culture, but the closeness of this relationship should be emphasized. John Blacking in his exceedingly provocative book *How Musical Is Man?* points out that "no musical style has 'its own terms': its terms are the terms of its society and culture, and of the bodies of the human beings who listen to it, and create and perform it." His is a musicological approach, but it's more than a mere study of music. For music is a "relatively spontaneous and unconscious process. It may represent the human mind working without interference, and therefore observation of musical structures may reveal some of the structural principles on which all human life is based."[1]

Susanne Langer, in *Philosophy in a New Key*, makes a similar claim. For her, "a work of art expresses a conception of life, emotion, inward reality. But it is neither a confessional nor a frozen tantrum; it is a developed metaphor, a non-discursive symbol that articulated what is verbally ineffable — the logic of consciousness itself." In particular, "music can reveal the nature of feelings with a detail and truth that language cannot approach."[2]

Of course, the music I have in mind is not just any old music; it's rock and roll music. But the closeness of the relationship still holds. David Pichaske, in *A Generation in Motion*, notes the following:

> A product of the new technology against which both the music and the Sixties rebelled, which both it and the Sixties took for granted, pop music is the most accurate reflection of the generation in motion. Folk, country, soul, but most of all rock are not merely a record of the new age, they were the age in all its multiplicity.[3]

What this means, of course, is that a cultural analysis can be conducted by means of a musicological analysis. The key, I think, is in the fact that music is an immediate and unreflective expression of consciousness, totally unlike the deliberate, self-conscious creations of ideology. This truth holds for rock music as well as for all other kinds. So, an investigation into the nature of rock music will inevitably tell us something about the culture from which it has originated — ours.

I should say something about the nature of rock music and how it is related to American culture. Many people have done this in a variety of ways, but what follows, I think, is a unique attempt. It culminates in Chapter 3's suggested typology, and while there is no category for the demonic per se, it should adequately illustrate the extent to which many people have been all shaken up.

1

Rock Music and Contemporary American Culture

In order to defend my claims that America is in the midst of a cultural revolution, and that this is best apprehended through an appraisal of rock music, the many interrelationships among culture, the arts, music, and revolution have to be thoroughly explored. I am convinced that music not only reflects cultural consciousness but also participates in creating, stabilizing, and changing it. If culture (and consequently cultural change) is the creation of our consciousness, then it's essential for us to know how this creative and re-creative process works. Only then will we be able to assess the peculiarities of present-day American culture and deal with the possibilities of a cultural revolution.

We can all agree on some things. First, artistic expressions are manifestations of culture. We can also agree that by examining artistic expressions we should be able to determine whether or not a revolution is in progress and, if so, its ideological tendencies. Finally, we can agree that these indirect, non-discursive expressions are more revealing than ideological writings and the like. In short, a cultural-artistic analysis is the best way to acquire this knowledge. It may even be the only way.

But why should we consider rock music to be more revealing about contemporary American culture than any other artistic expression? In answering this, we should keep in mind the following:

1. Arts and culture are dialectically related; the arts reveal the status of culture by expressing its fundamental values. Thus, artists can both reflect and re-create cultural consciousness — unpredictably and often unknowingly.

So it is with rock music, which reflects as well as brings into being a particular state of consciousness. More often than not, this occurs unintentionally. One of the most dramatic illustrations of this tendency is the creation of an "outlaw consciousness," which I'll discuss in Chapter 4.

2. Technological innovations (invented means for accomplishing chosen ends) stem from what humans value; that is, their ultimate goals determine the selection or creation of means. Conversely, these various technological means can affect the kinds of values that people hold and how widely they might be disseminated.

The desire to maintain (or create) a stable and reasonably peaceful, albeit economically competitive, society has made the relative uniformity of ideological convictions among Americans essential. From this has followed the encouragement of improvements in mass communication. Without underestimating the role of the individual inventor, the impetus for developing certain kinds of technology has depended very much on positive social support. Conversely, numerous innovations, culminating in the radio, recording instruments, motion picture photography, television, and a variety of other electronic marvels, have had effects unforeseen by their original supporters. Aside from ensuring greater conformity, these new and highly influential media have informed the vast and complacent middle class about the existence of America's social outcasts. Not only was the extent of their plight revealed dramatically and forcefully to an extensive audience for the first time, but their basic values were also shown to differ radically from those of the majority. Most important for our purposes, the enormous numbers of post–World War II adolescents had revealed to them the hitherto unknown consciousness of Blacks and poor White southerners through their music. The result: an unavoidable internal conflict between tradition and experience, the values they had been taught and the values they were encountering. The tension, as everyone who grew up then can remember, was explosive.

3. All artistic expressions are at least partially explainable in terms of available technology (or technique). Innovations make new kinds of expressions possible, but only insofar as artists choose to adopt them. Unlike virtually every other kind of musical expression, rock music has developed around electronic innovations. Although not definable as simply the result of this technology, rock music has nevertheless made such effective use of it that it's hard to imagine nonelectric rock. Simon and Garfunkel's "Sounds of Silence" on their first album was acoustic and pure folk; later, when electrified, it became a folk-rock classic.

4. The popularity of an artistic expression depends on its capability for reflecting or re-creating the consciousness (and thus the ideological commitments) of a mass audience. Using all of the electronic media, rock music has had the unquestioned capacity to appeal to (or create) a mass audience from the very beginning. The radio and the newly developed 45 rpm records, both comparatively inexpensive, were ideal means. Exploiting them to the fullest would come later, but the potential was obvious to everyone, including those whose only or main interest was personal profit. These varied devices for the creation of music and its propagation through modern mass communication were available for all musical expressions, yet only one chose, or perhaps could choose, to make successful use of them. Is rock music, therefore, no more than a media creation? In some way, it might be suggested that the nature of this music is intimately tied up with electric guitars, amplification, light shows and multimedia concerts. I agree, but this misses a more fundamental point: popular music must appeal to popular ideological convictions in order to be popular. It can't be created ex nihilo, relying only on modern technology in the service of greed (as was alleged during the payola scandals). With the conversion of White middle-class youths to a consciousness sympathetic to that of the social outcasts, a mass audience was brought into being that was responsive to rock music and only rock music. Obviously, the media had an impact, but they would have availed nothing had there not been a receptive audience. Technology didn't create this audience; in a very real sense, the audience created the technology.

5. While all artistic expressions reveal something about the culture in which they exist, the most effective one in doing this at any particular time will be the most popular one. It would be superfluous to point out that rock and roll has by now inundated the very meaning of popular music. In 1954, only the Crew Cuts' sanitized cover of the Chords' "Sh-Boom" in the top ten hinted at what was to come. By 1956, however, four of the ten were clearly rock and roll. Then, in 1959, despite the fact that many of the founding figures were tragically forced out of the game, you had to search down as far as number twenty-one before hitting a non-rock song. This trend has continued, and in increasingly varied ways.

6. Popular art, when irreconcilably in conflict with the art preferred by those holding social and political power (that is, elitist art), represents a revolutionary set of values. Until the inevitable Counter-Reaction, and the resulting conflict with an unpredictable outcome, this revolutionary art will necessarily be the most culturally revealing. (In its rejection of elitist values, it will — necessarily and paradoxically — express them at the same time.)

Though its meaning may be rigorously disputed, it simply cannot be ignored that rock and roll challenged and replaced a very different kind of music, relegating it to the status of total obsolescence in a matter of one or two years. Neither can the fact that, initially at least, a generational differentiation was involved. It is no accident that the term "generation gap" originated in the early 1960s, but this highly overstressed and under-reasoned term pointed to a mere superficiality. What really happened was a clash of fundamental values, although few would have articulated it in this way. Things are much clearer now, and the term is used far less.

Because rock music was initially in the position of negating the prevailing values, it necessarily had to exhibit the very values it opposed. When pleasure and sex, for example, were put forward as positive values in and of themselves, deliberately intended to replace the established values, we can rather easily infer the tenor of the prevailing values. Moreover, sex and pleasure as ultimate values would never have assumed such significance had they already been morally acceptable. Hence, in a paradoxical way, the values of rock music are contingent on the very values they reject.

7. Art that expresses revolutionary values is always more optimistic about a self-regulated society than the established art it opposes. Its inherent tendency is toward anarchism. Both proponents and detractors agree that rock music expresses anarchistic beliefs about the possibilities of a social life free from external authority. In all probability, this is the extent of their agreement. I'll discuss this in some detail in Chapter 10.

Should there be any lingering doubts that an understanding of rock music is essential for an understanding of contemporary American culture, they may be partially dispelled by a discussion of certain analogous situations in the history of popular music. Thus, if we were seeking to comprehend the consciousness of the seventeenth and early eighteenth centuries, we could hardly pass over the baroque music of Purcell, Vivaldi, Handel, and J. S. Bach. Should we find a fascination with the eighteenth century, we would turn to Haydn, Mozart, the sons of Bach, and the early Beethoven for clues. If our interests were then to wander into the nineteenth century, we would never question the importance of looking at the romantic music of Beethoven, Chopin, Brahms, and Tchaikovsky. And who would object to the serious consideration of the impressionist music of Saint-Saëns, Ravel, Respighi, Stravinsky, and Copland in any appraisal of the late nineteenth and early twentieth centuries? All of these composers wrote the popular music for their own times, producing one monster hit after another. In so doing, they not only reflected but also helped create recognizably distinct states of consciousness, all of which had their own unique and identifiable cultural manifestations.

Since this is so obvious, I wonder why it should be so difficult for some to admit that an understanding of contemporary American culture beginning with the mid-fifties is contingent on an appraisal of Muddy Waters, Chuck Berry, Elvis Presley, Bob Dylan and The Beatles. Perhaps there is the lingering suspicion that granting rock music even this meager amount of respectability might seduce the unwary into a seditious frame of mind, dangerous to the prevailing ideology and scandalous to everything holy. However, if there is even a germ of truth in this fear, any attempt to impute respectability, great or meager, is bound to fail. The very essence of rock music would seem to be a denial of respectability. It would be like Pat Boone struggling to emulate the pre-born-again Little Richard: Boone's attempt to make "Tutti Frutti" respectable was not only a failure, it was a travesty.

2

What Is Rock Music?

The first recording of the word "rock" associated with music was by Blind Blake, a Delta Blues singer, in a song called "West Coast Blues" in 1926. (The word "rock" was used well before 1926, as a naughty Blues verb, but this was the first time it was used this way in a song.) He sang about "country rock," but had a line in the song that left little to the imagination: "I'm gonna satisfy you if I can." Aside from that rather overt hint, there's nothing much to go on in terms of a definition. Felix Cavaliere, record producer and member of the Young Rascals, recently identified the entire genre simply as "liberation." This doesn't give us much to work with either, but both provide us with a couple of clues.

An entire book could be written about the many and varied attempts to derive and support such a definition, but it wouldn't be very helpful. Few of the definitions agree, and several are even contradictory. Selecting any one of them as authoritative could be nothing more than an arbitrary decision, since there's no possible basis for choosing other than on personal whims.

A clear obstacle to defining rock music is that it actually has no unique musical quality (or combination of qualities) that allows us to distinguish it from non-rock. Peculiarities of rhythm, instrumentation, voice, volume, lyrics, and so on have all been suggested, yet every one of them can be found in other kinds of music as well. Moreover, undeniable examples of rock exist that don't have any of these alleged peculiarities. So any standard definition would leave us with the absurdity of calling some things rock which clearly aren't and leaving others out which clearly are.

Given this problem, the closest we can probably come to the illusory ideal definition is to gather a large and varied collection of "family resemblances," a device that only acknowledges the futility of the effort. Even specifying the clearest, most universally acceptable musical characteristics will not provide us with an accurate understanding of rock music.

As a cultural artifact, rock music participates in the process of historical change. It is conditioned by and, in turn, conditions its total environment, and it cannot be understood apart from its relationship to culture. Cultural creations are born, they live, and they die; but above all, they change and effect change. So, a permanent, unchanging definition of rock music is intrinsically impossible; it would amount to an abstraction from a particular part of its developmental process and would thus contradict itself: a part would claim to be the whole. In the following pages, I intend to show why this holistic approach is needed and why a purely musicological approach fails.

A Holistic Approach

Of the three major components of music (melody, harmony, and rhythm), a distinctive rhythmic styling has been cited most often as providing the key to its uniqueness. In 4/4 time, for example, with four beats to the measure (rarely are there three), rock music accentuates the second and fourth. Similarly, in 2/4 time or cut-time, the up-beat (or back-beat) is emphasized. To hear this, simply compare a rock classic such as Jerry Lee Lewis' "Whole Lotta Shakin' Goin' On" with the decidedly downbeat emphasis in any country-and-western standard, as with Loretta Lynn's "Coal Miner's Daughter." Another rhythmic feature is the rolling or boogie-woogie ("Yancey") bass, first prominently used in 1948 by such blues artists as Sonny Thompson in "Long Gone." Shortly thereafter, pianists like Fats Domino popularized the use of triplets as a rhythmic feature, usually in the treble clef. (Listen to Fats Domino's "Ain't That a Shame" for a reasonably good example.)

Instrumental configurations have also been cited as distinctively different. For example, no one who has ever heard rock music could ignore the importance of percussive instruments, especially the drums. While none of the components of the typical drum trap are entirely unknown outside of the rock genre, their centrality in providing a driving beat is a bit unusual. Almost as decisive is the virtually universal use of guitars, acoustic and electric, although the latter have clearly assumed the prominent role. (Interestingly enough, after their invention and introduction into popular music in 1937, electric stringed instruments quickly became differentiated according to genre: the slide guitar was preferred almost exclusively by country and western; blues stuck with the standard guitar to carry the lead; and rock added an electric bass.) Not quite as prevalent as they once were, but still very significant, are saxophones: baritones, tenors, and altos. Played with gutsy insistence, often honking out the rhythm, they were virtually the epitome of early rhythm and blues. Finally, deriving primarily from honky-tonk, the technically percussive piano also has been an unquestioned presence in rock performances, then reincarnated initially as the keyboard, synthesizer, or Mellotron and later metamorphosed as a veritable plethora of electronic instruments.

Although the vocal characteristics of rock music have been far too diverse for anything distinctive to emerge as a defining feature, it has nevertheless given birth to at least one unique style, "doo-wop," present in no other kind of music as far as I know. I mention it because of its obvious cultural significance. In the early Fifties, Black youths too poor to buy musical instruments began to emulate various instrumental sounds, providing background accompaniment for the lead singers. Because of the way this street-corner a cappella music sounded, it came to be known as the doo-wop style. ("Get a Job" by the Silhouettes is doo-wop backed up instrumentally.) Other vocal styles were taken over and modified by rock: blues (Rolling Stones), gospel call-and-response (Isley Brothers), nasal country-and-western twang (Everly Brothers), operatic (Roy Orbison), and lush choral harmonies (Beach Boys). In other words, a distinctive rock vocal style does not exist.

Lyrically, one might at first find rock distinctive. In what other kind of music, after all, could you find something like "A Wop Bop A-loo Bop a Lop Bam Boom" (variously transcribed, from "Tutti Frutti") if not in rock music? Isn't unintelligibility a key feature of rock lyrics? Perhaps with some, but you also find Simon and Garfunkel's "Sounds of Silence," Dylan's "Blowin' in the Wind," and The Beatles' "Eleanor Rigby." Which type is more representative? Both, I think. Among detractors, however, the case is often made that rock lyrics do have certain distinctive themes, whether or not they are intelligibly expressed. Granted that sex, drugs, drinking, rebellion, and pleasure are emphasized, these themes are no more characteristic of rock than of blues and of C&W. So there's really not much to go on in terms of lyrics. Rock lyrics are certainly worth looking at for their own sake (within a holistic perspective, of course), but there is nothing definitional about them.

If rhythm, instrumentation, vocal qualities, and lyrics are, at best, only partially helpful in describing something as unquestionably rock, then maybe it is all of these things with the addition of excessive volume. Is loudness that little extra that can isolate rock music from other kinds? Certainly, no one would ever claim that volume is never an attribute, but this doesn't say very much. As I recall, *The 1812 Overture* is also quite loud. Besides, there are such things as volume controls; we can make our music as loud or as soft as we like.

Now, even without citing borderline cases and exceptions (which would far outnumber the examples actually captured by the preceding musical characteristics), this approach must inevitably prove unsatisfactory. Consider the fact that rhythmically and instrumentally (the only two musical characteristics with any hope of providing a definition), the most unlikely music qualifies as rock: much of the commercial music on radio and TV, the theme music from numerous TV shows, "Disco Duck," and the material done by Donny and Marie! Something is obviously wrong.

What is wrong is that the musicological approach fails to consider the other components of rock music: the artists and what they intend with their music, the audiences and how they interpret what the artists intend, the media and how they affect and are affected by the message, and the entire cultural context in which all of this occurs. Rock music encompasses all of this, not just its own musical characteristics. "Rock and roll" is not musical terminology after all.

Referring back to the musical styles mentioned at the end of the previous chapter, baroque, romantic, and impressionist, note that these too are not musicological characterizations. They connote instead something about what their respective artists and audiences intended, that is, the meaning the music had for them. The same is true with the modern styling of blues, jazz, and C&W. Nothing in these terms denotes anything at all musical. On the contrary, they are clearly intended to portray the consciousness of the participants, the way the music is interpreted, its meaning, the intentionality of everyone involved. An attempt to define any of these genres would run into the same obstacles that we've encountered with rock: they are much more than their alleged musicological features would give us to understand.

The term "rock and roll" was not originally intended as a dance reference. Instead, as all of us were more or less vaguely aware, it had to do with sex — plain, raw, and undisguised. Its linkage with dancing was a thinly veiled attempt to make it more acceptable to White America in the mid–Fifties. But sex wasn't the whole story either. The meaning of rock was, and always has been, more than what the specific term might suggest at any given time. Billy Ward and the Dominoes' "Sixty Minute Man" (1951) and Hank Ballard's "Work with Me Annie" (1954) may have represented the intentions of its earliest participants, but rock and roll very soon came to mean much more than this. (Nevertheless, Bob Seger's "Horizontal Bop" (1980) illustrates the fact that its original intent hasn't been lost on succeeding generations.) Today, with the advantages of hindsight, we must approach rock music as a gestalt, as a whole larger than the sum of its individual parts, and certainly not something to be identified with one of its historically conditioned components.

A Revolutionary Art

If we now reflect on the characteristics of art per se, there's simply no possible conclusion other than to see rock music as revolutionary. Herbert Marcuse had quite a bit to say about art and its relationship to revolution. In his short collection of essays entitled *Counter-Rev-*

olution and Revolt, he saw the political potential of art in its ability to communicate two things: an "indictment of the established reality" and an encouragement to seek the "goals of liberation." Authentic art, in other words, communicates the general attitudes of both negation and affirmation. This duality is a necessary condition for art to be genuine. To communicate successfully, however, a nonconformist language (understood in the widest possible sense) is necessary. It can't be an invented language because this wouldn't speak to people in their own life setting. Language form can only be a subversion of traditional material. Only in this way can it reach "a population which has interjected the needs and values of their masters and managers and made them their own, thus reproducing the established system in their minds, their consciousness, their senses and instincts." To put it in other words, the established language must be "spoken," but in unforeseen and subversive ways. Notice that negation and affirmation are contingent on a subversive language — one that uses the common tongue but in ways which do not conform. Rock music is just such a language. Not only has it not conformed to musical convention, it has communicated a negation of the established reality and an affirmation of the goals of liberation.

All forms of art are intrinsically capable of this subversive activity, because they necessarily involve illusions about the reality they represent. Illusions always transform the prevailing order by showing the established reality in a far different and antagonistic way. As Marcuse put it, "Words, sounds, images, from another dimension 'bracket' and invalidate the right of the established reality for the sake of a reconciliation still to come." What must emerge is a "new experience of reality, new values." Coming from this other dimension, artistic language is extraordinarily potent. "More effectively than its political goals and slogans, this 'existential' protest, hard to isolate and hard to punish, threatens the cohesion of the social system." The essence of art's revolutionary nature is thus its illusory character; whenever art "*wills* itself as illusion," it both preserves and transcends its cultural setting with the promise of liberation. For Marcuse, for example, the writings of Dickens, Ibsen, Defoe, Kafka, and Thomas Mann succeeded in this dual function. Today, we might cite Vonnegut, Mailer, J. D. Salinger, Doris Lessing, and Ray Bradbury. In every case, the writer speaks to us in our own language, yet at the same time opens up a new world to us. Obviously, this principle extends to art forms other than literature.

There is a danger, however, and much that passes for art succumbs to it: "Where the world no longer sustains the dialectical unity of what is and what can (and ought to) be, art has lost its truth, has lost itself." Art can fail by leaning too much in either direction; both its immanence in the revolutionary process and its transcendence above it must be maintained if the creation of illusion is to have its revolutionary impact. Marcuse saw guerrilla (street) theater, the poetry of the "free press," and the music of Cage and Stockhausen as having lost touch with the people experiencing the revolution. Being so immersed in the revolutionary process, they lost their capacity for a transcendent critique of society.

On the other hand, most television and most popular novels fall prey to the opposite temptation. They have become too far removed from the revolutionary process, losing the quality of immanence.

Negation and affirmation are thus the two dimensions of one transforming (revolutionary) process — a process that must relate to and yet transcend the status quo. In the next chapter, this double dialectic will provide the basis for a decidedly different kind of typology of rock music.

Art performs its innately subversive role through its creation of illusions, but this necessarily means that art is a cognitive activity: it makes knowledge claims about what is and what ought to be. This latter claim, of course, is always threatening to the prevailing order. But it is especially so since this knowledge claim is never rational. In fact, the less rational it is the more threatening it becomes. According to Marcuse,

> Art is recollection: it appeals to a pre-conceptual experience and understanding, which reemerge in and against the context of social functioning of experience and understanding—against instrumentalist reason and sensibility.
>
> When it attains this primary level—the terminal point of the intellectual effort—art violates taboos: it lends voice and sight and ear to things which are normally repressed: memories, longings—ultimate states of sensibility.... These extreme qualities, the supreme points of art, seem to be the prerogative of music.[1]

For some incredible reason, which Marcuse never disclosed, he found rock music to be a one-dimensional form of art. He saw it as being far too preoccupied with bourgeois culture—its loss of immanence in the revolution dooming it to almost total ineffectiveness. At best, it was an imitation of genuine revolutionary art—rock music had not yet developed the capacity for transcendence. However, Marcuse ignored the obvious. For example, he was seemingly oblivious to what was said about the transforming role of rock music by the very people in whom he placed most of his hopes for change—youth, students, the New Left, and Blacks. Didn't he know what music they were listening to? Didn't he trust or understand what they were saying about it? Why also was he unaware of the genuine ambivalence within rock culture itself about revolution? Even the most strident calls for action were coupled with fears for what might follow, as in "Won't Get Fooled Again," when the Who sang "Meet the new boss/Same as the old boss." And why wasn't he at all sensitive to rock music's almost total preoccupation with alienated human existence, expressed as a universal truth as well as in numerous examples? Could he, perhaps, have overlooked The Beatles' "Eleanor Rigby," Simon and Garfunkel's "Sounds of Silence," the Beach Boys' "In My Room" and Chuck Berry's "No Particular Place to Go"? In all of these songs, the alienation expressed is total, including the self-alienation of rock culture itself.

Despite his failure to understand the true import of rock music, Marcuse's discussion of the revolutionary potential of art and music is invaluable. His belief that "a subversive potential is the very nature of art" cannot be overestimated. For, at the very least, this potential must operate as an ever-present critique of the revolution itself. It cannot cease its negating/affirming posture in any sense without ceasing to be art. Thus rock music must stand with (immanent in), and yet above (transcendent to), the revolution, estranged from the very transforming situation it seeks to invoke.

The Implications of Revolutionary Art

Before leaving Marcuse, we should pause for a moment to reflect on what is implied by the subversive nature of art. Since he believed that "revolution is in the substance of art," we can—at the very least—infer that genuine art is necessarily revolutionary. However, there is more that can be said. First, because "art can and will draw its inspiration, and its very form, from the then-prevailing revolutionary movement," a mere revival of past expressions cannot ever be genuine, authentic. Art, in other words, is historically conditioned; to be true to itself it must emerge from or reflect its situation in life. This is the immanent dimension of art, and successful communication is contingent on satisfying its demands. Genuine art must speak the language of the people who are engaged in the revolutionary process, whatever form their "language" may take. Today the popular form of music is rock — in any one of its many forms.

Second, a genuine art must at the same time transcend the revolution it expresses. It cannot be so submerged in the movement that it forfeits its essentially subversive role. The revolution itself must be subjected to constant critical review; hence, the canons of authenticity include a fundamental estrangement of art from its cultural setting. Nothing can kill the revolutionary potential of rock more than crass commercialization. Of course, rock music has more than occasionally succumbed to this temptation.

The dialectic between immanence and transcendence must always be maintained. The loss of either one would necessarily condemn an artistic expression to the status of non-art. The loss of immanence would obviously involve a failure to communicate, for it would lack a true involvement with the revolutionary process. It could neither negate nor affirm as a result. Ultimately, music like this would be characterized by "selling out" — being co-opted or exploited by the established order. Its revolutionary substance would be removed and replaced by a substance antagonistic to change. It would have to use a language so far removed from the movement toward liberation that its speech would necessarily be that of the counterrevolutionaries. Prime examples of this failure just might be the four Bobbys (Darin, Rydell, Vee, and Vinton) from the age of the "teen idols." Of course there are such "idols" in every age. Most recently, of course, one of the most popular reality/talent shows is American Idol.

On the other hand, the loss of the transcendent dimension would result in almost total ineffectiveness; art would be relegated to a purely masturbatory enterprise, satisfying only to its proponents. Lacking the capacity to engage its own revolutionary movement from a critical perspective, it would as a consequence lose its capacity to engage the establishment as well. This in effect would be another way for art to "sell out," to be co-opted or exploited, but in this case it would occur by its having too much of a revolutionary consciousness. Art would become mere propaganda. By "selling out" to a particular historical embodiment of the revolution, it would cease to be genuinely revolutionary (and so the establishment encourages such moves). True art must not sell itself out to either side if its subversive character is to be maintained. (Keep in mind that the loss of one facet is not compensated for by increasing the other. Such an increase does not take up the slack but only magnifies the loss.) For example the first Lennon/Ono album, *Two Virgins*, filled as it was with various electronic noises, had little to say to anyone. It came to be regarded as a joke — exactly what the establishment wanted.

Third, as one facet of immanence and transcendence, authentic art will attempt to negate the established order, focusing on its fundamental values and the ways they may be institutionalized. (This includes the negation of how these values are allegedly known.) Of course, the negation must also involve a critical perspective on the historically conditioned embodiment of the revolution itself. The negation of art is total — all-encompassing. By far the best example of this is the ambiguous version of "Revolution" by The Beatles (on *The White Album*).

Fourth, another facet of authentically immanent and transcendent art is affirmation. Positive values must be proposed as replacements for what is being rejected (along with an alternate way of knowing). As I've mentioned many times before, this would not involve a wholesale substitution; only the basic values are at issue. Again, this must never be an affirmation of a specific, momentary part of the process. Affirmation is always from "beyond." Elvis Costello's "(What's So Funny 'bout) Peace, Love, and Understanding" epitomizes this aspect of rock music.

Obviously, nothing is ever negated without something being affirmed. Conversely, nothing is ever affirmed without something being negated. A less obvious truth is that negation should not be regarded as automatically "bad" and affirmation "good." This depends on what values are at issue. Attacking the accepted beliefs about race shows the role of negation in rock and roll at its moral best.

Finally, there is no necessary correlation between negation and anger or hate on the one hand and between affirmation and joy or love on the other. Negation and affirmation can be, and are, expressed with a variety of moods and feelings, often confounding our expectations and disturbing our sensibilities. The negation embodied in Frank Zappa's work is pure joy, while the affirmation in the Waitresses' "No Guilt" is one of the saddest in contemporary music.

My own beliefs about how these four implications relate to rock music ought to be rather obvious. Essentially, I maintain, à la Marcuse, that rock music should be understood as the artistic expression of America's cultural revolution. Hence, contemporary American culture provides the substance of rock music. The two are intrinsically related.

Since the mid–Fifties, the revolutionary language of America has been the language of rock and roll, and it has spoken at times with great effectiveness. At other times, however, it has lost either its immanence or its transcendence, winding up as a counter-revolutionary tool in either case. Musically, these losses have not always been apparent; musical characteristics can easily be duplicated and can thus be disguised an exploitive use of the art. So we have to pay attention to the entire culture of rock to see what's really been happening.

The same is true of the second dialectical pair, of course. The negative and affirmative facets of rock music are revealed only when we look at the whole, rarely (if ever) by the music alone. Moreover, when a holistic perspective is taken, a decidedly existential flavor becomes clearly evident. In the contemporary classic *Irrational Man*, William Barrett finds modern art to be a revealing testimony of modern consciousness.[2] And without altering one jot or tittle of his remarks, they might just as well be referring to rock and roll.

"Art," he says, "is the collective dream of a period, a dream in which, if we have eyes to see, we can trace the physiognomy of the time most clearly." Hence, rock music "touches a sore spot, or several sore spots, in the ordinary citizen of which he is totally unaware." Joined by "the learned and sensitive traditionalist," they all object to its content: it is "too negative or nihilistic, too shocking or scandalous; it dishes out unpalatable truths." It voices the impoverishment of traditional ideals, sometimes violently and aggressively, and it pictures "a world where man [kind] is a stranger." In such a world, there is no "final intelligibility"; human existence "is no longer transparent and understandable by reason." Reality is portrayed "as opaque, dense, concrete, and in the end inexplicable, and at the limits of reason one comes face to face with the meaningless." In its earliest manifestations, rock and roll was castigated for the unintelligibility of its lyrics — as if intelligibility would have redeemed it. And to many, it was beneath contempt, no matter what it "said." Further, in its stress on living for now, rock implies that there is no final goal, no purpose, no meaning. This is quite unpalatable for those stuck in the traditional order.

Barrett then claims, "This break with the Western tradition imbues both philosophy and art with the sense that everything is questionable, problematic." Hence, the themes that obsess him are alienation, finitude, and the encounter with nothingness. Not religion, nor reason, nor science can offer us any security, for the traditional certainty that there are timeless truths to guide and protect us is no more. We are on our own, the sole source of whatever meaning there is. Despite the enormous power we have developed, none of it is to any avail. On the contrary, it provides us with a frightening symbol for the "dreadful and total contingency of human existence: existentialism is the philosophy of the atomic age." Total annihilation is with us always as a permanent potential. One song, "Red Car" by the Trees, is such a stark portrayal of the specter of nuclear devastation that it voids all hope in powers political or religious.

From its beginnings, rock music has challenged the basic values of the culture in which it emerged, not all at once, not always self-consciously, certainly not programmatically, but surely and steadily nevertheless. First, there were challenges to the accepted beliefs about sex, race, and work; then, nationalism, war, and economics came under attack. By implication, of course, the entire conception of reality that supported these values was negated. Essentially, what was being rejected was a Protestantized incarnation of the Judeo-Christian tradition, with its firm convictions about destiny, inevitable progress, absolutist morality, fixed social positions, and eternal punishments and rewards. Max Weber and R.H. Tawney long ago explored the Protestant work ethic and its relationship to capitalism. More recently, theologians and sociologists everywhere have studied manifestations of this religiosity. Rock and roll, however, didn't propose to study this value scheme at all; rock and roll proposed to abolish it.

3

A Suggested Typology

By tying together several of the important strands of the discussion so far, we should now be able to create a typological scheme that may enable us to interpret the phenomenon of rock music accurately, that is, within its cultural context. In order to do this, the close correlation between contemporary American culture and its music obviously needs to be more specifically illustrated. I also need to pinpoint the crucial symbolic events within what I'm claiming to be a revolutionary process. Precisely where and when, for example, were the received values being negated and the new ones affirmed? And what of the alleged Counter-Reaction? Can it be identified? We need to take a collective look over our shoulders.

American Culture and Rock Music

A consideration of contemporary American culture starts no later than August 6, 1945 (the atomic bombing of Hiroshima), but earlier events must be kept in mind. These include the first widespread commercial uses of radio (1920 for AM, 1939 for FM), film (1900s) and audio recordings (1900s). Also vital is a rough indication of the beginnings of jazz (1900s), ragtime (1900s), blues (1910s), country music (1920s) and swing (1930s). But there are a lot more. Here are a few to keep in mind: FDR and the New Deal (1932–45); Pearl Harbor (December 7, 1941); World War II (for the United States, 1941–45); the Great Depression (1929–World War II); the rise of the modern Ku Klux Klan (1920s); the labor movement (1920s–1930s); the first major Black protest march on Washington, D.C., led by A. Philip Randolph (1941); the Harlem and Detroit race riots (1943); and perhaps even the heyday of Hollywood (1920s through the early 1950s).

1945

CULTURE • Prior to 1945, the American consciousness was almost universally preoccupied with the war. One of the problems with our society today is that most people holding political power still view events in these terms, a perspective that ceased to have much validity after Hiroshima and Nagasaki. Together with the death of FDR and the ending of the war, the atomic bomb dragged America out of the one era and into another.

MUSIC • Aside from the established music of the period (big bands, show tunes, crooners and the like), songs like "The Honeydripper" by Joe Liggins were beginning to hint at a new set of sexual values. But explicit references, like this one, to the pure joy of sex were at this time confined to the "race" market. Many unconventional ideas about race, sex, and work, kept in check by a unified concentration on the war effort, would be released after the war ended, to the chagrin of many.

1946

CULTURE • The Cold War began in earnest despite the hopeful founding of the United Nations. Bad feelings about the Yalta Conference would release the hatred and fear of Soviet communism held back by the wartime anti–Nazi alliance. Dr. Benjamin Spock published *Baby and Child Care*, a book that would have an enormous impact on postwar babies, the generation that would begin reaching adolescence in the mid-fifties. Spock sowed the dangerous seeds of a free consciousness by encouraging parents to allow a child a decisive role in its own development. The "baby boom" was, as a consequence, inherently subversive. Television programming also began — a development that would eventually end the dominance of the film industry in popular entertainment and cause the radio industry to emphasize music in order to survive.

MUSIC • Black blues music, still called "race music," recovered nicely from its temporary eclipse. (The Great Depression hit its audience harder than it did any other group.) In addition, Black migrations into northern urban areas began giving this music a different character: rawer, gutsier, and angrier. Much of it sounded a lot like what we later called rock and roll, but at this point, it was just called "urban blues."

1947

CULTURE • Americans did not quickly adjust to the fact that FDR wasn't around any longer. Loved or hated for almost thirteen years, Roosevelt had become the primary symbol for American hegemony. No one expected his likely successor, Harry S (the letter stood for nothing) Truman, to compete with the late president's stature and image. Meanwhile, partially obscuring the political developments, Jackie Robinson became the first Black to play major league baseball, winning Rookie of the Year honors.

MUSIC • The thinly disguised sexuality of rhythm and blues was becoming more and more open. Black Americans were asserting themselves more clearly in their music than perhaps anywhere else. Both "Shake Your Boogie" (Sonny Boy Williamson) and "We're Gonna Rock, We're Gonna Roll" (Wild Bill Moore) were released; the latter included the first clear reference to "rocking and rolling." A dance reference this was not, unless it is remembered that "dancing" was a euphemism for sex.

1948

CULTURE • Presidential electioneering dominated this year, with no one expecting Harry Truman to beat Thomas E. Dewey — not even Truman. Nevertheless, his scrappiness and earthiness appealed to more people than Dewey's elitist diffidence. Ominously, the Democratic Party was split when Truman pushed his beliefs in civil rights at the convention. The "Dixiecrats" walked out and ran Strom Thurmond as their candidate, and he picked up more than a few electoral votes. Henry Wallace's Progressives did pretty well also. The Soviets blockaded Berlin, hoping that it would force the Western powers to cede their sectors of Berlin to them. The West responded with a massive airlift. The United Nations created the modern state of Israel, as a partial response to the Holocaust. Alfred Kinsey published his first sex report (on males), and *The Ed Sullivan Show* aired for the first time.

MUSIC • Continuing the trend toward sexual explicitness, "Good Rockin' Tonight" by Wynonie Harris was released (later covered by Elvis in 1954). It served to popularize the association of the term "rock" with the music. Specific musical developments included the characteristic rolling, boogie-woogie bass (originally introduced by a person named Jimmy Yancey, a groundskeeper for the Chicago White Sox); it achieved prominence in Sonny Thompson's "Long Gone." Technologically, the 33 rpm long-playing record was placed on the market, but it was reserved almost exclusively for classical music.

1949

CULTURE • Now elected, Truman kept himself busy. He desegregated the armed forces by executive order and kept the Berlin airlift alive. Feeding the fires of an already virulent anti-communism, the Chinese communists pushed the Nationalists off the mainland onto Taiwan. Hence began the mutual recriminations as to who was responsible for "losing" China to Mao and his communist hoards. Meanwhile, flying saucers were sighted, Gorgeous George's wrestling shows competed with roller derbies for the new TV audience, and various Levittowns were built. The Soviet Union made its own atomic bomb, and nuclear testing was underway with all deliberate speed. Some people were getting worried.

MUSIC • While "Chicken Shack Boogie" (Amos Milburn) and "Boogie at Midnight" (Roy Brown) represented the growing openness about sexuality unsullied by romance and love, "Drinkin' Wine, Spo-De-O-Dee" (Stick McGhee, a.k.a. Sticks Mcghee) represented a new avenue of dissent; now, outrageous drinking and uninhibited language were aggressively proclaimed with unashamed abandon. (The nonsense lyric "Spo-De-O-Dee" replaced a scurrilous phrase having to do with the sexual proclivities of some unspecified "mother.") A couple of other happenings were important as well: the term "rhythm and blues" began to replace "race music," and the 45 rpm record was introduced.

1950

CULTURE • The Cold War turned hot: the Korean police action began along with McCarthyism and the Internal Security Act. Not only was the Communist Party of the United States of America harassed, but anything or anyone perceived to have even the faintest leftist leanings was suspect, and many were officially blacklisted. To many, America had now become the land of the repressed and the home of the cowardly. Few were willing to voice an objection, especially those without power and influence.

MUSIC • Fats Domino's career began about this time, establishing him as one of the earliest major figures of the rock era. Meanwhile, something was happening in White music that would produce significant waves later: the top song of the year was the innocuous "Goodnight Irene," recorded by the Weavers, one member of which, Pete Seeger, was blacklisted for his outspoken socialist sympathies. A revolutionary had achieved cultural prominence—through popular music. It would not be the last time for such an occurrence.

1951

CULTURE • Again, a war consciousness prevailed, but this time the war was ambiguous. Not only was the popular General Douglas MacArthur relieved of command in Korea, no clear threat to U.S. security was perceived. Further, no symbolic affront to America's dignity had set off the war (as had been the case in so many earlier wars — Pearl Harbor, the sinking of the *Maine* and *Lusitania*, the Alamo, Fort Sumter, and so on, all of which Americans were encouraged to remember). Americans, however, were losing their moorings; the "lost generation" was emerging, that is, American youths were increasingly perceived as having no guiding orientation in their lives; and J.D. Salinger published *The Catcher in the Rye*, which expressed this development perfectly.

MUSIC • Something curious was happening. After the FCC lifted its freeze on new TV licenses, radio began its inevitable shift to music programming. Alan Freed began his *Moondog Show*, using the term "rock and roll" on the airwaves for the first time. He played such songs as "Sixty Minute Man" (Billy Ward and the Dominoes) and "Rocket 88" (Jackie Brenston), the latter covered immediately by Bill Haley and the Saddlemen. Haley also covered Jimmy Preston's 1949 R&B hit "Rock This Joint," beginning a process that was to reach its apogee from 1954 to 1957. Alan Freed and Bill Haley were picking up on something significant. White adolescents were finding in this music a kind of freedom not available to them anywhere else in American society. An underground, barely discernible, halting fascination with Black culture was in its infant stages — and rock and roll had presided at the birth.

1952

CULTURE • With the election of President Dwight D. Eisenhower, America revealed its continuing attachment to the clear World War II distinction between good and evil; the unquestioned truths of duty, honor, country; the simplicity of a nondenominational civil religion; and the stability afforded by a moral code that kept all the passions in check. In short, Americans wanted security. More than anything, they feared unsettling questions and disquieting problems — things like that had to be kept out of sight. The only cloud on Ike's horizon was the disclosure of a slush fund kept by his vice-presidential candidate, Richard M. Nixon. However, after Nixon's confessional "Checkers" speech in the midst of the campaign, Adlai Stevenson didn't stand a chance; he was overwhelmed. Security had a price, however, for a new cloud appeared on the horizon: the hydrogen bomb.

MUSIC • While sexual themes were becoming more explicit ("Rock Me All Night Long," "5-10-15 Hours," "Lawdy Miss Clawdy," "No More Doggin'," "Have Mercy Baby," and "Middle of the Night"), rock and roll was acquiring a wider meaning, threatening to challenge and negate still other traditionally accepted values. Amos Milburn's "Thinkin' and Drinkin'" juxtaposed two activities usually regarded as contradictory. Elsewhere, the infamous House Un-American Activities Committee suppressed Pete Seeger and the Weavers; a concert in Cleveland's arena, organized by Alan Freed and attracting far more than the hall could possibly hold, developed into America's first rock and roll riot; and *Bandstand* had its debut on Philadelphia television.

1953

CULTURE • Joseph Stalin died, and the Korean War ended, giving rise to some speculation that these two events were related. A popular uprising in East Germany pointed out that the Soviet Union's "steel" grip ("Stalin" means "steel" in Russian) had been severely shaken. Kinsey released his second sex report (on females), showing as before that something disconcerting was lurking beneath the surface of social calm. Three-D movies had their brief life span, suggesting that technological innovations succeed only when they're really wanted. (It would take over 50 years for this technology to re-emerge.)

MUSIC • More food for controversy was provided by the increasing popularity of rhythm and blues with White middle-class youths. They were listening to songs such as "Crying in the Chapel" by the Orioles, "Good Lovin'" by the Clovers, and "Money Honey" by Clyde McPhatter. Bill Haley continued to pick up on this trend with his first hit, "Crazy Man Crazy." He knew what he was doing; the year before he had renamed his group the Comets, leaving behind his C&W image forever.

1954

CULTURE • If ever there was a big year, this was it — it was the very voice-in-the-wilderness of years, baptizing all those who had ears to hear and eyes to see. The established order was mortally wounded by a series of events with far-reaching implications. The French were decisively defeated at Dien Bien Phu in the region called "Indochina," then little known in the States; the resulting peace treaty divided the northern and Southern parts of the newly created Vietnam into communist and non-communist segments, ending Western influence in the area for a brief moment. More apparent to the typical American was the crushing of Sen. Joseph McCarthy in the televised Army-McCarthy hearings, a spectacle that dominated American consciousness and gave the United States its first TV phenomenon. Furthermore, the Supreme Court's decision in *Brown v. Board of Education* called for an end to segregation in public education with "all deliberate speed," a legal and moral watershed. Not as obvious, but just as influential, the drug-oriented *Doors of Perception* by Aldous Huxley was published — giving a positive perspective to chemical epistemology as well as providing the name for one of California's (and rock's) most important groups. Adding to this, the exceedingly controversial movie *The Wild One* was released. Starring Marlon Brando as the leader of an amoral motorcycle gang that pillaged a small town, the film portrayed no just retribution for their deeds. Accordingly, having no redeeming quality in the eyes of the established order, it was banned in England (having only one showing) and in many other places as well. Something was afoot.

MUSIC • In order to capture the allowances and part-time earnings of the vast and growing audience of White middle-class youths, White performers began quite consciously to cover Black music as soon as it came out (in the process, smoothing it over and cleaning it up to make it more palatable and thus more salable). An unintended side effect was to popularize the originals far more than would have been possible otherwise. As with country music, small regional labels with no capabilities for mass distribution produced Black music. The cover artists performed on national labels that did have this capability, so those who hadn't yet heard the news soon did. Most notorious was "Sh-Boom" by the Chords (Cat), covered by the Crew Cuts (Mercury); "Tweedlee Dee" by LaVern Baker (Atlantic), covered by Georgia Gibbs (Mercury); and "Sincerely" by the Moonglows (Chess), covered by the McGuire Sisters (Coral).

Yet crossovers began to kill the cover business almost immediately. (It had about two more years to go.) The original Black versions began to outsell the covers and appear on ("cross over" to) the pop (White) charts as well as the R&B (Black) charts. What the Supreme Court had just proclaimed as a desired future goal — integration — was already a reality in rock and roll. Whites were now listening to Blacks, unmediated. The songs mentioned above illustrate both the covering process and the crossover reaction (produced, in good dialectical fashion, by the cover itself). White America still wasn't ready for Hank Ballard's sexually obvious "Work with Me Annie" in any form, but it wouldn't be long. (Too blatant even to be sanitized effectively, it was later recorded by Etta James in a revised version as "Dance with Me Henry," itself instantly covered by Georgia Gibbs.) A technological transition occurred, with enormous implications: the wholesale conversion of the popular music business to 45 rpm records from 78s. (LPs were still being reserved for classical music.) In addition, that summer, a part-time truck driver walked into Sam Phillips's Sun Studio in Memphis to record a few of his country favorites in a style he had picked up from listening to Black music and gospel. His name was Elvis Aaron Presley when he walked in, but he walked out as the "King of Rock and Roll." His early recordings were only regional hits, but to perceptive executives at RCA they told the story of the future. Elvis was not to remain a regional phenomenon much longer.

1955

Note: My conviction is that the demarcation of decades is an interpretive act, with dates and events playing a symbolic, not a literal, role. Hence, 1955 is when I see the "fifties" beginning. Symbolically, then, 1955 can now be seen as the beginning of America's cultural revolution and, as such, a key turning point in American history.

CULTURE • Internationally, America began its intervention in Vietnam as an effort to halt the election we agreed to by treaty, an election that was clearly going to be won by Ho Chi Minh, the communist candidate. Secretary of State John Foster Dulles was largely responsible for this turn of events. Ike's heart attack forced the nation to consider the possibility of a Nixon presidency, but the Davy Crockett craze diverted its attention.

Meanwhile, in Montgomery, Alabama, Rosa Parks refused to move to the back of a segregated bus, and the bus boycott under the leadership of Martin Luther King, Jr., was underway. The boycott captured the imagination of all those people who had developed a fascination with Black culture through its music. On the fringes of American society, a small group of disaffected "hipsters" was reading Allen Ginsberg's newly released book of poetry, *Howl*. And in backyards everywhere, bomb shelters were being built and made ready for what everyone knew was the inevitable outcome of the arms race and continued nuclear testing. All the ingredients for revolution were now set; America's consciousness was divided and in conflict. A youth culture had developed that was antagonistic to the traditional culture of the adult world. Blacks had finally made their organized move against White repression. The established order, with its quasi-religious ideology, had removed all legitimate avenues for the expression of alternate views within the system. Technological innovations, however, had brought into being new media and had altered the character of the older media, providing different means for the expression of counter-traditional ideas. Underlying all of this was the fact that a conflicting set of fundamental values had emerged in opposition to the traditional ones, and a very large and diverse group of people shared these new values. Racism was rejected; sex was seen as good in itself; and the work ethic was considered irrelevant. Granted that these anti-traditional beliefs were often semiconscious, voiced for the most part negatively and not carefully reasoned out, they were nevertheless real and potentially explosive. All that was needed was a catalyst.

MUSIC • Then it happened, suddenly, unexpectedly, and coming from a most unlikely source: "Rock around the Clock." As the theme for the film *Blackboard Jungle*, it became "*The Marseillaise* of the teenage revolution," according to rock historian Lillian Roxon in her *Rock Encyclopedia*. Bill Haley was not the stereotypical revolutionary by any stretch of the imagination, and he was hardly young (thirty in 1955). Moreover, the song had already been out for a year and besides it was a cover. Despite all of this, "Rock around the Clock" became a genuine revolutionary phenomenon — it became the de facto anthem. Whether or not they were aware of it, when teenagers bought this 45, they were taking a stand against the established order. Even today, the song has considerable symbolic power. Whenever *Blackboard Jungle* played, rioting was likely, and teenagers often attended just to join in. Slashing seats in the theater was common — at least in the often exaggerated press reportage. Riots did not always happen, which came as a disappointment to at least one young "Teddy Boy" attending its Liverpool showing. Nevertheless, he found it inspirational enough to form his own band, comprised of classmates from Quarrybank High School. We would soon hear more about this Ted a few years hence. Two other significant films were released, *Rebel without a Cause* and *East of Eden*, both starring James Dean. The complementarity they provided for *Blackboard Jungle* was enormous. Together they overshadowed the emergence of Chuck Berry, Ray Charles, and Bo Diddley.

1956

CULTURE • On the international scene, de–Stalinization was getting underway in the Soviet Union, with its effects being felt in the Hungarian revolt and in Polish anti–Soviet elections. In the non-communist world, England and Israel jointly invaded Egypt and temporarily occupied the Suez Canal. At home, the "I Like Ike" supporters overwhelmed Stevenson for a second time. America wanted the peaceful, stable, secure and ordered mythic past more than ever. However, C. Wright Mills was exposing the undemocratic workings of America in *The Power Elite*, and Jack Kerouac was expressing the will to be free in *On the Road*, suggesting and giving voice to the revolutionary dialectic between negation and affirmation. It became increasingly prudent to keep abreast of current events, which threatened daily to break open the established and repressive social order. Hence, *The Huntley Brinkley Report* came into being (sending the *Camel News Caravan* into retirement and John Cameron Swayze to do Timex commercials).

MUSIC • The Elvis phenomenon had now begun, initiated symbolically by his appearances on *The Ed Sullivan Show*. The facts about these appearances somewhat belie the mythic tales about his being shown only from the waist up; nevertheless, it was something not to be equaled in intensity by anything in American culture for another seven years. Even at this moment, "skiffle" groups were forming in England in the wake of "Rock around the Clock." Based on a newly awakened interest in the American blues tradition, Elvis, Bill Haley, and rockabilly in general, these amateurish jug and washboard bands were causing all sorts of musical havoc along the Mersey and the Thames. One skiffle group formed in Liverpool called themselves The Quarrymen. Seven years later, they too would appear on *The Ed Sullivan Show*, finally accomplishing what Lord Cornwallis had failed to do so long ago — the reconquest of the Colonies. When Black artists became increasingly recognized as the originators of much of the music White middle-class youth were listening to, "covering" for commercial purposes came to an abrupt end. This was the year of Little Richard, Fats Domino, Carl Perkins, and Chuck Berry. But it was also the year that an ominous note was sounded: Gene Vincent ("Be Bop A-Lula") was in a near-fatal car wreck, portending that rock and rollers did indeed live in the fast lane. Movies of consequence included *Rock around the Clock* and *The Girl Can't Help It*. The former had more to do with musical performance than with plot. The latter, however, was a dazzling satire of the music business that also included some fantastic footage of Little Richard and Gene Vincent, among others. Moreover, it included a brief shot of Little Richard obviously casting a barely disguised lascivious glance at Jayne Mansfield, thus violating one of America's most sacred taboos — any suggestion pertaining to interracial sex.

1957

CULTURE • Tension was everywhere. Eisenhower sent federal troops to Little Rock, Arkansas, in order to ensure the integration of public schools, and he somewhat reluctantly signed the Voting Rights Act. The Soviets launched *Sputnik*, the first artificial earth satellite, stunning Americans, and they shifted their educational emphases to science and mathematics. As a result, short shrift was given to the humanities and the arts. Soon afterward, America's first attempt to duplicate the Soviets' achievement exploded on takeoff at Cape Canaveral. People were reading Paul Goodman's anarchistic book *Growing Up Absurd* and were beginning to believe it.

MUSIC • *American Bandstand* premiered on national television, playing daily with Dick Clark as host. Alan Freed held his first rock-and-roll show in New York and appeared in the film *Don't Knock the Rock*. Elvis made *Jailhouse Rock*, one of his best films. Rockabilly added Buddy Holly, Jerry Lee Lewis, the Everly Brothers, and Ricky Nelson to its ranks. R&B added Sam Cooke. But the first skirmishes of the cultural revolution were about to come to an end.

1958

CULTURE • As if to counteract the threatening noises of America's troops landing on the coast of Lebanon to shore up a friendly government, Ban the Bomb parades began in both America and England. SANE (Committee for a Sane Nuclear Policy) was beginning a very diverse movement that continues to this day. Nuclear testing, however, went on unabated, its proponents unimpressed with the increasing opposition provided by the likes of Bertrand Russell. The John Birch Society was also founded this year, and Nixon was pelted with stones in Caracas, Venezuela. But millions of Americans had something else on their minds: the Hula Hoop.

MUSIC • In response to the growing political awareness, an older style of music was resurrected that seemed better able to express the new ideological sentiments: folk music, which had been highly successful advancing the cause of labor. Now, however, it was increasingly wedded to a pop style, and thus came into being such groups as the Kingston Trio. Distinguishing folk from the developing rock tradition was the fact that it was almost always recorded on the new stereo LPs; rock was still recorded on 45s. The established order was now fighting back in earnest; the values put under attack by rock were being reasserted with a heavy hand. Work, not sex, was again proclaimed as an end in itself, and anything hinting at racial mixing was quashed. Alan Freed's concert in Boston turned into another riot, and Freed was accused of inciting it. Elvis was drafted and went willingly, thus ending his active role as a revolutionary negation. Symbolically, however, he would always retain this meaning.

Jerry Lee Lewis's marriage to his fourteen-(or thirteen-) year-old cousin led to his premature retirement from rock. And anti–rock-and-roll demonstrations were held throughout the country. Rock and roll, and the cultural revolution, was on the defensive.

1959

CULTURE • Fidel Castro came to power in Cuba, overthrowing the unpopular, American-supported Batista regime. When his communist sympathies became clear, the CIA began plans to remove him. Nixon and Khrushchev exchanged visits, each with enormous TV exposure. Sullying his image forever, Charles Van Doren, confessed to being "prompted" on TV's *$64,000 Question*. We soon learned he wasn't alone.

MUSIC • A two-year series of congressional hearings on "payola" in the music industry began, focusing on rock and roll. Somehow its popularity had to be explained, and the prevailing theory was that disc jockeys were being paid to play it. (Why else would American kids listen to such trash? It was the only music available. Rock and roll was being forced on them, and teenagers simply weren't strong enough to resist it.) Chuck Berry was arrested for technically violating the Mann Act. Buddy Holly was killed in an airplane crash along with Ritchie Valens and J.P. Richardson, the "Big Bopper." To top it all off, Little Richard converted to Christianity after a nearly fatal accident aboard an airplane, becoming the first "born again" rock and roller. Still part of the reaction, the music industry began its attempt to co-opt the form of rock music without adopting its substance, killing its revolutionary potential in the process. Hence, there emerged the tame, bland "schlock rock" favored by *American Bandstand* and the established order. Some of the premier examples were Fabian's "Tiger," Connie Francis's "Lipstick on Your Collar," Paul Anka's "Put Your Head on My Shoulder," Frankie Avalon's "Venus," and Dodie Stevens's "Pink Shoelaces." As if to counter this development, the folk trend continued: the first Newport Folk Festival was held, giving an emerging singer, Joan Baez, national recognition.

1960

CULTURE • The narrowness of John F. Kennedy's presidential victory over Vice President Nixon, indicated a fundamental uncertainty in America, but Kennedy's New Frontier symbolized something other than Nixon's clear identification with the old order. No matter that Kennedy himself was far different than the image he projected. The image was the important thing. Even the marginal preference expressed for this image in the election sent America in a new, as yet unspecified direction. JFK represented innovation, change, the hope for a better future, and a way out of America's domestic and foreign travails. Yet national and international travails were to follow him into office. Sit-ins gave the Black liberation movement a new and effective tactic — and good publicity as well. Caryl Chessman was executed despite the growing opposition to the death penalty. The production and sale of birth control pills introduced a new factor into the struggle for sexual liberation. And hopes for peace were dampened when Francis Gary Powers's U-2 was shot down on a spy mission over the Soviet Union.

MUSIC • Elvis was discharged from the service but never regained his active revolutionary stature. Much of his later material was schlock or worse. Broadway's *Bye Bye Birdie* (based on Elvis's induction) reflected his almost total co-optation by the established order. Eddie

Cochran, a minor rockabilly rebel, died in a London taxi accident. And the "payola" hearings continued, absolving Dick Clark and castigating Alan Freed.

1961

CULTURE • This was not a good year for realizing much of the Kennedy promise. He watched the Berlin Wall being built (making a lot of political hay out of it, nevertheless), permitted the CIA's debacle at the Bay of Pigs, and sent America's first combat troops ("advisors") into Vietnam. Meanwhile, back in the United States, the race revolution was taking an even more aggressive turn; freedom rides into the South pushed Kennedy farther than he was willing to go. Books published included Updike's *Rabbit Run*, Heller's *Catch-22* and Heinlein's *Stranger in a Strange Land*; they portrayed anomie, negation, and affirmation, respectively.

MUSIC • Both schlock rock and folk continued, but the latter picked up one Robert Zimmerman from Hibbing, Minnesota. America would hear more from him. The revolution, suppressed in one of its forms (rock) was emerging in another (folk). Neither was to remain static, however. The pressures of social change would not allow it: schlock was counter-revolutionary, and pure folk was outdated. It had lost its connection with the revolution underway.

1962

CULTURE • Kennedy emerged a hero after the Cuban missile crisis, but this would prove to be the last popularly approved Cold War act in America. He would be more favorably remembered as one who boosted America's space program, with John Glenn's orbit of the earth. Another very traditional value came under attack when the Supreme Court struck down school prayer. New values were introduced with Rachel Carson's *Silent Spring*, a warning about the abuse of the environment with modern technology (DDT in this case). Other books published were Burdick and Wheeler's *Fail-Safe* and Knebel and Bailey's *Seven Days in May*. James Meredith, still referred to as a "Negro," could register at the University of Mississippi only with the help of military force. As a preview of coming attractions, the Students for a Democratic Society was organized around the idealistic principles of its founding charter, the Port Huron Statement. And when Marilyn Monroe died under suspicious circumstances, the sad event seemed to symbolize the end of an era.

MUSIC • As in American culture as a whole, new things were happening in music. Schlock and folk both died a quiet death, and in their place came folk rock (e.g., Peter, Paul and Mary), contemporary protest music (e.g., Dylan, Joan Baez, Tom Paxton, Phil Ochs, and another Newport Folk Festival), surfing music (e.g., The Beach Boys), Phil Spector's "wall of sound" and the twist phenomenon. LPs were now becoming the preferred medium, suggesting a new degree of seriousness for the values being affirmed through the music—an excellent example of the message being conveyed by the medium.

1963

Note: The fifties had by this time come to an end, their function being primarily to negate the established order. Since the election of Kennedy, however, something amorphously new was being affirmed. More than anything else, this is what the sixties were about: the affirmation and clarification of a new set of fundamental values, such as radical individuality, freedom, pleasure, pacifism, non-nationalism, and a nonreligious spirituality. The period lacked only a symbolic beginning, but 1963 was to provide one.

CULTURE • The sixties began on a Friday in Dallas, at 12:30 P.M. (local time) on November 22, with the assassination of John F. Kennedy, tragically ending a year of high promise and grim foreboding. The values of the established order and those of the revolution were about to clash far more openly and more violently than had earlier been the case. The optimistic symbol of peaceful, cooperative, and nationally unified change was gone. But the ideals arising earlier in the year were not: the civil-rights march on Washington capped with Martin Luther King, Jr.'s "I have a dream" speech; the Nuclear Test Ban Treaty; Vatican II; and the Re-actualization of feminism with the publication of Betty Friedan's *The Feminine Mystique*. Unfortunately, the forebodings remained: the assassination of civil rights leader Medgar Evers; the murder of four Black children attending Sunday school in Birmingham; the televised police-led attack on civil-rights marchers in Birmingham; the death of Pope John XXIII; the CIA assassination of South Vietnamese President Diem, and the firing of Timothy Leary from his teaching position at Harvard for advocating the use of LSD. James Baldwin's *The Fire Next Time* was published. To report it all, network TV news expanded its daily coverage from fifteen minutes to thirty.

MUSIC • The conflict was already a reality in the folk-rock scene, the third Newport Folk Festival providing a veritable tour de force of revolutionary expressions ("Blowin' in the Wind" and "The Times They Are a-Changin'" being not the least of them). Protest music had now reached its peak. Motown was on the rise despite Sam Cooke's shooting death, and Diana Ross was to become the first openly acknowledged Black sex fantasy for White males. The R&B charts were abolished — illustrating that integration had been accomplished ... in music, at least. Very shortly the naïveté of this ideal would also become evident, a truth that would again be revealed first in music. The big story, however, was somewhere else, in England — Liverpool, to be exact.

1964

CULTURE • Despite his innate contradictions and enormous ego, Lyndon Johnson won the presidency as the peace candidate — and brought us war. He led the tough Civil Rights Act through Congress, proclaiming "we shall overcome" on prime-time TV — to the cheers of millions and the scorn of other millions. But he also forced through the Gulf of Tonkin Resolution, placing America firmly in the Vietnam War. Aside from the continuation of civil-rights murders in the South and the Berkeley free speech movement, however, it appeared that Johnson had things pretty much under control. Yet, this was also the year that Cassius Clay became Muhammad Ali, *That Was the Week That Was* appeared on TV, and *Dr. Strangelove* was released. Obviously, some people were not quite so happy with LBJ and his Great Society.

MUSIC • We met The Beatles! Beginning with their appearance on *The Ed Sullivan Show* early in February, their first tour of the United States overwhelmed everyone — including The Beatles themselves. With the first five singles on the charts — "Can't Buy Me Love," "Twist and Shout," "She Loves You," "I Want to Hold Your Hand," and "Please Please Me") — they completely dominated popular music. However, Beatlemania was far more than a mere phenomenon of music; it was charged with quasi-religious significance. The four musicians became demigods. They thumbed their noses at authorities of every kind; they were joyous, free, and they took nothing seriously — least of all themselves; and they gave us hope. Soon, even the establishment fell in love with them, thus conceding to them the most effective role possible: a symbolic stature. The Quarrymen had come a long way.

1965

CULTURE • Antiwar demonstrations began in earnest, right along with the continued and progressively larger military escalation in Southeast Asia. (In 1987, Wallace Shawn's character, Vinzzini, in *The Princess Bride,* would proclaim this to be the most famous of the classic blunders, namely, to "get involved in a land war in Asia.") Somewhat lost in the shuffle, however, was the American invasion of the Dominican Republic. A Quaker's self-immolation at the Pentagon dramatically and tragically illustrated a growing popular reaction against war in general and the Vietnam situation in particular. Even with another strong Civil Rights Act and Bill Cosby being featured in TV's *I Spy,* Black discontent was still on the rise: thus the Selma marches, the Watts riots, and the outrage at the assassination of Malcolm X (followed immediately by his publication of his *Autobiography*). Seemingly, the only hopeful events were urban peace during the New York City blackout and the beginning of Frank Herbert's *Dune* trilogy (later to become a far longer series).

MUSIC • The Beatles, Dylan, Simon and Garfunkel, the Byrds, soul (featuring James Brown, Otis Redding and, consequently, the reinstatement of the R&B charts), and psychedelia dominated the year. Protests against the war and racism were becoming increasingly "the messages," and their media of expression were becoming increasingly TV and films as well as radio and records. Dylan changed his musical style to rock with *Bringing It All Back Home,* to the consternation of the fans of pure folk music, and Alan Freed died. It was a year of gradually developing bitterness.

1966

CULTURE • The Black Power movement competed for attention with more and more war protests, and "death of God" theologies began calling traditional religion into question more publicly than ever before. Christian and Jewish atheism became fashionable, but a spiritual dimension to existence was at the same time paradoxically affirmed. Sex and drugs were in the news too: Masters and Johnson's report was released and the use of LSD was placed under government regulation. Bad news was aplenty: the Richard Speck murders in Chicago; "race" riots in Chicago, Cleveland, Brooklyn, Baltimore and even Omaha, Nebraska; Lenny Bruce's death by a heroin overdose; and the shooting of James Meredith in Mississippi. There were some curiosities too: hippies were flowering; *Star Trek* was on TV; and the Red Guards' idealism, based on *The Quotations of Chairman Mao,* shook almost everyone's naive understanding about China.

MUSIC • The Beatles, with their existentially oriented album, *Revolver,* entered a much more serious stage. (Look at the album cover!) Other notable happenings included The Rolling Stones, Dylan (and his near fatal motorcycle accident), soul ("Say It Loud — I'm Black and I'm Proud" by James Brown), the Fugs (who united the fifties beatdom with the sixties hippiedom), and the arrival of FM rock. All were clearly responding to a time of turmoil but at the same time giving it direction. The Beatles performed their last live concert in San Francisco, and Lennon made his infamous "We're bigger than Jesus" statement. On the lighter side, but just as controversial, the Monkees appeared regularly on TV. (To their credit, they eventually did learn to play their instruments and their songs.) Finally, the only pro-war song to come out during the Vietnam War era hit the top of the charts: Barry Sadler's "Ballad of the Green Berets."

1967

CULTURE • Opposition to the war and racism continued as cultural negations, while alternative lifestyles were affirmed as part of the positive side of the revolution. Communes of every conceivable type were set up, and modifications of the traditional marriage relationship to greater or lesser degrees were tried. The year included an antiwar march on the Pentagon (countered by a pro-war march in New York), *The Smothers Brothers Comedy Hour* on TV, *MacBird* on the stage, Muhammad Ali's dethronement as heavyweight boxing champion (because he didn't have anything against "them Viet Congs"), the release of *The Graduate*, and the massive Newark riot. San Francisco's Human Be-In and Tom Wolfe's *Electric Kool-Aid Acid Test* pointed to "the summer of love," despite the "Hippie Funeral" and chartered tours through the Haight-Asbury ("Hashbury") district. Elsewhere, Che Guevara was killed while trying to incite another Cuban-style communist revolution in Bolivia, and the Israelis defeated the Arabs in the Six Day War.

MUSIC • The Beatles' *Sgt. Pepper's Lonely Hearts Club Band* outdid everything, including *Hair,* Monterey Pop, the Jefferson Airplane, the Doors, the Grateful Dead, Country Joe and the Fish, Jimi Hendrix, Sly and the Family Stone, and underground radio. Sly and the Family Stone deserve a special mention. Comprising Blacks and Whites, males and females, they presented a rare sight in 1967 and a pretty rare one today as well. Some unfortunate deaths: folk singer Woody Guthrie, soul singer Otis Redding, and The Beatles' manager Brian Epstein — all losses of the first magnitude.

1968

CULTURE • There is no way a mere list of events can convey how it felt to live through this year — but here goes: both Robert Kennedy and Martin Luther King, Jr., assassinated; the police riots at the Democratic National Convention in Chicago; the Tet Offensive in Vietnam; the My Lai massacre, also in Vietnam; the Berrigan brothers' war protests; the "National Mobilization" against the war, created by a coalition of many antiwar organizations; "Resurrection City," the massive "tent-in" on the Mall in Washington, D.C., to protest poverty; the Paris student protests; the Czech uprising; campus demonstrations too numerous to mention; Black Power; the seizure of the USS *Pueblo* by North Koreans; the election-forced retirement of LBJ; and the election of Nixon as the new president. *Laugh-In* emerged on TV, *2001* on the movie screen, and Norman Mailer's *Armies of the Night* and Kurt Vonnegut's *Slaughterhouse-Five* on bookshelves.

MUSIC • Always The Beatles (*The Beatles,* was released, better known as the "White Album"), Dylan, the Who, the Rolling Stones, incipient heavy metal rock (Led Zeppelin), country rock (the Band), a blues revival (Janis Joplin) and, in general, the search for something new in something old. Elvis's return, with a spectacular pre–Christmas TV special, showed us the past really wasn't dead after all. However, it was hardly a Christmas show. Instead, his manager, Colonel Tom Parker, designed it to demonstrate that Elvis hadn't lost anything in the previous ten years. And he hadn't — he could still do it all. Maybe, we all thought, the reports of his demise as an actively symbolic figure had been greatly exaggerated.

1969

CULTURE • The disruptions of the previous year continued, both negative and affirmative: violent antiwar demonstrations in Washington, D.C., and elsewhere; the Weathermen; police raids on the Black Panthers; the soldiers' strike in Vietnam; the Chicago Eight trial; Senator Frank Church's antiwar bill; cancellation of the Smothers Brothers show; UCLA's firing of Angela Davis (a feminist, anti-war, anti-racist communist); the seizure of Alcatraz by Native Americans; the Charles Manson murders; the death of Ho Chi Minh; Chappaquiddick; the *Apollo XI* moon landing; Charles Reich's *The Greening of America*; and more. There was no end in sight; the dialectic continued.

MUSIC • Woodstock and its negation, Altamont, headed the list, but The Beatles were a close second (with Paul McCartney's alleged death, their internal legal battles, and their last album, *Abbey Road*). It's worth noting that Woodstock began with Richie Havens singing several extended verses of "Freedom" (a spontaneously improvised rendition of an old negro spiritual, "Motherless Child," because no other acts were prepared to go on) and ended with Jimi Hendrix singing a heavily "wah-wahed" version of "The Star Spangled Banner." There you have it: America's cultural revolutions distilled to its essence: Freedom. Meanwhile, country rock continued (Creedence Clearwater Revival; Crosby, Stills, Nash and Young), and a rock-and-roll revival was in full swing. Meanwhile, *Easy Rider*, starring Jack Nicholson, Peter Fonda, and Dennis Hopper on a drug-laced motorcycle trip across America, surprised the film industry with its low cost and high quality. With an extraordinary sound track (the Band, the Byrds, Jimi Hendrix, and Steppenwolf, among others), it demonstrated the culture-music linkage as few films have ever done.

1970

CULTURE • Still the traumas of race and war continued and, if possible, intensified with the killings of students at Kent State and Jackson State by the National Guard and police respectively; the U.S. invasion of Cambodia; nearly universal campus demonstrations and even a few bombings; the repeal of the Gulf of Tonkin Resolution; and the election of socialist party leader Salvador Allende Gossens in Chile. The mood of the country had now shifted almost entirely to an antiwar posture, and the linkage between the peace movement and the struggle against racism was no longer questioned. The film *M*A*S*H* premiered; ostensibly a dark satire about the Korean War, it mentioned Korea only once, in the opening scroll, and was understood to be actually about Vietnam. Universities began recruiting minorities for the first time.

MUSIC • Tragedies here too: The deaths of Janis Joplin and Jimi Hendrix and the dissolution of The Beatles. Simon and Garfunkel's last album, *Bridge Over Troubled Water*, was the top album of the year, and a fitting commentary it was.

1971

CULTURE • It seemed endless: the Attica prison riots; the unsanctioned publication of *The Pentagon Papers*; the invasion of Laos and the resulting massive antiwar march on Washington, D.C., with thousands of illegal arrests. Meanwhile, *All in the Family* began a new TV era with its portrayal of fundamental values in conflict.

MUSIC • The deaths this year included Jim Morrison and Duane Allman, but hope was expressed in ways that would develop in years to come: *Jesus Christ Superstar,* George Harrison's *Concert for Bangladesh*, and John Lennon's *Imagine*. Led Zeppelin replaced The Beatles as England's most popular group; an era was winding down.

1972

CULTURE • During the sharply divided presidential campaign, the shooting of George Wallace in Maryland ended his candidacy but not his life; in the following months, Nixon overwhelmed George McGovern to win a second term. Nixon then visited China and the Soviet Union but began his own downfall by overseeing, and helping to cover up, the Watergate break-in. Still the war continued: massive saturation bombings of North Vietnam preceded a United States–initiated cease-fire. Elsewhere, the death penalty was temporarily halted and *M*A*S*H* began as a TV series.

MUSIC • Country rock continued and diversified, and the Rolling Stones toured the United States. But another Britisher, Elton John, was the big news. His fourth album, *Honky Chateau*, perhaps his best, was released. Although it attacked an old enemy, racism, it also expressed an underlying fear that the revolution had begun to stall (in "I Think I'm Going to Kill Myself").

1973

CULTURE • The climax of the "sixties": the Paris Peace Accords were signed, ending direct American military intervention in Vietnam; Spiro Agnew resigned the vice-presidency in disgrace; Congress passed the Equal Rights Amendment; the Supreme Court legalized abortion; and the Watergate hearings got under way.

MUSIC • Already looking to the future, reggae (for example, in the film, *The Harder Come* with Jimmy Cliff) and disco emerged with contradictory messages. Jimmy Cliff was warning that liberation would require a renewal of the struggle with "You Can Get It If You Really Want It," as was Johnny Nash with "Stir It Up." But the Spinners, with "One of a Kind (Love Affair)," the Stylistics, in "Rock 'n' Roll Baby," and Manu Dibango's "Soul Makossa" were advising us to dance our troubles away. As if to keep Woodstock alive, 600,000 rock fans came to Watkins Glen, New York, for another peaceful concert. Bruce Springsteen was looked to as the new Dylan or Elvis, and fifties nostalgia erupted with the highly regarded and highly mythic film *American Graffiti*, an interpretive portrayal of the period.

1974

Note: Another symbolic year, bringing an end to the "sixties" but not the cultural revolution. The fact that revolutionary values were not formally institutionalized is not important. What mattered above all else was the fact that they had been voiced in a coherent way; they achieved legitimacy. The denouement was to last for the next several years.

CULTURE • Nixon's resignation, after a threatened impeachment, was the symbolic event that closed the tumultuous era. Neither the bad feelings created by Gerald Ford's pardon of Nixon nor the diversion provided by the Patty Hearst kidnapping could spoil the relief. But the relief was hardly joyous; it was just relief.

MUSIC • Nothing really new or eventful was happening on the surface. Elton John's popularity continued, but the incipient reggae and disco trends were more significant. Stevie Wonder's "Boogie on Reggae Woman" and Eric Clapton's cover of Bob Marley's "I Shot the Sheriff" illustrated the former, while MFSB's "TSOP (The Sound of Philadelphia)," Betty Wright's "Where Is the Love," and George McCrae's "Rock Your Baby" illustrated the latter.

1975

CULTURE • There were only aftershocks now; as Cambodia and South Vietnam were overrun, the remaining Americans were unceremoniously snatched from the top of the U.S. embassy in Saigon. Nixon's cohorts were convicted for assisting him in covering up the Watergate break-in. And future U.S. international problems were presaged in the Cambodian seizure of the U.S. merchant ship *Mayagüez*.

MUSIC • Something genuinely new, *Saturday Night Live*, one of the most remarkable shows ever to appear on TV, made its debut. It featured classic and soon-to-be classic rock performers (such as Randy Newman in 1975, Jimmy Cliff in 1976, Joan Armatrading and Elvis Costello in 1977, Devo in 1978, and the Talking Heads in 1979), introduced new variations in music (such as the Lockers, Toni Basil, the Roches, the B-52's, Leon Redbone, Brick and Kate Bush), spawned a series of clones, and invited The Beatles to reunite on the show — for $3,000. (Lennon and McCartney, watching the broadcast together in Lennon's New York apartment in the Dakota, almost drove over on a lark — an event portrayed interestingly in the 2000 film *The Two of Us*.)

1976

CULTURE • Aside from Jimmy Carter's presidential election, nothing much happened. The country was preoccupied with the bicentennial and the repression of the Vietnam experience in our collective consciousness. A space feat helped to do the job as well — two *Viking* space probes landed on Mars and sent back spectacular photographs.

MUSIC • McCartney was back, illustrating through his world tour that The Beatles and what they symbolized were far from dead — dormant, perhaps, but hardly dead. Despite their personal desires, The Beatles' legend lived on in each one of the four. Otherwise, Fleetwood Mac was becoming a phenomenon; Elvis's *Sun Sessions* was released; Parliament/Funkadelic, the film *Car Wash*, and *Dr. Buzzard's Original "Savannah" Band* signaled the rise of funk; and the *Outlaws* album pointed to a new trend in C&W.

1977

CULTURE • Carter's major action was to pardon Vietnam draft evaders. Inflation increased, John Irving's *World According to Garp* was the book to read, the *Roots* phenomenon on TV illustrated the historic plight of Black Americans under slavery, and with Gary Gilmore's execution, capital punishment was reinstituted for the first time in ten years.

MUSIC • Reggae developed (or devolved, perhaps) into a cult phenomenon; but with the punk rock groups the Ramones (in the U.S.) and the Sex Pistols (in the U.K.), a renewed revolutionary awareness was also growing. Disco was at its peak with *Saturday Night Fever*, which starred John Travolta as Tony Manero, a Brooklyn youth seeking recognition and self-fulfillment in a discotheque. The movie illustrated, as others had so many times before, that the intricacies of dance are directly proportional to social divisiveness. Whereas earlier the dances were simple and unsophisticated enough to allow everyone to participate, now they required lessons. Punk rockers countered with the ultra-unsophisticated pogo (jumping up and down). The death this year was a big one: on the eighth anniversary of Woodstock, Elvis was found dead at Graceland, burned out as his music had been for years. The negation he symbolized, however, would endure. Other music was getting interesting: Elvis Costello, the Ramones, Steely Dan, David Bowie, Talking Heads, Randy Newman, and Little Feat all released critically acclaimed and thought-provoking albums. The only official live Beatles album was also released, *Beatles at the Hollywood Bowl*.

1978

CULTURE • Billy Carter was beginning to embarrass his brother, Jimmy, as was the uncontrollable inflation. But Jimmy Carter had spectacular success in bringing Israeli prime minister Menachem Begin and Egyptian president Anwar Sadat together, setting in motion the peace process between their two countries. The international horror created by the Vietnamese "boat people" refugees, however, presented Carter with insoluble problems. The Supreme Court set back affirmative action programs with the Bakke decision. And an ugly travesty occurred with the mass suicide of Jim Jones and his People's Temple followers in Guyana.

MUSIC • Dormancy and waiting. With no clear embodiment of the established order, there could be no catalyst, no enemy to spark the stalled revolution. The old order had been banished in Nixonian luxury to San Clemente, and the new order had no clear direction. The death of rock and roll was both lamented and celebrated, but as with Mark Twain's, its death was highly exaggerated. Blondie's *Parallel Lines*, Bruce Springsteen's *Darkness on the Edge of Town*, Warren Zevon's *Excitable Boy*, Funkadelic's *One Nation Under a Groove*, Patti Smith's *Easter*, Elvis Costello's *Armed Forces* and Teddy Pendergrass's *Life Is a Song Worth Singing* are a few notable counterexamples.

1979

CULTURE • The Iranian takeover of the U.S. embassy in Teheran dominated American consciousness, providing an illusory unity. The civil war in El Salvador, the Sandinista takeover in Nicaragua, and the Three Mile Island nuclear accident, however, showed the cracks beneath the surface. Sixty-five thousand people protested against nuclear power in Washington, D.C., and Jerry Falwell's "Moral Majority" portended something really ugly — declaring those holding "nontraditional" values as both non–Christian and un–American. His anti-abortion, anti-gay, anti–ERA and anti–nuclear freeze positions almost made him a parody of the revolution's opposition.

MUSIC • The antiwar movement now took shape in the emerging "no nukes" sentiment. The *No Nukes* concert and album helped keep the movement alive. Present were Bruce Springsteen; Crosby, Stills, and Nash; Tom Petty and the Heartbreakers; Chaka Khan; Bonnie Raitt; the Doobie Brothers; Jackson Browne; and Gil Scott-Heron among others. Also, Dire Straits' *Dire Straits*, Pink Floyd's *The Wall*, and Prince's *Prince* were pointed reminders that the revolution was far from dead.

1980

Note: Again a symbolic event, indicating this time the beginnings of the Counter-Reaction — a revived, renewed, and reconstituted version of the old established order delivered an enormous counterpunch. Having learned its weaknesses and profited from its mistakes, it would be a formidable opponent for the stalled revolution for many years to come.

CULTURE • With Reagan's election, the Counter-Reaction had begun, embodied by someone almost always underestimated. He would not provide an easy target as had LBJ and Nixon. The bitter memories of Iran's holding American hostages, the strikes in Poland, and the Soviet Union's invasion of Afghanistan (along with Carter's boycott of the Olympics in Moscow) would provide convenient, external foci for American attention, and Ronald Reagan would make wise use of them. His domestic program ended the last vestiges of FDR's welfare liberalism and brought back into the limelight Classical 18th century liberalism (à la Adam Smith) supported by a healthy dose of Social Darwinism (à la Andrew Carnegie). Moreover, to top this off, he revived the puritan ethic as well. Meanwhile, the revolutionary values of liberation were not being adequately expressed, headed off at the pass by Reagan and his wealthy and security-conscious supporters. "Reaganomics" was on the horizon. But problems were developing: three American nuns were murdered by government troops in El Salvador; Ku Klux Klan and American Nazi Party members were acquitted of murdering communist demonstrators in North Carolina; and Miami experienced serious race riots.

MUSIC • There was really only one event. It came late in the year in New York, on December 8: John Lennon's murder. The public reaction showed, as the McCartney tour had shown already, that what The Beatles symbolized was living still and maybe not quite as dormant as it had been. Lennon, after all, was immersed in the movement more than all of the other Beatles combined (as his solo albums more than adequately demonstrate). The reunion rumors were finally laid to rest. Many thought Lennon *was* The Beatles; so without him, there would be no second coming. A few albums, however, do deserve mention for helping to preserve the revolutionary consciousness: the Clash's *London Calling*, Lennon/Ono's *Double Fantasy*, Rockpile's *Seconds of Pleasure*, the Police's *Zenyatta Mondatta*, Stevie Wonder's *Hotter Than July*, Bob Marley and the Wailers' *Uprising*, Adam and the Ants' *Kings of the Wild Frontier*, the Bus Boys' *Minimum Wage Rock and Roll*, and the Ramones' *End of the Century*.

1981

CULTURE • Although the big story was Reagan's program of massive government deregulation, his support for the MX missile and El Salvador's government with money and advisors was even more significant. Solidarity Day in Washington, D.C., attracted over a quarter of a million protesters. But attention was diverted by the assassination of Anwar Sadat and the wounding of Pope John Paul II and of Reagan himself. On TV we were watching *Hill Street Blues*. And we were getting to know our first woman Supreme Court justice, Sandra Day O'Connor — a major development in manifesting revolutionary values.

MUSIC • Kim Carnes's "Bette Davis Eyes" was the song of the year, but Prince's *Controversy* (which included "Ronnie, Talk to Russia Before It's Too Late") would be remembered far longer. Less explicit but equally effective albums of negation were *The Blasters* and *Was (Not*

Was), the former updating the past and the latter manifesting the present. Two documentary films performed the same function: *This Is Elvis* and *The Decline of Western Civilization* (about the Los Angeles punk scene).

1982

CULTURE • The beginnings of an economic recovery disguised the emergence of several serious and long-term conflicts: the CIA's support for the anti–Sandinista "Contras" in Nicaragua, right-wing victories in El Salvador, a proposed constitutional amendment permitting public-school prayer, the official defeat of the ERA, the EPA scandal caused by zealous deregulators, and the MX missile—all of which had Reagan's support. The dedication of the memorial to Vietnam War veterans in Washington, D.C., threatened to open old wounds. (It actually performed a healing function.) However, we were distracted by the British-Argentinean war in the Falkland Islands, the Tylenol poisoning scare, another race riot in Miami, and the death of John Belushi.

MUSIC • Antiwar sentiment was undergoing a revival with a "no nukes" concert in New York's Central Park; Billy Joel's "Goodnight Saigon" on his *Nylon Curtain* album; the Clash's *Combat Rock*; Crosby, Stills and Nash's "Wasted on the Way"; and the film *Atomic Cafe*. There was an appeal to the old (in albums by Marshall Crenshaw and George Thorogood) and to the new (in albums by the Waitresses, Juluka, X, and Elvis Costello). We danced (to Michael Jackson's *Thriller*), we brooded (to Bruce Springsteen's *Nebraska*), we laughed (to the Go-Go's *Vacation*) and we cried (to Paul McCartney's *Tug of War* with his farewell to John Lennon in "Here Today"). Technologically, compact discs and players were introduced, providing the clearest reproduction of sound to date. Many of the latter were shown off at the U.S. Festival (originated by Apple's Steve Wozniak), which resurrected the large rock festivals called to a halt by Altamont.

1983

Note: It was "20 years ago ('today')" when the "sixties" began, and it's worth noting that people remembered this November 22 as especially significant.

CULTURE • The renewal of the conflict was now well under way. Reagan's policies in Central America seemed to be more and more like those of Vietnam. (Posters, for example, were distributed with the names of one area superimposed on the map of the other.) In numerous cities throughout Europe, over two million people gathered for a day of protest against Reagan's military policies. Catholic bishops in the United States voted overwhelmingly to oppose Reagan's reliance on nuclear weapons. Over two hundred American soldiers were killed by a terrorist's bomb in Lebanon. We had a "splendid little war" in Grenada. The government was forced to buy the entire town of Times Beach, Missouri, because of uncontrolled toxic wastes. The Reagan administration was also forced to accept January 15 as a federal holiday commemorating the birth of Martin Luther King, Jr. Over a quarter of a million gathered at the Washington Monument to remember the 1963 civil-rights march at which King gave his "I have a dream" speech. Numerous other events acknowledged the symbolic significance of John Kennedy's assassination and The Beatles' first American tour. Meanwhile, there were other serious developments: the outbreak of AIDS, the Soviet downing of Korean Airlines flight 007 and a steadily improving economy (which many felt did not include the poor).

MUSIC • There were some more pointed blasts from the past (Dylan's *Infidels*, Paul Simon's *Hearts and Bones*, Pink Floyd's *Final Cut*, and Randy Newman's *Trouble in Paradise*), all having antiwar messages. There were also previews of coming attractions: neo-protest (Peter Schilling, the Blasters, and Talking Heads), neo-psychedelic/paisley underground (the Bangles, Dream Syndicate, Rain Parade, and the Three O'Clock), country-punk (Jason and the Scorchers, Rank and File, the Long Ryders, Lone Justice, and Blood on the Saddle), Latino rock (Tierra, Los Illegals, the Plugz, Los Lobos, and the Brat), to say nothing of hardcore punk (Suicidal Tendencies) and African rock (King Sunny Adé). As Huey Lewis and the News sang, "The Heart of Rock and Roll (Is Still Beating)." Clearly, it was. With the increasing conflicts in society at large, rock was entering one of its most active and creative periods. Music videos were coming into their own to capture all of this visually (Randy Newman's "I Love L.A." and Michael Jackson's "Billie Jean" being two superlative examples). The film *The Big Chill* maintained ties with the sixties by dealing with the apparent loss of ideals — its soundtrack comprised some of Motown's finest. Not to be forgotten was the second installment of the U.S. Festival, wherein each of the three days was devoted to a particular style: new wave, heavy metal, and rock.

1984

CULTURE • There was no lessening of conflict. For the first time, a Black American (Jesse Jackson) was a relatively serious contender for the presidential nomination, and a woman (Geraldine Ferraro) was nominated for vice president on the Democratic ticket. The Democratic Party, because of its opposition to Reagan, also came to embody the more explicitly political aspects of the cultural revolution. Carly Simon's "Here Comes the Turning of the Tide" was adopted as the party's official theme song. But a still-improving economy made a Democratic victory virtually impossible, especially since the Democrats had been unable to separate Reagan's personal popularity from his increasingly unpopular policies. A travesty of a trial was held in El Salvador to convict some underlings for the murder of three American nuns, and a demented gunman slaughtered over twenty people in a McDonald's near San Diego. Tragic deaths included Marvin Gaye and Dennis Wilson.

MUSIC • The Re-actualization of the revolutionary conflict over fundamental values was evident in the film *Footloose*. Its theme was a contemporary conflict between an irrational, repressive establishment and liberated youth, and the music was an essential component of the plot. The past recharged the present in Bruce Springsteen's *Born in the U.S.A.*, Lou Reed's *New Sensations*, and the Rolling Stones' *Undercover*. Newer artists, of course, were even more active: UB-40, Prince, Cyndi Lauper, X, Grandmaster Flash, Elvis Costello, the Alarm, Billy Idol, Culture Club, Laurie Anderson, and Kate Bush. Prince and Culture Club's Boy George deserve special attention. Together they illustrate the intrinsic connection between negation and affirmation — in their negation, they affirmed something positive about sexual roles and sexual orientations. People either loved them or hated them; no one ignored them. The torch was being passed.

1985

CULTURE • Reagan's "Teflon coating" began to wear a little thin, with attacks being mounted against his policies on the budget, tax reform, trade, the Strategic Defense Initiative ("Star Wars") and his "constructive engagement" approach toward South Africa. Opposition to South Africa's apartheid policy became increasingly vociferous, with campus demonstrations and protest marches dredging up memories of the sixties. Some of the most active participants were quite familiar, albeit a little older. When Rock Hudson's battle against AIDS became public knowledge, it suddenly became respectable to voice concern and sympathy for AIDS victims, and there emerged an increasing awareness of the need to end the repression of gays and lesbians. The plight of drought-ridden and starving Africans also caught widespread attention and sympathy.

MUSIC • Collaborative charity efforts manifested a groundswell of concern throughout the year, beginning with the British Band Aid project, continuing with the American U.S.A. for Africa performers, and climaxing with the gigantic, worldwide, multi-venue and universally televised Live Aid concert, and its offshoot, the Farm Aid concert. Some of the most popular albums provided a mix of old and new artists, diverse themes, and styles: Bruce Springsteen's *Born in the U.S.A.*, Tina Turner's *Private Dancer*, John Fogerty's *Centerfield*, Huey Lewis and the News's *Sports*, Madonna's *Like a Virgin*, Prince's *Around the World in a Day*, and Bryan Adams's *Reckless*. Springsteen's "No Surrender" exhibited an antiwar theme, as did Turner's "We Don't Need Another Hero" (from the apocalyptic movie *Mad Max Beyond Thunderdome*). The fifties and sixties were revived with Fogerty's "Big Train from Memphis," Adams's "Summer of '69," Huey Lewis and the News's "The Heart of Rock and Roll (Is Still Beating)," and Springsteen's "My Hometown." And Sgt. Pepper was resurrected with Prince's album. More specifically, and despite the passage of ten years since the "end" of the war, anti–Vietnam War songs became even more prevalent: "19" by Paul Hardcastle, "Stars and Stripes of Corruption" by the Dead Kennedys, "The Wall" by Bernie Higgins, "Clean Cut Kid" by Bob Dylan, and "Born in the U.S.A.," by Springsteen, a song often misunderstood as merely a patriotic anthem. All of this kept us aware that the war had an "aftermath." Madonna and some heavy metal groups came under attack by the PMRC (Parents' Music Resource Center) for their allegedly obscene, blasphemous, violent, occult and degrading music and videos. The PMRC's ostensible purpose was to encourage placing "warning labels" on albums. Much of this is symptomatic of the renewal of the revolutionary struggle, and more like it was to be expected.

1986

CULTURE • The horror that was bound to happen, given the dangers of space exploration, finally did: The shuttle *Challenger* exploded on lift-off for the entire world to see. Other disasters this year included the nuclear explosion at the Chernobyl Nuclear Power Station in the Ukraine (then part of the Soviet Union) causing the release of radioactive material across much of Europe, and the discovery and spread of mad cow disease in England. A political scandal for the Reagan administration, Iran-Contra, deepened suspicions about the American government's activities. But there were optimistic events as well: the Human Genome Project was begun, approximately seven to eight million people joined together in "Hands Across America," the USSR successfully placed the *Mir* space station in orbit, email came into being, IBM produced one of the first laptop computers and there was talk of nuclear disarmament between the U.S. and the Soviets.

MUSIC • There was a wide diversity of music this year, which might indicate a lack of unity or direction — something undesirable. However, the accomplishment of diversity might more aptly be seen as something positive. Janet Jackson's soulful *Control*, the pop success of the all-female group the Bangles, genuine rap artistry with Run-D.M.C. (their album *Raising Hell* being the first rap album to go platinum), Dwight Yoakam's punk-country song "Honky Tonk Man," Cameo's techno-funk, the light metal of Bon Jovi, the art fusion of Sade and the quirkiness of Cyndi Lauper taken all together seemed to presage something good. Overall, more seemed to be affirmed this year than negated.

1987

CULTURE • It was a year of continued foreboding. A new drug for AIDS, AZT, was introduced, as was the controversial antidepressant drug Prozac. French agents sank a ship of the environmental activist group Greenpeace. The stock market plunged 22.6 percent in one day. And Rupert Murdoch set in motion the Fox News Channel that would become the de facto communication vehicle for "traditional" values and the political personalities who espoused them. There were some rumblings of something new as well: The Cambridge Z88 lightweight computer entered the marketplace and began to win a cult-like following. Also entering the mainstream of culture was the first use of DNA in court to convict a criminal. The "Chunnel" (English Channel tunnel) was started, metaphorically promising a significant change in how we think about national boundaries. More amusing than significant, the not-so-good Reverend Jim Bakker was caught with his hand in the proverbial till and would later be indicted for mail fraud.

MUSIC • The Beatles' first five albums were released on CD. U-2 did a Beatlesque rooftop concert for a video to advertise *The Joshua Tree*, the big deal of the year. Also Michael Jackson's *BAD* yielded a record five #1 singles; Guns N' Roses made it big with their *Appetite for Destruction;* and George Michael's first album, *Faith*, sold 11 million copies. Although not in the rock idiom, it should be noted that Andrew Lloyd Webber's *Phantom of the Opera* opened in London. It would become the most seen and longest running musical in history. The story's appeal had a lot to do with the sympathy we have for the downtrodden and social outcasts. It took the telling of this story through music for it to have such a massive impact. The top music of this year was varied, and for the first time listed two "raps" by Public Enemy (with Chuck D and Flavor Flav), newly signed to Def Jam Records. U-2, R.E.M., The Cure, Guns N' Roses and Prince were on that list too. The U.K. and Black America were both well represented. Rock music was no longer merely an American phenomenon — nor was the cultural revolution. As if to reinforce this notion in a curious way, the Beastie Boys became the first group to be censored on *American Bandstand*.

1988

CULTURE • Following in the wake of Oliver North and President Reagan's Iran-Contra scandal, George H.W. Bush and Dan Quayle beat out Michael Dukakis and Lloyd Bentsen for the two top jobs. Soon after, the Dan Quayle jokes began in earnest. There were ominous rumblings overseas: The Soviets finally admitted defeat in Afghanistan after an 8-year war. The U.S. bombed Iranian oil platforms in retaliation for an earlier Iranian attack. Popular uprisings in Bratislava, Slovakia, against the communist regime foretold the imminent collapse of the Soviet state. The Iran-Iraq war ended with over a million killed. There were I.R.A. killings of British soldiers in Ireland, and Pan Am flight 103 was sabotaged over Lockerbie, Scotland. Deaths included porno legend John Holmes, 12-year-old Tempest Kayne Smith by suicide, allegedly prompted by bullying in school, Harris Glenn Milstead (a.k.a. Divine), and Roy Orbison.

MUSIC • African American music, especially rap, began to dominate the charts, with recordings by N.W.A, Public Enemy, Rob Base & DJ E-Z Rock, and (of course) Michael Jackson. But punk (Fugazi), metal (Def Leppard), alternative (Sonic Youth) were present and accounted for as well. It was a big night at the Rock and Roll Hall of fame, too, when The Beach Boys, The Beatles, The Drifters, Bob Dylan, and The Supremes were all inducted. The 1987 mini-tribute concert to Roy Orbison, *A Black and White Night,* was aired on television—soon to become a major item in everyone's collection of recordings. The iconic Motown song, "I Heard It Through the Grapevine" made it big again by advertisers who used animated raisins to sing it. Plus, for the first time ever, CDs outsold vinyl albums. The end for vinyl would come very quickly.

1989

CULTURE • Times were beginning to change: Ron Brown was the first African American to head a major political party (the Democrats), New York City had its first Black mayor (David Dinkins) and Barbara Harris was ordained the first female Bishop of the American Episcopal Church. Still, Robert Mapplethorpe's photo exhibit, which included explicitly sexual (and homosexual) images, was removed from the Corcoran Gallery of Art. In entertainment, Sega released Genesis and Nintendo released Game Boy. Plus, both *Seinfeld* and *The Simpsons* premiered on TV. The nasty and infamous *Exxon Valdez* spilled oil in Alaska. Alas, Abbie Hoffman and Gilda Radner died. Yet bigger news came from afar. On the downside: the Ayatollah Khomeini placed a $3 million bounty on the head of author Salman Rushdie, author of *The Satanic Verses,* and many of the students protesting for freedom in Beijing's Tiananmen Square were massacred. Both events foreboded greater troubles to come. On the upside: at long last there was an apt example of the much ballyhooed "domino theory"—first Hungary, then Poland, the three Baltic states, East Germany, Czechoslovakia and finally Romania all declared their independence from the Soviet Union—ending Soviet domination in eastern Europe. The Cold War was over, seemingly in the blink of an eye. Symbolizing it all was the mutual dismantling of the Berlin Wall by East and West Berliners.

MUSIC • Woodstock '89 tried to recapture the spirit of the 1969 original, but more important events occurred this year. Madonna's "Like a Virgin" video debuted amid lots of controversy. Also of interest, Michael Jackson was crowned "King of Pop," The Monkees reunited for a few concerts and Ringo formed Ringo Starr and His All Starr Band. Finally, an event surely to cause Lenin to roll over and give Stalin the news, the Moscow Peace Fest went on without a hitch, with several heavy metal bands headlining the show (Mötley Crüe, Ozzy Osbourne, Bon Jovi, Skid Row, Cinderella and the Scorpions). Oh yes, James Brown got six years in lockup for his high-speed chase through two states. (Rock and Roll!)

1990

CULTURE • Some positive signs of the times: Douglas Wilder was the first elected African American governor (Virginia). Nelson Mandela was released from Victor Verster Prison after 27 years behind bars. Antonia Novello was sworn in as the first female and Hispanic American surgeon general of the United States. The World Health Organization removed homosexuality from its list of diseases. In space, the "Pale Blue Dot" photo of earth was sent back from *Voyager 1,* then 3.5 billion miles away, and the Hubble telescope was successfully launched. East Germany and West Germany reunified into a single Germany—a further clue that the Soviet state was mercifully coming to an end. However, ominously, the Gulf War loomed ahead. In technology, Microsoft presented Windows 3.0 to the world.

MUSIC • Something old became new again when The Byrds reunited with Bob Dylan in concert. Both Depeche Mode and MTV's *Unplugged* signaled something new. Milli Vanilli borrowed a little lip-synch technology and rode it into oblivion. And Madonna faced the threat of arrest in Canada for acting out a little something blue in her concert. (The authorities backed down.) On that same note, a judge in Nevada decided that Judas Priest was *not* responsible for two mentally tortured youths committing suicide. And how could you classify this? The musical drama *Cop Rock* made its [tragically, in my opinion] short visit to prime time television. Farm Aid IV in Indiana and a tribute concert in Wembley Stadium to Nelson Mandela brought older and newer performers together. Big songs of the year included Sinéad O'Connor's "Nothing Compares 2 U," Madonna's "Vogue" and MC Hammer's "U Can't Touch This." Tragic deaths included Del Shannon, Stevie Ray Vaughan, Johnnie Ray and Jim Henson.

1991

CULTURE • As the year began, so did the First Gulf War (a.k.a. Desert Storm). The Provisional I.R.A. created terror in London, attacking 10 Downing Street and several train stations. In Los Angeles, a bystander's video of police beating Rodney King was made public. Jeffrey Dahmer was arrested for at least 17 murders and mutilations. On a much better note, after a failed coup attempt against Mikhail Gorbachev, the U.S.S.R. formally ceased to exist; the Supreme Soviet voted itself out of existence, and Boris Yeltsin was elected president. Also, in South Africa, apartheid was formally repealed. The future dawned with the creation of the World Wide Web utilizing hypertext, and Linus Torvalds invented Linux, a free open-source operating system. Gamers, of course, had something to look forward to with Sega's Hedgehog series.

MUSIC • This year yielded a few more subcategories for an already swelling list of rock genres, a process that would soon call the intelligibility of the categorization process into question. New subgenres included the following: grunge (Nirvana, Pearl Jam, Alice in Chains, Soundgarden and Stone Temple Pilots); glam metal (Def Leppard, Mötley Crüe, Poison and Ratt—their categorization created as their popularity declined); death metal (Suffocation); trance music (Dance 2 Trance and Resistance D); alternative rap (De La Soul, Dream Warriors, Gang Starr and the Poor Righteous Teachers); pop/crossover country (Garth Brooks); and even contemporary Christian (Amy Grant and Michael Smith). Notables included Metallica, Guns N' Roses, Janet Jackson, Michael Jackson, Whitney Houston, Tupac Shakur, U-2 and the Red Hot Chili Peppers. That's a pretty eclectic list, if you ask me! Oh yes, there was another suit, this one in Macon, Georgia, against a "metallurgist" for allegedly inducing suicide with music—Ozzy Osbourne this time. Like the others, it was also dismissed. The first Lollapalooza happened. The surviving members of Bill Haley and His Comets began performing again. Leo Fender died. (He invented the Stratocaster!) So did Tennessee Ernie Ford and Freddie Mercury.

1992

CULTURE • A year before Bill Clinton's turn at the top began, George Bush vomited and then fainted in the lap of the Japanese prime minister in Tokyo. Not to be outdone, Dan

Quayle blamed America's "poverty of values" on people like the TV character Murphy Brown, a single mother, and then later erroneously chastised an elementary school student's "misspelling" of "potato" without an "e" at the end. Better news: The Kentucky Supreme Court held that laws criminalizing same-sex sodomy were unconstitutional. Pope John Paul II (at long last) issued an apology for the Roman Inquisition's persecution of Galileo Galilei, but it didn't stop Sinéad O'Connor from ripping up his picture on *Saturday Night Live*. Nevertheless, the Church of England did decide to allow women to become priests. Bad news: riots of considerable size and intensity ensued in Los Angeles after a jury acquitted four LAPD officers of using excessive force in arresting Rodney King.

MUSIC • Dr. Dre released his groundbreaking and critically acclaimed album, *The Chronic*, which began the mainstream popularity and success of gangsta rap, g-funk and West Coast hip-hop. Note that this added yet more subgenres to the mix. Other music of note included the record-breaking success of Boys II Men, being at #1 for 12 weeks. Farm Aid Five and the Freddie Mercury Tribute Concert produced significant mixes of musical genre, and raised significant coinage for charities as well. Sam Kinison, Mary Wells and Eddie Kendricks all died this year.

1993

CULTURE • The beginning of the year saw a new beginning for Europe, as the European Community began dissolving old barriers. Women achieved a victory as Clinton decreed that they should be deemed eligible to fly warplanes in the air force, and a mixed notice with Lorena Bobbitt's "bobbing" of her husband's male extension. Gays achieved marginal success with Clinton's questionable "don't ask, don't tell" policy, and a mixed blessing of their plight with the film *Philadelphia*. Ugly stuff happened in Waco, Texas, when the Branch Davidian farm was torched by FBI and AFT agents to end the siege of the cult's headquarters. Even more ominous, a terrorist bomb killed six and injured over a thousand at the World Trade Center in New York. Elsewhere, American's youth began playing *Doom*, a new generation of 3-D, computerized gaming. And *The X-Files* debuted on Fox TV amid suggestions that the FBI was not innocent in covering up things it didn't like.

MUSIC • The year began with the issue of an Elvis stamp by the U.S. Postal Service, and continued with Whitney Houston's "I Will Always Love You," the longest running #1 single — maybe of all time. Janet Jackson, Ace of Base and the Wu-Tang Clan had mega-hits too. Nirvana, Meat Loaf, UB-40, Four Non-Blondes and Björk rocked the critics and the audiences. A Christian rock label, Tooth and Nail Records, came into being — to attempt the impossible: the coexistence of "traditional" and revolutionary values. Prince announced that his name, "Prince," would henceforth be replaced by an unpronounceable symbol: ⚦ Michael Jackson proclaimed himself innocent of all charges of child molestation; we would hear his protestations again ... and again. Portending something of significance, the band Jamiroquai, their name adapted from the Iroquois, achieved significant popularity throughout the world. Why significant? Because they were quite clearly impossible to categorize. And, finally, the world of rock lost Buddy Red Bow (a Lakota folk-rock singer), Conway Twitty and Frank Zappa.

1994

CULTURE • Trends were beginning, both desirable and not: The Church of England ordained the first female priest. Nelson Mandela was inaugurated as South Africa's first

Black president. The first conference devoted exclusively to the World Wide Web was held in San Francisco. Netscape Navigator, the first practical Web browser, was born. Apple released its first version of the Power PC microprocessor. V.G.O.L (video games on line) was formed. And civil unions were legally recognized in Sweden. Here are some of the "not so desirable" items: a series of monstrous high school arsons in Minnesota and the O.J. Simpson murders. In popular entertainment: *Pulp Fiction, Forrest Gump, The X-Files*—all groundbreaking.

Music • The biggest-selling singles had an interesting mixture of styles and performers, continuing the trend begun several years earlier: Bruce Springsteen's "Streets of Philadelphia," Rednex's "Cotton Eye Joe," All-4-One's "This I Swear," Mariah Carey's "Without You," Nirvana's "All Apologies," Stone Temple Pilots' "Big Empty" and Machine Head's "Bush." Through the years, the eclecticism of rock music had done nothing but grow and expand, and it would continue to do so and be assisted by the new media then coming into being. Deaths of significance included Kurt Cobain, Harry Nilsson, Papa John Creach and Cab Calloway. Although not a musician, Charles Bukowski's death was a loss to many in all the arts, his negations and affirmations mirrored the cultural revolution. (Rock and Roll!)

1995

Culture • There were some radically disturbing events this year. One of them, a curiosity at the very least, was Mississippi finally ratifying the Thirteenth Amendment—thus becoming the last state to abolish slavery! (And some say the Civil War is ancient history!) McVeigh and Nichols bombed the Alfred P. Murrah Federal Building in Oklahoma City, killing 197 people. Another oddity, to say the least, O.J. Simpson was found not guilty of the murders for which he was tried. (And some say "jury nullification" is a myth.) But there were some welcome events too. Dr. Bernard Harris became the first African American to walk in space. British soldiers ceased patrolling the streets of Belfast as they had been doing for 26 years. Canada's Supreme Court outlawed discrimination based on sexual orientation. Beijing sponsored the Fourth Annual Conference on Women with 181 countries participating. And the Million Man March took place in Washington, D.C., focusing on the responsibilities of African American men. In technology and media, this was the year for Windows 95, eBay and Yahoo!

Music • Illustrating the rising importance of rap and hip-hop, Tupac Shakur's album, *Me Against the World*, made it to #1 on Billboard's Top 200—while he was doing 1½ to 4 years on sexual abuse charges. Illustrating how rapidly music from those whose ancestors had been so recently liberated from slavery in Mississippi had overwhelmed all American culture, Michael Jackson's *HIStory* became the bestselling multiple album of all time. Illustrating the recognition of the place of rock music in American culture, the Rock and Roll Hall of Fame opened in Cleveland Ohio. The losses this year included Selena Quintanilla Perez by murder. By natural causes we lost Burl Ives, Dean Martin, and Maxene Andrews from the "old school"; and Jerry Garcia, Wolfman Jack, Melvin Franklin of the Temptations and Jerry Daniels from the Ink Spots from the "new school." Meanwhile, the top songs of the year continued to illustrate a growing diversity of styles and genres: Coolio's "Gangsta's Paradise," Shaggy's "Boombastic" (reggae), Take That's "Back for Good" (British pop), Michael Jackson's "You Are Not Alone" and U-2's "Hold Me, Thrill Me, Kiss Me, Kill Me."

1996

CULTURE • As always, there were ominous things to worry and disturb us. The Brits introduced us to mad cow disease, while in Scotland, "Dolly" the sheep became the first cloned mammal to be born. Osama Bin Laden declared a jihad on the United States. The "Unabomber," Theodore Kaczynski, was arrested at his Montana cabin. There were also a couple of notorious murders: Tupac Shakur and JonBenét Ramsey. However, there were some hopeful events as well. In *Romer vs. Evans*, the U.S. Supreme Court struck down a Colorado law that threatened gay rights. The Communications Decency Act of 1969 (which would severely curtail freedom on the Internet) was struck down as well for threatening the First Amendment. The Truth and Reconciliation Commission hearings were in full swing in Cape Town, which helped South Africa to move past apartheid. The Comprehensive Test Ban Treaty was signed by more than forty nations. But most hopeful of all in many ways was the gorilla Binti Jua (the niece of Koko of sign-language fame). She retrieved a three-year-old boy who had fallen into her enclosure and handed the unconscious boy to zoo personnel. In the category of presaging events, the computer "Deep Blue" defeated world chess champion Gary Kasparov for the first time.

MUSIC • There were a lot of "firsts," "lasts" and "biggest" this year: Canadian singer Alanis Morissette's album *Jagged Little Pill* won Album of the Year award at the 38th Annual Grammy Awards. She was the youngest person ever to win that award. The Prince's Trust fundraiser concert, held for the first time in Hyde Park and headlined by The Who, drew almost 200,000 people. The three remaining Beatles along with a recorded John Lennon released "Real Love." The Mariah Carey/Boyz II Men collaboration "One Sweet Day," lasted for 16 weeks at number one on Billboard's Top 100. Tupac released the first ever double rap album, *All Eyez on Me*, and it went platinum in four hours. The Spice Girls had a gigantic hit with "Wannabe," the biggest-selling single ever from an all-girl group. David Bowie became the first performer to release a copy of a song ("Telling Lies") as a free digital download. The Ramones played their last gig at Hollywood's Palace. Other prominent songs included Beck's "Where It's At," Backstreet's "No Diggitys" with Dr. Dre, Björk's "Hyperballad," and "Ready or Not" by the Fugees. More and more genre-busting eclecticism was evident. Then there were some deaths, including Brownie McGhee (blues), Timothy Leary of LSD fame, Ella Fitzgerald (jazz), Tiny Tim (ukulele player) and Les Baxter (big band).

1997

CULTURE • I suppose oddities occur all of the time, but this year seemed to specialize in the somewhat bizarre. This includes both positives and negatives as far as revolutionary values are concerned as well as some random events. Not so odd were Madeleine Albright being named the first female secretary of state (so much for assumptions that women weren't up to the task) and divorce being legalized in Ireland (so much for atavistic thinking about human relationships). Not to be ignored as a positive was the discovery of DNA evidence showing that all humans had African origins about one or two hundred millennia ago (so much for "creationist" nonsense). Also arguably positive was the mass suicide of 39 Heaven's Gate cultists who were awaiting extraterrestrial "transpo" they believed was hiding behind the Hale-Bopp comet (so much for the rationality of cultists). Negatives included Kelly Flynn, the first female to be certified as a bomber pilot (B-52s no less), who was tossed out of the air force for adultery (so much for equality of treatment in the military). The accidental death of Lady Diana, princess of Wales, resurrected the dormant debate about the value of the British monarchy. While *Titanic* became the largest-grossing film of all time (until *Avatar* in 2010)—both directed by John Cameron—much overlooked (except by sci-fi nerds) was the fact that 1997 was the year HAL, the computer in *2001: A Space Odyssey*, became operational. On TV, both the ratings system and *South Park* debuted, an interesting juxtaposition of events. The controversial FDR memorial opened on the Mall; it was controversial as it didn't show him in his wheelchair. (See 2001 for a correction of this omission.) Finally, a Pegasus rocket carried the remains of 24 people into earth's orbit for the first burial in space. Oh yes, the first book in the Harry Potter series was published.

MUSIC • New musicians and reunions and revivals of older ones seemed to dominate this year. The promise that rock and roll will never die (à la, Sha Na Na, Neil Young, King Missile and Wesley Willis, among others) seemed to be borne out. David Bowie turned 50 with a giant party in Madison Square Garden. Madonna successfully did a turn at acting (*Evita*). The Spice Girls went gigantic (kissing Prince Charles on the cheek and pinching his butt). The Monkees reassembled for a while and did a couple of massive concerts. Fleetwood Mac got back together as well. McCartney was knighted. Phish, perhaps in an attempt to reinvigorate themselves, used a newly named ice cream by Ben and Jerry as a funding source for their Lake Champlain initiative. The Black Crowes, Radiohead, Oasis, Björk, Everclear, Puff Daddy and Shania Twain all became gigantic along with the Spice Girls. In addition, not to be forgotten, KLF (Kopyright Liberation Front) did their Fuck the Millennium tour, celebrating a kind of offbeat anarchy. Performers who passed on included Townes Van Zandt (folk), The Notorious B.I.G. (rap), LaVerne Baker ("Tweedlee Dee"), Laura Nyro (folk), Lawrence Payton (The Four Tops), Jimmy Witherspoon (blues), John Denver (folk/pop/rock) and Mrs. Miller (novelty). Although not musicians, Allen Ginsberg and William S. Burroughs (both Beat writers) left this plane of existence. So did Jacques Cousteau (explorer of the ocean depths) and Anton Szandor LaVey (founder of the Church of Satan and explorer of the depths of religion).

1998

CULTURE • Sex was an ongoing theme this year: orientation, roles, abuse and plain old philandering. At the top of the charts was a lot about Monica Lewinsky's lips, often illicitly associated with President Clinton's "southern hospitality." For his "contributions" he was summarily impeached, then summarily acquitted. On an ugly note, Matthew Shepard was tied to a fence in Wyoming and left to die for being gay. Also ugly was another episode in the ongoing scandal about some Catholic priests' predilection for young boys. On the other hand, Sharon Cohen (Dana International), an Israeli transsexual, won the Eurovision song contest in the U.K. NASA approved Lt. Col. Eileen Collins to command the space shuttle *Columbia*, the first woman to be given the job. The U.S. Supreme Court extended sexual harassment protection to gays. And, lest I forget, the FDA approved Viagra for sale. In other news, White separatists were nabbed before they could wreak biological havoc on New York subways. Jesse Ventura was elected governor of Minnesota. Some culturally significant deaths included Dr. Benjamin Spock, Barry Goldwater, Roy Rogers, Buffalo Bob Smith, Gene Autry, Shari Lewis, and Flip Wilson. (There is a lot of children's television going down on this list.) A death not to be missed was James Earl Ray.

MUSIC • Continuing the theme of increasing diversity of styles, groups, ages and individuals, those prominently mentioned included almost everything. Included were Yoko Ono,

The Bee Gees, George Michael, Elton John, Van Halen, The Stray Cats, Shawn Colvin, Radiohead, John Lee Hooker, Sarah McLachlan, Jamiroquai, R. Kelly, Erykah Badu, Will Smith, Puff Daddy, Ziggy Marley, Fiona Apple, The Wallflowers, Smashing Pumpkins, Tool, and of course Bob Dylan. The latter was referred to as "Bill Dylan" by Usher during the Grammy Awards this year, giving rise to the notion that his mind may not have been completely on the history of music. The deaths of note included Sonny Bono, Junior Wells, Carl Perkins, Carl Wilson, Judge Dread, Wendy O. Williams, Linda McCartney and Charlie Feathers. Dead also was Frank Sinatra. Although not exactly a rocker, he once did a spot with Elvis on TV.

1999

CULTURE • This year there were many things about death to note. The murders at Columbine High School revived the attack on goth and metal as alleged causes. Marilyn Manson and a few German metal bands were singled out, and trench coats were banned in schools around the country. (The killers wore them.) A White supremacist was convicted of dragging an African American to death behind his truck. Warner Brothers Television was found liable in a reality TV gay-crush murder case. Another White supremacist spent three days in Indiana and Illinois killing non–Whites. And still another in Los Angeles wounded five and killed one at a Jewish community center. Dr. Kevorkian was declared guilty of second-degree murder, and was perhaps himself the victim here. John F. Kennedy, Jr., crashed his plane and died along with his wife and her sister. There was one glimmer of hope for change: The Citadel, "The Military College of South Carolina," began admitting women. And there were other curious events to observe: The euro came into being. The king of Bhutan finally allowed television into his country. The world population reached 6 billion. Not to be overlooked, on 11/19/1999 was a phenomenon that would not recur until the year 3111—all odd numbers. In entertainment there were departures of note: Gene Siskel, Stanley Kubrick and (where have you gone) Joe DiMaggio.

MUSIC • Napster arrived on the scene — and the scene would never be the same. Woodstock 1999 also arrived, but possibly more significant was the first Callatis Festival — Romania's largest music festival ever. New music was taking the stage everywhere: Prince ("1999"), Megadeth ("Set the World Afire"), Britney Spears' first album (...*Baby One More Time*), Eminem's *The Slim Shady LP*, B*Witched (an Irish all-girl band) with *Blame It on the Weatherman*, the Backstreet Boys with *Millennium*, Christina Aguilera's self-titled album, Dr. Dre with *2001*, KoЯn with *Issues* (and played it live at the Apollo — the first White band to do so), Nine Inch Nails' *The Fragile*, Limp Bizkit with *Significant Other* and Jennifer Lopez's *On the 6*. Other musicians in the news: Garbage, Santana, Eurythmics, Hikaru Utada (with Japan's best-selling album ever, *First Love*), *NSYNC, TLC and Kid Rock. Rock and roll departures included: Buddy Knox ("Party Doll"), Guy Mitchell ("Singing the Blues" and "Heartache by the Numbers"), Rick Danko (of the Band) and Curtis Mayfield (singer, songwriter, producer of R&B, soul, funk and blues).

2000

CULTURE • Numbers sometimes drive people crazy—as with the Y2K scare that turned out to be a non-event. Perhaps because stupidity always seems to involve an inane confusion between pedophilia and homosexuality, the real problem, the former, has never been dealt with effectively. This year, a "naming and shaming" of convicted sex offenders in England and "Sara's Law" in the U.S. did little to resolve the issue. It was also the year of the Elián González imbroglio wherein super-patriotic souls felt the need to prevent the 6-year-old child from returning to his father in Cuba — because it was Cuba. It was, after all, a remarkable year in politics wherein the Supreme Court decided the contested election in George W. Bush's favor. Technology was in the forefront with the largest corporate merger ever, between AOL and Time Warner, the creation of Nupedia (forerunner to Wikipedia), the first permanent crew arriving for the International Space Station, and the "resurrection" of the 136-year-old Confederate submarine *H.L. Hunley*. Sadly, for many, Charles Schulz died along with the comic strip *Peanuts*. So did Douglas Fairbanks, Jr., Walter Matthau, Steve Allen and Alec (Obi-Wan Kenobi) Guinness.

MUSIC • Rage Against the Machine was big this year, but *NSYNC, Eminem, Oasis, Bon Jovi, Madonna, Limp Bizkit, Destiny's Child, Britney Spears, the Backstreet Boys and Santana (winning 8 Grammys) were just as big. Even The Beatles were still selling in the millions. The Coen brothers' movie *O Brother Where Art Thou?* reintroduced America to bluegrass; it was also a pretty good movie. There was a giant tribute to Joni Mitchell in New York, emblematic of Canada's giant contributions to rock music throughout the years. Of significance in many other ways was Metallica's legal wrangling with Napster over copyright infringement. This would shortly have enormous consequences. Those passing on included Screamin' Jay Hawkins, Doris Coley of the Shirelles, Tito Puente and gospel great Roebuck "Pops" Staples.

2001

CULTURE • George Bush (the younger) took over from Bill Clinton early in the year, yet everything this year centered around the terrorist attacks of September 11. In our collective minds' eyes, we now see everything through this horrific prism. The attack on the World Trade Center was followed up by anthrax attacks on newspapers and TV stations, but the twin towers ever since loom over everything. In entertainment, fittingly, the major events seemed to be only deaths: Perry Como, Stanley Kramer and Ken Kesey. Usually overlooked, but not insignificant, was the placement of another statue of FDR in the memorial on the Mall — this one clearly showing him in his wheelchair.

MUSIC • Music, too, was affected. Earlier in the year, Jennifer Lopez was the first female artist to have a number one album and film simultaneously. Manic Street Preachers, a rock band, played in Cuba (the first such event ever). Both Michael and Janet Jackson's albums (independently produced) hit number one. "Lady Marmalade" (from *Moulin Rouge*) goes really big for Christina Aguilera, Lil' Kim, Mya and Pink. Aaliyah was big also, and even bigger after her death in a plane crash in the Bahamas. Of considerable interest was the Armenian American, art-metal and critically acclaimed band System of a Down. They illustrated that rock's influence now extended far beyond the ethnicities of its birth. Britney Spears and the Backstreet Boys kept the pop-rock circuit alive. But mega-benefit rock concerts the month after 9/11 dominated: The Concert for New York City, two Volunteers for America benefits, and the United We Stand benefit all combined to present a list of rock performers from virtually every era of rock and roll. A plain old concert with a multiplicity of musicians, Area One, rocked out the following month. And Napster was at its peak of popularity — it was still operating quasi-legally, but its days were numbered. Aside from

Aaliyah, there were some major departures: Rufus Thomas, John Lee Hooker, John Phillips, Joey Ramone, and George Harrison.

2002

CULTURE • Aside from some ugly reminders of the 9/11 attack, there was other ugliness as well to occupy our attention: The war in Afghanistan, the "Beltway Sniper" in the Washington, D.C., area and a United Nations report stating that at least 40 million people were infected with AIDS. A massive "Godless March on Washington," however, demonstrated that the "freedom of religion" proviso of the First Amendment includes "freedom from religion" as well. Elsewhere, literally, the *Mars Odyssey* found signs of a large deposit of water on the planet. This planet lost Milton ("Uncle Miltie") Berle, Linda (*Deep Throat*) Lovelace, Billy (*The Apartment*) Wilder and Rod (*In the Heat of the Night*) Steiger.

MUSIC • Women ruled this year. Avril (*Complicated*) Lavigne, Kelly (American Idol) Clarkson, Kylie ("Can't Get You Out of My Head") Minogue and Christina ("Dirrty") Aguilera to name a few. But there were more: Missy Elliot, Pink, Girls Aloud, Sheryl Crow, Shakira, Alanis Morissette, No Doubt, Nelly, Vanessa Carlton, Michelle Branch and Jennifer Lopez. Notice the growing variety among them—diversity, in other words, a lot of it. The men were busy too: Justin Timberlake, Red Hot Chili Peppers, Eminem, Jimmy Eat World, Linkin Park, Coldplay, Creed, Nickelback and Johnny Cash. Again, more and more diversity. Elsewise, John Waters' *Hairspray* was acknowledged—finally—in the guise of a knock-off Broadway show. And consigned to the netherworld were Dee Dee Ramone, John Entwistle, Lionel Hampton, Lonnie Donegan and Joe Strummer.

2003

CULTURE • Some significant tragedies and ominous rumblings marked this year. As for the former, the Space Shuttle *Columbia*'s disintegration on reentry, killing all seven aboard, tops the list. The rumblings were more plentiful: scary diseases (SARS and mad cow disease), 10 million protesters against the Iraq War around the world (followed by George Bush's infamous "Mission Accomplished" sign) and repressive laws (Article 23 in Hong Kong and the Department of Homeland Security in the U.S.). On the good side both the U.S. Supreme Court (*Lawrence v. Texas*) and the Massachusetts Supreme Judicial Court (*Goodridge v. Department of Public Health*) struck down anti-gay laws. Things more hopeful than good right now were a proposed European constitution, the former Soviet state of Eupatoria sent a METI message to five nearby stars, and *Pioneer 10*, now 75 billion miles on its journey, finally lost contact with the earth. Dead people included Mr. (Fred) Rogers, David Brinkley, Gregory Peck, Art Carney, Bob Hope, John Ritter (son of Tex), Gordon Jump (WKRP's Mr. Carlson) and Timothy ("Grizzly Man") Treadwell (you guessed it, eaten by a bear).

MUSIC • Paul McCartney's concerts in Red Square and St. Petersburg Palace Square demonstrated to the world that the cultural revolution begun in America in 1955 was alive and well in 2003. Avril Lavigne was making hit after hit after hit. So were OutKast, Beyoncé, The White Stripes, Radiohead, 50 Cent, Coldplay, The Yeah Yeah Yeahs, The Strokes, Nora Jones, Dido and Linkin Park. To illustrate the eclectic mess here, The Yeah Yeah Yeahs have been described as an art rock, edgy, post-punk, dance floor confection. Several notable concerts, aside from Paul's were a SARS benefit in Canada (with a crowd of nearly a half million, Canada's largest ever), Glastonbury in the U.K., Bruce Springsteen's Rising Tide Tour, and a Simon and Garfunkel world tour. There was a mega-tragedy: a fire in a Rhode Island nightclub where Great White was performing killed 100 and injured another 160. There was some seedy stuff too: Michael Jackson was arrested on child molestation charges and Phil Spector was arrested for murder. The dead included a mixture of the old and the new: Hank Ballard, Edwin Starr, Little Eva, Maurice Gibb, June Carter Cash and Johnny Cash, Barry White, Sam Phillips, Warren Zevon and Bobby Hatfield.

2004

CULTURE • One of the most horrific natural disasters of the modern age occurred in December: a massive 9.3 earthquake in Indonesia that produced a giant tsunami — almost 200,000 killed and over 50,000 missing. Another kind of tsunami was brewing: gay marriage. San Francisco (by an act of civic civil disobedience) and Massachusetts (by law) allowed same-sex marriage, and 11 states banned it. Ronald Reagan died. The World War II memorial in Washington, D.C., was finally completed and opened to the public, amid controversies about its seeming resemblance to Stalinist or even Nazi art. In the Mojave Desert, *Space Ship One* became the first privately funded "spaceplane" to achieve legitimate space flight. In the world of entertainment, the deaths included Jack Paar (the second host of the *Tonight Show* after Steve Allen), Marlon Brando, Isabel ("Weezy") Sanford, Fay (*King Kong*) Wray, Julia (OSS operative and cook) Child, and Susan Sontag (whose ideas I've used herein).

MUSIC • I suppose after 12 years it's time to mention the infamous "weenie roasts" sponsored by KROQ in Los Angeles. It always favored presenting "alternative" rock and still does. (This year The Killers, Modest Mouse, Bad Religion, Velvet Revolver and the Beastie Boys downed a few dogs.) Much like the roasts, Lollapalooza was to be in its 14th year, but was canceled for the first time due to "poor ticket sales." (It later recovered its verve and teamed up with *Austin City Limits* and now has a contract through 2018.) Eminem was still going strong, as was Brian Wilson — who finally completed his long-stalled project SMiLE which received unprecedented acclaim as one of the best albums ever made. On a sort of "downer" note, Janet Jackson's "wardrobe malfunction" disturbed a nation's sensibilities beyond all rational expectations. (The music didn't soothe *this* woman's savage breast!)

2005

CULTURE • A series of 10 concerts in July called *Live 8* was dedicated to "making poverty history." Meanwhile a Danish newspaper published a few drawings of Muhammad to the righteous outrage of Muslims who decry such depictions as blasphemous. The United Nations held a major climate change conference that decried the use of hydrocarbons as equally blasphemous. Elton John "married" his lover, thus taking advantage of a new British law that recognized gay unions as equal to straight marriages — which traditionally religious people found blasphemous. And to cap off all of the significant events, a "leap second" was added to this year — the first one added since 1998. No one found this to be blasphemous. The "Deep Throat" of *All the President's Men* fame was revealed to be Associate FBI Director William Mark Felt, Sr. Some blasts from the past ceased breathing: Shirley Chisholm, Johnny Carson, Arthur Miller, Hunter S. Thompson, Johnnie (get killers off at any cost) Cochran, Peter Jennings, Richard Pryor, Simon Wiesenthal, and Pat ("Arnold's" and *The Karate Kid*) Morita.

MUSIC • Lots of people were breaking all sorts of records with their records. Here's a top ten list: Mariah Carey (*The Emancipation of Mimi*), 50 Cent (*The Massacre*), Kelly Clarkson

(*Breakaway*), Green Day (*American Idiot*), The Black Eyed Peas (*Monkey Business*), Coldplay (*X&Y*), Rascal Flatts (*Feels Like Today*),Gwen Stefani (*Love. Angel. Music. Baby*), Kanye West (*Late Registration*) and The Game (*The Documentary*). Madonna's 36th top ten single, "Hung Up," tied her for most top-tens ever. (In comparison, The Beatles have 34.) The deceased included Luther Vandross, Little Milton, Robert Moog (his name says it all) and Clarence "Gatemouth" Brown (who merged blues and country to perfection).

2006

CULTURE • It seems that demonstrations took the front pages by storm this year. There was a massive one against the war in Iraq that proceeded down Broadway in New York. In 130 cities around the world, the Global Night Commute tried to point out the invisibility of children in Uganda. The Great American Boycott struggled for immigration rights. And a demonstration for gay rights in Moscow was broken up by police. The London bobbies broke up a broke up a terrorist plot aimed for planes going from the U.K. to America. (No more bottles of liquid on board as a result.) And Blu-ray disks made their debut. We lost Ed Bradley, Robert Altman, Mickey Spillane, Betty Friedan and Coretta Scott King.

MUSIC • There were quite a few "firsts" this year. Bon Jovi's "Who Says You Can't Go Home" was the first rock song to make it to number one on the country charts. Three 6 Mafia was the first African American hip-hop group to win an Academy Award for "It's Hard Out Here for a Pimp." Mary J. Blige's "Be Without You" spent 15 weeks at number one, making it the most successful R&B song ever. Gwen Stefani's "Hollaback Girl" has the greatest airplay in a week for any song ever. And 1,951 guitarists simultaneously played Jimi Hendrix's "Hey Joe" in Poland, breaking the Guinness world record. Others doing big things this year: U-2 (at the Grammys), the Rolling Stones (in Rio de Janeiro) and Dylan (with the album *Modern Times*). Here are some of the dead: Billy Preston (a "Beatle" among other things), Arthur Lee (of the group Love), Wilson Pickett (soul), Lou Rawls (also soul), Ruth Brown (blues), Desmond Dekker (ska and reggae) and Gene ("Town Without Pity") Pitney. And it was the 150th anniversary of Mozart's birth.

2007

CULTURE • In recognition of the anger and hatred that religious symbols are wont to arouse, the Red Cross and the Red Crescent adopted a nonreligious alternative symbol for both of them for overseas operations: the Red Crystal. The final Harry Potter book was released and it became the fastest selling book in 24 hours ever. The coma of Comet Holmes flared up to become visible to the naked eye. Roscoe Lee Browne, Boris Yeltsin, Tom Snyder, Norman Mailer, and Evel Knievel all died this year.

MUSIC • It seemed to be a year of festivals all around the world: Salzburg (Austria), Sasquatch (Washington State), Peel Bay (Isle of Man), Rádio Expres (Slovak Republic), Glastonbury (England), Heineken Open'er (Poland), Live Earth (worldwide), Summer Sonic (Japan), Reading and Leeds (Reading and Leeds!), Bryn Terfel Faenol (Wales), Manifest (Mexico) and the Decibel Festival (Seattle). If nothing else, this demonstrates conclusively that rock and roll is here to stay. Others were not to "stay": Denny "Papa" Doherty, Joe "Funk Brother" Hunter, Boots (saxophonist) Randolph and Lucky (African ska and reggae mega star) Dube. Big this year were the Dixie Chicks, Mika, Shakira and Joss Stone.

2008

CULTURE • Obviously, the political campaign leading to the election of Barack H. Obama as the first African American president utterly dominated the year's news and commentary. In Canada, the prime minister formally apologized for the nation's mal-treatment of its "First Nations." And yet another leap second was added to the year. Bobby (the chess man) Fischer died. So did William Buckley, Jr. (a genuine conservative), Charlton Heston (actually a classical liberal), Albert Hoffman (Mr. LSD), George Carlin, Betty (pinup) Page, W. Mark ("Deep Throat") Felt and Paul Newman.

MUSIC • Let's take a look at the groups and artists making it big on the charts and at an increasingly number of festivals, celebratory occasions and commemorative events: Coldplay, AC/DC, ABBA (because of the movie, *Mamma Mia!*), Duffy, Metallica, Leona Lewis, Amy Winehouse, Katy Perry, Rihanna, Alicia Keys, Sugarland, Pink, Elbow, Erykah Badu and Portishead. Need I even mention that the musical and stylistic eclecticism had at this point become too pointless to re-overly emphasize again and again still more?

2009

Note: For perhaps obvious reasons, I see this year as the beginning of the re-actualization. However, the event symbolizing this, the inauguration of America's first African American president, should be correctly understood as a symbolic event. This means that the event, person or object must point to something beyond itself, something ultimate, and to do so it must carry within itself its own self-negation. Just as John F. Kennedy was not "the Messiah," neither is Barack H. Obama "the second coming." Both are flawed, but both elicited something from the masses, namely, various formulations of the desire for freedom along with the hope that such freedoms could be actualized. After all, Obama did not receive the Nobel Peace Prize for his accomplishments in 2009; he won it for what he symbolized. Again the message of hope and fundamental (revolutionary) change is in the medium, not necessarily in what his administration may or may not accomplish. *That* he was elected speaks volumes.

CULTURE • Houston, Texas, became the largest American city to elect an openly gay mayor (Annise Parker), New Hampshire's law recognizing gay marriage took effect, and a nearly universal health care bill passed both houses of Congress. (Its ultimate disposition was still an open question as of the publication of this book.) The rights of assorted socially and culturally oppressed minorities were being gradually, or perhaps begrudgingly, more widely acknowledged. Elsewhere, Sweden assumed the presidential function of the European Union, perhaps illustrating that "ultra-nationalism" may be on its way out. Swine flu made its way around the world, and (this is bigger than merely a musical event) Michael Jackson was inadvertently killed by his doctor. John (*Rabbit Run*) Updike also died. So did Marilyn (porn star) Chambers, Walter ("And that's the way it is") Cronkite and John (*Breakfast Club*) Hughes.

MUSIC • More and more variety entered or reentered the rock arena: Lady Gaga, Kings of Leon, Adele, Blink-182, Ke$ha, Tool, Blur, Bone Thugs-n-Harmony and Flo Rida. Rage Against the Machine's "Killing in the Name" was adopted as the anthem of a Facebook campaign opposing state-sponsored racism. Survivors from the past as well as newer "oldies" have continued to maintain an audience while the ultra-newbies have begun to introduce a newer generation to the music of rock and America's cultural revolution in the process. Suffice it to say, as I write these last words of yearly summaries, Dave Matthews of the Dave Matthews Band is being actively solicited to run for Congress, as a conservative. Al Franken is already in the U.S. Senate and who knows how many more may cross over from the "culture" category to the "music" category

Is The Future Really So Bright?

Perhaps. Shades, however, are not at the moment necessary (the protestations of Timbuk3 to the contrary notwithstanding). Nevertheless, although the future is unpredictable, I wouldn't be surprised to see the continued reactualization of both traditional and revolutionary values — albeit in manners and forms modified to fit the times — for the foreseeable future. Consequently, we should expect an intensification of the conflict between the revolutionaries and the reawakened values of the Counter-Reaction. The so-called "Tea Baggers" (originating in late 2009) are one dramatic instance of the reawakened Counter-Reaction. So also is the rejuvenation of the yearly Conservative Political Action Committees (C-PACs). Make no mistake, although many in this crowd are clearly reminiscent of the blatantly racist and sexist "Know-Nothing" movement in the mid-nineteenth century (See William Kristol's editorial in *The Weekly Standard*), there are many others in this movement who still have the power of thought to use in the service of traditional values.[1]

Just as the reaction is not merely a clone of the earlier established order, but something newer and stronger, the resurgent revolutionaries cannot be the same as their past embodiment either. They too must prove stronger and renewed — or die. There are strong indications that this is indeed the case. One thing that should be unmistakable is the steady (albeit often slow) manifestation of individuality and freedom *for* everyone, and in many similar ways freedom *from* everyone. The other side of the coin is particularly apt for minorities and those without political power. This, after all, is what the cultural revolution is all about. As for the "end" of the cultural revolution, I'd say it will end when the thirst for these values is quenched, that is, when (not if) it succeeds.

In the previous pages, I've made several references to the media and the messages they have conveyed. Unlike many people, I feel that the revolutionary message actually subverted the media as often as the reverse, perhaps more often. The subject of this first part of the book has been the dialectic between music and culture, and it really deserves a much larger and more complete analysis elsewhere; nevertheless, the mutual influence of one on the other, and consequently the similar, mutual influence of the message and the media, should now be unmistakable, at least in its conception.

The second part of this book will explore more theoretically this relationship between the various media and rock music. At this point, however, I only want to stress that this effect on each other does in fact exist. To delve into the relationship still further, I plan in Part Three to illustrate this mutuality by calling attention to several key moments in the revolutionary process: the inception of the revolution's negation in the fifties, its affirmation in the sixties, an interim period for its re-creation, the counter-reaction to it and its defense, and finally, its rebirth and reactualization. At the book draws to a close, I'll suggest a paradigm for revolutionary cultural change in America as I see it — in the "state" of California.

The Typological Scheme

Recalling some of the ideas from the previous chapter is essential at this point. Here's a quick review: an authentic communication of a revolutionary message through art entails both negation and affirmation — inseparable facets of the dialectic between art and culture.

First of all, "negation" has nothing to do with "being negative." The former has to do with a certain type of action. The latter is a trait of character or personality. To be clear, the act of negation herein refers to the rejection of the traditional value scheme (and an affirmation to the support of a new scheme of values). Artists, being artists, can accomplish these tasks in the most creative ways: negation with a smile, so to speak, and affirmation with a sledgehammer. Every act of negation entails an affirmation, and every affirmation entails a negation. We have come to see that some artists tend to stress one over the other in what they do, but those of symbolic stature tend to stress both with equal vigor. In any case, authentic artistic negation and affirmation must arise from the historical situation and yet not be captive to it. They must be immanent within the historicity of moment in order to participate in the cultural revolution, and at the same time transcend the moment in order to maintain a critical perspective on the revolution's pretensions to ultimacy.

However, the popularity of some artistic expressions engaged in the cultural revolution (in this case rock music) has made their creators ripe targets for co-optation and exploitation by the established order, and not a few artists have been seduced by these blandishments and have "sold out." (The inducements to do so — money, sensual delights and fame among others — are not inconsequential.) The inevitable result is that the artists either are completely out of touch with the revolutionary movement (loss of immanence) or completely submerged within the cultural dynamics of the revolution with no overall critical perspective (loss of transcendence). In either case, the communication of revolutionary values is weakened or rendered altogether impossible; hence, the capability of the artist to negate and affirm cannot be fully realized. For example, a loss of immanence can occur when the music is so ethereal that it has no grounding in the revolutionary struggle (for instance, "The Song of the Sybil" on *Aion* by Dead Can Dance). Or it can happen when the music expresses counter-revolutionary values, clearly outmoded values or has simply "sold out." (Third Day's "Saved" on *Offerings: A Worship Album*) Similarly, a loss of transcendence can happen when the music is so fully engaged within the revolution that it has no self-critical perspective (the Sex Pistols' "God Save the Queen" on *Never Mind the Bollocks: Here's the Sex Pistols*). Or it can happen when it is so self-absorbed that it has no revolutionary perspective at all (Yes's "Roundabout" on *Yessongs*). Of course, it's completely possible to lose touch in both senses at the same time, and this just may be the best possible characterization for "schlock rock."

To complicate things, all musicians fall prey to one or more of these weaknesses at various times, and some are more prone to it than others are. These lapses merely illustrate that they are not the ultimate; and it may be that great artists tend to lapse greatly. Nevertheless, I still regard such artistic lapses as authentic to the rock music phenomenon. It's all part of the revolutionary process. Schlock, for example, did not cease being rock; it just ceased being effective. Those musicians of symbolic stature, however, never succumb to these lapses for long. They know (whether consciously or not) that their art must rise from the immediacy and point beyond, then it must look back with a critical eye on the movement it represents.

I want to stress in the chart that follows (see pages 60–61) that, while I stand by and defend my categorizations, the examples I use are purely subjective and subject to alteration.

(In fact, I have rethought and changed several of my examples in the chart for this new edition. And in all probability, I will continue to do so!)

Other American Music

Obviously, not everyone has been devoted to rock music during this period, a fact that can be very informative. Since people tend to identify with the kind of music that best portrays their values, the music they listen to can reveal the existence and character of the divergent groups in society. Although it is not possible to explore fully how these other musical expressions relate to America's cultural revolution, I do need to suggest how such an exploration might proceed. Using some of the same categories I've developed for the typological scheme of rock music, I'll discuss in turn classical, jazz, blues, country and western, and pop — keeping in mind that these labels are easily as question-begging as rock and roll.

The first thing to notice about all of them is that despite the numbers of people who listen to and identify with them, their styling all originated prior to the mid-fifties. They reflect the culture of an earlier time, in other words, not the time of cultural turmoil in which we now live. Hence, though they might have originated in a different period of cultural change, they cannot possibly communicate negation and affirmation today. As Marcuse so correctly observed, past traditions cannot be revived as revolutionary art. The only real effect they can have is to represent and support the established order to one degree or another. Put simply, they are all counter-revolutionary.

Classical music is the most difficult to deal with, involving as it does so much diversity, so many cultural groups, and such a long stretch of time. What interests me, however, is the classical music that has grown out of the American experience, the music of Copland, Piston, Ives, Rogers, and Gershwin, for example. Perhaps the most striking feature about this music is its almost total absence of both transcendence and immanence. Using the ingredients of a past language and tradition, it attempts to relate to a present with which it has no real connection. Its contemporaneity notwithstanding, its representatives are atavisms, their language incapable of revolutionary (subversive) communication. In its extreme form, it even loses its connections with the past, becoming virtually pure transcendence in the process (as with the formless and spontaneous sounds and non-sounds of John Cage).

Much the same is true of jazz. Its dialect, so to speak, is outdated, even though it may have been authentically revolutionary at one time. Actually, it spoke quite effectively to the Beat Generation of the late forties and early fifties. Unfortunately, the Beats were far too small in numbers to bring off the revolutionary changes they all too cautiously and metaphorically suggested. Besides, the fundamental value orientation revealed by jazz is not as clearly contrary to the established order as that of rock music. In any case, like American classical music, it too no longer has any genuine dimension of immanence or transcendence. Unlike classical music, however, it once did exemplify both. Today, with some minor and interesting exceptions, it remains outside the actual movement of history. (A contemporary California group, for example, Nutty Jazz, mixes cool jazz with essentially sixties rock to form a clever and entertaining amalgam.)

Blues and C&W are similarly disabled, but their failure to communicate stems from being too fully immanent to negate or affirm anything. Both, when expressed authentically, exhibit acquiescence to the trials and miseries of life and a resignation that nothing can

A Typology of Rock Music as Revolutionary Art

The Dialectic	The Fifties (1953–1963)	The Sixties (1963–1974)	The Interim (1974–1980)	The Counter-Reaction (1980–2008)	The Reactualization (2009–?)
Revolutionary					
Negation	Elvis Presley/ Chuck Berry/ Jerry Lee Lewis/ Little Richard/ Bill Haley / Bo Diddley/Coasters/ Midnighters/Billy Ward/ Penguins Race Music /R&B/Doo Wop/ Rockabilly	Beatles/Rolling Stones / Doors/Randy Newman/ John Prine/Jimi Hendrix/ Bruce Springsteen/Janis Joplin/Alice Cooper/Bob Dylan/Jefferson Airplane/ David Bowie/Santana/ Frank Zappa/Led Zeppelin/Kinks Folk-Protest/Heavy metal/ Blues Rock/Acid-Rock/Soul	Steely Dan/Lou Reed/ B-52's/ Warren Zevon/ Patti Smith/ZZ Top/ Blondie/Kiss/Heart/ Rolling Stones/Clash/ Sex Pistols/Pink Floyd/ Billy Joel/ Devo/Tubes/ Bob Dylan Punk/Southern Boogie/ Outlaw Country	B-52's/Public Image Limited/ Blondie/Clash/ X/Billy Joel/Violent Femmes /Robert Gordon/ UB-40/Rockpile/ Pink Floyd/Adam & the Ants/ Bruce Springsteen/ Stray Cats/ Devo/Rick James/ Dead Kennedys/ Bangles/ Prince/Randy Newman/ Crass/Rank & File/ Blasters/ Billy Idol/Alarm / Grandmaster Flash/Quiet Riot/Rolling Stones Neo-rockabilly/ Punk-Country/ Punk/Funk/ Heavy Metal/ Neo-protest	Limp Bizkit/Marilyn Manson/Machine Head/ Pink/Indigo Girls/ HammerFall/Korn/ OutKast/Eminem/ Strokes/Lady Gaga/ K'Naan/The Ting Tings/ Katy Perry Nu Metal/Emo/Metalcore
Affirmation	Elvis Presley/Ricky Nelson/ Ray Charles/Buddy Holly/Drifters/Roy Orbison/Alan Freed Beach Music	Beatles/Moody Blues/Sly & the Family Stone/Beach Boys/Mamas & Papas / John Denver/Harry Chapin/Carly Simon/ Bob Dylan/Joan Baez/ Byrds/Stevie Wonder/ Love/Grateful Dead / James Brown/Joni Mitchell/Supremes/ Simon & Garfunkel/ CSNY/CCR	Elton John/ Fleetwood Mac/ Jimmy Buffett Supertramp/Al Stewart/ The Band/Rufus/ABBA/ ELP/Bob Marley /John Lennon/Kool & the Gang/ Paul McCartney/Eagles/ War/Santana/Stevie Wonder/Bob Dylan New Wave/Funk, Country–Rock/ Reggae	Elvis Costello/ Waitresses/ Talking Heads/Go-Go's/ John Lennon/ Joan Jett/ Paul McCartney/ U-2/ English Beat/ Michael Jackson/ Human League/ Big Country/Juluka/Bus Boys/ Police/Los Illegals/ Culture Club/Cyndi Lauper/Peter Tosh/Bob Dylan/ Pointer Sisters/ Stevie Wonder	The Killers/Ben Harper/ Passion Pit/Stevie Wonder Fugazi/White Stripes/ Strokes/Kings of Leon/ Pink/Radiohead/Girls Aloud/Nickelback/Missy Elliot/Brad Paisley/Brandi Carlile/Neko Case/Yeah Yeah Yeahs/Pearl Jam/ Darius Rucker/Scissor Sisters/ Taylor Swift

	The Fifties (1953–1963)	The Sixties (1963–1974)	The Interim (1974–1980)	The Counter-Reaction (1980–2008)	The Reactualization (2009–?)	The Dialectic
		Folk-Rock/Jazz-Rock/ Motown/Hair		Neo-psychedelia/Latino Rock Reggae/New Wave/Female Rockers/African Rock	Electronic/Dance Punk/ Latin	
						Co-opted
Loss of Immanence	Pat Boone/Bobby (Darin-Rydell-Vinton-Vee)/ Annette Funicello/Paul Anka/Dick Clark/Frankie Avalon/Connie Francis/ Dead Can Dance/Third Day	Monkees/Petula Clark/Peter & Gordon/Peter Frampton/Bobby Darin/ Cliff Richard/Amy Grant/ Blood Sweat & Tears	Chicago/Knack Carpenters/ Bee Gees/Shaun Cassidy/ Village People/Neil Diamond/Jefferson Starship	Manhattan Transfer/Rick Springfield/Rush Journey/ AC/DC Foreigner/REO Speedwagon/ Linda Ronstadt/ Sheena Easton/ Orchestral Manoeuvres in the Dark	Jonas Brothers/Kelly Clarkson/Miley Cyrus/ Avril Lavigne	
	Christian Rock/Pop/Schlock Rock/covers	*Pop/Schlock*	*Bubblegum/Disco, Soul Train/ Religious Rock*	*Pop-Rock/Top 40 Radio Avant-Garde/Techno-Rock*	*House/Trance/American Idolists*	
Loss of Transcendence	Screamin' Jay Hawkins *Garage Band Rock*	Fugs/MC5/Lennon–Ono/ Velvet Underground/ Georgie Fame/Yes/Sex Pistols/Screaming Lord Sutch *Jesus Christ Superstar* *Art-Rock*	Bob Dylan/Holly Near/ Tom Waits/Brian Eno *Feminist Rock/Folk-Rock*	The Teardrop Explodes/ Japan/Suicidal Tendencies/ Cabaret Voltaire/Killing Joke *Hard Core Punk*	Mariah Carey/Jennifer Lopez/Usher/Britney Spears/Marilyn Manson *Death Metal*	

really be changed. Drinking, carousing, fighting, cheating, traveling, and the like, themes common to both genres, are merely efforts to suppress the pain and hurt of an unfriendly world. Despite the similarities with many themes in rock, these two styles lack the anger necessary for genuine negation and the enjoyment necessary for genuine affirmation. Insofar as they function as an expiation or catharsis, they drain off any revolutionary energy that might be present and thus play into the hands of the established order. Actually, C&W quite often reflects and re-creates traditional values directly and seemingly offers the established order positive support. I do not intend to ignore the distinctions, however, between the "C" part and the "W" part — Nashville and Austin, to simplify it. Negation is still living in some of the "outlaw" elements of the "W." Nevertheless, to the extent that either is influenced by pop music, both transcendence and immanence are lost.

Of the styles noted so far, "pop" is the only one intrinsically inauthentic, and this only to the extent the term is used to describe music deliberately created exclusively for monetary gain and for no other reason. (*All* musicians, like all artists in general, want their music to pay! But that's not the sole reason they do it.) "Pop," therefore, reflects no one's present experience and thus has no immanence whatsoever. Nor does it convey with any conviction any particular set of values (except perhaps plutocratic values), so it is totally devoid of transcendence as well. Pop music is best described as early rock and roll once was, namely, music consciously contrived to make money by appealing to the widest possible audience. Whatever is currently popular is imitated and marketed, and as such, it is form without substance, mere empty calories. All styles of music have fallen prey to deliberate financially motivated popularizations of course — classical, jazz, blues, C&W, and even rock; nothing is sacred. Muzak and the material played by the numerous "EZ" listening radio stations across the nation are only the most blatant examples. Others are revivals of earlier styles with no attachment to their experiential bases. I once took Sha Na Na to be the paradigm par excellence of this practice, yet I freely admit that I was too hasty. They may express little transcendence, but they do exemplify immanence. Top 40 radio is a better target; it is obviously not immune to the "pop" disease. In all cases of "pop," however, imitation (not merely making money) is pop's key distinguishing feature, no matter how difficult it might be accurately to diagnose its presence.

To summarize, except for pop music, all musical expressions are or have been authentic in expressing the human condition. Rock, however, is for our age the sole revolutionary styling. Blues and C&W are too immanent to be subversive, while classical and jazz are too transcendent. All of these forms, then, can only function as counter-revolutionary, despite the fact that rock has made enormous use of them (and owes them a considerable debt as a result).

Part Two

MEDIUM AND MESSAGE

Everybody experiences far more than he understands. Yet it is experience, rather than understanding, that influences behavior, especially in collective matters of media and technology, where the individual is almost inevitably unaware of their effect upon him.
— Marshall McLuhan

>Do you remember Hullabaloo,
>Upbeat, Shindig and Ed Sullivan too?
>Do you remember rock 'n' roll radio?
>...
>Do you remember Murray the K,
>Alan Freed, and high energy?
>...
>Do you remember lying in bed
>With your covers pulled up over your head?
>Radio playin' so no one can see
>— The Ramones

Once the darling of academic sophisticates, the media observer and guru Marshall McLuhan is now no more than a scholarly version of the Hula Hoop. (His sin was having become too popular, the kiss of death in the academic world.) However, dead though he may be, Marshall McLuhan cannot be ignored. Granted, he was pretentious, opaque, absurd, and frequently given to contradictions. At the same time, he was insightful, provocative, original, and, more often than not, right on the mark. He clearly saw America in the midst of a cultural revolution; he regarded the artist as partly a reflection and partly a shaper of the future; and he looked forward to the harmony of all in a new, more perfect world. This is my McLuhan.

The overall theme of McLuhan's *Understanding Media: Extensions of Man* (1964) is precisely the prediction that the new electronic media have "wholeness, empathy and depth of awareness" as their "natural adjunct." McLuhan was confident that, no matter how long it took, a new world was in the process of being born. It couldn't be stopped short of returning to a pre-electronic age, and he was well aware of how that might occur.[1]

With the invention of the printing press, Western thought and culture assumed the logical structure we've come to accept uncritically as the nature of rationality itself. The revolution it brought about he called the Gutenberg Galaxy, and in a book of the same name, he added the subtitle, "The Making of Typographic Man." Typographic people, from that time until the present, have attached the highest value to such things as uniformity, continuity, discreteness, specialization, and, perhaps above all, detachment. Among the many blessings of the Gutenberg technology has been the creation of nationalization, warfare, and selfish individualism. Literacy in the West, based on the incredibly flexible phonetic alphabet and made endlessly repeatable with typography, has held these rather disconcerting messages for us (along with their more positive results).

All of this, however, is slowly and inexorably coming to an end. With the introduction of electronics, another revolution has occurred. The possibility of instantaneous communications has expanded our perceptions and has thus made the world a very much smaller place. The term "global village" is McLuhanesque in origin, and it foreshadows a higher level of civilization in which the harmony of the tribe will be returned. Yet this harmony will recognize and even encourage individuality and diversity. (No wonder he was such a hot item during the sixties.) Unfortunately, as with all radical transformations, the process is bound to be painful at times and maddeningly slow; it takes cultures quite a while to catch up with new technologies and their concomitant values. The fact that these changes have come about far more slowly than he anticipated, imperceptibly, some would say, should not lead us to conclude that he was wrong about everything. Cultural revolutionaries are notoriously impatient, and McLuhan was no exception.

Perhaps if he had paid more attention to what he himself was saying, he would have been able to discern more accurately the character of radical change, namely, that it does proceed imperceptibly and, for the most part, subliminally. Few are aware of what's happening until later, and some not even then. Only they have within them the capacity to know, in advance, which way the wind is blowing. On this, I think McLuhan was right on the mark; however, as he admits, this is not really a startling revelation: "The power of the arts to anticipate future social and technological developments, by a generation or more, has long been recognized.... This concept of the arts as prophetic, contrasts with the popular idea of them as mere self-expression." However, there's more than prophecy in McLuhan's notion of the artist's role: "It is the artist's job to try to dislocate older media into postures that permit attention to the new ... even though the majority of his audience may prefer to remain fixed in their old perceptual attitudes." Artists, in other words, are nothing less than the vanguard of the revolution.

They perform this function most effectively, however, when their work is manifested in commercial entertainment, and again I think he was right on target. Far from rendering the media universally inoffensive and neutral, entertainment ensures that program content will receive maximum exposure, pervading every aspect of our psychic and social lives. And even more pointedly, "entertainment pushed to an extreme becomes the main form of business and politics." (All of a sudden, entertainer-politicians become almost comprehensible.) Yet too much recognition and acclaim, as is the wont of those in the entertainment business, can be counterproductive. "To reward and to make celebrities of artists can ... be a way of ignoring their prophetic work, and preventing its timely use for survival." Although McLuhan never expanded on this idea, in all probability he meant that a narrow fascination with personalities would inevitably blind us to the meaning of what artists create.

In what is perhaps the most suggestive (and confusing) slogan associated with him, "the medium is the message," McLuhan attempted to capture the essence of his complex and often unfathomable thought. Unquestionably, according to any reasonable measure, he failed. For the phrase remains almost as cryptic today as it was when he first introduced it. It always seems to require further clarification.

McLuhan intended to equate all media with technologies, and technologies with extensions of our bodies, senses or mind. Put a bit differently, but still in his own terms, media translate the human presence into other forms, thus linking the individual and society in an organic way. Technological innovations accomplish the translation with increasing speed and to a greater extent; hence, new media expand our social awareness and bring the world closer to us. Just about anything can qualify as a technology, according to McLuhan. He likened clothing to an extension of our skin, the telegraph to an extension of our hormonal system, and the credit card to an extension of our grasp. Therefore, the message of media per se is the extension of ourselves into time and space.

New technologies force a readjustment of all existing patterns of human relationships, and they cause all existing media to change so as to accommodate the new. In short, technological innovations are disruptive, accompanied by greater or lesser degrees of stress and strain. Since society is in effect the organic extension of humanity, social stress and individual stress are essentially undifferentiated.

Media, as extensions, also provide us with perceptual apparatus, so that new media introduce new perceptual tools. They alter our perceptions and thus our very consciousness. The meaning conveyed by this (its message) is nothing short of the creation of a new world. What we "see" is what we get.

The ostensible "content" of any medium is simply another medium. Speech, for example, is the content of writing, writing the content of print, and print is the content of telegraphy. Hence, it should be obvious that there can be no such thing as the study of "content," for there is no such animal! There are only media, with their varied specific messages. Every medium has something particular to "say," so media study should focus above all on the characteristics of the form in question.

When you put all these interpretive comments together, they add up to the fact that media are never neutral, with the capability of being used in many and various ways. Rather, the media themselves are value laden, communicating and often "imposing [their] assumptions on the unwary," irrespective of "what" is being communicated. The medium, as it were, is indeed the message.

McLuhan distinguished between "hot" and "cool" (or "cold") media. Usually, hot media involve the extension of but one sense; yet the really key feature is their intensity. They convey a lot of well-organized, highly structured information. As a result, there is little need for audience participation to "fill in the blanks." Generally, the Gutenberg (or print) technology is hot. Cold media, on the other hand, are not nearly so well organized and structured. An example is electronic technology. Unlike its warmer kin, it has no fixed "point of view," no thematic perspective to be foisted already developed on the audience. Cold media are more like mosaics, necessitating a high degree of involvement and participation. What they present must be actively created and grasped; organization and structure are imposed, not passively received. Only under these conditions can genuine learning take place; coolness is an indispensable condition for the assimilation of any kind of data. (Seminars are, accordingly, far better than lectures as pedagogical techniques.)

The temperatures of the included media can apparently vary. For example, sometimes McLuhan saw radio as hot; at other times, he described it in cool terms. In these latter instances, he seemingly had in mind the features that differentiate radio from some form of the print media, like newspapers. Newspapers, however, he often characterized as fundamentally a mosaic in nature! But he did so when referring to books and film, both having a decidedly fixed point of view.

Mixed media make the interpretation of McLuhan exceedingly complicated, with the results being unpredictable at best. In the most general sense, he felt that electronic media have now begun to mix with the mechanized, print media; and the message being sent by the hybrid forms is charged with energy. His analogy for the entire process was nuclear fusion (as opposed to fission); so he clearly anticipated a dramatic impact. "The hybrid or meeting of two media is a moment of truth and revelation from which new form is born ... a moment of freedom and release." Apparently, out of the conflict something new is born, as when film emerged from the marriage of mechanical and electronic technologies, and the phonograph from the telegraph and telephone. But the electronic invasion of our overheated American culture has yet to transform our thinking fully and completely. In one of his most interesting series of observations, McLuhan said, "We have confused reason with literacy, and rationalism with a single technology. Thus in the electronic age, man seems to the conventional West to become irrational." IQ testing was a particularly good example of this tendency: "Unaware of our typographic cultural bias, our testers assume that uniform and continuous habits are a sign of intelligence." The West isn't prepared for the transformation of thought that it is presently undergoing.

Music, of course, is a medium, and it functions both as a "content" for other media (radio, records, film, etc.) and as a medium with "contents" of its own (language, sound, dance, etc.). Music as medium and message is the concern of this second part of the book, and McLuhan will be popping up in various places throughout.

Though he never acknowledged rock music, he was nevertheless aware of the contrasts between the (hot) specialization and fragmentation of the symphonic idiom beginning in the sixteenth century and the (cool) participatory and unifying mosaic of jazz. He also stressed that the highly intense and ordered music of the symphony found embodiment in the waltz, while jazz dancing (and the twist) exemplified involvement and improvisation.

In any case, McLuhan was convinced that the impact of electronics would eventually bring about the revolution. Maybe McLuhan was right after all.

In the second part of the book, I've chosen to recollect my own experiences of the media and assess how I came to know and identify with rock culture through them. As will become quite evident, there has been a common element throughout all of my encounters with rock music; however, it's only become apparent to me after years of listening to and reflecting on the music and its attendant culture. I have in mind the almost always unexpected results of the dialectic between media and culture, especially when rock music is involved. This suggests the revolutionary power of this kind of music, which, when you really think about it, is merely another medium.

4

Radio: The Creation of a New Community

As with virtually every historical and personal turning point, this one, too, happened quite unintentionally. The specific events leading up to such changes can never be planned, and the results of these changes are most certainly unforeseeable. Turning points, especially the most important ones, are like this. Even conscious and deliberate efforts to control the flow of events are destined to be disappointing, perhaps all the more so for having been attempted. For all such attempts tend to be fundamentally mistaken: they center their efforts on the highly visible events thought to be "causes," when in fact the genuine causes are likely to seem so insignificant as to be invisible. Concentrating on the pseudo causes is inevitably self-defeating. Of course, all of this is evident only in retrospect, and even then, I'm not so sure we can really know why things happen.

In any case, as I continue to look back over my shoulder, here is what happened to me and likely to millions of others. No doubt, the specific, invisible events differed in every case, but the eventual consequence was pretty much the same for all of us. For a variety of reasons, we had all reached a turning point in our lives; we had coalesced into a new, revolutionary community, despite all the efforts made to prevent it.

In the fifties, while most of my preteen peers in Baltimore had recently abandoned their radios for the newest toy on the market, television, I still enjoyed listening to the radio, especially at night. I was hardly immune to the seductive glow of the tube, but television pretty much went off the air in the early evening ("prime time" was then somewhere around 6:00 P.M. to 8:00 P.M.), rendering our brand-new, twenty-one-inch Muntz TV totally useless at bedtime. I would go to sleep listening to the likes of *Fibber McGee and Molly*, *Burns and Allen*, *The Great Gildersleeve*, *The Jack Benny Show* and, my only musical selection, *American Patrol*. Every once in a while, I'd pick up a late-night talk show with some exotic guest who had just returned from Venus with proof that death was the most effective means of space travel. "Long John" from New York tended to emphasize or perhaps encourage the unusual (and sometimes dangerous) denizens of the night. (Rumor has it that early in the sixties one of his guests was none other than Lee Harvey Oswald, proclaiming something about aid for Cuba.) I realized that my interests were somewhat outside the norm, but I did pursue them in private at least. What I didn't realize was that I was listening to the dying gasps of radio as America had come to know it.

The decisive event for me seemed innocuous enough—troublesome, but hardly the kind of thing that could possibly alter the course of my life. Somehow, perhaps because my radio was cheap as well as ancient, the little station pointer broke off of the tuning knob, rendering the search for the desired station something of an acquired skill—a skill I never completely mastered. I had to twist the knob until I heard something familiar and proceed from that point. And that's how it happened.

It was during one of my evening searches for the proper station that this seemingly insignificant event had its effect. Numerous other invisible events were having the same effect all across the country: random occurrences without a doubt, but no less momentous for their being part of no master plan. As the direct consequence of having to search for my desired station, I had chanced upon some music the likes of which I had never heard before—music I knew for certain I shouldn't be listening to.

I was familiar with the songs on the Hit Parade of course. Everyone knew them: Perry Como's "Don't Let the Stars Get in Your Eyes," Patti Page's "(How Much Is That) Doggie in the Window?," Les Paul and Mary Ford doing "Vaya Con Dios," Eddie Fisher's "Oh My Papa," and the latest, "Sh-Boom" by the Crew Cuts (or so I thought). All these ditties were harmless enough. But the music I had happened upon was different, incredibly different. All at once, it was raw, sexy, exciting, gutsy, angry, scary, and unquestionably dangerous. I loved it.

As luck would have it, I had happened upon one of Baltimore's few Black radio stations. And they were playing such songs as "Lawdy Miss Clawdy" by Lloyd Price, the Chords' (original) version of "Sh-Boom," and, unbelievably, the Dominoes' "Sixty Minute Man." With a swiftness unparalleled by anything other than a teenager's change of moods, I knew with absolute certainty that my parents wouldn't appreciate this discovery with the same degree of ardor. Their reactions would have been nothing short of apoplectic, disclosing instantaneously (and perhaps even helping to create) a gap of understanding between us that would never be fully bridged. Within days, for the first time in my life, I felt a camaraderie with my peers that I had never believed possible. I had never really liked very many of my fellow preteens, but at least most of them were now listening to same kind of music as I was—and we were doing it in secret, needless to say, a fact that further bonded us.

We all knew without ever having it spelled out for us that this "nigger music" would be regarded by our parents as an imminent threat to our White, middle-class well-being. They were right, of course, although this was hardly something we were capable of admitting to ourselves, much less to them. In any case, even if we had been conscious of this threat, it wouldn't have made any difference in our behavior. To us at the time, all we were doing was listening to music, nothing more. Such is the extent of adolescent naïveté. Had we realized what was happening to us, I'm not sure we would have continued, not all of us, that is. I'd like to think that I would have been one of the few, but the traditions of centuries are not so easily overcome. In a very real sense, our naïveté was our salvation.

It became the "in" thing to do, listening surreptitiously to Black radio stations and cluing in our friends. The practice had become quite extensive, completely apart from anyone's intending it so. However, with millions of teens and preteens tuning into and turning onto Black music, it was not to remain an underground phenomenon for very long.

As early as 1951, Alan Freed was on the air on WJW in Cleveland, with his *Moondog Show*, an R&B ("race music") program oriented to Whites. As the decade moved on, more and more disc jockeys followed suit, which in a sense validated our vaguely disconcerting behavior (at least to ourselves). We could now listen to Black music on White stations. Nevertheless, to even the most casual observer, something was afoot, and to the overwhelming majority of American society, it was something insidious. For if nothing else, Blacks were communicating with Whites through the language of music, and the medium of radio was largely responsible.

Black Fascination

Alan Freed wasn't alone for very long; he had tapped into something he himself probably never understood, something momentous; and others were exceedingly quick to pick up on it. Almost every major city had at least one station devoted to playing Black music for Whites, and they were usually placed at the ends of the AM dial. In Baltimore, I remember two Black stations (WSID and WEBB) and two White imitators (WCAO and WITH), but I don't want to create the impression that these latter were exact duplicates. Far from it! Only some Black music was acceptable to our parents, and a radio station would have been crazy to ignore the unspoken guidelines.

Much of the music played by these White stations was imitation as well. For some time, perceptive White artists had begun to "cover" Black originals, usually cleansing them in the process. "Sh-Boom" is the paradigm, but the examples of this practice are plenteous. Other White musicians tried to duplicate the sound and sense of Black music by sanitizing anything that seemed "negroid." For example, LaVern Baker's "Tweedle Dee" was covered by Georgia Gibbs; Fats Domino's "Ain't That a Shame" by Pat Boone; Smiley Lewis's "I Hear You Knocking" by Gale Storm; and Gene and Eunice's "Ko Ko Mo" by Perry Como. (It goes without saying which versions made the most money, a situation that on reflection seems to have verged on larceny.) The White airwaves were filled with this kind of material. Not that all of it was bad, of course; it was, however, derivative and "sanitized" where necessary. Black music had to be made "safe" before it could be aired. From the perspective afforded by the passage of more than a few years, it might justifiably be wondered why such imitation stations were necessary to begin with. Why didn't we just listen to the Black stations and be done with it? In reply, it must be remembered that this was still before Orval Faubus departed the governorship of Arkansas. Times were not yet a-changing.

Radio, contrary to portions of McLuhan, is a unifying medium; in no way does it isolate us from one another. Even while listening alone we are aware of others doing the same, even if this awareness isn't always conscious. The medium itself overcomes the physical separation and is, in a sense, its fundamental message. It re-tribalizes our diversified and alienated culture, creating empathy among listeners where none existed, bonding people who would otherwise remain alienated. Therein lay radio's revolutionary import: Whites were becoming involved and unified with Blacks.

In Baltimore, as elsewhere, rock-and-roll radio attracted an intensely loyal following. Though defections most assuredly took place, a fickle listener would never be so foolish as to admit to such dissolute behavior. We proclaimed our allegiance while reviling all other stations not so fortunate as to have earned our favor. (The more contemporary practice of affixing bumper stickers is merely a continuation of the less formal protestations of allegiance.) A typical activity after a dance or movie was for aficionados of a particular station to co-opt one section of the local drive-in, open all the windows, and turn up the volume so high as to render the all-pervasive steak subs and French fries into cinders.

If any of us made a habit of listening to Black radio, we most assuredly wouldn't admit it publicly. Very few of us would admit it privately. Most of us hadn't even met a Black person outside of a service occupation. Our schools and (of course) our communities were rigidly segregated, and while many of us had mixed feelings about this, we weren't about to open ourselves to the accursed invective "nigger-lover." Listen to Black radio? It would have been tantamount to inviting ostracism if not worse—especially since their songs included the Midnighters' "Work with Me Annie" and the Drifters' "Money Honey," pretty rough stuff for the early fifties. Prior to the late sixties, to identify in any way with Blacks was not only a social abomination, it was positively dangerous and potentially life threatening. Contrary to what might have been intended, the White imitators kept us in contact with genuine Black music.

I wonder to this day how many of us were aware of the subtle contradiction involved in our attitude. We mirrored our parents' racial prejudices while at the same time we became devoted to Black music and indirectly to Black culture. Imagine, if you will, a typical high school dance in the fifties, in a typical white middle-class neighborhood: a sea of White faces writhing to the strains of decidedly Black music. A consciousness thus divided is inherently unstable. Sooner or later such contradictions are bound to bring about changes, and we were teetering on the precipice of a dramatic conversion. We didn't think very much about it at the time, but the taste of Black culture we were getting via the radio was addictive. It offered us something we couldn't get anywhere else.

McLuhan wrote that "radio affects most people intimately, person-to-person, offering a world of unspoken communication between writer-speaker and the listener. That is the immediate aspect of radio — a private experience. The subliminal depths of radio are charged with the resonating echoes of tribal horns and antique drums." Even more to the point, "The message of radio is one of violent, unified implosion and resonance." It can and does create community where none before existed. Hence, "Our teenagers in the 1950s began to manifest many of the tribal stigmata.... To the teenager, radio gives privacy, and at the same time it provides the tight tribal bond of the world of the common market, of song, and of resonance." McLuhan even noticed that this "independent isolation of the young makes them remote and inaccessible." However, this inaccessibility was not from one another, as these words might suggest. Far from it. The inaccessibility he had in mind was from the adult world. He mentioned also in this connection that radio created the disc jockey and, not long thereafter, the disc jockey cult: "The natural bias of radio to a close tie-in with diversified community groups is best manifested in the disc jockey cults," a fact that served to magnify and reinforce this isolation and inaccessibility.[1]

The unavoidable consequence of radio in the fifties was the creation of a new community, a community beginning to be fascinated with the Black experience in America, regardless of whether or not its members were fully aware of what was happening to them. And most assuredly, they weren't.

Something had to give, and soon. The internal contradictions were becoming increasingly intolerable and had to be resolved one way or another. Yet no matter what the outcome, it had to have been something entirely different, something new. And most assuredly, it was.

The Backlash

Considering the values intrinsic to the kind of music that White middle-class youths were listening to, there was no way a reaction could have been avoided. And it wasn't long in coming, in the form of the payola hearings of 1959 and their assorted clones throughout the country. Everywhere it seemed that somebody was castigating and banning "that nigger music." In what is perhaps the only genuine instance of Soviet-American agreement, rock and roll was found by both to be responsible for almost every lamentable social condition. If civilization were to crumble into dust, the blame would no doubt rest entirely on this new music of the young, so they proclaimed. Curiously enough, however, each side accused the other of instigating this insidious sound.

Accordingly, moves were made to destroy rock and roll or, at the very least, keep it under strict controls. By 1959, these tasks had suddenly become much easier. With Elvis willingly submitting to the draft, Chuck Berry jailed for a Mann Act violation, Jerry Lee Lewis disgraced by his marriage to his young cousin, Little Richard converted to the ministry, and Buddy Holly dead in an airplane crash, the way was clear for a major attempt to co-opt the heart and soul of rock and roll. Soon we began hearing something strangely different on our radios. Not that all of it was bad; it wasn't. It was, however, cleaned up and less raunchy. It was more about love and less about sex. From what we were hearing, drinking had apparently come to an abrupt end in American life. Perhaps more significant than anything else, it wasn't angry anymore.

Among rock historians and authorities, it has become a commonplace, if not a divinely revealed truth, that nothing of any consequence was produced during this period before The Beatles. Fortunately, Dave Marsh and Kevin Stein help to discredit this idea in their *Book of Rock Lists.* Citing some of the number one hits from this period makes their point quite well: Lloyd Price's "Stagger Lee," Wilbert Harrison's "Kansas City," the Drifters' "Save the Last Dance for Me," Del Shannon's "Runaway," Ernie K-Doe's "Mother-in-Law," Dion's "Runaround Sue," Little Eva's "The Loco-Motion," the Crystals' "He's a Rebel," and Stevie Wonder's "Fingertips—Pt. 2." There is certainly enough in this list alone to shatter the myth.

On the other hand, beliefs of this kind (no matter how literally unsupportable they may be) originated and still have currency for some reason. In other words, there are more than a few grains of truth to the allegations made about this period. It wouldn't take too much effort to construct an even longer list of sanitized rock—music acceptable to those who intuitively understood the revolutionary meaning of genuine rock, and who just as intuitively feared it. Such a list would no doubt include David Seville's "The Chipmunk Song," Frankie Avalon's "Venus," Percy Faith's "Theme from a Summer Place," Connie Francis's "Everybody's Somebody's Fool," Pat Boone's "Moody River," Bobby Vee's "Take Good Care of My Baby," Shelley Fabares's "Johnny Angel," Bobby Vinton's "Roses Are Red," Little Peggy March's "I Will Follow Him," and, rounding out the year 1963, giving credence to the charge as perhaps no other song could possibly do, "Dominique," by the Singing Nun. To be sure, there is certainly nothing dangerous in this crowd.

Actually, a survey of the hits for any year would in all probability yield a comparable division: some treasures, some trash. Sincere minds are likely to differ on precisely where to locate the dividing line, but this dispute is not nearly as significant as the fact that this period was and still is perceived as being productive primarily of trash. This perception is what is crucial.

Although the period from 1959 through 1963 has been interpreted as stiflingly inauthentic and repressive, and although this is generally thought to be responsible for the poor quality of the music, this conviction has only become clear in retrospect. To be sure, there was a vague uncertainty gnawing away at our collective consciousness (which has only become apparent in retrospect). We were all perfectly aware of the tragedies, defections, and attacks with which this period began; we just didn't reflect on them very deeply, if at all. Not surprisingly, given our merest of overtures toward maturity, we weren't exactly perspicacious about any potential threats to our freedom. We sang to, danced to, hung out with, and necked to the schlock just as we did the good stuff. All we had to do if we didn't like a particular song was to switch to a different station. (As I recall, no one was in the least reluctant to voice an opinion about musical preferences, and such opinions were usually very strong.) Schlocky tune? No sweat. Just punch in something different. Yes, we were ignorant; yet our ignorance hardly mitigated the reality of the times. They were repressive, and all the more so for our blindness.

The effort to inhibit the growth of rock and roll or make use of it for non-revolutionary purposes — in short, to defang and declaw it — is beyond dispute. The payola hearings epitomize the effort, yet they were merely the most visible symptom. The effort was widespread and thorough. Concerts were banned, disc jockeys smashed records on the air, and ministers of the gospel preached against rock as the work of the devil. The White middle-class establishment was frightened; its actions were confused, uncoordinated, and generally ineffectual. Yet they were not without some impact. As far as radio is concerned, one of the most significant actions was the creation of top 40 programming, which took the choice of what was to be played out of the hands of individual disc jockeys. Executives, who were (and still are) much more amenable to the influence of the established order, now made up the playlists, and security and profits guided them in their selections as much as ideology. Together, these values led to the creation of an ironclad list of "safe" hits, the continual playing of which reinforced their sales, of course, making it doubly difficult for anything "dangerous" to succeed.

Despite the pervasiveness of this practice, however, radio had helped produce an audience on which it now depended for its very existence. No matter how offensive rock music seemed to be, its audience would have to be served. (The seventies TV program *WKRP in Cincinnati* was this reality incarnate.) Therein lay the seeds of self-contradiction, followed by conflict and change.

Switching Stations

Listeners to rock-and-roll radio were intensely loyal to the point of chauvinism, but not always to only one station, and not by any means forever. It was a little like remaining faithful to one spouse at a time. Actually, radio listening habits weren't nearly so restrictive; loyalty to more than one station at a time was acceptable without the accusation of being indiscriminate, so long as the stations were musically compatible.

What interests me is the process whereby loyalties were changed, the process of conversion. How was it that devoted fans abandoned one station and committed themselves to another? Even more interesting, and perhaps more significant as well, was how they converted from one type of station to another, that is, from one type of music to another.

Of one thing I'm sure, and that is that disc jockeys had very little, if anything, to do with it. Loyalty was given to the music that was played, not to the personality who played it. I don't mean to suggest that disc jockeys did not become cult figures (as McLuhan suggested they were). On the contrary, on occasion they were as popular as some of the musicians they chose to broadcast. All I mean is that their popularity was derivative. Allegiance was given first to a kind of music, and only then to the jockeys who play it — because they play it. Where would Alan Freed have been without R&B? Who would have mythologized Wolfman Jack if he hadn't been playing rock? Obviously, if it hadn't been for Liverpool's major contribution to the civilized world, very few would recognize the name of Murray the K.

My explanation for this process presupposes certain technological innovations and legislative reactions, but alone these are not sufficient. Some other factor is necessary if we are to grasp how and why such conversions take place. To illustrate, it is undeniably true that the rise of television destroyed the kind of radio programming that had existed so successfully from its inception to the years between 1949 and 1951, when radio, practically en masse, converted to a music and deejay format. Also beyond dispute is the impact of the payola controversies in elevating the program director to a position of almost absolute authority in selecting which records would be played (if not their exact order). The restrictive playlists and top 40 programming that resulted were no doubt a prime cause of album-oriented rock and underground radio, which came into being in the sixties. No less certain is the questionable role of market research in designing very limited programming for audiences defined with increasing specificity (thereby contributing to a resegregation of rock listeners). None of these developments, however, singly or in combination, can account for why any given listener might switch stations or alter listening habits.

Actually, the very success of AM radio (along with massive commercialization) and the invention of the push-button radio (especially since such radios are almost exclusively located in the family car, which has always provided a place of refuge away from the adult world) go deeper in helping to explain the conversion process. Push-buttons make it unnecessary to submit to the interference of commercials; more desirable songs can be sought out with a mere press of the fingertip. Yet neither the push-button nor commercialization can explain why a different kind of station might be punched into the radio, why someone might buy an FM tuner to avoid the AM dial, and why such intense loyalty is at the same time fickle.

The clue is contained in the counterproductive strategy of the radio networks and independents in the wake of the payola scandal. By this time, radio was fully and completely dependent on a vast teenage audience for its continued existence, so there was no question that their needs would be met. Yet at the same time, the traditional values of the established order had to be protected, for the radio stations were legally dependent on the political establishment for their existence as well. So radio found itself in the midst of two contradictory forces: On the one side were the vast hordes of American adolescents with a barely suppressed fascination with Black culture, the values of which were anathema to the White middle-class establishment. On the other side were the "powers that be," manifested in the FCC — the agency that grants licenses to broadcasters — and, of course, their own personal sympathies.

The solution to these conflicting pressures, unbeknownst to all parties, was to result in strengthening the fledgling community of adolescents far beyond what any intentional effort to do so might have accomplished. Schlock rock and playlists were supposed to be the means for controlling the influence of undesirable music and what it represented; they were supposed to produce nothing more than "entertainment" and hence be completely inconsequential and most certainly harmless. McLuhan had some interesting observations about just such a tactic:

> The commercial interests who think to render media universally acceptable, invariably settle for "entertainment" as a strategy of neutrality. A more spectacular mode of the ostrich-in-sand could not be devised, for it ensures maximal pervasiveness for any medium whatever.... The commercial entertainment strategy automatically ensures maximal speed and force of impact for any medium, on psychic and social life equally. It thus becomes a comic strategy of unwitting self-liquidation, conducted by those who are dedicated to permanence, rather than to change.[2]

To put it a bit differently, schlock and top 40 were destined to produce their own downfall. They were programmed to self-destruct, much to the consternation of their most fervent advocates.

Radio for McLuhan was "the tribal drum" because it inevitably caused unification to occur. In the American environment of the fifties, this unification was disturbing to many. Radio, he felt, "provides the tight tribal bond of the common market, of song, and of resonance.... Our teenagers in the 1950s began to manifest many of the tribal stigmata." By stigmata, he meant the indicators of the unified group; among them are isolation from others, a self-identity, and the instinct for self-preservation. The first thing that comes to mind regarding these characteristics might be the teenage gang phenomenon of the fifties, but this is to miss the essential point, namely, that teenagers themselves, as an entire category, were unified into a definable group. Prior to the fifties, the term "teenager" simply did not exist, for there was nothing to which it could refer.

Why people converted from one kind of music to another (from one station to another) had to do with the self-consciousness that radio has helped create. Given group identity and the instinct for self-preservation, it seemed only natural for stations to be selected with these criteria in mind. When a particular station no longer offered support, another would be found (or brought into being by radio executives interested in their own self-preservation). Obviously not every adolescent was self-consciously a member of the same group; it's hard to conceive of any contention more ridiculous. Nevertheless, they did see themselves as members of the same *kinds* of groups, since they, for the most part, have the same kind of consciousness. This is what radio has helped bring about: a similarity of consciousness, a consciousness defined by its opposition to the established order.

An Outlaw Consciousness

No one knows better what can and cannot be broadcast over the air than the musicians themselves. I sincerely doubt that the MC5 expected the full, live version of their "Kick Out the Jams" to be played on any radio station. (They used the word "fuck.") Similarly, the Rolling Stones were hardly kept awake at night waiting to hear "Sweet Virginia." (The forbidden word "shit" is used throughout.) And how many times was the Velvet Underground's "Heroin" aired on any station's playlist? Or anything from Prince's *Controversy* album?

This is hardly surprising. In each of these cases (and the list of unplayable music could be expanded to become a book of its own), the offense against "community standards" was egregious. The wonder is that they were recorded in the first place. Some musicians are content to be heard only in a live performance; others, however, want as much exposure as possible, for a variety of reasons. Money and fans are obvious goals, and few artists of any kind are immune to such seductions. When these become the sole reasons for desiring mass exposure, it is not unreasonable to allege that a sellout has occurred (especially since such artists are likely to take great pains not to offend anyone who might possibly contribute to their care and feeding). In any case, there are many others who want the exposure for reasons in addition to these flagrantly materialistic blandishments, reasons having to do with the propagation of values. Now it is probably obvious, but it is worth pointing out anyway: whenever people see the need to propagate their cause, it is because their cause is not presently receiving much support. Hence, their music will almost inevitably be counter to the prevailing values and offensive as a consequence. Therefore, like the establishment in the radio industry, this latter group of musicians found themselves in an apparently impossible position — trying to satisfy demands from two different directions: the values of the established order (as reflected in the radio industry) and those of their audience (which they shared).

An uneasy alliance was created by this coincidence of dilemmas. Radio executives and rock musicians both sought a way to play over the airwaves a kind of music that was threatening to the prevailing ethos. As mentioned above, the solution was to strengthen the community that radio had inadvertently brought into being.

This kind of jointly faced dilemma was not always the case, however. Not only was there a rigid segregation of music programming by race (with a relaxed standard for what could be broadcast by Black stations), but until the mid-fifties there was also no mass adolescent audience on which most stations depended for their existence. Prior to the inception of America's cultural revolution, radio audiences simply mirrored the values of those in charge of broadcasting, to say nothing of their racial characteristics. The color lines were rigid and, for all practical purposes, teenagers didn't yet exist.

The solution to the mutually felt dilemma was no doubt obvious to everyone: tone down the expressions of antagonistic values without exactly denying them. To carry through with this solution, however, was another matter, requiring considerable skill and talent. For what was needed was an indirect method of communication, a way of saying it all without quite saying it all. Perhaps another way of putting it is that the form of the music needed to be softened so that the content could "pass" more easily. I don't mean to suggest that anything conspiratorial took place; much of what happened was probably unconscious. Indirect communication is simply a way of using the language (understood in the broadest possible sense) that suggests its meaning through a variety of literary, dramatic, auditory, and visual devices. Symbols, puns, double entendres, euphemisms, innuendos, ironies, surrealistic imagery, and the like have all been employed in the cause. Further, the sound of the music, the style of the performers, the context of the performance and even their costumery all "say" something, but they "say" it indirectly, and often unconsciously.

The effect of all this indirect communication — unintended, unanticipated and no doubt barely recognized by anyone — was nothing less than the creation of an outlaw consciousness, the often vague but nevertheless real awareness of oneself as being in some way illegitimate. In "I Dig Rock and Roll Music," Peter, Paul and Mary sang, "But if I really say it/The radio won't play it/Unless I lay it between the lines." They were only making explicit something everybody already knew, for laying it between the lines had by then become no less than the tribal language. The term "rock and roll" itself originated as a sexual reference, while "dancing" functioned as a more general sexual euphemism. So, when Elvis sang "Good Rockin' Tonight" and Bobby Freeman "Do You Want to Dance?" there was little doubt as to what was being communicated. The Coasters, however, warned us about the consequences of indiscriminate sex with "Poison Ivy," a veiled reference to VD.

Sexual aberrations and alternative lifestyles have provided some interesting themes as well: "Lola" by the Kinks and "Walk on the Wild Side" by Lou Reed are both rather celebratory of transsexuality and homosexuality. The proverbial generation gap is exacerbated by the Coasters' "Yakety Yak" and the Silhouettes' "Get a Job," while the Who did the same with "My Generation" and Chuck Berry with "Almost Grown." Although this content is obvious, these latter songs also attacked more subtly the puritan notion of work and its alleged direct correlation with rewards. The Drifters despaired of the same correlation, with "Money Honey."

Naturally, political change was emphasized, especially as the sixties came into full swing, but with a particular slant: "Revolution" on The Beatles' "White Album" was ambiguous about the desirability of revolution; "A Hard Rain's A-Gonna Fall" by Bob Dylan has a specific meaning only if the listener attributes one to it; "Thank You (Falettinme Be Mice Elf Agin)" is Sly and Family Stone's double-edged commentary about personal suppression, for the song appeared also in a very dark version as "Thank You for Talkin' to Me Africa." And the Who's "Won't Get Fooled Again" has those wonderful lines "Meet the new boss/Same as the old boss." These are hardly naive sentiments, but neither are they obvious to the casual or alien listener.

Also attacked was religion: "With God on Our Side" by Dylan (sung by Joan Baez and Manfred Mann, among others as well) questions the basis of Western religion; for if god is on the side of all disputants in a war, then this god is absurd — it cannot exist. Groups such as Black Sabbath openly portrayed devil worship (probably to confound fundamentalists and to affect the guise of outrageousness), and numerous others have slyly advocated obeisance to Satan as a way of rejecting the received traditions, as with "Friend of the Devil" by the Grateful Dead and "Sympathy for the Devil" by the Rolling Stones. However, none of this is an advocacy of Satanism — it was the rejection of the Western religious tradition. As with "Revolution," only a careful listening will reveal that it's not spirituality but the Judeo-Christian (and Islamic) spirituality that's being denounced. Again, this was not exactly a naive distinction.

Finally, the attitude toward drugs was not nearly as simplistic as detractors were likely to think, for here, too, sophisticated distinctions were drawn. "The Pusher" by Steppenwolf and "Sam Stone" by John Prine are decidedly against drug use, while "Coming into Los Angeles" by Arlo Guthrie and "Let's Go Get Stoned" by Ray Charles are clearly advocating only one kind of recreational drug: marijuana. Other ambiguous songs include "Cracklin' Rose" by Neil Diamond, "Witchy Woman" by the Eagles, "Eight Miles High" by the Byrds, and numerous others. Perhaps it's a bit too neat, but the antidrug songs were mostly about hard drugs, pro-drug songs were about marijuana, and the ambiguous songs were about alcohol, cocaine, and hallucinogens, respectively. And the preceding is but a small, sketchy sample.

Sometimes, of course, the lyrics and every other element of indirect communication are profoundly unintelligible, a fact that serves to illustrate an important point about this tribal language (and any language for that matter): namely, it is not so much what's said but how it's interpreted that counts. "Louie, Louie" by the Kingsmen is an excellent illustration. No one to my knowledge has ever been able to make sense out of what the Kingsmen were singing (assistance provided by other, interpreted versions of the song doesn't count). Yet this terminal uncertainty didn't halt the flow of reputedly "real" lyrics from circulating on college campuses across the country, few of which agreed; nor did it prevent radio stations from banning the record for a long time. All this when no one knew what was being sung! In essence, the true meaning of the song was its interpretation, regardless of what the Kingsmen might have actually sung. Without question, the song was interpreted as clearly counter to the prevailing values. The film *Animal House* used it as its de facto anthem, and to this day, it still evokes the feeling of genuine revolution.

This is precisely the process by which an alternate, underground consciousness arose. It came into being as a peculiar way of receiving or interpreting the sometimes cryptic musical messages. Whether the music caused the consciousness or the consciousness was there to begin with, having arisen from other causes, is probably impossible to recover.

Probably they were mutually influential. In any case, it makes no real difference whether or not "Lucy in the Sky with Diamonds" is a reference to LSD; what matters is how it was interpreted by its listeners, and on this there is little doubt.

The consequence of all of this was, and continues to be, a reinforcement of a particular sense of self as outsider or outlaw. Of course, some of the music of today is much more explicit than music was in the fifties, and censorship over what can and cannot be played has been relaxed, but the damage, so to speak, has already been done. This outlaw consciousness no longer depends on musical obscurities to reinforce its existence. On the contrary, the reverse is probably more the case for today. Berlin's "Sex," Prince's "Controversy," and Cyndi Lauper's "Girls Just Want to Have Fun," for example, leave little to the imagination. The various expressions of alternative values (both direct and indirect) result now from a sense of already being outside the mainstream of American culture; yet it remains true that the music still serves to strengthen this consciousness. The effect is still reciprocal.

It is worth remembering that our conception of reality is largely determined by our consciousness. Outlaws, being what they are, must inevitably see themselves in conflict with the established order, antagonistic to the status quo. And, in turn, the established order will inevitably see itself as threatened, and it will necessarily respond with hostility. In this kind of atmosphere, is there any wonder why a cultural revolution has come about?

Commercialization

A perennial critique of claims such as this concerns the allegedly overpowering lure of money. Supposedly, the pursuit of wealth is too strong for any revolutionary movement to withstand, especially in America where materialism is magnified to monstrous proportions. It is no doubt true that many revolutionaries do "sell out," but this reasoning alone misses the point. Cultural revolutions are more complex, more enduring, and more subtle than we are led to believe by equating them with political struggles. They have a life and power of their own, completely apart from any of their participants (proponents and opponents). Once set in motion, change is inevitable; nothing ever remains the same. To paraphrase Heraclitus and Bob Dylan, we can never watch the same river flow.

So, no matter how much money is used to reestablish the status quo ante, the effort can never work out as intended. It is not that the revolutionaries prevent it from happening, or that the allure of money is not as strong as feared, or that the establishment is weaker than one might hope. The fact is that the movement of history is in no one's control; the future is not a mere product of deliberate manipulation — not anyone's.

Consider the various attempts to seduce and co-opt genuine rock and roll with covers and imitations. Such attempts, along with restrictive playlists, led not to a diminution of its impact but rather to the relocation of creative programming to FM, the hitherto forgotten child of radio. Thus, an outlet was provided for the increasingly sociopolitical commentary of the music that began to characterize the mid-sixties. Covering in particular had the effect of publicizing the relatively unknown Black originals, and it wasn't long before this practice ceased to exist.

History continues to move, often contrary to our wishes, and certainly without giving us any advance warning. With the enormous increase in FM's popularity, commercial interests again entered the scene and brought with them the formulas that worked so well on

AM: playlists and a top 40 format. With the exception of its being broadcast in stereo, FM became little different from AM. This trend pretty much characterized radio during the Interim period.

As the revolution became confronted with a newly reinvigorated and more potent opposition (and consequently was forced to make itself viable again), radio, too, underwent yet another change. Stations began devoting some of their airtime to what was increasingly being called "new music," including new wave, punk, techno-rock, avant-garde, neo-rockabilly and the like; as a result, they found a sudden and unexpected surge in their popularity. From 1979 to 1981, for example, the *Rolling Stone* readers' poll found Cleveland's WMMS, which had a new-music format, to be the nation's top station. In 1982, KLOL in Houston, WNEW in New York, WMMR in Philadelphia, and KROQ in Los Angeles, all of which played a variety of new music, joined WMMS.

In the 21st century, radio has, perhaps reached its figurative and literal zenith in satellite radio, XM and Sirius. Free, ostensibly, from many FCC controls (being so far "offshore") they have the opportunity to play anything they want—and often do. Yet there are still strong commercial interests at work, and these pressures have yet to be played out.

Consider also how commercialization has affected our perceptions about race relations. As radio in the fifties more or less capitulated to rock and roll, segregated programming was ended for all practical purposes—only on rock radio, of course. Integration had occurred in music and on the radio, if not in society. Then, by means of an exceedingly complex process, the attempt to exploit the popularity of this kind of racially indistinguishable music led to the semblance of resegregation. Although it was a genuine meeting of the races, this early achievement of integration was accomplished by Whites allowing Blacks to enter White society; White radio was the active agent, Black music was passive. The commercial support for rock-and-roll radio then acted as an encouragement for Blacks to develop apart from the now unnecessary White support. Hence, in the sixties, along with the rise of Black power and Black pride movements, came Motown and soul. When this trend continued into funk and disco, radio stations again began exhibiting racial distinctiveness, but this time the separation was largely the result of Black initiative. As this development, too, became popular, commercial interests stressed the creation of narrowly defined radio stations so as to cater to these "separatist" demands, further strengthening and encouraging Black consciousness.

With the Re-actualization of a revitalized establishment, the revolutionary opposition was forced to respond with a revitalization of its own, and this meant a reformulation of the old coalition of outcasts. This time, however, Blacks joined on more equal terms, and most definitely with a stronger sense of self. The resulting merger was then, as it was in the fifties, a source of renewed creativity and energy, giving new life to the revolutionary values. This mutual rediscovery was a part of the new programming just now beginning to emerge (especially on satellite radio stations where diversity can be maximized), but it had a significance all its own. For during their period of separation, Blacks and Whites developed their musical traditions independent of one another, a situation that served to produce an enormous dynamism when again they met. Today, Whites are listening to Black music and Blacks are listening to White music. (Beginning with McCartney's "Say, Say, Say," and continuing with Eminem's *Slim Shady* album, for example.) As in years before, the primary medium of communication has been the radio. The resulting experience is remarkably similar to the excitement of the fifties, and we can thank commercial pressures for allowing us to recapture this revolutionary impetus. Many Black Americans have long since recognized and appreciated Elvis Costello, the Jam, and the Clash; Whites have long since come to know the likes of Prince, the Pointer Sisters, Rick James, Patti Austin, the Gap Band, Skyy, the Sugarhill Gang, Angela Bofill, and Maze.

A genuine breakthrough happened with Michael Jackson's *Thriller* album; its top singles, "Billie Jean" and "Beat It," topped both Black and White charts, as did the album. The Jacksons' 1984 "Victory Tour," as well as their *Victory* album, was as popular with Whites as with Blacks. Perhaps even more significant, Michael's sex appeal was unselfconsciously biracial. Prince has had the same kind of biracial appeal and a bisexual appeal as well, but with a harder and sharper edge. Michael Jackson is cute, but Prince is dangerous. Another significant breakthrough concerned Hall and Oates, a White duo with a large Black following, evident in their performing and recording with Eddie Kendricks and David Ruffin of the original Temptations. A portent, I think.

Little needs to be said about the enormous impact of rap and hip-hop. Originating in the African American community, it has spread to be, perhaps, the dominant form of rock in many ways. When the East Coast/West Coast conflict burst into the open in the paradigmatic murders of both Tupac Shakur and Biggie Smalls (The Notorious B.I.G.), the result was a monumental shift of attention to both the styling and the lyrics of their work.

So, the allegedly deadening hand of commercialization has not had the kind of effect so often attributed to it. It has neither stifled the creativity of rock nor corrupted the basic values of the cultural revolution. On the contrary, a good case could be made for the opposite. It seems that whenever pressure is applied at one location, another path is found or created to release the suppressed energy. Hence follows the temptation to observe: the greater the repression, the more creative, and often unanticipated, the eventual response. After all, the real message in many ways is the medium.

5

Records:
The Newest Testament

The message of radio is records: it plays them, sells them, overexposes them, and eventually disposes of them. Along the way, the essential meaning of the electronic media is reinforced. It makes little difference which records are played or even what kind of music is on them. What is important is that they are records.

Every age has had its method for communicating the important news of the day. In the long period before the invention of movable type, oral communication was the dominant means. The ancient Greeks favored the allegory, and Jesus used the parable. Later, with stringed accompaniment, the troubadours of the eleventh through the thirteenth centuries entertained and passed along the latest news. With the introduction of the printing press, however, society became far more hierarchical and closely organized, and as a consequence, the masses became decidedly more passive. An increasing differentiation and isolation of one society from another also occurred. Such was the impact of a common culture spread through the medium of print. So said McLuhan.

The electronic media have changed all of this, not instantaneously of course. Nevertheless, a steady revolutionary transformation has occurred since the inception of this new technology (this, too, according to McLuhan). All these changes have been in the direction of decentralization, unification, and retribalization — tendencies that McLuhan regarded as inevitable. The term he used to describe this movement was implosion, a rather graphic term. As the very opposite of the overheated explosive media of print, implosion suggests the contraction brought along by cooling.

If we understand implosiveness in terms of the values implicit in rock music, it is bound to include such stances as opposition to nationalism, religions, the military, authoritarianism, racism, sexism, and ignorance. Correspondingly, the values affirmed include freedom, individuality, happiness, mutuality, and harmony. All the electronic media tend in this direction; some, of course, more so than others, depending largely on how purely electronic they are (or how mixed they are with mechanical media). In addition, specific media perhaps necessarily emphasize certain values over others. Not all implosive values are equally expressed, in other words. Therefore, it is important to keep in mind which electronic medium is under discussion — in this case, audio recordings.

Unfortunately, McLuhan himself was not very helpful when it came to a consideration of records. He did offer a few tantalizing suggestions regarding the phonograph, but he seemingly ignored his own notion that, as a medium, the message of the phonograph was necessarily another medium — records. I certainly do not wish to disparage what he said about record players, but I'm convinced that it is more important to concentrate on what they are designed to play. Nevertheless, there are some points to keep in mind about the equipment, namely, the progressive improvements in sound quality. From the earliest mechanical devices, through the perfection of tape (as the means for making records), to hi-fi and stereo, the enhancement of sound has contributed enormously to our developing revolutionary consciousness. McLuhan termed this "sound in depth," the multiplicity of sensory factors in one unified experience: "When a medium becomes a means of depth experience the old categories of 'classical' and 'popular' or of 'highbrow' and 'lowbrow' no longer obtain." He went on to add that anything approached or acquired "in depth" inevitably has the quality of seriousness about it, regardless of what it is. Total involvement makes this possible, so the development of stereo (and continuing improvements) cannot be overlooked.[1]

One of the maddening things about McLuhan was his refusal to offer sufficient evidence for some of his more provocative claims, and this idea about an in-depth experience was no exception. Yet, if we reflect on the time when stereo was introduced, there is an amazing coincidence between this and a new attitude toward rock music. Of course, it is equally possible that the new sound potential inspired rock musicians to new heights in artistry, but even if this were the case, it would serve only to provide an explanation for McLuhan's idea; it wouldn't call it into question. In any case, my interest is in the recordings themselves and how they aided the implosive process in its creation and propagation of revolutionary values.

Having gone through adolescence in the fifties affords a unique perspective on this development and can provide as much confirmation of the impact of records as is perhaps possible. I can still recall, for example, buying my first few 45s almost as if it were earlier this afternoon. What really mattered was having my own personal record collection, something different from my parents', something that would establish my linkage with others of my own age and experiences. (Since what few records my parents owned were all 78s, this wasn't hard to accomplish; just owning those few 45s was sufficient.) Thinking back to the records I actually bought, the selection gives enormous credence to the medium's truly being the message. Since it was 1955, I bought a copy of "Rock around the Clock," but that was it as far as rock and roll was concerned. (Elvis wouldn't make it nationally until the following year.) The others included "Lisbon Antiqua" (Nelson Riddle), "The Yellow Rose of Texas" (Mitch Miller), "Cherry Pink and Apple Blossom White" (Perez Prado) and something taken from a Disney TV show called "The White Buffalo" by musicians long since faded from my memory. I did have some discretion, of course; I didn't pick these at random. They represented what I was hearing on the radio. Yet, while I was secretly listening to the new and dangerous Black music, to actually purchase one of these recordings was out of the question, no matter how much I liked it. There were limits to how far you could go with this new music, and no one had to tell me what they were. Besides, having my own collection was the significant thing, not so much what was in the collection. Only later would I begin to realize the effect that owning records had had on me, and by then the content of my collection would matter very much.

The War of the Revolutions

Today, few people remember the "Battle of the Speeds" that occurred in 1948. Very shortly, after tape recordings made possible vast improvements in sound quality, CBS

(Columbia) introduced the 33⅓ rpm disc, mainly in order to produce symphonic music more cheaply and thus make it more attractive to consumers. At about the same time, RCA introduced its own highly improved disc, the 45 rpm. The spectacular increase in fidelity evident in both rendered the 78 rpm recording obsolete almost immediately, and by 1957, the record industry ceased making these fragile relics entirely.

The record-buying public was now confronted with a rather curious dilemma because of this rather sudden transformation in the technology: all existing equipment had to be replaced, or at the very least potential consumers had to contemplate which kind of equipment to buy. Initially, neither disc was compatible with the other's equipment. Unfamiliarity with the rapid succession of technology was yet another cause for hesitancy. (When my parents bought me my first LPs, all classical, we initially played — or rather tried to play — them on my grandparents' 78 rpm machine, which had a tone arm as heavy as a brick and a stone needle that mercilessly plowed through the grooves. We simply didn't know any different.) However, to the rescue came the ever-popular law of supply and demand. Both CBS and RCA soon offered their new equipment practically at cost, and Capitol began pressing both sizes, thus setting the trend for the future. From that time on, the newest equipment was designed to play all three speeds.

Sales took off. Jerry Hopkins, in *The Rock Story*, traces a steady, sharp rise from about 1954 on — precisely the year when rock music entered the American consciousness. (From 1921 to 1948, the growth in sales had increased significantly, yet it was hardly at a rate likely to attract much attention.) The only significant exception to this meteoric rise (until the recession in the 1970s) occurred in 1959, when sales plummeted 25 percent, coinciding with the tragedies, defections, and scandals of the immediate period in rock music. Nevertheless, the new technology made possible the dissemination of this new form of music, which just happened to make its entrance onto the American scene at about this time.

Certainly Columbia did not intend for popular music to be the prime beneficiary of this new technology, let alone music largely influenced by Black culture and that of other assorted outcasts. Peter Goldmark, the president of CBS Labs, hoped that the LP would make classical music more appealing. It took about five 78s, for example, to record an entire symphony, something that could be accomplished on a single LP. Apparently, Goldmark and others like him thought that this and poor sound quality presented prohibitive difficulties for the enjoyment of classical music; however, while this is not untrue, it is only a small part of the explanation. Times were a-changing.

At first, classical music was the content of most LPs. "Pop" sounds were relegated to the 45, with a resulting three-minute or so time limit for any given song. In fact, the "song" itself was just about the only musical structure available for popular music. Significantly, ever since, the LP retained this connotation of importance, while the 45 continued to be the epitome of superficiality. Relating this to radio, "serious" rock music since the sixties has been associated with FM, which has always favored the LP and thus has helped to define a new genre of broadcasting: album-oriented rock. Until recently (with the introduction of CDs), top 40 stations were almost exclusively limited to playing 45s. These acquired qualities should be kept in mind when considering the kind of message being conveyed by a given medium, for in many ways album rock inherited the mantle of significance from the classics.

However, history never pauses, and the technological changes just keep coming. Two new developments promised to have an especially important impact on values. One was the twelve-inch single, and the other was the new compact laser disc and player.

The former really did not involve any new technology; it was more or less an elaboration of the single. Since it played longer than the typical 45, its AM airplay turned out to be somewhat limited, but the twelve-inch disc did become very popular in dance clubs — and later as a de facto musical instrument available to a new group of "spinner" DJs. Its real importance, however, concerned its impact on race relationships, and I'll comment on this in the next section.

Compact discs are another matter entirely; they were a genuine advance in technology and as such carried a decidedly new message. Although McLuhan never offered any observations about records per se, his theory about sound is helpful at this point. Referring to the introduction of high fidelity, or hi-fi, he maintained that "realistic sound" merged the senses of hearing and touch, with the result that the distance between performer and audience is largely overcome: "For the sensation of having the performing instruments right in the room with you is a striving toward the union of the audile and tactile in a finesse of fiddles that is in large degree the sculptural experience. To be in the presence of performing musicians is to experience their touch and handling of instruments as tactile and kinetic, not just as resonant." Thus he characterized the "in depth" experience mentioned earlier.

With still greater improvements in sound quality, it makes sense that the sensory involvement was likely to become correspondingly greater. According to every audiophile and rock fan whose hearing is reasonably intact, the compact disc has provided a quantum leap in this direction. As such, once the price for the equipment dropped, the CD virtually overnight replaced the vinyl medium. Most important, it has had the potential for creating an even more complete merger between performer and audience. It quite literally sounds like the musicians are barely three feet from your skull: you not only hear them, you can almost see, feel, smell, and even taste them. Finally, it must be kept in mind that the more perfect the merger, the more complete the identification of ideas and feelings. Such improvements as these tend to give the performers an enormous degree of influence over their audiences.

One other aspect of the CD revolution should be emphasized, and as far as I know, this factor has received little or no attention. CD players soon boasted a feature whereby the user could select specific songs to play, and with players that could handle multiple disks, literally an entire day could be programmed according to an individual's particular taste. This was not at all practicable with LPs, since with most record players a person would have to manually move the arm of the record player to the desired song — and continue to do so ad infinitum.

The importance of this capability, to be magnified exponentially by music being made available on the Internet, cannot be overstressed: One of the major goals of the cultural revolution has been its desire to support and increase individuality and diversity. Now, as never before, each and every person could plan, program and listen to his or her own choice of music. The record producer or radio program director — the "middlemen," so to speak — have largely lost their control over the individual's choice of music. Both individuality, and the other side of the coin, diversity, have emerged unintended and virtually unnoticed from these technological advances.

Race and the Little Labels

Exclusion has its curious advantages — one hopes to the chagrin and consternation of those doing the exclusion. For those living on the outside, the prevailing norms weigh less heavily, and sometimes they can be successfully ignored altogether. Outsiders have a certain freedom that those on the inside can never possess; after all, social pariahs have no power to threaten the established order, so they aren't considered dangerous. Their comparative freedom costs society little. (Of course, they receive no social benefits either.) One needs only recall Ralph Ellison's *Invisible Man*, published in 1953. (I read it inadvertently, thinking it was a contemporary update of the H. G. Wells book.)

Prior to the advent of the cultural revolution marked by the rise of rock music, this was precisely the situation with record companies that were producing Black music (at that time called "race" or "sepia," and later "cat" music). They were outsiders, excluded, barely existing in the enormous shadows of the then big three (Decca, Columbia, and RCA Victor, with Capitol trailing as a poor fourth). These outsiders included such labels as Aladdin, Argo, Aristocrat, Atlantic, Chance, Chess, Cobra, Dot, Duke, Dunhill, Federal, Gee, Herald, Imperial, Jubilee, King, Rama, Savoy, Specialty, Stax/Volt, Sun, Vee-Jay, and many others that have long since faded from memory. Much of their output was devoted to Black music, and it isn't hard to imagine the extent of their distribution capabilities—just about nil. If you wanted to buy something they produced, you pretty much had to go to where they recorded.

Because of its relatively high degree of freedom from the prevailing cultural norms, Black consciousness was permitted to express itself in an almost undiluted form. Music has always provided this kind of outlet, from the time of slavery up to and including the present. In fact, music has been one of the few means of Black expression available to White audiences. This is the kind of material that disc jockeys like Alan Freed began playing for White adolescents in the early fifties.

The rapidly increasing popularity of this music caught the attention of the majors and forced them to revise their practices in order to compete. The competitive struggle that ensued was obviously unequal, and many of the small companies were bought out or otherwise put out of business (for example, Jubilee, Herald/Ember and Savoy). Only a few survived, and fewer still went on to become majors in their own right (for example, Atlantic, Roulette, and Dot).

Despite the fact that financial success did not follow the popularity of the music they recorded, there was nevertheless success of another kind. A different and conflicting set of fundamental values was introduced into American culture, acquainting White adolescents with the Black side of America in the process. Yet more important than even this was the fact of the communication itself: the years of slavery and segregation had made it virtually impossible for the races to communicate honestly face to face. Now, for the first time in American history, Whites were authentically hearing what Blacks were saying. (Blacks were always capable of knowing what Whites were saying and thinking, for it was rarely risky for Whites to reveal themselves to Blacks, much as servants are often privy to knowledge about their employers that even the employers' families never know. Again, the powerless need not be feared.) To be more accurate, it was principally White youth who were doing the listening; White parents were mainly becoming apoplectic because of what their children were hearing.

Prejudice, ignorance, superstition, hatred, and fear can only exist in the absence of genuine communication. With the invention of cheap 45s, authentic communication between the races began to take place. I don't mean to give the impression that White adolescents, en masse, bought into Black culture. Hardly. This no doubt would have been quite dramatic, but not altogether significant. What was significant was the fact that they were

5. Records: The Newest Testament

truly listening. It should not seem so strange, then, that it was precisely this generation that found itself uncomfortable with the whole ideology of racism and all its attendant beliefs. Not that racism immediately came to an end with the listening to Black music. Far from it. But White youth could no longer feel secure with the attitudes bequeathed to them; they now knew too much. One incredibly naive belief shared by most Whites throughout American history was the notion that Blacks were either happy with their lot in life (no doubt since they realized their innate inferiority and were grateful for whatever blessings were bestowed on them) or were too stupid to know anything different. Listening to virtually any Black recording would dispel those beliefs almost instantaneously. Well, maybe you'd need to listen to several. Certainly, by the mid-seventies on, listening to any recording by Grandmaster Flash, the Bus Boys, or Run-D.M.C. should have done the trick. Anyway, the nagging suspicion gradually, but inevitably, arose that other beliefs about Blacks were equally absurd. No, racism didn't magically die with a few records, but at least for the adolescents of the fifties and the decades that followed, racist ideology could never again provide one of the unquestioned building blocks of American society.

As always, interracial communication is vital, and as before it has often occurred through music. Partly because of Black Americans withdrawing from mainstream (White) society for reasons of pride and integrity, isolation of a different kind developed. Since the mid-sixties, rock music has reflected and has served to reinforce this separation. In this case, the separation has not been all bad; the reestablishment of self-esteem was its major initial accomplishment. Yet something new was afoot and, as before, it had to do with technology. Only a few artists, at first, recorded twelve-inch singles (at 33 1/3 or 45 rpm) as well as on the standard LP and 7-inch single. Although this may have been nothing more than a clever marketing device (since it gave them exposure to the dance floor in preference to the other two), note well what rock critic Robert Hilburn had to say about them in 1983:

> The lure of the 12-inch single is partly functional. The large discs generally allow better sound because the discs utilize wider grooves. In most cases, they also provide a longer and even punchier rendition of the song...
> The 12-inch revolution also is tied to a musical style: a disco/new wave merger that may turn out to be the biggest commercial and creative force in pop over the next few years.
> Besides providing many of today's most exciting and adventurous records, this "dance" or "modern" music hybrid could also be enormously helpful in breaking down much of the racial and cultural isolation that has plagued pop music since the early '70s.
> The best of the new music combines the sensual urgency of the peppy, R&B-affiliated sound that first found favor in disco with the wry sensibility of punk and new wave rock.
> Once outspoken enemies, disco fans and the electro-pop new wave followers have now discovered a common meeting ground in the hot pulse of 12-inch dance records...
> Indeed, the 12-inch single could be as integral a part of pop in the '80s as 45 rpm singles were in the '50s and long-play albums were in the '60s.[2]

Hilburn's optimism might have been considered excessive when he wrote it, since there really had not been enough time to assess the impact of the twelve-inch disc. Nevertheless, there was again communication across racial lines, and this did give some basis for hope. Also worth noting is the possibility of genuine communication between straights and gays. One of the unspoken reasons for the widespread antipathy against disco was its association with homosexual dance clubs; so with this new musical merger, some of the ignorance about sexual preference might have been dispelled as well that about the races.

Even more significant was the development of major corporate conglomerates devoted to African American music in all of its contemporary manifestations. Often established and run by African Americans, these organizations portend something about the future. Motown Records and its R&B flavor is well known. Def Jam Records emphasizes rap and hip-hop. Island Records originally had a calypso orientation, followed by reggae and ska, but its list of musicians now includes virtually everything by everybody. As the years passed, each of the three has gone through multiple changes of location, ownership, orientation and so on, so that the original flavor of each has long since evaporated. In an odd way, however, these originally Black-oriented music conglomerates have been fully integrated into American society and culture, thus fulfilling one of the original dreams of the early Civil Rights movement.

Looking back at all these developments from the perspective of the 21st century, I think Hilburn hit the proverbial nail on the head — with the caveat that this 12-inch phenomenon has had as much to do with sexual preferences as with racial groups. His only error, in other words, was to *under*estimate its impact. With its close association with disco, rap and hip-hop, this 12-inch disc, properly and effectively used by a DJ — an artistic profession made possible by the disk, if not wholly created by it — has had a cultural influence far exceeding its physical characteristics. I don't think it's stretching the truth to say that the initial success (promising more to come) of proponents of legalized gay marriage proponents owe a lot to that curious 1877 invention of Thomas Edison in Menlo Park, New Jersey.

And to proceed one step further, Hilburn just might have generalized that recordings themselves — regardless of their composition, speed or technology — have had and will continue to have a revolutionary impact on American culture — and beyond.

Sex and the 45

One of Hilburn's points was undeniably correct to readers even then: the 45 was indeed an integral part of the fifties, and probably to a greater extent than even he had in mind. For its impact, in good McLuhanesque fashion, had as much to do with its form as with its content.

It is hard to image what the fifties would have been like without the doughnut-shaped seven-inch disc. Quite simply, the fifties, as we've come to know them, would never have existed were it not for the 45. Consider for a moment the challenge it presented to the puritan notion of sexuality and the traditional conception of the family. These were among the most important pillars of pre-fifties American culture, and the Samsonian task of pulling them down was accomplished to a large extent by this seemingly innocuous novelty.

With regard to its impact on sexual morality, the ends-and-means relationship was simply reversed. The preponderant attitude toward sexuality in the Western religious tradition has always been one of barely suppressed suspicion, especially in Christianity. Although the dualism between flesh and spirit had long ago been declared heretical, and despite the fact that sex was regarded as part of the goodness of God's creation, it was, and continues to be for many, good only as a means. Roman Catholics have traditionally viewed sex solely as the means for the propagation of children; more recently, however, the Catholic Church has begun to interpret this goal more broadly. Protestants and Jews have almost always acknowledged a wider role. Nevertheless, for them, too, sex is properly a means and only a means. Propagation is only one facet of its intended end; the enhancement of love in marriage and the strengthening of family life in general are its other goals. In no case has sex been regarded by Western religious thought as a valuable end in and of itself. This notion, however, is precisely what emerged as a result of the 45 rpm record.

The typical teenage party was a case in point. In the fifties, and no doubt still today, a necessary prerequisite for any valid party was and still is music, and this may actually be, in some instances, sufficient as well. In any case, a "stack of platters" on that little RCA record player would permit uninterrupted dancing for quite a while. No one but the most prodigious, of course, could maintain such a pace for very long, and besides, there were other things to do — necking, to be specific. When the parents frequented the downstairs rec room less often (or wherever else the party was held), the real party could begin. Couples would take turns being stationed by the door to warn of the parents' impending return; then the lights would be lowered or simply turned off. The key deception was provided by those easily handled 45s, since from upstairs it would still sound like dancing was going on. The "stack of platters" would now provide uninterrupted cover for necking and even some heavy petting; the giant holes in the records and the configuration of the player made turning them over in the dark "no sweat."

To modify a proverb, opportunity may be the mother of invention; in this case the opportunity allowed for the invention of sex as something desirable (valuable) in and of itself—apart from the constraint of being a "means" to some "end." The party was merely one of the means to accomplish this end, and parties were rated as to how effective they were. Sex had become, for many, the sole measure of success. The party was the medium, and sex was its message.

"Record hops" (or "sock hops" when held in the school gym, since leather shoes and the wood floor were deemed incompatible) became yet another way to approximate the goal. The measure of success or effectiveness in this case, however, was partly in terms of whether a party date could be arranged. Another measure concerned what could be arranged for after the dance, at the local "passion pit." The record hop has always been "hormone city," everyone restlessly maneuvering for position (literally and figuratively). Take the "dance" for example: the slower and closer the dancing, the greater likelihood that "things" would bode well for afterwards. ("Need a ride home?") The adult authorities, of course, didn't stand idly by, allowing this to go on unimpeded. There were rules! One was that dancing must always include perceptible movement (presumably to prevent pure, uninhibited embracing on the dance floor; the semblance of a dance had to be retained after all). Often a yardstick or a plumb was used to assess the degree of compliance, and just as often, it became a joke to see who could comply with the least amount of motion. Another rule prohibited the so-called dirty boogie, the jitterbug with suggestive pelvic gestures — an undisguised portrayal of copulation. The "dirty boogie" would always attract an appreciative audience that would circle around the offending couple and thus provide them with a temporary protective screen. The fact that this practice no longer occurs to any appreciable extent merely illustrates how threatening any open display of sexuality was in the fifties.

So, you ask, what has this to do with the 45 rpm record? They weren't called "record hops" for nothing! Their very raison d'être was to play and dance to the latest recordings. Often, local disc jockeys would be hired as a special attraction, but their appearances were incidental. Sex was the goal, and the records provided the means.

The family was affected just as much, although the impact was more indirect. Prior to the advent of the infamous record hop, the whole boy-meets-girl courtship ritual was carried out under the auspices of the family. I don't mean to suggest by this that parental control was either complete or even very effective. If this were ever true, it was characteristic of an age long before the emergence of the automobile. What I mean is that courtship was at one time legitimated by being carried out under the guidance and patronage of the family; the effectiveness of this guidance and patronage is another issue entirely.

Prior to the record hop, dances were major events requiring planning, organization, and cooperation. For dancing to take place, the group needed a live band, which has always given such occasions a decidedly different flavor. Parents necessarily had (and still have) a greater role: they gave permission to use the car (or they drove the couple), provided the funds, met the date, took the pictures for posterity, and waited up late hoping for the couple's safe return. Record hops were something entirely different. Their casualness and informality obviated the parental role almost completely. Many were held immediately after school or after a sporting event, ruling out any possibility of formality. Others were sponsored by the local department of recreation ("recs" or "teen centers") and were held every weekend, eliminating their uniqueness. Rarely was dating practiced (and no "stag or drag" pricing), so meeting parents and having them take pictures became irrelevant. Since the events were held early in the evening and/or regularly, parental worrying was minimized. Sometimes parents didn't even know their children had gone to a record hop: it didn't seem important enough to be concerned about; so parents didn't ask and their children didn't tell. Yet what neither clearly recognized was the fact that the accepted pattern of courtship was being flagrantly violated: the parents were unaware because the interactions were all happening out of their sight, and their children because they didn't know any different.

When this challenge to the family's authority is added to the value reversal regarding sex, there is considerable evidence for the impact of the 45 — quite apart from the songs recorded thereon.

Politics and the LP

Without the LP, rock would have remained essentially apolitical and would have provided no real threat to the established order. The LP has always connoted an element of seriousness, so when rock music was first recorded on LPs in about 1960, it was inevitably regarded differently. To be specific, I have in mind only those rock albums designed intentionally as such, not collections of previously released singles. The creation of an album of rock music is not at all the same as the production of a single, and the implications of this difference are extremely important.

The production of rock LPs became well-nigh universal by 1963. Singles became the derivative medium as a consequence (with very few exceptions). Some popular music, in addition to classical, had been recorded on albums prior to this period, but, significantly, not blues, C&W, or rock and roll. These latter were thought (perhaps unconsciously) not to necessitate such quality treatment. The Beach Boys were the first rock performers consistently to break through the barrier and make it onto the charts, beginning with *Surfin' USA* in 1963. (Elvis, Ricky Nelson, Dion, and Chubby Checker had a few entries prior to this, but they lacked the album orientation of the Beach Boys.) Then in 1964, the floodgates were opened with *Meet The Beatles*, the year's top album and the first time a rock album made it to the number one spot. Soon there emerged the "concept album," an LP devoted to the expression of a specific theme. While The Beatles are usually given credit for this development with *Sgt. Pepper*, the practice has become comparatively common among rock musicians today. (From its outset, Pink Floyd, for example, has done little else.) What is important, however, is not whether an album is intended as a concept album; it is the album medium itself that carries the message of seriousness.

Some clarification is needed. First, seriousness should not be understood to imply dourness, humorlessness, or anything of the sort. On the contrary, seriousness can easily encompass humor, satire, joy, pleasure and all sorts of fun. Early on, *Talk Show* by the Go-Go's exemplified this perfectly. True seriousness is merely the opposite of triviality and frivolity, and it need not have been consciously intended as such. What is important is that it be interpreted as such. The vital aspect of messages is not how they're sent but how they're received. Second, as far as possible, I want to focus on the qualities of the 33⅓ rpm recording itself, not on the peculiarities of its contents. (Keep in mind that what is true of the vinyl LP is also true of its technologically superior descendant, the CD.) And third, while what naturally comes to mind is high definition or stereophonic sound (at the very least high fidelity), most of the following can just as easily apply to the early monaural recordings as well.

Individually, the following characteristics may seem relatively unimportant, but together they make a convincing case, and the "case" has to do with the message of the medium, "the LP." One characteristic has to do with the price of an album in comparison with that of a single. Because of this, it has never been an easy decision to buy an LP; buying a 45 can almost be done on a whim, but buying an album takes some thought. It is not simply a matter of the amount of time spent in deciding; it's more a matter of the source of the decision. Singles are bought mostly as the result of caprice, prompted by forces outside of the deciding agent (usually the force in question is the familiarity created by excessive airplay). Few albums are bought like this. Most are purchased on the basis of reviews, hearing them first, trusting what others say about them, and the artists' past performances. In other words, the decision to buy a single stems largely from external causes, while the decision to buy an album originates internally. (In Chapter 8, I'll deal with how all of this is affected by the existence of the Internet.)

It is also significant to consider where the album is kept once it's purchased. Singles are packed away in those little carrying cases or in some other inconspicuous place. Albums, however, require their own furniture. Hence, even small collections necessarily become part of the home's decor. Because of their size, they can never be an incidental feature of the room; they have to be deliberately placed into their setting (like the sound equipment itself), available to anyone interested in checking out the collection.

Yet another distinguishing quality is the album's artwork. The jacket's size and relative permanence permit some rather elaborate endeavors of various kinds, and there are quite a few books devoted exclusively to album art as a field in its own right. However, regardless of the quality of any given album cover, the artist must give some thought to how the art relates to the contents of the album. Further, since this is "commercial" art (as if there were any other kind), some consideration is inevitably given to the effectiveness of the artwork in selling the album. The art, in other words, is never the product of accident.

A related quality concerns the liner notes. Something has to fill up the backside of the album, if not further art, and the liner sleeve isn't usually allowed to go to waste either. (Cheap re-pressings are another matter entirely.) As with the artwork, thought has to be given to the notes' relationship with the contents as well as to potential sales; again, nothing is left to chance. Interestingly, the punk movement of the late 1970s and early 1980s quite self-consciously avoided notes, and sometimes art, as a symbolic rejection of the kind of image and attitude that had at that time become associated with the album medium. Of course, this very denial was the result of a calculated decision; this, too, was not done by happenstance.

Thus, the decisions as to what will be included (or not) on the album require careful thought, aesthetic as well as commercial. Moreover, attention has to be given to which cuts should be released as singles because they will receive most of the airplay. If the singles make the charts, the chances increase that the album will do well too.

The kind of station that's likely to play cuts from the album directly, without relying on singles, is obviously one devoted to AOR (album-oriented rock), and this means FM almost exclusively (despite the fact that FM programming has tended to emulate AM in recent years). This, too, contributes to the connotation of seriousness. As if to resurrect this quality, almost every city has a local or syndicated FM station devoted to the free-spirited individualism that once populated the higher end of the frequency spectrum. (At this writing, Los Angeles has a "Jack FM" and "The Sound"—both doing eclectic and seemingly "free spirited" album rock.)

One element common to all these various qualities is thought, or more specifically, the reasoning process—at the very least, this impression is created. The reasoning may not always be very good, but it is unavoidable, and it is essentially political. Thought, after all, is intrinsically connected with the act of choice, the making of decisions, and choices are nothing other than evaluations: goodness and badness might even be defined as our affirmations and negations. The evaluation of alternatives, to continue, is at basis the political process itself—its heart and soul.

The fact that the kinds of decisions relating to rock albums—which albums to buy as well as which to broadcast—have been remarkably consistent is obviously significant, and this consistency is largely what this book is about. People who produce, broadcast and purchase rock albums share certain fundamental values or deliberately appear to share them (and appearances—even if sham—are important), and as it happens these values are in conflict with the traditional values of our culture. Why this is the case has a lot to do with the historical context, and this will be the theme of the third part of the book.

The Counterculture and the Record Store

A certain kind of record store epitomizes the dialectical relationship between the values of the traditional culture and those of the counterculture. By "records" I mean recordings, of course. Just as the vinyl 45s and 33⅓s replaced the shellac 78s, these, too, have been replaced by CDs. But there are still places to buy them; they haven't changed so much. Some features are obvious. In addition to an emphasis on rock music, there are clothing, books, and magazines as well—all with an identifiable antiestablishment character. Some record shops sell drug paraphernalia as well, depending on the local ordinances. Virtually every city or town has such a store or a chain of such stores. Of course, just as brick and mortar movie-rental establishments have precipitously declined, so also have all kinds of record stores. Much of the distribution of music is now, in one way or another, associated with the Internet. Nevertheless, this notion of the "record store" is still significant.

What makes these particular record stores essentially different from other record stores is their attitude toward the records. On the surface, all record stores are doing the same thing—selling records for a profit. Whereas in the traditional record store the records are merely the commodity to be sold, having only extrinsic value, in the counterculture store the records are regarded as intrinsically valuable. To put it differently, in the former, the records exist for the business, and in the latter, the business exists for the records. In the Los Angeles area, for example, there are Walmarts and Kmarts and Targets — oh, my!— that sell recordings along with household products and clothing. On the other hand, there are the likes of Rhino Records, Fat Beats, and Vacation. (Unfortunately, in 2005, Aron's Records succumbed to newer media — downloading and iPodding. They and stores like them are missed.) Profit isn't denied; it's just relegated to the status of a necessary means for the distribution of records. I realize that this is a bit simplistic, but the idea is nevertheless valid. (As a small caveat, I have in mind the attitude conveyed more by the sales personnel and not by the owners, who must in any case be aware of the image being presented.) The film *High Fidelity* (2000) conveys this image perfectly, using the record store as the mise-en-scène for a romantic comedy. *Empire Records* (1995) does so as well with a somewhat predictable story about trying to save an independent record store from a corporate takeover.

Thus understood, the counterculture record store functions as a haven, a sanctuary from the oppressiveness of established order. To see this, the observer need only witness the discomfort of "straights" (participants in the traditional order) who enter this alien environment. If ever there were a litmus test for values, this might be it: a discomfort index for customers. In any case, it is here, if nowhere else, those rock-and-roll recordings can properly be appreciated for what they truly are: The principal means for the dissemination of revolutionary values — the latest form of the testimonial, or, "the newest testament." After all, the message is conveyed by the medium.

6

Film: A Creative Tension

Film is a hybrid medium according to McLuhan, "a spectacular wedding of the old mechanical technology and the new electric world." Visually, film is closely associated with hot, intense technology and the lineally structured rationality of print; whereas the presence of sound places film squarely within the revolution brought about by electronic technology. This was more than merely an aesthetic development. According to McLuhan, the electromagnetic sound track already forecast the substitution of an electronic implosion for a mechanical explosion.

The inevitable result of all such hybrids is internal tension and the consequent release of energy. The way energy is released, however, depends on the cultural context in which the hybrid develops. In the highly literate West, for example, an electronic implosion must inevitably lead to the steady transformation of fragmentized cultures into ones that are highly interdependent. Nuclear fusion was McLuhan's analogy. Human relationships could be expected to undergo a similar change.

With this idea in mind, there are two key elements to consider about film as a medium for rock music. One is the dichotomy between the visuals and the sound track. The other is the enormous tension produced by film in our highly literate society and the possibility of serious conflict as a result. Rock music has exacerbated this tension and has speeded the transformation along.

The object of this chapter is to investigate the interrelationships among rock music, film, and culture. To do so, there are several things to keep in mind.

First, I'll be concentrating only on those films that have as their thematic content the periods in which they were produced. So there won't be any analyses of documentaries (for example, *Woodstock* and *Monterey Pop*), concerts (for example, *The Last Waltz* and *Shine a Light*), retrospectives (for example, *American Graffiti* and *Hairspray*—the original John Water version, of course), biopics (for example, *The Buddy Holly Story* and *Notorious*), and non-period films using post synchronous rock music as interpretive of the plot (for example, *Apocalypse Now* and *Boogie Nights*). All of these are secondary or derivative; they do not permit us to view the period directly, as if we were actually there. To do this, we have to concentrate on films that (1) portray the period in which they were made and (2) are fictional in their narrative. The first of these two is obvious: self-examinations like this make direct access to the period possible. It might be objected, however, that no film can do this. All films are the products of the collaborative efforts of everyone involved (writers, directors, actors/actresses, editors, producers, cinematographers, etc.); so they are all necessarily derivative. Obviously, there's a point to this objection: portrayals of events are not the events themselves. This, however, is precisely why I've specified the second condition. For what interests me, and what I find directly revealing of the times, is the collaborative effort itself—

as interpretation, not as factual reportage, which it could never be. These film interpretations are direct manifestations of the periods in which they took place. Authenticity, not accuracy, is the ultimate criterion for selecting a film for consideration, and the sustained narrative of a fiction film provides the most authentic cultural artifact. With fiction, after all, there need be no attempt to have the narrative correspond with brute facts (even if there were such raw uninterpreted data); nothing need interfere with the interpretive effort. In short, the interpretation itself is the artifact.

The second factor to keep in mind it that we shouldn't get bogged down with aesthetic criteria. Even if there actually were such standards, and even if they could be distinguished from mere personal taste, they would be irrelevant. "Bad" films can be just as revealing as "good" ones. Some will always be more revealing than others, of course, but this has nothing to do with their quality.

Third, the time periods I've already suggested will provide the structure for the analysis: the fifties (1955–63), the sixties (1964–74), the Interim (1975–79), the Counter-Reaction (1980–2008) and the Re-actualization (beginning in 2009). Each of these periods is characterized by a certain attitude toward fundamental values, attitudes that should not be confused with any particular set of emotions. Negation and affirmation can be expressed in a variety of ways, including various feelings and emotions that may seem paradoxical and even contrary to the fundamental attitudes. However, this is not a psychological analysis of the cultural revolution — it is, at bottom, a phenomenological analysis.

Finally, by utilizing the dichotomy between visuals and sound, I want to suggest how the revolutionary process has been reflected in film. Basically, each stage of thought and history eventually produces its own negation, which causes internal conflict. This antagonism eventuates in the creation of a new stage, which then undergoes the same process as the earlier stage. And so it goes.

The Fifties

As a period of negation, the prevailing value structure was often attacked vigorously. Some of the earliest youth films of this era had the attack itself as the principal theme. Most important were *The Wild One* (1954), *Rebel without a Cause* (1955), and *The Blackboard Jungle* (1955), beginning a new genre, teenage *film noir*. With the notable exception of *The Wild One*, they wound up reaffirming the traditional values. The attack was portrayed as superficial, ineffectual, and most certainly evil; the initially appealing bad guys always got what was coming to them, their threats having been thwarted by the reawakened virtue of the established order. Society was then returned to its previous state, stronger and wiser for the experience. We need only reflect on the conflict between Glenn Ford and Vic Morrow, the teacher and the teenager, in *Blackboard Jungle*. There was never any doubt as to the eventual victor. Rock music, however, was absent from the soundtrack of these films (*Blackboard Jungle* being a special case), a fact that called attention to its existence and presence all the more. Nobody was fooled.

When it was explicitly introduced as the focus of the film, an interesting contradiction began to emerge. Support for established values was maintained in the narrative, but the music in the sound track simultaneously called them into question. Some of the more interesting internally divided films include *Rock around the Clock* (1956), *The Girl Can't Help It* (1956), *Don't Knock the Rock* (1956), *Shake, Rattle and Rock* (1956), *Loving You* (1957), *Jailhouse*

Rock (1957), and *King Creole* (1958). A scene from *Don't Knock the Rock* illustrates this point beautifully. Ostensibly, the message of the film is that rock and roll is simply the most recent expression of youthful exuberance, no different from that embodied in the dance crazes of earlier generations. Its bad rep is undeserved and based on ignorance, easily enough overcome. Yet, at an impromptu party at one of the kids' homes, while the parents are away no less (the ideal teenage party), the dancers get so carried away with the music that they dance all over the furniture to the strains of Bill Haley's version of "Rip It Up." This is not the kind of action likely to carry the film's traditional message very effectively. In *The Girl Can't Help It* (a romantic comedy–satire exploiting the common belief that rock and roll was a gimmick of the music industry and a passing fad so simplistic that anyone could perform it), there's a scene in which Jayne Mansfield sinuously sways across a nightclub floor accompanied by the rhythms of Little Richard singing the title song—all the while seeming to ogle her every movement. The narrative suggests the essential harmlessness of rock, but the music celebrates miscegenation, one of America's most fiercely defended taboos.

This kind of tension couldn't last for very long; some kind of resolution had to be effected. One way for this to occur was through a narrative expressing the dangers of rock, thus harmonizing the plot with the dangers implicit in the music. A number of films took this tack. *High School Confidential!* (1958) was perhaps the best of the lot, but there were many others, including *Hot Rod Gang* (1958), *Girls Town* (1959), and *Daddy-O* (1959). Teenage film noir was clearly at its nadir. With greater or lesser degrees of artistry (usually the latter), all of these films consistently ground out the idea that rock and roll was responsible for every social evil imaginable (sexual aberration, violence, drug abuse, miscegenation, and laziness). This accord between music and narrative, however, was no less superficial than the films themselves. For whereas the narrative lamented this deplorable situation and the threatened loss of American youth to demon rock and roll, the music was positively celebratory. Who could take seriously all of the horrors attributed to rock when the likes of Jerry Lee Lewis, Gene Vincent, and the Platters were blasting forth with some of the most playfully exciting music of all times? In *High School Confidential*, for example, Jerry Lee comes rolling across the screen, pounding on his piano on the back of a truck. What kind of warning is this? The moods of the music and narrative are incongruous, yielding conflicting messages.

Another attempt to effect a resolution to the internally divided film was to deactivate the music, force it to fall in line with the traditional narrative. Selective use of genuine rock and the production of quasi rock was how it was accomplished, and the result was another seeming harmony between music and narrative. Consider these examples: *Go, Johnny, Go* (1959), *Where the Boys Are* (1960), *Wild in the Country* (1961), *Twist around the Clock* (1961), *Play It Cool* (1962), *Bye-Bye Birdie* (1963), *Beach Party* (1963), *Bikini Beach* (1964), and *Muscle Beach Party* (1964). Although there were legitimate rock artists in some of these films, their role and music were incidental to the narrative. If a musical performance was essential to the plot, we could always count on the Hondells, the Walker Brothers, Jimmy Clanton, Connie Francis, Billy Fury, Bobby Vee, Bobby Rydell and, as the epitomes of this kind of musician, Frankie Avalon and Annette Funicello. There was nothing at all threatening about these films; all of the traditional values were strongly supported by the narrative and sound track. The revolutionary essence of rock had been co-opted, defused in order to serve counter-revolutionary purposes. The form was retained, but its substance had been unceremoniously removed. Nevertheless, and this is the internal contradiction, all these films unabashedly glorify youth culture, which by this time was profoundly influenced by rock and roll. The very lack of authentic rock created a striking incompatibility between their portrayal of youth and what the youthful audiences knew to be true. The more these films succeeded, the more they failed.

Both attempts at a resolution had reached an impasse, and both had done so for essentially the same reason. Existing rock and roll had not yet sufficiently distinguished itself from the culture it was negating. Lacking the affirmation of an alternative set of values, the revolution wound up negating itself as well. Self-negation, however, did provide the opportunity for something completely different.

The Sixties

The affirmation of a revolutionary set of values in the sixties resulted partly from the decline of authentic rock music in the immediately preceding period combined with a simultaneous legitimization of the youth culture. It also resulted partly from the fact that, somehow, authentic rock music was preserved throughout this period. Together, these factors helped set the stage for the explosion that followed.

It happened with the release of *A Hard Day's Night* in 1964, a film that coupled this new attitude toward youth with a decidedly positive and far more energetic style of rock (and it was about this time that we stopped calling it "rock and roll," preferring just "rock" instead). From this point on, films having rock culture as their principal textual content were inscribed with the affirmation of new values, making them far more antagonistic to the established order than those expressing the attitude of negation. For by making the conflict clearly evident for the first time, the antagonism was necessarily heightened. Consider these other films: *Help!* (1965), *Blow-Up* (1966), *The Graduate* (1967), *Yellow Submarine* (1968), *Easy Rider* (1969), *Alice's Restaurant* (1969), *The Magic Christian* (1969), *Zabriskie Point* (1970), *Performance* (1970), *Shaft* (1971), *200 Motels* (1971), *The Harder They Come* (1972), *Five Summer Stories* (1973), *Heavy Traffic* (1973), and *Claudine* (1974). In a list of this diversity, it probably needs to be restressed that the attitude of affirmation does not imply any particular emotional vehicle for its expression. On the surface, the early Beatles films are joyous; however, there is an underlying, subtle anger. *Shaft* tends to reverse this relationship. *Easy Rider* and *The Harder They Come* incorporate a progression of feelings from euphoria and irony to fear and loathing. All, however, are films of affirmation. Closer attention to these films might also help dispel the damaging illusion that the sixties was a period of carefree abandon, Edenic innocence, communal warmth, and utopian zeal. There was a lot of this, of course, but there was also hatred, selfishness, racism, and sexism, both within the movement and in society at large. Moreover, of course, there was the overwhelming presence of the Vietnam War, international militarism, imperialistic nationalism, and the repressive triple entente of Hoover, LBJ, and Nixon. A period of sweetness and light it was not.

The best of these films were not so naive. Their optimism about a new age was tempered by an acknowledgment of how difficult it would be to actualize it. Opposition from the established order and disagreements from within were coupled with the inevitable problems of bringing into being a completely new cultural orientation. Dustin Hoffman's portrayal of alienated youth in *The Graduate* is a good illustration. Confronted by the incomprehensible and impenetrable world of his parents' generation, Benjamin is immobilized. The enticements offered to him (success: "Plastics" and sensual pleasure: Mrs. Robinson) make sense only in terms of the prevailing value structure. With no clear alternative in mind, and probably unconscious of what he is rejecting, he remains ambivalent to the end (his running off with Mrs. Robinson's daughter notwithstanding). His future is still indeterminate; the film ends, but the problem persists. (Interestingly, Rob Reiner's 2005 film, *Rumor Has It*, fictionally portrays the story as having been based on actual persons, according to rumor. The critics largely hated it — often because it in some way violated the "spirit" of the original. In other words, it made the subtle affirmation of *The Graduate* unimportant.)

The Harder They Come, just as valid a sixties film as any other on the list, actually ends in tragedy. Jimmy Cliff portrays an aspiring reggae musician who finds brief success in the face of establishment opposition (embodied in governmental, criminal, and imperialistic forces). David Ehrenstein and Bill Reed, in *Rock on Film*, describe Cliff's character as "the pop star as cultural guerrilla," and with his death in the final scene it is crystal clear that the transformation of culture will not be accomplished easily or rapidly, and perhaps not at all.

No assessment of film in the sixties would be complete without some mention of *A Hard Day's Night*. Aside from representing perfectly the harmonious marriage between narrative and music, this time affirming a new set of values (and doing it so subtly that while pervading the entire film they are never consciously the object of attention), the film's spectacular success served to create an antagonistic reality that would eventually confront all rock films: profit. Surprising to perhaps everyone, including The Beatles themselves, no doubt, was the film's unprecedented critical acclaim. When combined with its wholly expected financial success, the result was the sincerest form of flattery: imitation. Some attempts to cash in were so obvious and direct as to border on plagiarism, as with the Monkees. More important, however, was the general recognition that films about rock music and its attendant culture were potentially the most profitable things going.

Imitations of The Beatles' successes continued throughout the sixties; it was inevitable that the film industry would try to capitalize on them. *Head* (1968) was the most blatant example of this trend since it starred the Monkees — the most blatant imitation of The Beatles. But there were others: *Having a Wild Weekend* (1965) with the Dave Clark Five, *Seaside Swingers* (1965) with Freddy and the Dreamers, and *Good Times* (1967) with Sonny and Cher. The cloning was partially successful: many films were artistically and financially rewarding, but they were no longer authentically revolutionary. The form had been retained, but the substance had been subverted. Coinciding remarkably with the end of the sixties, these imitations managed to supplant the real thing almost entirely.

The Interim

Characterized not only by imitation but also by remakes, the avoidance of controversy, and the sublimation or repression of any value that might smack of revolution, the films of this period simply gave expression to the nearly universal exhaustion everyone was experiencing. Nothing was ventured and nothing was gained, but on the other hand, nothing was lost. There exists no better way to describe this than as a holding period, a time for the licking of wounds and the regrouping of scattered forces.

The Interim was often referred to as "the me decade," but this little slogan should not automatically be understood as a simple allusion of selfishness. While selfishness was certainly a part of it, a concentration on the self also had reference to psychological survival. Given the traumas of the sixties, it should be obvious that the self was in need of repair. Only if the self is intact can it manifest a concern for others, and recreation is an essential component of keeping it intact. After all, "recreation" means to "re-create." Nothing frivolous about this, and certainly nothing selfish either. Essentially, re-creation is healing, the revitalization of the body and spirit and the opening of the self to the future. A key component in the process of emotional healing is the often-underrated dimension of entertainment, literally the pause that refreshes. Looked at in this light, the films of the Interim weren't all that bad.

This relative quietus could hardly last for very long. Once the restorative function of this period had its effects on the combatants, the struggle would continue where it left off. Placidity would inevitably produce its own opposite, a renewal of the cultural revolution.

The non- (but not anti-) revolutionary character of this period is evident in both music and narrative, as the following films illustrate: *Mahogany* (1975), *Tommy* (1975), *A Star Is Born* (1976), *Car Wash* (1976), *Saturday Night Fever* (1977), *Looking for Mr. Goodbar* (1977), *The Wiz* (1978), *FM* (1978), *Almost Summer* (1978), *Sgt. Pepper's Lonely Hearts Club Band* (1978), *Thank God It's Friday* (1978), *The Rose* (1979), *Can't Stop the Music* (1980), *Times Square* (1980), and *Xanadu* (1980). The concentration on self is readily apparent in *Saturday Night Fever*, but selfishness is not all there is to it. John Travolta plays a Brooklyn youth struggling to achieve self-worth in a world that consistently ignores individuals without power or wealth. The quest for self-respect and identity is not selfishness: it's a matter of psychological survival. Tony sees only one way to achieve a worthwhile identity—through dancing. And, as everyone knows, the kind of dancing he does is the much-dreaded disco. Disco, as everyone also knows, is not exactly the music of revolution (and Travolta's character is not exactly a Jimmy Cliff–style cultural guerrilla). Nevertheless, the film is in no way an updated version of the late fifties beach movies. While the text of the film is hardly an incarnation of the revolution, neither is it a manifestation of the established order, facts that ought not to be ignored when disco as a phenomenon of the 1970s is reconsidered. Also part of the disco craze were the aesthetically inferior *Can't Stop the Music* and *Thank God It's Friday*, which were just as noninvolved (not to be confused with value-free, since a concern for the self in any understanding is highly evaluative).

Success pervades *Mahogany*, *The Rose* and *Times Square* as the ultimate goal, but this is not simple selfishness either. The achievement of personal aims is incompatible with social aims only when the value to be achieved is scarce, when others necessarily become a threat. Neither psychological survival nor self-worth nor success is in any way a scarce commodity. Everyone can achieve them at the same time; they are not contraries and certainly not contradictories.

Notice finally the plethora of rehashes: *A Star Is Born*, *The Wiz*, *Tommy*, *Sgt. Pepper*, and *Xanadu*. This hints at an unwillingness and/or an incapacity to venture into something new. There has always been an inclination in the film industry to rely on the successful formulas of the past, but this need not imply only a fear of the new or a lack of imagination. It just might suggest a subconscious need for recapitulation, a desire to make the history of the revolution explicit in the consciousness of individual participants. Each of the five reaches into the past (even the pre-rock past) for its source of inspiration, and by so doing establishes a connection, possibly a healing connection. This shouldn't suggest an attempt at some kind of reconciliation, which can only occur when the parties at odds are clearly manifest. With these films, however, the conflict is suppressed.

Actually, the conflict of values is suppressed in virtually every film produced during this period, resulting in a general lack of direction and an apparent stagnation. However, if I'm right, this period did contribute to a renewal of energy; but the first to benefit from this pause were not the cultural revolutionaries. The first to benefit were the traditionalists.

The Counter-Reaction

In 1980, with the opposition clearly identified in the person of the newly elected president, the revolution was also revived. Cinematically, the non-revolutionary rock films of the Interim called forth the only conceivable response: a renewal of negation. It couldn't simply be a reaffirmation of the positive revolutionary values; this would ignore the fact that the established order had meanwhile been rejuvenated. No, the first order of business was to attack the reconstituted establishment and to do so in a relevantly new way.

Hints of the new negation had already been lurking in the wings, as if waiting for the propitious moment. *The Rocky Horror Picture Show*, for example, was released in 1975 but only later achieved its status as the premier cult movie of all times. Its significance for our purposes, however, is the way it has been viewed and interpreted since the election of 1980, as illustrated by a positively brilliant opening sketch done by the cast of *Fridays* (ABC's short-lived version of *Saturday Night Live*). As the film begins, the super straight Brad ("asshole," yells the audience) and Janet ("slut"), after leaving their friends' wedding, have a flat tire and become lost. They see a light up ahead in the castle of Dr. Frank N. Furter, and proceed to seek assistance. Soon they are confronted by the "sweet transvestite" himself, in drag, descending in an open elevator. In the *Fridays* version, as Frank N. Furter comes into view, singing "(I'm a) Sweet Transvestite," his net stockings gradually give way to a black corset and finally to the unmistakable face of Ronald Reagan. What follows is a biting satire, completely erasing the apolitical mood of the Interim. Understanding the film this way is a comparatively recent phenomenon — a part of the Interim.

Another hint was the total lack of any rock music at all in the excellent film *Return of the Secaucus Seven* (1980), which concerns the reunion of several close friends from the sixties. Their get-togethers are apparently held yearly; this one occurs at the end of the 1970s. The friends still maintain their earlier ideals, so the striking omission of what would have been contemporary music for them suggests a fundamental incompatibility between the sixties and their present. A still more revealing aspect of this omission is the implicit admission that no music yet exists to carry forth with the cause. The music of the fifties and sixties had accomplished its mission; newer revolutionaries require newer music. Nothing can last forever.

A final cinematic hint, *Rock and Roll High School* (1979), reveals with precision exactly what kind of musical styles would begin this renewed negation. Culminating with the students' burning their school to the ground, the theme of the film is a celebration of punk rock, specifically the music of the Ramones, who accompany the burning with an impromptu performance on the school lawn. With the exception of one defector from the teachers, the film portrays the sharp confrontation between two cultures, with little pretense to subtlety. As if to suggest whose music is now in charge of the revolutionary negation, one scene has school authorities comparing various kinds of music on a "rockometer." Naturally, the Ramones are found to be the most destructive, causing mice to explode, but notice who follows them (in descending order): the Who, the Rolling Stones, Ted Nugent, Led Zepplin, Jethro Tull, Foreigner, Peter Frampton, Kansas, Donny and Marie, Debby Boone, Pat

Boone, and Muzak. In a dream sequence, the mise-en-scène includes various records and posters connoting the negation of the fifties and sixties, but P. J. Soles's character conjures up Joey Ramone for the erotic interlude. In both scenes, as well as in the sound track, the music of negation predominates; yet it is completely clear that punk is the new force in rock. Significantly, nowhere in the film was there any reference (except by omission) to The Beatles, the symbol par excellence of sixties affirmation. This just wasn't the time for affirmation.

Again, there was a harmony between narrative and music, and as these three films suggest, the harmony was initially expressed as a negation of the Reaganite sociopolitical program as reflected in the new styling of punk. (Obviously, much of this new musical form harks back to the fifties; no development is ever entirely new.) Other films expressing negation include *The Great Rock and Roll Swindle* (1980), *Heavy Metal* (1981), *American Pop* (1981), *The Wall* (1982), *Eddie and the Cruisers* and *Footloose* (1984). *The Great Rock and Roll Swindle* seems so negative as to make the expression of anything positive impossible. Starring the Sex Pistols as themselves, in their version of *A Hard Day's Night*, the film takes on The Beatles and Elvis as objects of derision. (Sid Vicious does perhaps the best parody/imitation/homage of Elvis ever when he sings "My Way.") On closer inspection, however, it is really just a matter of who is now in charge of the revolution; in no way is the revolution derided. "Anarchy in the UK" and "God Save the Queen" make this perfectly clear, as if the Sex Pistols themselves didn't. The other interesting film in this list is *American Pop*, because of its attempt to establish a continuity with the past, ranging from vaudeville to the present — and the present is heavy with the music of negation.

Yet if there was to be any hope of continuing the revolution with any degree of success, this negation had to be followed up with a strong reaffirmation of positive, alternative values. *Radio On* (1979) provides the contrapuntal hint in the year prior to the Reagan election. It's a murder mystery set in England in the latter stages of the Interim. Although the mood of the film is definitely *noir*, what comes across is the crying need for something positive. The very absence of hope is an effective commentary on the period and serves to prepare us for the inevitable re-expression of revolutionary values. Paul Simon's *One-Trick Pony* (1980) asks the musical question, Can the sixties be revived for the 1980s? It recounts the tale of a sixties rock star trying to rekindle both his personal and his professional life — a kind of parable. Again, the need for affirmation permeates the subtext of the film. On the surface, both these films are depressing, but this is so because they are both self-consciously lacking something.

With *Fame* (1980) we finally get the reaffirmation so desperately needed, and it is the kind of reaffirmation that does not in any way ignore its historical context. The issue of race is a clear example. While the fifties negated racism and the sixties affirmed racial harmony, *Fame* portrays race as an irrelevancy, a reality worth preserving in all its diversity but no longer an issue one way or another. Obviously, this is not really the case (then or now), but reality is not the point. The film affirms an ideal, something specific to strive for. At the same time, the Interim's emphasis on personal success is also affirmed.

Three other films of affirmation deserve mention: *Star Struck* (1982), *Baby It's You* (1983), and *Flashdance* (1983). The first, a new-wave musical set in Australia, of all places, serves to point out the difference in attitude between punk and new wave. It, too, finds value in the struggle for success. *Baby It's You*, although a period piece from the fifties and sixties, illustrates the absurdity of maintaining class and ethnic prejudices in our contemporary American culture, showing them to be hopeless atavisms even then. *Flashdance*, crippled by a thin and often incredible story and weakened further by unconvincing acting, nevertheless links the notion of success with the most energetic and promising of all Counter-Reaction issues — sexism and human liberation. The principal character is a woman driven by a desire to perfect her unorthodox (and apparently untutored) dancing style at a local saloon while supporting herself by working as a welder. Along with both male and female friends, she acquires a lover, using the kind of assertiveness that we all wish we had (firm and sure, without the slightest hint of stridency or resentfulness). Interestingly and not accidentally, the sound track is mostly women: Laura Branigan, Donna Summer, Joan Jett, Kim Carnes, and Irene Cara, among others. Maybe even more interesting is the film's clear affirmation of eroticism, portrayed without the slightest trace of baseness.

In 1984, there were a series of affirmative films: *Breakin'* and *Beat Street* both celebrated ethnic diversity and a new urban music form; Prince's *Purple Rain* showed how these same values could be manifest in the eighties in perhaps the most remarkable rock film since *A Hard Day's Night*; and *This Is Spinal Tap*'s satire of "rockumentaries" warned revolutionaries not to take themselves with ultimate seriousness.

Affirmation with a subtle, hard edge characterized three films released in 1985. *The Breakfast Club* illustrated that the acquisition of a new, revolutionary set of values must be undertaken anew with each generation, and that the process is often painful. *St. Elmo's Fire* pointed out that holding these new values is no guarantee against the loss of motivation and purpose. Furthermore, *The Coca Cola Kid*, with its gentle, erotic satire of American imperialism, reminded us that the cultural revolution is implicitly a worldwide phenomenon.

The Beginnings of the Re-actualization

In all of these previous instances, the complementarity of narrative and music is aimed at the affirmation of revolutionary values. Together with the films of negation, they indicate the general direction taken in response to the reawakened embodiment of traditional values — moving ever closer to liberation and Individuality. This process, aiming toward the achievement of these values, will characterize the Re-actualization of the revolution, and evidence of both negation and affirmation should become progressively clearer as the movement continues.

The films that followed the Counter-Reaction can be categorized accordingly, and I make no pretense of this being an objective endeavor — this is just how I see them. The important thing, however, is to recognize that such a categorization of negation and affirmation is even possible! Collectively, then, the films of this period portray a part of the ongoing revolutionary process leading to a full Re-actualization.

Films of Negation

Films which directly confront the traditional values include the following, and as is often the case, the more subtly this is done, the more effective the negation. War was one particularly obvious target — especially unjustified wars (*Platoon* in 1986, *Born on the Fourth of July* in 1989, *Three Kings* in 1999, *The Quiet American* in 2002). Even justified and perhaps necessary warfare was lamented as undesirable (*Saving Private Ryan* in 1998, *Flags of Our Fathers* and *Letters from Iwo Jima* both in 2006). Quentin Tarantino's *Inglourious Basterds* (2009) reinforced the fact, as did *The Hurt Locker* (2008).

Racism provided a similar target (*Mississippi Burning* in 1988, *Glory* and *Do the Right Thing* in 1989, *American History X* in 1998 and *Antwone Fisher* in 2002) and Clint Eastwood's *Gran Torino* (2008). Closely associated with racism was a new focus on genocide that rose from or together with the rise of "world music" in this period. There were many instances to work with and they included *Dances with Wolves* in 1990, *The Last of the Mohicans* in 1992, *Schindler's List* in 1993, *Life Is Beautiful* in 1997, *Hotel Rwanda* in 2004, *Blood Diamond* and *The Last King of Scotland* both in 2006). Even the science fiction action film *District 9* (2009), raised the issue as it might arise in the future as it pertains to aliens coming to earth. Similarly, *Avatar* (2009) dealt with earthlings going to the aliens.

Not so much capital punishment per se, but the abuses of capital punishment were confronted (*The Shawshank Redemption* in 1994, *Dead Man Walking* in 1995, *The Green Mile* in 1999 and *Monster's Ball* in 2001). The abuse of power and authority — political, economic, parental, legal and military — was another new dimension of the negation (*Wall Street* in 1987, *A Few Good Men* in 1992, *Nixon* in 1995, *Wag the Dog* in 1997, *Bulworth* and *Primary Colors* in 1998, *Erin Brockovich* in 2000, *Training Day* in 2001 and *Little Miss Sunshine* in 2006. With greed and ambition as its focus, *There Will Be Blood* (2007) was a striking exhibit of what the revolutionary negation is all about.

Films of Affirmation

Although it is clearly a simplified schema, I've been referring to the affirmative values of the cultural revolution as "freedom" (also "liberty" and "liberation") and "individuality" (also "diversity" and "tolerance"), so I'll make use of these two fundamental values here for categorization:

Freedom involves both a negative (freedom from...) and a positive (freedom to...) quality. The former offers assurance or protection from unjust interference, while the latter affords opportunities to act justly as one wishes. Often the portrayals of freedom focus on the unjust denials and not so much on the opportunities, so they may appear to be negations. However, the goal — what *should* be the case vs. what *is* the case is clear. In *Thelma and Louise* (1991) the tragic consequences of the denial of freedom to women is the focus. *Courage Under Fire* (1996) shows how subtle this denial can be. Both sexism and racism are obstacles in *The Joy Luck Club* (1993). A repressive culture in *Pleasantville* (1998) and in *Billy Elliot* (2000) is the culprit responsible for denying freedom. In addition, the repression of forms of sexuality other than that narrowly defined by tradition is captured in *Philadelphia* (1993), *People vs. Larry Flynt* (1996), *Brokeback Mountain* and *Capote* (both in 2005). Ending the prohibition on marijuana use is not always the sole theme of a film; often smoking grass is presented a regular part of normal life — the viewers being able to draw the obvious conclusion for themselves, as in *Homegrown* (1998), *Dazed and Confused* (1993), *Cash Crop* (2003), *Sideways* (2004), *Harold & Kumar Go to White Castle* (2004), *Humboldt County* (2008), *The Wackness* (2008) and *Adventureland* (2009). *The Wackness* is particularly interesting since it portrays marijuana users as more than youth. In fact, every age, income, race, and sex is shown as participants. Moreover, without self-consciously doing so, the story told in the film "recapitulates" (in the sense of palingenesis) the sense of anomie experienced by Benjamin Braddock in *The Graduate* (1967) and Harold in *Harold and Maude* (1971), and, like them, celebrates the "freedom from" the weight of traditional values and practices. Explicit portrayals of the "freedom to" are found in Clint Eastwood's *Million Dollar Baby* (2004), which dealt with expanding the role of women in society, and in *Ratatouille* (2007), which playfully suggested that we can all be what we want to be (even if you happen to be a rat)!

Individuality is often portrayed in seemingly negative ways as well, focusing more on the obstacles inhibiting it than on its positive expression. *My Left Foot* (1989) and *A Beautiful Mind* (2001) made it clear that some obstacles are not of anyone's evil intent or of our own doing. Some are natural in origin. The need for privacy for genuine individuality and its fragility is a frequent concern, as in *Sex, Lies, and Videotape* (1989), *The Truman Show* (1998) and *Minority Report* (2002). Yet there were clearly films that celebrated individuals overcoming various kinds of obstacles in expressing their own uniqueness. Here "individuality" as "diversity" becomes obvious: *Field of Dreams* (1989), *Pretty Woman* (1990), *Fried Green Tomatoes* (1991), *Malcolm X* (1992), *Forrest Gump* (1994), *Ed Wood* (1994), *Hoop Dreams* (1994), *Good Will Hunting* (1997), *Ali* (2001), *School of Rock* (2003), *Million Dollar Baby* (2004), *Cinderella Man* (2005), *Into the Wild* (2007), *Juno* (2007), and *Man on Wire* (2008). Sometimes the celebration of individuality is expressed in the variety of music available: *Almost Famous* (2000), *High Fidelity* (2000), *8 Mile* (2002), *A Mighty Wind* (2003), *School of Rock* (2003), Ray (2004), *Walk the Line* (2005), *Dreamgirls* (2006), *I'm Not There* (2007). *Up* (2009) is a delightful animated film showing that you're never too old — or young — to follow your own particular dream.

Finally, there are some films that defy categorization — in fact, the attempt to categorize may itself be the target. If so, this may be the ultimate expression of both freedom *and* individuality. Here's one in particular: *Borat: Cultural Learnings of America for Make Benefit Glorious Nation of Kazakhstan* (2006).

The Theater as Theater

The most interesting and significant interpretations, the ones that are immediate and not self-conscious, do not occur in the columns of reviewers or in the numerous and thoughtful scholarly articles, nor even in the often lively discussions that take place following a showing. Rather, they take place in the theater, during the showing, as the film is happening. Interpretation is the way we have of perceiving something, the mental slot into which we place what we experience. In so doing, we attribute a meaning to that which we are in the act of perceiving. The meaning is not in that which we perceive; the meaning is in the act of perception itself. Not that it is a conscious activity; if anything, it is preconscious. It is the emotional reception that greets the experience on which the later rational commentaries are based.

Recalling McLuhan's claim that the combination of mechanical and electric technologies is analogous to the release of nuclear energy, it just might be that this release occurs in the immediate interpretive process itself. The amount released may even correspond directly with the relationship between music and narrative. The former is cool, and the latter (which McLuhan associated with all the print media) is hot. The locus of their meeting is inside the theater, and that's where we have to look.

With the release of the first movie to make use of rock and roll in the sound track, *The Blackboard Jungle* in 1955, teen audiences went crazy, ripping up the seats (preferably with forbidden switchblade knives). Audiences viewing many of the later teenage *film noir* epics continued the trend by cheering the supposed villains, and quite a few of these movies were banned because of how the audiences responded to them. The more musical films prompted audiences to dance wildly in the aisles. None of this should be very surprising, since the essence of the electronic revolution is participation (as it is for all cool media).

The inauthenticity of the beach movies and their kin led to the almost instantaneous decline of participation. Teenage audiences responded to them no differently than to traditional films (which in many ways they were): they sat and watched, lost in their individual thoughts. Commenting on how film was received in highly mechanized Western cultures, McLuhan said: "Typographic man took readily to film just because, like books, it offers an inward world of fantasy and dreams. The film viewer sits in psychological solitude like the silent book reader." Thus ended the fifties on film.

The way music and narrative were interwoven during the sixties led to new depths (or heights) of participation. Rock films were frequently accompanied by the smoking or ingestion of controlled substances; participation had advanced to the state of mystical oneness. Filmmakers, not unmindful of this trend, and being influenced by McLuhan directly, took to producing films that demanded viewer participation: split screens, composite images, stream of consciousness, speed changes, dialogue with the audience (remember *Alfie* in 1966? It was one of the originals), and the like. *More American Graffiti* (1979), a very good film in its own right, nevertheless seemed so very out of place because of its use of a '70s style of filmmaking to portray the '60s; George Lucas failed to be authentic to the period in form as well as in content. The film got generally poor reviews.

During the Interim, participation ended again. The sound track began to be conceived of as something separate from the film, an entity in its own right. Nothing illustrates this better than the practice of relying on the film to sell the sound track album. Concerning *FM*, Ehrenstein and Reed note that "more people bought the soundtrack than actually saw the movie." Participation continued, of course, but not in the theater; it happened at the disco.

Since the beginning of the Counter-Reaction, there has been a reassertion of participation in the theater, but something new has been added. The midnight cult film has made the theater a social gathering place for various kinds of social "deviants." *The Rocky Horror Picture Show* epitomizes this new style, for not only do audiences come dressed as their favorite characters and dance and sing to the music, they have also developed a counter dialogue, which makes them an integral part of the film experience. Obviously, not all cult films have evolved to this point, yet they all share the same setting—the theater at midnight, the only respectable hour for a cult film. Even if the cult-film phenomenon never becomes very large (and by definition this would probably kill the phenomenon), everyone knows about it; this is nothing to be sneezed at. *Fame*, which is not a cult film, includes a scene in which the characters attend a showing of *Rocky Horror*, and they pass around joint too. This links the small cult audiences with the vast majority of nonparticipants and makes the cult phenomenon more significant as a result. Other linkages have been established with past manifestations of the revolution, for rock films of the fifties and sixties are now being shown at the midnight hour, thus converting them into quasi cult films of the present.

It is impossible, of course, to predict which films will achieve cult status. (It is also impossible to set out to make them deliberately.) However, one 1984 release stands out and has good chance in the future: *The Adventures of Buckaroo Banzai*. In this absurdist science-fiction satire, the major character is a neurosurgeon, a test-car driver, a physicist, and a rock singer from another dimension. It hasn't happened yet, its ultimate importance may be still determined in years to come, at midnight. This may also be the case for another science fiction absurdist satire, *Repo Man* (1984), which toys with the punk phenomenon.

One major obstacle to the continuation of movie cult-hood is the new computerized technology. After all, if the movie-going experience in the theater can be replicated for all practical purposes in the home, then "theater as theater" may be one of those media that evolve out of existence (in McLuhanesque fashion). On the other hand, it may be that the computerization and the Internet may re-create the experience in our living rooms.

Finally, it's worth noting that, despite its lack of size, the cult phenomenon symbolizes a renewed dichotomy between the cultural revolutionaries and the established order — no matter where it may take place. After all, it's simply a jump to the *left*. As always, the message of this lyric is contained in the message.

7

Television: Bringing It All Back Home

The scandal caused by Dylan's apostasy from folk music toward rock at the 1965 Newport Folk Festival is not sufficiently explained by a change in either his style or his lyrical material. What outraged folk purists was the electrification of his music. When he dropped acoustic instrumentation and picked up the electric guitar, his music acquired an authenticity and power it could never have had otherwise. His audience was right in sensing this to be the crucial defection, but they were wrong in accusing him of selling out. On the contrary, what he did was to introduce their common themes to the most radical form possible and thereby brought it all back home where its effectiveness would be multiplied.

In a manner of speaking, this is precisely what happened when rock and roll began appearing on television. No longer was it something that could be safely ignored, something kept securely apart from the family setting and the protection it afforded. Now it was being brought directly into the home, and with an unparalleled seductiveness.

McLuhan's chapter on television in *Understanding Media* is subtitled "The Timid Giant" because of the medium's alleged tendency to avoid or play down controversies and clashes of well-defined and sharply opposing views. While he agreed with this assessment, he was quick to add that this did not imply that television lacked either a value orientation or influence. Its impact is subtle, he observed, but much more thoroughgoing as a result. To understand how this is so, one must keep constantly in mind that the medium itself is the bearer of the message.

Noting some of the technological features characteristic of film and television might be helpful in making some sense of this claim. For unlike all forms of photography (still and motion), the TV image is never still. Rather, it is a ceaselessly forming series of dots (about three million per second), which the viewer mentally (and unconsciously) constructs into an intelligible pattern. Said McLuhan, "The TV image requires each instant that we 'close' the space in the mesh by a convulsive sensuous participation that is profoundly kinetic and tactile, because tactility is the interplay of the senses, rather than the isolated contact of skin and object." The relatively high definition of film imagery, providing an enormous amount of information, requires much less viewer involvement for the picture to make sense; whereas, television's low definition demands that the viewer participate. The result is the creation of a unity between the physical senses and the imagination (which McLuhan called "synesthesia"), a goal that artists have always regarded as unattainable. The effects of this merger have been enormous. As an extension of our central nervous system, television has affected our lives in every conceivable way. The development of HD (high definition) television does not affect this notion of the viewer's participation, but it certainly affects his explanation of how the unity takes place. Rather than "low definition" being the "culprit," it seems much more likely that the "setting" itself — in the intimacy of the home — is responsible. Here, a high degree of involvement comes about naturally, where — by definition — there is already an established involvement in the form of the "family."

It would be absurd, of course, to claim that everything televised has had the same degree of effectiveness. The "content" does make a difference, with the important caveat that the "content" of any medium is simply another medium. The resulting mixture of media makes the difference. Media more suited to television (the cooler and more electronic ones) are likely to emphasize its effects much more than those less complementary. Television demands a high degree of audience involvement, so the most effective programs are those that require participation — programs that are not whole unless "completed" by their viewers. The portrayal of intimacy requires completion in this respect, for the program is an utter failure unless the viewer becomes deeply involved with the characters. It is especially helpful toward this end if the characters are cool and not very well delineated: "Anybody whose appearance strongly declares his role and status in life is wrong for TV.... When the person presented *looks* classifiable ... the TV viewer has nothing to fill in." You *get to know* a guest invited into your home, and hence the guest is assimilated into the family setting.

Similarly, the viewer's participation is necessarily required for programs constructed as a mosaic; otherwise, there will be no unity to the show, and it will appear as no more than a mishmash of disconnected segments. Closely related is the kind of program that makes a viewer's interpretation vital, as when the superficial account (comprehensible and enjoyable for its own sake) contains a deeper meaning that is not immediately obvious. So, broadly conceived, there is a distinction between television programming that requires viewer involvement and that for which the viewer is essentially irrelevant, the former being the more effective of the two in communicating the message of television. It is the difference between the viewer being a participant or a mere witness, and when it comes to a consideration of televised rock and roll, the distinction indicates where we should look for its primary impact.

Without denying this difference, the greater one's exposure to all kinds of television programming, the more it will affect one. McLuhan described its overall impact as "the power to transform American innocence into depth sophistication." This being the case, it is to be expected that the generation that has grown up with television will be the one most influenced by it. Writing in 1964, McLuhan observed,

> The young people who have experienced a decade of TV have naturally imbibed an urge toward involvement in depth that makes all the remote visualized goals of usual culture seem not only unreal but irrelevant and not only irrelevant but anemic. It is the total involvement in all-inclusive *now-ness* that occurs in young lives via TV's mosaic image.... The TV child expects involvement and doesn't want a specialist job in the future. He does want a role and a deep commitment to his society.[1]

Since he wrote these words, there have been more than forty-five additional years of viewer experience, and more than forty-five additional years for television to have its way with us. The youth of McLuhan's time are now in their fifties and sixties, and only a few of them (the lucky ones) have ever had a role to play in this ideal sense. Most are no doubt frustrated to one extent or another — a fact that yields an interesting implication: the greater the exposure to TV, the greater the general level of dissatisfaction in society.

The impact of television may very well be subtle and indirect, but its message is nevertheless revolutionary. With each new television generation, the social discontent will increase until the bonds of the traditional order snap under the strain. Hence, the great mollifier of controversy is likely to continue mightily its contribution to the overthrow of the prevailing value structure. In addition, it's worth noting that the first television generation was also the first generation to be exposed to the insidious blandishments of rock and roll.

The Viewer as Witness

Rock music and its attendant culture have been the focus of several TV formats, and all of them have reflected the developments within the overall revolutionary process. Some, however, have utilized mixed or non-electric media as their content and, as such, have tended to reflect cultural changes more than further them.

The Record Hop

The earliest manifestation of rock and roll on television was Philadelphia's own *Bandstand* in 1952, with Bob Horn as the TV disc jockey. Soon after its inception Dick Clark, a local radio DJ, replaced him (allegedly because of some impropriety involving Horn and one of the young female dancers on his show). ABC quickly picked it up and began to broadcast it nationally as *American Bandstand;* the rest, as they say, is history. In the wake of its success, every city with television facilities and enough teenagers to pose a threat to civic and gastric peace came up with a clone of its own. In my varied necks of the woods, there was *The Buddy Dean Show* (Baltimore), *The Milt Grant Record Hop* (Washington, D.C.) and *The Clay Cole Show* (New York). With the possible exception of *The Lloyd Thaxton Show* (Los Angeles), Clark had no real competitors, and Thaxton was a woefully poor second at that. *American Bandstand* was on the air every weekday from three to five in the afternoon, an incredible saturation of the market for then, or any time. Clark's influence was enormous, as much as for whom he didn't invite to lip-synch on his show as for whom he did. Whether or not his guest list was suspiciously heavy with those in whom he had financial investments (or those who sang the songs in which he had invested), as some people alleged, the list was certainly composed of the most sanitized and least threatening performers available. No Elvis or Jerry Lee Lewis, nor Chuck Berry, Little Richard, or anyone else "too Black" ever darkened the stage of *American Bandstand*. Instead, we got the likes of Frankie Avalon, Bobby Vinton, and Fabian Forte. Single-handedly, Dick Clark virtually defined the essence of "schlock rock," and still today, he symbolizes the hardcore sellout. Nevertheless, through his agency, rock and roll was legitimized and brought into our living rooms, and has forever after been accepted as a part of our lives—and our family.

Soul Train continued the televised record hop into the 1970s, only in this instance, reflecting later cultural developments, the audience and performers were Black. Soul had become a definably separate entity within the rock genre during the sixties, resulting from the militancy and pride of a new Black consciousness. The music played on the show was still pretty clean-cut, but Black Americans now had access to the nation's living rooms. It didn't make a dime's worth of difference that most Whites didn't bother to tune in; what mattered was that the show was programmed equally along with every other show and that it allowed for the expression of Black culture as a legitimate component within the larger American culture.

The disco craze of the Interim manifested itself perfectly in *Dance Fever*, a Saturday Night Fever kind of show minus the story. It had large enough audience, but it was rarely watched all the way through. I've never met anyone who has ever watched it for more than a few minutes at a time. Ditto for *Solid Gold*, which played the week's top tunes accompanied by a troupe of interpretive dancers who seemed to be not terribly talented. Perhaps its inexplicable popularity depended more on the dancers' sex appeal than on their dancing.

The highly successful MTV and syndicated shows like *MV3*, *Friday Night Videos*, *Music Magazine* and *Black Music Magazine*, which relied heavily on then-new video technology, were a different matter entirely. Still essentially reflective (and not furthering) of cultural change, they tended to open the way to the many varieties of new music, with the problematic exception of some contemporary Black music (rap and hip-hop). Although some people have denied that racism is the explanation for this exclusion, it does seem to have stemmed from their ignorance and narrowness of taste brought about by the separate musical developments up to that point. And while this was perilously close to racism, it did not continue for very much longer. Musical mergers were already taking place on radio and in recorded music, and this continued unabated. Aside from this, the video shows lent strong support to a developing art form: the "music videos" and mini-video movies (for example, Michael Jackson's "Thriller"). Most of them present some form of interpretive mini-drama along with the music, and awards have been given to the most creative of these productions since 1984. (Madonna's "Like a Virgin" won hands down!) The fact that many could be purchased or rented for home use (on recorders or disc players) led some people to speculate that the visual performance would eventually replace the audio recording as the principal means for the transmission of rock music. I doubted this very much at the time and still do: visuals require too extensive a commitment of time and concentration to appreciate fully. Nevertheless, I was wrong about how significant MTV would become as a way of introducing new music. Audio transmission allows other things to go on simultaneously (as the iPod and similar devices have demonstrated); it does not demand the kind of total concentration characteristic of television, a visual medium. Furthermore, recordings do not restrict the free play of imagination as videos must do in principle. Videos are a separate but related art form — not a substitute.

Despite their apparent diversity, all televised record hops and video performances are fundamentally non-involving. The performers on the set or in the video do the dancing, not the viewers at home, who are no more than passive observers.

The Variety Show

The next major manifestation of rock on TV began just a few years after the televised record hop, in 1956, when Elvis appeared on *The Ed Sullivan Show*. He had appeared on some other nationally televised shows prior to *Sullivan*, but this one symbolized his emergence as "the King." In terms of significance, his appearance was second only to that of The Beatles not eight years later. The televised variety show has never been an important vehicle for the discovery of emerging talent (this, despite the enormous popularity of *American Idol* and the few stars who have been created therefrom), but it has been remarkably perceptive in highlighting the current trends, whatever they might be. Sullivan's indignant statement that "Elvis will never appear on my show" underwent a dramatic conversion to "This is a real, decent, fine boy" when he did appear two months later — after Sullivan was smashed in the ratings by Elvis's first TV appearance on *The Steve Allen Show*, which ran opposite

Sullivan's. It turns out that his entertainment instincts were far stronger than his convictions regarding the protection of traditional values.

Another show of some significance, reflecting the mood of the sixties, was *The Smothers Brothers Comedy Hour*. Heavily weighted toward traditional folk in the music it presented, it had a decided tendency toward the expression of social concerns and protest—factors which eventually led to its demise in 1969, only a little over two years after its debut. When the Smothers Brothers took on America's policies in Vietnam and had as a guest the blacklisted Pete Seeger—who sang the forbidden "Waist-Deep in the Big Muddy (and the Damn Fool Says to Push On)"—cancellation was no less predictable than the sun's rising in the east. An interesting and curious contrast at the end of the sixties was the highly innocuous *Sonny and Cher Comedy Hour*, starring the "hip" couple of the sixties. Suffice it to say that nothing more controversial than Cher's navel ever appeared on their show.

All of these variety shows came equipped with a studio audience to whom the shows were directed. The audience at home was necessary for the ratings game, but little else. Interestingly, since the sixties, this format has not been very successful. Almost every attempt to breathe some life into it has failed. This should not be very surprising, since the format is essentially vaudeville, bound to lose out to more electronically oriented programming. In any case, it's still worthwhile thinking back to those first appearances by Elvis and The Beatles on *Sullivan*. What a contrast they presented to acts such as Algernon Vim and His Blind Dancing Dogs from New Oxford, Pennsylvania, and the guy from Paramus, New Jersey, who could play the national anthem on his head with wooden spoons! (Ok, I made these acts up, but chances are the real acts were even weirder!) With the contrast between Elvis and The Beatles on the one hand and the novelty acts on the other, the emergence of revolutionary values couldn't have been clearer.

The Concert

Beginning in the mid-sixties, live concerts were staged for broadcast, and they were specifically intended to capture the style and flavor of the contemporary scene. Every once in a while, we'd be treated to an "oldie but goodie" (a term which I find as offensive and deplorable as "boy," "the little woman" and "senior citizen," for all of them exemplify a patronizing attitude that the perpetrator seems unable to recognize as such). As can be ascertained from their titles, *Hullabaloo* and *Shindig* were folkie flavored, but they never completely excluded rock. (This was the sixties, after all.) *Hollywood a Go Go*, another mid-sixties entry, catered more to rock-oriented tastes but tended to stress danceable music over anything that might appear to be controversial. As the sixties came to an end, the late-night concert scene began to develop and enjoy a modicum of popularity: *Midnight Special, Don Kirshner's Rock Concert, In Concert*, and *Rock'n'Roll Tonight*. Their success was temporary; it depended largely on the shows leading into them—almost exclusively late-night talk and variety shows with ample comedy and satire. But their success was temporary. As a participatory medium, the TV concert was intrinsically flawed; passively watching was about all you could do. Nevertheless, a few survived and continued (ABC's *In Concert*), and several filmed concerts aimed at television have continued. One of the latter is worthy of notice: *Austin City Limits* is one, and maybe the best. Austin has always tilted toward a far more eclectic presentation of music than its northeastern C&W counterpart in Nashville. Public television and VH1 have also continued the format but direct their shows toward smaller and more specialized audiences, as with *The Chris Isaak Show, Soul Stage* and *Sound Stage*. At the opposite end of the spectrum is *Later with Jools Holland*, one of the most eclectic music shows ever to appear. One interesting television channel has taken advantage of all the latest technology to present an eclectic musical experience in high definition: Palladia TV. It presents concerts, videos and assorted live performances from MTV, VH1 and CMT. It broadcasts virtually everything and anything resembling or akin to rock music. Its elaborate show-transitions alone make the channel worth watching. In a real sense, this kind of show has rendered all previous forms of concert TV obsolete. As of 2009, there is simply no equal to Palladia.

As for the major live concerts designed exclusively for television, they could not compete with the broadcasts of live concerts from around the world as exemplified by one of the earliest and best of the lot: *The Prince's Trust All-Star Rock Concert*, which began in 1986 and continues up to the present, albeit peppered with controversies all along the way. In addition, most of these often charitable concerts were quickly made available on video (first on tape and later on DVDs). These, Palladia and VCRs have obviated the need to watch them live.

The Film

Films produced specifically for television are different in many important respects from theatrical releases; they differ in terms of structure, concept, theme, technique, and in numerous other ways. My comments will concern the former category only, and I include in it such apparently diverse forms as miniseries and cartoons. Even though all have qualities suiting them uniquely for television, the viewer is nevertheless more of a witness than a participant, comparatively speaking. As such, these programs reflect more than motivate, and give direction to cultural change.

TV films about rock music were first produced toward the end of the Interim, including *American Hot Wax* (1978), *Deadman's Curve* (1978), *Elvis* (1979), *The Birth of The Beatles* (1979), and a documentary, *The Heroes of Rock and Roll* (1979). Together, they possibly signaled the rebirth of revolutionary fervor. This being so, it is significant what meaning is implicit in these films. *American Hot Wax* is about Alan Freed and his persecution (yes, persecution) by the established, traditional order, and it establishes clearly that a genuine cultural conflict is underway. *Deadman's Curve* portrays the tragic and apparent end of Jan and Dean, yet it ends with their tumultuous resurrection after a period of desperate struggle. The analogy with the then-current state of the cultural revolution was striking, to say the least. *Elvis* and *The Birth of The Beatles* were portrayals of the two major symbols of the revolution, both dealing with the earlier part of their careers and each leaving the finale and the future open-ended. Elvis's negation is clearly reestablished and The Beatles' affirmation is just as clearly revealed as their destiny. The final film is one of the best historical surveys of rock ever done, and, significantly, it links the music to cultural change (though it tends to overemphasize its present, 1979). Interpretations of this kind may seem to be rather farfetched and more the product of wishful thinking than anything corresponding to the facts. Yet, if the Interim is most accurately understood as the result of exhaustion and the loss of an appropriate symbol for the opposition, then a renewal would seem to be the next likely stage following a period of rest and recreation, especially since the established order has again acquired a symbolic head.

There are only two rock-oriented miniseries I know of during this time: *Rock Follies* (1975) and its sequel, *Rock Follies 77* (1977). (I consider these as one.) The second is *Shake Rattle and Roll: An American Love Story* (1999). The first deals with a fictional "girl band" making it big in England and the second follows a "boy band and singer" making it big as they move through the fifties and sixties. Both illustrate perfectly the various sensual and financial seductions offered by success in the mass market. Authentic revolutionary anger is portrayed as pretty much selling out to the allurements of money and fame (rock becomes disco, in other words) but eventually climbing out of the pit to reestablish the original fervor. Another miniseries, *The Sixties* (1999), had the cultural revolution at its heart, and it even won an Emmy.

Several interesting questions come to mind in conjunction with this theme. Do these blandishments account for the decline of rock during the Interim? Is a genuine recovery adequately suggested? Is anything significant indicated by the fact that *Rock Follies* centers on a female trio? Most important, where else can you see performing the one and only Rula Lenska (unless you just happen to be one of her friends whom she used to show around London)? Of equal importance is the suspicion that "retrospectives" imply the demise of the phenomenon.

If we look briefly at some of the TV films of the Counter-Reaction, I think a reasonably apt conclusion will result. There is definitely a "look back" throughout the entire period, with a heavy emphasis on biopics: *The Jacksons: An American Family* (1992), *The Temptations* (1998), *Ricky Nelson: Original Teen Idol* (1999), *The Beat Goes On* (about Sonny and Cher, 1999), *Hendrix* (2000) and, most interesting of all, *The Two of Us*, about Paul McCartney's 1976 impromptu visit to John Lennon's Dakota apartment one Saturday afternoon (2000). Do these, and films like them, portend the death of the cultural revolution? Hardly! A revolutionary movement's taking stock of its history and chronicling it is an act of recapitulation making it ready to move on.

Think about the early Christian movement, once it realized its deified founder was not about to "return" soon. Christians began to recapitulate (and of course reinterpret and make sense of) their history — all this done in preparation to move forward. Moving forward, however, always entails the "conversion of the heathen and the indoctrination of the young." Much of the historical retrospective is intended (not necessarily consciously) to accomplish the former — as was the historical framework constructed by the early Christians. Who are we? Where did we come from? What are we about? All these questions and more need to be addressed in order to "build the church." As for the indoctrination of the youth, consider such films as *Shake Rattle and Rock* (1994), which retells the story of a culture unfriendly to rock music, and *Blue Seduction* (2009), which recounts the pitfalls of success. Then there are the more optimistic films, epitomized by *High School Musical* (2006) and the sequel, *High School Musical 2* (2007)

Television cartoons have obviously catered to the kiddy trade, inducing us to coin the expression "micro bopper" to describe the audience. Throughout this period, they've included *The Bay City Rollers, The Monkees, The Jackson Five,* and *The Beatles.* Even though the groups are watered down so as to be unrecognizable except for their songs and visage, the existence of rock music and its message is now evident to even the youngest of us. With The Beatles, of course, they are introduced to one of the major symbols of the cultural revolution. (The very young learn Beatle songs and stories simply as a part of growing up.) With *The Archies, Josie and the Pussycats* and *The Doodlebops,* new fictionalized groups are introduced. The message here is, "You can play this music yourselves," and the message continues with the implicit injunction "Go ye therefore, and teach all nations, baptizing them in the name of rock and roll." The infiltration of rock throughout our culture is, for all practical purposes, complete.

The Talent Show

Beginning with Major Bowes' *Original Amateur Hour* on radio (1934–1945) and then continuing with Ted Mack's version eventually winding up on television, talent shows have been a staple of television. *Arthur Godfrey Talent Scouts* (1948–1958) and then, after a hiatus, *The Gong Show* (1976–1989), Ed McMahon's *Star Search* (1983–1995) and *Showtime at the Apollo* (1987–present) have made the same format work in one way or another. Despite the success of these latter efforts, the crowning jewel of this enterprise is clearly the collection of "Idol" shows, with *American Idol* (2002–present) being the king of the heap.

In an interesting mixture, the medium of television has in this way taken an older medium (the live amateur show) as its message. In turn the performers (media in their own right) have as their message the music created by others. Originally, the musical message was pop music of the pre-rock era, but today, it has become almost universally rock and roll. Granted, the rock and roll suitable for this medium is not the kind to offend or disturb anyone; nevertheless, rock music is by its very nature disturbing as a medium. Given the rather robust history of the talent contest, this is not likely to end soon — if ever. The format will continue to be a major medium for presenting (albeit by the practice of covering or through "karaoke-izing") the music of America's cultural revolution.

The Viewer as Participant

Television was bound to produce some formats uniquely its own, designed (consciously or unconsciously) to take advantage of the peculiarities of the new medium. As varied as they might be, they all have in common the necessity of an audience; without it, they are unable to accomplish the kind of communication for which they were designed. Some of these formats have been used for the expression of rock music, and the results have been dramatic.

Situation Comedies and Dramas

Although the situation comedy is hardly exclusive to television, there are several reasons why the televised version is now much more effective than its predecessor on radio. In every case, this is so because the viewer has become absolutely essential for the completion of the comedy situation. Like television itself (and unlike radio), the characters manifest a coolness, a lack of definition, which the viewer must supplement for the sake of intelligibility. This was only a potentiality for radio, which television has exploited fully. Next, because these series are intended to continue week after week with no specified conclusion, viewers must stick with the show if the events and developments are to be fully understood. This incompleteness produces a fundamental distinction between loyal viewers and all others, a distinction that becomes even sharper when the visual element is considered. Yet since most people watch more than one show, there is no absolute separation between and among various groupings. Finally, because we are able to see the characters (and all of us are seeing the same thing, unlike radio listeners), the intimacy thus created is magnified. Not only do we become more closely involved with the people we meet on the TV screen, but a show establishes a closeness among viewers who meet on the street. The characters necessarily become very real to us, the same characters for all viewers, and we await their visits with us as eagerly as we would guests or favorite members of our families. (Seeing one of our

TV personalities out of character is often distressing to us; it's not at all like seeing a film personality who plays no regular role. Nor can seeing a radio personality be as universally distressing, since we all have a different image of the character in our individual imaginations.) All of these factors have combined to have an enormous impact on and within the family, and the impact has been both more complex and more effective for its being essentially subliminal. To put it as simply as possible, situation comedies provide us with a series of relationships to emulate, guidance for dealing with problems by means of the comedy paradigm, and a validation for whatever is found acceptable on the show.

When the theme is wholly or even partially concerned with rock music, a sellout is likely to be alleged, as with Dylan at Newport. In both cases, the initial impression is that something authentic has been sacrificed for the sake of popularity and/or money. After all, if someone were to look for the epitome of defanged and declawed rock and roll, the television sitcom would seem to be the first thing to investigate. When the music is considered in isolation from the medium, this is no doubt true; TV executives would probably abandon their hidden expense accounts before risking any advertising revenue by broadcasting genuine, bloodcurdling, revolutionary rock and roll. Also like the Dylan episode, there has been an entirely unanticipated consequence stemming from this alleged sellout: an enhancement of the revolution. No matter how "schlocky" the music, rock and roll has become an invited guest in the home, brought in by friends whom America had come to trust. No television "family" (and every situation comedy has a family of some kind) was ever threatened by the introduction of rock, so why should the family on this side of the screen be worried? Rock and roll has been consistently portrayed as something the family, the protector of traditional values, need not fear. So, if rock is compatible with the model family, why should its existence within the imperfect but actual family cause any concern? Why indeed?

Here is why. It was the fifties, and the first rock and roll guest to be invited into our homes was none other than Elvis. It wasn't really Elvis, of course; it was Ricky Nelson. But we all knew an imitation when we saw one; nobody was fooled — not even Ricky Nelson — except maybe our parents who no doubt saw Ricky as the ideal, if irrepressible, son they never had. How could little Ricky do anybody any harm? He was everyone's kid brother; he grew up with us and was probably as much a part of our families as our real siblings. Not only was he safe, he also did what we all wanted to do: he eventually became a rock star on the show as he grew up. Of course, he had a slight advantage over us, since *The Adventures of Ozzie and Harriet* (1952–1966) featured his real-life parents as actors, writers, producers, and directors. Somehow they worked his performance into the show (usually at the end) so that he could sing one or two of his latest songs, and in the process our parents were lulled into thinking that the rock-and-roll phenomenon was nothing more than the latest dance craze.

Significantly, our next important visitors were none other than The Beatles, coming to us in the form of *The Monkees*, in their eponymous show (1966–1968) that was modeled so closely after *A Hard Day's Night* and *Help!* that it's still a wonder no massive lawsuit was brought against its creators for plagiarism. In terms of making The Beatles acceptable to American sensibilities, these four antiseptic imitators were hardly necessary. By this time, the Liverpool originals had become the lovable mop-tops who delighted everyone with their wit, enthusiasm, playfulness, and merry melodies. (They would not remain this way very much longer.) Instead, contrary to expectations, *The Monkees* actually preserved a residual hardness and anger to The Beatles' image that might otherwise have been lost. If anyone ever thought that The Beatles had degenerated into mere pap, they had only to look in on a weekly episode of *The Monkees* to recognize the difference. (Later, the Monkees themselves acknowledged their artificiality and tried hard to become an authentic rock group — by actually learning to play their instruments, for one thing.) When The Beatles metamorphosed again, into something obviously dangerous, they had already become welcome guests in our homes, no longer held at a safe distance. However, all the while, because of the Monkees, we should have known what was going to happen.

Exhaustion often produces a need for diversion from the source of the exhaustion, so during the Interim, most situation comedies ventured nothing and succeeded admirably. *The Partridge Family* (1970–1974) and *The Brady Bunch* (1969–1974), both with contemporary settings, appealed primarily to the very young and to all those who wished the world contained nothing more threatening than what confronted the characters on these two shows. It might strain credulity to call the music performed on these programs "rock," yet it did serve to introduce the younger generation to its form (if not its substance); from then on, American youth would never know a world without rock and roll. Every revolution, bar none, has had a problem with the succeeding generation, since only the first generation, by definition, can possibly experience the beginning and what preceded it. The loss of this element of consciousness has always tended to lessen the passion so necessary for a revolution to continue, for there is no longer any basis for comparison. Hence, there arises a dilemma: the new generations must become acquainted with the revolution and its history, yet the spirit and fervor of the original generation are forever lost to them. With these two situation comedies, the demarcation between the generations was established.

Happy Days (1974–1984) and its spinoffs, *Laverne and Shirley* (1976–1983) and *Joanie Loves Chachi* (1982–1983), came along next. Set in the fifties, they familiarized this new generation with the idea that rock had a history. They depicted not the facts of this history but the fact of the history itself. This distinction is crucial, and missing it is largely why the significance of these shows (especially the first) has never been properly appreciated. "The Fonz," for example, is in no way an accurate portrayal of a fifties "greaser" (or "drape" as we called them in Baltimore), but the character does accurately indicate that there were, in fact, rebels and that they were somehow associated with rock and roll. Moreover, as this generation grew in maturity and sophistication, it was bound to ask why this guy was considered so ominous. He was portrayed as part of the super square Cunningham household after all. The more they watched the show, the more this contradiction would gnaw away at them: either Fonzie had to represent a genuine threat, or everyone else on the show was insane. Those interested in what the facts really were just might have populated the ranks of mods and punks, who came along shortly thereafter as the inheritors of what Fonzie represented.

As the Counter-Reaction got underway, the networks responded (again, no doubt unconsciously) with two critically acclaimed shows. One, *WKRP in Cincinnati* (1978–1982), dealt with rock history with surprising accuracy and sympathy. It even portrayed the conflict between traditional and revolutionary values, leaning heavily toward the latter. Yet at the same time, there was the clear impression that America's period of cultural unrest was over and done with. (Johnny Fever was a burned-out sixties freak, and Venus Flytrap's continual attempts to be a Black revolutionary were laughably and hopelessly outmoded. Moreover, both of these disc jockeys wanted into the system; they didn't want to change it.) This parody produced a certain energy, which suggested that the reports about the demise of the revolution were highly exaggerated. Though *WKRP* expressed its values murkily if at all, it left no doubt as to where to find them expressed with clarity: in authentic rock and roll.

Its undisguised implication was that these values wouldn't be found in anything resembling disco, that being the craze at the time.

The other show, *Square Pegs* (1982–1983), also set within its contemporary time period, was aimed directly at the generation reaching maturity in the early 1980s, just after Reagan's election. Although references to the history of rock were not infrequent, the music was heavily oriented toward new wave (punk being perceived as far too negative for the family hour, and probably for any hour). Its portrayal of high school life was egregiously saccharine, but no one has ever accused situation comedies of approaching too closely the literal truth. What mattered about this show was its portrayal of a revolutionary response to the Counter-Reaction and the idea that the responses was linked with the new developments in rock music. The theme for the show was written and sung by The Waitresses, whose commitment to revolutionary values is unquestioned. And Devo actually performed on the show, leaving little doubt as to the show's orientation. Further, it was developed by one of the writers for *Saturday Night Live* and a former editor of *National Lampoon*, Anne Beatts, whose revolutionary credentials are impeccable. Neither *Square Pegs* nor *WKRP* lasted very long; both were canceled because of low ratings — but then again, so was *Star Trek*.

Dramas with a rock music component have been more rare, but specimens of this type of television actually existed and flourished. Although incorporating rock and other performing arts as well, *Fame* (1982–1987) is probably the best known, and one of the best. Born from the movie of the same name — about a New York high school of performing arts — it had a rebirth in the 21st century in film. One of the most bizarre shows of any kind ever to be on television was *Cop Rock* (1990), which combined musical theater and police drama and was created by Steven Bochco. It may not have been good, but everyone still remembers it! After a period marked by a dearth of shows with a rock music sensibility, the 21st century produced a new entry, *Flight of the Concords* (2007–2009). The mere fact that it is created by New Zealanders points out that rock music and perhaps its revolutionary message is not limited to the United States. While this may be obvious in some ways — the music and musicians have been internationalized almost since its inception — the effects of the music may not yet be fully appreciated.

Satire

Of the four shows I'm about to mention, two of them — *Rowan and Martin's Laugh-In* (1968–1973) and *Saturday Night Live* (1975–present) — have presented some of the most innovative programming ever to appear on the tube. The two others, *Fridays* (1980–1982) and *Second City TV* (1976–1984), while equally good in many ways were in some ways derivative (*Fridays*, whose first show opened with a hilarious sketch about *not* being derivative as the camera pulled back to reveal a complete cast mirroring that of *SNL!*) or inherently limited (*Second City*, which is named after Chicago, its place of origin). *Second City* did manage to break out of Chicago in that some of the original members of *Saturday Night Live* had their roots in Second City's live act. In all four cases, however, the format came as close to McLuhan's vision of television's mosaic as anything ever scheduled. Actually, *The Ernie Kovacs Show(s)* (1949–1962 in a variety of TV formats — his career a mosaic in itself) came pretty close, winning an Emmy for outstanding achievement in electronic camerawork for a series of specials during 1961–1962 season, as if to offer a tantalizing foretaste of what was possible. However, his shows rarely did very well in the ratings; Kovacs obviously lived and died (in an automobile accident) ahead of his time.

Riding the crest of McLuhan's popularity and influence, *Laugh-In* emphasized the mosaic style to a degree never seen before or since. Still, the other three are also best described in terms of a mosaic. Comprising distinct elements, each one left it to the audience at home — neither *Laugh-In* nor *SCTV* had a studio audience — to establish the connection, if any. The audience was required to integrate and thus interpret what was perceived: The relationship among the disparate parts was not given in the experience. It had to be intentionally supplied. The mosaic is not something visually accessible. McLuhan wrote, "The mosaic can be seen as dancing can, but is not structured visually; nor is it an extension of the visual power. For the mosaic is not uniform, continuous, or repetitive. It is discontinuous, skew and nonlineal, like the tactile TV image." McLuhan meant here that the viewer must form the pattern, much as a sculptor forms a shape from whatever materials are available.[2]

Not surprisingly, given the similarity of "the materials" made available, the viewers of these four shows came up with similar interpretive patterns or structures. Much of *Laugh-In* was affirmative of something new (mirroring its 1968–73 dates). Its very format told us this much. Even though there was no recognizable rock music either performed or recorded on the show (it relied instead on some kind of simulated and synthesized rock), its influence was unmistakable and all pervasive. Horace Newcomb, in *The Most Popular Art*, attributes much of the power and popularity of *Laugh-In* to its attack on the traditional values associated with politics, religion, sex, the military, and the family. All of its segments "were clearly intended to shock, to challenge accepted values, to call certain beliefs into question." Even when some of the favorite objects of its derision actually appeared on the show (John Wayne, Billy Graham, and Nixon, for example), the satire was not thereby lessened or blunted. Yet the attitude of affirmation need not focus its attention, and expend its energy, on an enemies list. It was apparent to cast and viewers alike that there were alternatives to everything they satirized; for the moment, the opposition could be safely ignored. (Such naive optimism carries a mixed blessing, since the taste of success that's so necessary for any social movement tends to be accompanied by a dangerous underestimation of the opposition.) In any case, some of the delightfully pointed episodes of *Laugh-In* should be remembered: The "Flying Fickle Finger of Fate Award" (given for all sorts of social and political outrages); the "Farkle Family" (the many children of which suspiciously resembled the neighbor); Goldie Hawn's writhing, bikinied body (painted with social, political, and scatological graffiti); the opening party scene (in which the dancing would stop for short, one-line, commentaries) and Lily Tomlin's Ernestine (whose phone company sketch was a devastating parody of corporate America).

The rumblings of a new negation began to occur toward the end of the 1970s, and NBC's *Saturday Night Live* captured this mood and encouraged it along perfectly. In its first two or three years, the satire was positively brutal. Nothing this aggressive had ever appeared on television before, and its anger was directed squarely against the established order. Playing in the same time slot as *The Tonight Show*, *SNL* underlined the contrast in audience sympathy; very few people watched both shows, since their points of view were so obviously at odds. The focus of attack of *SNL* is plainly evident in a few selected examples of sketches and other bits: the "Claudine Longet Men's Open Invitational Ski (Shoot) Tournament" (the injustice of the judicial system), Dan Aykroyd's imitation of Jimmy Carter confessing lust in his heart (the stupidity of most sexual restrictions), a pseudo-union advertisement for the United Marijuana Growers of America, Inc. (the stupidity of most drug laws), Laraine Newman as Squeaky Fromme (the stupidity of having no effective gun laws),

Jane Curtin as Baba Wawa (the pretentiousness of everyone with status and authority), Garrett Morris's summer job as a "Black boy" lawn ornament (the continued existence of racism), Don Novello's Father Guido Sarducci (the continued existence of religion), Chevy Chase as Gerald Ford (the continued existence of politics), Aykroyd as sexual object in the "beefcake" sketch (the continued existence of sexism), Aykroyd and Belushi as Nixon and Kissinger in "The Final Days" sketch (the continued existence of Nixon and Kissinger), Gilda Radner as Patti Smith, and Lorne Michaels's invitation to The Beatles to appear on the show for the incredible sum of $3,000 (the music business), the Spud Beer advertisement (the medical business), the sketch about the cancellation of *Star Trek* (the television business), Michael O'Donoghue (anything), and John Belushi (everything). Further, only once was there a guest host with an unambiguous establishment orientation, Ron Nessen (Carter's press secretary); most were decidedly of the opposite persuasion, including George Carlin, Richard Pryor, Sissy Spacek, Paul Simon, Buck Henry, Ralph Nader, Lily Tomlin, Eric Idle, Steve Martin, and Jodie Foster. The musical guests have also been even obviously cultural rebels, and through thirty-five seasons, there have been approximately 700 shows with musical representation from every period and genre of rock and roll.

The negation of the Counter-Reaction blossomed fully with the satire on *Fridays*, as illustrated by the Rocky Horror sketch mentioned earlier. Its attack on traditional values was actually more scathing than those of *SNL*, and its affirmations of new values associated with sex, drugs and rock and roll were more direct. For example, unlike *SNL* at the time, it often featured new wave music, with even an occasional punk group invited to perform (slam dancing and all). It has also clearly portrayed marijuana usage, alternative sexual practices and often graphic violence in its parodies.

Even more explicit was the short-lived *Richard Pryor Show*, which lasted only four episodes in 1977. The first show opened with Pryor apparently nude (he wore a body stocking)— a visual commentary on NBC's censorship. The major musical act was The Pips (sans Gladys Knight) doing the background singing (and only that) to "Midnight Train to Georgia." The country wasn't ready to accept satire this striking.

SCTV was always less direct in its satire than either *Fridays* or *SNL*, and originally it had no musical guests at all. When they finally were added, the emphasis was pretty much a balance between music from the sixties and contemporary music, suggesting an attitude closer to affirmation.

Three of the four shows under consideration were linked in ways not apparent from merely watching what they broadcast. The commonality had to do with the performers' personal lives and how the shows were viewed. First, the persons associated with *SNL*, *Fridays*, and *SCTV* all knew each other rather well from having a common background, and many were close friends. The similarity among the shows is thus hardly in need of careful investigation. Second, since they were telecast well past the family hour (*SCTV* even followed SNL at one time), they were likely to interfere with the weekend parties often scheduled by members of their viewing audiences; however, their popularity was such that it was acceptable to interrupt the festivities to watch them. It is probably unnecessary to add that the viewing of these shows was often chemically enhanced, an experience providing yet another dimension to their participatory qualities, to say nothing of their antiestablishment orientation.

Saturday Night Live, of course, lives on, now accompanied by other, newer shows which have the same social and cultural bent. *Madtv* (1995–present) is the longest running and is often on a par with some of the best work of *SNL*. Of course, many of the more recent shows (especially *SNL*) are now available on DVD, and despite the fact that much of the material is dated, the best of the shows still have a certain zing to them. There is something timeless about first-rate satire, something worth preserving in the best as well as the worst of times. With the loss of John Belushi, their preservation is all the more important, for he symbolizes better than most what these shows are all about.

The Impact of Television

McLuhan remarked that, since the arrival of television, "there is scarcely a single area of established relationships, from home and church to school and market, that has not been profoundly disturbed in its pattern and texture." He must have meant it. His jumbled list of affected areas is seemingly endless, especially when all the complex implications are recognized. By noting what kinds of values are involved, however, one can bring some organization to his chaotic ruminations.[3]

Among the most important are an appreciation of differences with a corresponding opposition to imposed uniformity, the encouragement of individuality without the corruption of individualism, a unification that recognizes both harmony and diversity, and a deeply committed life instead of a life of fragmented superficiality. If these sound a lot like the fundamental values of the cultural revolution, there shouldn't be any real surprise. The arrival of television as the key electronic medium happened at just about the same time as the release of "Rock around the Clock," and never was television a more unifying medium than in the days following November 22, 1963. At those key points in the development of the revolution, television was there, not only to record but also to participate.

Now, maybe some of the manifestations of these values can be perceived and comprehended as the outcome of rock and television's joint impact. Concerning race and sex, McLuhan believed that integration was bound to fail, based as it was on literate culture's positive evaluation of uniformity. The goal was and is the eradication of both racial and sexual differences to achieve conformity. Electronically influenced cultures, on the other hand, have diversity as one of their primary goals. In both the fifties and the sixties, rock music exemplified this latter notion, and it has continued to do so in ever greater depth and complexity, most recently involving itself with the problems of sexism and sexual orientation. The repression of normal sexuality he saw resulting from the linear, structured consciousness of literate cultures: Western culture has "fostered the institution of prolonged adolescence by the negation of tactile participation that is sex," which has led to political and moral conformity. The reversal of this is so obviously associated with rock and roll that there is no need to belabor the point. Television's contribution, however, ought not be overlooked. Its emphasis on touch has made the reversal of sexual repression and conformity to sex roles practically inevitable.

In education, the revolution against specialization, selfishness, and materialism was one of the hallmarks of the early New Left. McLuhan saw the "Montessori educational strategy," the "beatnik rejection of consumer mores and of the private success story," and the demand for relevance and involvement as partially the result of television. Further, as is perhaps obvious, the New Left comprised the first television generation. Musically, the dissatisfaction with traditional education has been a major theme in rock, from Chuck Berry's "School Days" to Alice Cooper's "School's Out" to Pink Floyd's album and movie *The Wall*, to "I Don't Wanna Be Learned" by the Ramones, to "Mark Me Absent" by the

Clash, to "Principal's Office" by Young MC, to Eminem's "Brain Damage," to Dead Prez's "It's Bigger Than Hip hop" and to Black Star's "Astronomy (8th Light)." It is a tendency not likely to pass away.

Furthermore, politics (both domestic and international), guided traditionally by nationalism, imperialism, and militarism, has suffered perhaps its severest challenge ever. McLuhan claimed that television involves us in a depth experience, but it does not excite, agitate, or arouse, all of which are essential ingredients for the "old politics." Additionally, due largely to television, modern warfare is becoming a morally unthinkable (not, unfortunately, a physically impossible) idea. Along with all the electronic media, television has produced new opinions and feelings that result in our now having instant, global information literally at our fingertips. These new beliefs have to do with political universalism; even modern weaponry based on electronic technology serves to make more vivid the unity of the human family. Simply and graphically put, "the electronic techniques cannot be used aggressively except to end all life at once, like the turning off of a light." Nothing says it better than the corresponding imagery of John Lennon's "Imagine," but here again, rock's outrage at "politics as usual" is far too ubiquitous to need documentation.

Among the many other areas affected simultaneously by rock music and television are clothing styles (which reveal a person's musical preferences), automobile aesthetics (highly individualized), books (a preference for paperbacks), sports (football over baseball) and religion (ecumenical and non-ideological). Having such a pervasive impact, television (especially when coupled with rock and roll) just might deserve all the fear and loathing it so often attracts. For, like Dylan, it has expressed the values of the cultural revolution (the message) in the most far-reaching and dangerous of all possible forms (the medium of television). In a very real sense, one *is* the other.

8

The Internet: You Say You Want a Web-o-lution

With apologies to Elmer Fudd and appreciation to my daughter for suggesting the above title, we now have to consider the enormous technological developments within the past decade or so and the impact that they have had on the cultural revolution. I have no inclination to regale anyone with the admittedly important and no doubt interesting history of the birth of the personal computer, its emergence into adulthood and its flowering in the electronic ether. Others have done that elsewhere. Rather, I'm going to regale you with the tale of my own gradual immersion into this new world and how I see the Internet affecting rock music and hence America's cultural revolution.

Long before the personal computer was as commonplace as the telephone, there were people hidden away in garages tinkering around with musical instruments and making music—or something passably similar to music. It was rock and roll, of course, and the standards for what qualified weren't very high. Semi-organized noise with a discernable beat was pretty much all you needed back in the day when Bill Haley was the mainstay of the Comets. In other garages in the neighborhood, there were other people tinkering around with other kinds of instruments, electronic instruments with vacuum tubes, and clicking key pads that put them in touch with people doing the same thing in still other garages far away. All of these folks would soon emerge from their respective garages and present something new to the world, something the world had never before seen or heard—something revolutionary.

My encounter with the musicological garage-o-philes happened indirectly, late at night listening to forbidden radio stations. My encounter with the technological garage-o-philes also happened indirectly, in an early morning lecture hall at the Lutheran Seminary at Gettysburg. Some guest professor was opining excitedly about something he called "the impending cybernetic revolution," wherein all academic and scientific disciplines are understood as complex, interrelated self-regulatory systems. I vaguely recall some references to systems theory, robotics, artificial intelligence and the instantaneous exchange of information. I also vaguely recall the name Buckminster Fuller. However, nothing really resonated with me; there were other things on my mental agenda. It was 1966, and America was at war with people half the world away for reasons that didn't make sense. What made sense was to stop the war. However, America was also at war with itself over the status of American citizens whose ancestors used to be the property of other American citizens, and that didn't make sense either. It just made sense to correct the problem. So I just filed cybernetics away in the dark recesses of my memory, to be recalled at that time when I would undergo a conversion experience. Besides, Arthur C. Clarke's *2001: A Space Odyssey* was still two years off;

we hadn't met HAL yet. We wouldn't meet "Data" for an even longer period of time—19 years. Later, however, these two fictional creations of artificial intelligence would strike a chord, and it would begin to resonate when I naively asked my girlfriend a question about her new computer: "What does that "C:" mean?

So, for me, it didn't start as a love affair in a garage. Nor did some geekazoid believers come a-knockin' at my front door to proselytize me. My conversion to computerization happened as the result of necessity—in the early 1990s. Working with an old dedicated word processor (an electronic typewriter with a screen but no hard drive) to write a book, I arrived at a choke point when it came to printing the manuscript. I had to feed each page into the typewriter separately then stand by while the machine typed it out. At its swiftest, it took about a minute for each page (double-spaced in 12-point Courier). Clearly, I needed an alternate method. That's when I asked my friends, colleagues and girlfriend if printing with a computer would be faster. They laughed ... and laughed. The next day I went to the nearest computer store and joined the revolution.

It took little imagination to realize, immediately thereafter, that this beast had other applications that could assist me in the world of higher education. I could write and save my barely legible lecture notes on 3.5-inch floppy disks. In the process of so doing, I discovered I could revise, edit, spell-check and even add graphics with the greatest of ease. Most of all, it helped me get organized (a work still in process, by the way). Then I discovered that the modem inside the belly of the beast was more than a frill; it allowed me to communicate with all sorts of people in all sorts of places doing all sorts of things. It was text-based, but you could actually colorize the messages to "fancify" them. Not long after playing around with all sorts of chat boards (yes, all kinds), I wondered if I could actually try teaching a class this way. With the invaluable assistance of some key faculty members at El Camino College, we eventually got a logic class up and running. Not too long after that the graphics-heavy World Wide Web came into being and online education along with it.

During this process of making education genuinely and completely available to online students via the Internet, it became abundantly clear that this was not a development favored by the vast majority of faculty members and educational institutions. In fact, there was vociferous and strident opposition to it. Usually these "contrarians" (one might prefer the term "Luddites") maintained that online teaching was not academically respectable. Not only would proper intellectual standards not be maintained, but the persons engaging in such frivolous activity would, in so doing, express their own intellectual inadequacy. The fight was on.

As the ensuing struggle in academe between the Luddites and the Computeroids became increasingly nasty, it gradually dawned on me that there was an almost perfect correspondence between the Luddites and the proponents of traditional values on the one hand and the Computeroids and the cultural revolutionaries on the other. Was it just me? Hardly! One thing was beyond question: there was a fundamental conflict within academia over online education, but beneath the surface there was an even more fundamental conflict. As early as 1992, the lines were clearly drawn. In a study entitled "Faculty Support for Distance Education in a Conventional University," Evelyn Joyce Black, in her doctoral dissertation, addressed the controversy in terms of the credibility of distance education:

> Faculty skepticism has slowed the development and expansion of distance education despite increased demands for it.... There is little empirical evidence about the reasons for the antagonism between the supporters and opponents of distance education.... [So] the conceptual framework drew on studies of faculty attitudes towards ... academic culture and change.... There were sig-

nificant differences in faculty support by discipline and gender ... [and] about distance education as promoting social justice, as an educational method, or as the distribution of information. Faculty who were supportive held the beliefs and values associated with mass education while those who were opposed tended to believe in an elite approach to university education.[1]

Since then depictions of the conflict have become a lot clearer, but Dr. Black's basic observations still hold true. The conflict is and always has been over fundamental values.

In a 2008 compendium edited by Margaret Elliot and Kenneth Kraemer, *Computerization Movements and Technology Diffusion: From Mainframes to Ubiquitous Computing*, eight chapters alone are devoted to the basic values of "Freedom" and "Democratization," and many others suggest the complementary values of "Individuality" and "Diversity."[2] Furthermore, in one article (by Mary J. Culnan) the author uses an online Bruce Springsteen community to illustrate the inherent democratization fostered by this revolutionary technology. Like all of the other scholars contributing to this book, rock music does not figure into their assessment in any way. Yet, they all understand the essence of "Computerization Movements" as having to do with grand utopian visions that have become part of the "ether" of our society — much as has rock music.

So, what should we make of this new medium, the Internet, which might be better understood as an assemblage of related media. In a sense, we're on our own here, but not quite. Although McLuhan never had much to say about the Internet, having died in 1980, his ideas still speak for themselves. Were he alive today, I'm sure he would vociferously agree that the best way to understand the impact of the sudden and complete computerization of virtually the entire world is to see the computer and the Internet as new — and revolutionary — media. He died shortly after the beginning of the personal computer revolution and well before access to the Internet was widely available. Nevertheless, his basic notions about the impact of a medium on society and culture (apart from the message it conveys) still hold true.

I realize that I've listed, mentioned or otherwise referred to the fundamental values of the cultural revolution throughout, but maybe it would be helpful to allow this new medium to organize or perhaps reorganize them. After all, if the medium truly is the message, and if this medium truly is in accord with the cultural revolution as I allege, then these values should be implicit. The terms used in the aforementioned compendium might prove useful here, so I'm going to adopt some of its conceptual tools to express the message expressed by this medium.

Computerization Movements

In the foreword, Dr. Susanne Iacono describes a "Computerization Movement" in terms reminiscent of a cultural revolution: "Its advocates claim that [it] will be instrumental in bringing about a new social order, e.g., a more collaborative or productive organization or even a new organizational form."[3] She continues by characterizing this process as "social reform" proposed by "activists," and mentions "uncooperative people" and "countermovements" as the main barriers. Obviously, these terms hark back to the features of a cultural revolution. Although the immediate focus of this compendium is the business environment, it could easily describe the introduction of the computer and the Internet into the academic environment as well. Of single importance is her stress on the "gap" between the utopian visions proposed and the actually implementation of reforms. This often-overlooked aspect of a cultural revolution is perhaps the key reason for disillusionment among its activists and for woefully premature pronouncements of its failure. With experience and dedication, however, an infusion of pragmatism allows for a recommitment to the cause. In particular, where possible, the use of existing structures is likely to be more productive of reform than disrupting and transforming them. Again, this is remarkably similar to how I've portrayed America's cultural revolution.

In a very real way, all of McLuhan's ideas are tied up with this "Computerization Movement." He expressed the process as an electronic revolution that was gradually replacing the "Gutenberg Galaxy" inhabited by "typographic man." All of the four previous chapters in this section (Radio, Records, Film and Television) have their culmination in the process of computerization, perhaps the purest form of the electronic revolution. The computer, in essence, distills and recapitulates the earlier technologies and in so doing revolutionizes them. The sound track for this process is, of course, rock and roll.

While the values implicit in the music of rock are often expressed metaphorically and are sometimes just simply obscure, on occasion they can be as clear (and sometimes as literal) as a clarion call. Take, for example, the issue of ultra-nationalism and its by-product, war. Simon and Garfunkel's 1966 "(Are You Going to) Scarborough Fair," in the counterpoint lyrics, tells of a "child of the mountain" sleeping unaware of the "clarion call" while generals order their men to kill for "causes they've long ago forgotten." It's hard to avoid the conclusion that true love of any kind and war do not mix. More recently, Falconer (a Swedish power metal band) in 2002 said pretty much the same thing in their song "Clarion Call," when they wonder whose side God is really on when our visions of a "sweet tomorrow" are "cracking" and "fading away" and when they warn us that "our blood will be spilled" for the visions of the nobles. Yet, I think no one put these values clearer than did John Lennon in "Imagine": freedom from religions threatening hell and promising heaven, freedom from nations to kill and die for and freedom from the greedy quest for sustenance and possessions. Rather, we should live for today, in peace and in brotherhood with all the world. It is, he sang, only a dream but a dream we can try to fulfill. Elliot and Kraemer would no doubt call this a utopian vision — as would almost anyone. However, they, along with McLuhan, would also say that progress towards its accomplishment, no matter how slow, is inexorable.

What could possibly give them this hope? Let's look at some of the specific ideals implicit in the overall "Computerization Movement" looked at as a whole. Elliot and Kraemer strongly urge us to look not at singular instances of adopting a new technology but at the "macro social and cultural environments." To overuse again an already overused platitude, we must not miss the forest by concentrating on the individual trees. In their book, they seek to accomplish this in the book's organization, and it's worthwhile mentioning four of their themes before we proceed any further: Democratization, Death of Distance, Freedom and Information Rights, and Ubiquitous Computing. Together they spell out a somewhat confusing collage of ultimate values implicit in all forms of the Computerization Movement. Certainly, they coincide with the implicit values of America's cultural revolution, and although reasonably understandable as they are, we need to back up and take a look at the medium itself, as a whole, and not so much the message expressed by it. In other words, we can ask how the computerized Web manifests these fundamental values.

Two of McLuhan's books, published posthumously, *The Laws of Media: The New Science* (1988) and *The Global Village* (1989) give us a clue as to how we might proceed in evaluating the effects of the Computerization Movement as a medium. He developed a set of four criteria to guide any such evaluation, which he termed "a tetrad of media effects." But we must be careful here. These so-called laws should not be seen as akin to the law of non-contradiction (a logical principle) or even Newton's description of the laws of motion (empirical descriptions). They are more like "suggestions" or "tools." In *The Digital McLuhan*, Paul Levinson issues this kind of warning as well, and stresses that McLuhan never fully thought them out. Levinson actually believes Hegel's dialectic is a good way of understanding them.[4] This comes very close to the familiar proverbial characterization of "the blind leading the blind." Nevertheless, as long we consider them as tools to provoke inquiry, we should not be led too far astray into the wilds of philosophical gobbledegook. McLuhan posed these "laws" questions, perhaps as a way of reminding us that they are tools and only tools. He also stressed that these four characteristics are not sequential; they are simultaneous!

What Does the Medium Enhance?

Every technology or medium extends or otherwise enhances a bodily organ, as the radio enhances the ears and television the eyes. As with all of the specifically electronic media, distance is overcome and people are brought together. Referring specifically to the Computerization Movement, Elliot and Kraemer termed this effect, rather colorfully and aptly, "the death of distance." It's hard to imagine how monumental this development is and what may be the long-term consequences. Today, anyone can be in instant communication with anyone—and even everyone—else! Distance really has "passed away." "Twittering" may seem extreme to some, but it is an inevitable consequence of the technology; we can (and many do) report, to one and all, every single facet of our daily activities—as they are happening. Elliot and Kraemer refer to this as Ubiquitous Computing. This is most certainly enhanced by the Computerization Movement.

I referred earlier to the impossibility of separate categories for American and British rock music and, by extension, the entire English-speaking world. Obviously, this has to do with our common language, but computerization has overcome linguistic separation as well. Translation programs allow communication across cultures and ethnicities. Music, of course, has always crossed these barriers, but until the specific medium of rock music came into being, there remained ethnically and culturally separable types of music. Rock music is radically different. Because it speaks to the currents of revolutionary change everywhere, the different languages of rock lyrics are rendered impotent as devices of separation—it's the form, the medium, that's important, not so much the content, the message. Most of the Russians initially attracted to The Beatles' music didn't understand English; what appealed to them was freedom expressed by the music. The message is inherent in the *medium* itself.

Major benefit concerts have for several years been simulcast around the world, the very first, of course, was the "All You Need Is Love" B.B.C. television special *Our World*, hosted by The Beatles in 1967. Over four hundred million people in twenty-six countries watched it at the same time. Such events quickly became commonplace. Live Aid in 1985 reached sixty countries, and Freddie Mercury's tribute concert had a worldwide audience of over 1.2 billion viewers. Live 8 in 2005 included eight concerts in eight different G-8 cities. Yes, distance is indeed dead. Again, it is more than physical distance that is deceased. The conceptual and ideological distances, so long reinforced by national borders and languages, have also departed this life.

McLuhan characterized this in his notion of a Global Village created by the new electronic media, because it dramatically contracts distances between peoples. But this enhancement has its risks:

> Instead of tending towards a vast Alexandrian library the world has become a computer, an electronic brain, exactly as an infantile piece of science fiction. And as our senses have gone outside us, Big Brother goes inside. So, unless aware of this dynamic, we shall at once move into a phase of panic terrors, exactly befitting a small world of tribal drums, total interdependence, and superimposed co-existence.... Terror is the normal state of any oral society, for in it everything affects everything all the time.... In our long striving to recover for the Western world a unity of sensibility and of thought and feeling we have no more been prepared to accept the tribal consequences of such unity than we were ready for the fragmentation of the human psyche by print culture.[5]

Perhaps this is what worries the thousands of anti-globalization protesters at G-8 and G-9 summits — the threat to any hope of genuine democracy by multinational industries and the like. If so, they should be aware that neither McLuhan nor any of his descendants have ever alleged the inherent moral goodness (or evil) of any form of technology. It's what we do with it that makes it moral or immoral. Globalization itself, or the Global Village, is not a good or a bad thing in and of itself. It just is.

Computerization and the Internet not only permit but also actively encourage a dramatic enhancement of our individuality. The technology that enhances of our ability to communicate with anyone and everyone entails a concomitant requirement that we introduce ourselves. MySpace and Facebook were and still are major vehicles for accomplishing this. Furthermore, personal blogs and websites are available to everyone and every business, and it will not be long before virtually everyone and every business takes advantage of it to broadcast themselves, their ideas and their wares. In so doing, each individual necessarily expresses his or her individuality with few if any restraints. What we inevitably see on the Web, therefore, is the massive diversity of humankind. YouTube and other Web-based video sharing programs allow individuals to express their individuality still further — by presenting themselves as performers in some way as well as by their choices of what to contribute featuring others. We are no longer isolated individuals; we are individuals in contact with all other individuals.

Although perhaps obvious, all of this new technology has enhanced the listening and viewing experience beyond anything possible with previous technologies. A theater-in-the-home has become a reality for significant numbers of people, and promises to grow exponentially in coming years. Hence, every one of our senses are dramatically enhanced.

What Does the Medium Make Obsolete?

Although it will take some time for this to work itself out, "nations" as we have come to know them will cease to exist. After all, there was a time when there were no such things as nations, and there is no reason to suspect they have somehow acquired immortality. Take, for example, the many and varied nations of Europe. In a very real way, these nations have, during a few short years, ceased to exist. The European Union came into being with the Maastricht Treaty (the Treaty on European Union, TEU) on February 7, 1992. This new creation has resulted in a common monetary system based on the euro, and has led to a completely different way of understanding nationalities. The process was surprisingly easy, given the complex history of these nations. With a little reflection, however, it's not so difficult to understand. The communication across borders via the Internet prepared the way for this both practically and psychologically. A mere few years ago (historically speaking) most of these nations were at war with one another. Now such a turn of events is inconceivable. We can expect developments like this to take place elsewhere as well.

All of the earlier, previously mentioned technologies (recordings, radio, television and film) are also becoming obsolete in that they are being forced to change dramatically.

Consider the recording industry: the programmed album (once recorded on vinyl and now on plastic optical disks). Of course, individual bands will still record and distribute albums through record stores, but for the audience, obtaining music is no longer restricted to this method of delivery. Shawn Fanning, a Northwestern University college student, created a free file sharing service in 1999 called Napster. Everyone, anywhere, could share their MP3 music with all other members. This outraged some biggies in the music creation business: Metallica, Dr. Dre and Madonna, to name three, plus A & E Records. As a result, Napster quickly succumbed to all the legal niceties about copyright infringement in 1991, but it started a revolution in the wake of its demise. Other, far more decentralized file sharing services exist now which are far more difficult to prosecute—Kaaza, Limewire, Gnutella, eDonkey 2000 and Freenet, for example.

What has developed because of this technology? Now everyone can be his or her own record producer! You can now create whatever mixture of songs you want and download them to your iPod, Samsung, Zen, Archos, Zune or any one of the other portable audio (and video) players. Mostly the sites for downloading charge a minimal fee for the service, although some sites are still free. Nevertheless, there is no longer a necessity to rely on industry record producers to stand between the music and the individual. Diversity and individuality—two fundamental values of the cultural revolution—are intrinsic developments of this new technology.

This kind of change is also evident in radio broadcasting (consider the development of satellite radio as a way of getting around the formatting pressures of typical AM and FM radio). Film and television in many ways have merged, now that rental films can be downloaded directly and immediately to your large-screen TV equipped with high definition and accompanied by surround sound. These older technologies are not what they used to be. Individual choice in terms of what we watch and listen to has dramatically expanded, and we like it!

Along with this is the fervent desire of "Web-o-philes" to maintain freedom of access to all kinds of information on the Web. This, in turn, derives from the fundamental value of freedom itself. Elliot and Kraemer's organizing principle of freedom and information rights comes immediately to mind and along with it democracy. Again, America's cultural revolution is in synch with the new technology. The implicit effect of this is to render all forms of totalitarianism obsolete—not instantaneously, of course. It will take a while and a half. This is a monumental undertaking, but there are signs of it having already begun. Aside from the downfall of the Marxist-Leninist Soviet Union (it was not a "Marxist" state by any means), there was the Philippine People Power Revolution of 1986 and the Tiananmen Square protests of 1989. All of them gained considerable power because of the participants being able to communicate with the entire world. As of early 2010, there are stirrings of democracy in Iran by the usual "students" and "intellectuals" as well as otherwise dissatisfied citizenry against the fundamentalist mullahs and ayatollahs who have generally distorted the Islamic tradition. (See Wilfred Cantwell Smith's *The Meaning and End of Religion* for an insight into this history.) Giving this movement strength and courage is its access to the world through the Internet, while feeding and fueling it is rock music. Unlike the so-called Tehrangeles rock born of Iranian emigrants in Los Angeles, this rock is indigenous, albeit mostly underground. Although its roots are most certainly American and British with a tad of Germanic techno thrown in for flavor, it is clearly expressive of Iranian culture and its political and social conditions. The band called 127 displays a bit of rock and jazz in their music; Kahtmayan uses heavy metal styling; Abjeez has a reggae and Latin synthesis; and Barad is basically an alternative group. Kahtmayan's album *Virtual Existence* is suggestive of social critique on its own, as are some of its songs: "Broken Promise," "Cold Reflection" and "Utopia." It will not be easy for the Ministry of Culture and Islamic Guidance to stop this movement, although they will certainly try ... and "there will be blood."

The typical categorizations and sub-categorizations of rock music are also rapidly becoming unserviceable. They may not become, strictly speaking, obsolete, but their heuristic function has pretty much ended. Not only do genres come and go almost daily, it is increasingly the case that any attempt to describe a performer or a group in terms of their "type" quickly devolves into a dispute over the typological term itself. Sam Dunn's "flow chart of metal" in the film *Metal: A Headbanger's Journey* is an instance of this very notion. One of his sub-categories of metal is "grunge"— a rather question-begging notion, I would say! Grungers would probably be the first to protest their placement.

The approach I am suggesting, as an alternative (see my chart in Chapter 3), is equally question-begging, of course. At least it has the virtue of locating the disputes squarely on the proper target: the effect the group has within the overall scheme of the cultural revolution — affirmation or negation. This is a subjective judgment and, as such, it guarantees disputation. Moreover, these two facets are more or less two sides of the same coin, in that every negation implicitly proposes an alternative, and every affirmation implicitly rejects what is currently the case. Whenever there is something implicit, thus not immediately apparent, disputations are bound to arise.

It is pointless, for example, to try to characterize effectively artists such as Alecia Beth Moore (better known by her stage name Pink and often printed as "P!nk"). She does everything, as if she were the progeny of Freddie Mercury, The Runaways, AC/DC, the entire history of rhythm and blues and then bathed in the cauldron of Cirque du Soleil. No one really cares where to "place" her; they just listen and watch — in massive numbers. One thing, however, is exceedingly clear: she *affirms* a whole series of values associated with freedom and diversity — sexual identity, minority rights, animal rights, for example — and she *negates* a whole series of values associated with war, unrestrained capitalism and poverty, for example.

Having less of a mass appeal but coincidentally being one of the numerous influences on Pink, the Indigo Girls also defy categorization. Although they started out as kind of a folk duo, they do hard rock and country as well, and often cover another category-unfriendly artist, Bob Dylan. No one really cares where to "place" them any more than for Pink. As for what they *do*, however, they clearly share in the affirmation and negation of the same set of values as Pink. As a small aside, they came in second for the 1990 Grammy Award for Best New Artist to another duo — Milli Vanilli — and I suppose it's worth noting that no one has be able to categorize their music either (but for very different reasons, of course — the problem being whose music were they playing).

Maybe the best illustration of all is the 2007 film *I'm Not There*. "Inspired by the music of and the many lives of Bob Dylan" is the opening caption, and as the surrealistic story proceeds, we are introduced to six different "Bob Dylans" played by six different actors: Christian Bale, Cate Blanchett, Marcus Carl Franklin, Richard Gere, Heath Ledger, and Ben Whishaw. The fact that this list includes a Black youngster and a woman underscores the meaning of the title: The "real" Bob Dylan is impossible to categorize — you may seek him, but you will not find him. Everyone should have seen this coming in 1965 at the Newport Blues Festival when he "went electric" and forced the invention of a new genre, "folk rock."

My approach in dealing with categorizations is to mention them whenever they seem useful, but otherwise ignore them. For me the important thing is what they *do* — I regard Pink and the Indigo Girls, Metallica and Machine Head, The Beatles and Elvis, Tupac Shakur and Notorious B.I.G., as well as the Clash and Rufus, primarily as media. And their most important message is not at all what they sing; it's who they are.

So, my approach is not going to end disputes; it just relocates them to a place where they might be more heuristic. I see Pink as more or less affirmative of revolutionary values and the Indigo Girls as more negative toward old values; and I would expect around ten to fifty percent of everyone to agree. The film *Big Stan* (2007) has an interesting sequence where a smallish (but extremely well trained in martial arts) prisoner, Stan (Rob Schneider) commands that all the various prison gangs give up their constant fighting and raping and, instead, spend their time learning to dance to mariachi music. As if to point out the inevitable absurdity of the "creeping categorization" of rock genres, Stan faults them for mistakenly playing "Afro-Cubano" dance music. No one in the prison yard understands or cares about this nicety. Stan himself admits that the genre is of no significance. The intended effect is what counts ... and the intended effect is to affirm mutual respect among all groups.

Also facing obsolescence is the traditional educational system — at all levels from preschool to graduate work. There are, for example, few remaining classes taught that do not utilize some aspect of the computer and the Internet. This may initially seem a bit far afield from our immediate concern, but ... not so! The traditional face-to-face methodology of music education is affected, as well as every other field or discipline. This goes for music theory, history and practice as well. Now, anyone can learn the rudiments of playing an instrument without having to shell out massive amounts of cash. It's free, and equally available to everyone. It is understood, of course, that older forms of electronic instruments are almost daily being replaced by newer and better versions. This kind of evolution clearly suggests new instruments in the making for future expressions of rock.

What Does the Medium Retrieve That Had Been Obsolesced Earlier?

Just as radio "resurrected" oral storytelling and television "retrieved" the live performance, so also do all forms of media bring older media back into play. I put this differently earlier, when I stressed that every medium has as its content another medium, and this in turn has yet another medium as its content — in a kind of never-ending regress. Another way to put it is that each new medium comes into being as a way of utilizing more fully all of the media that have preceded it. Consider the older media that the computer and the internet have made more useful: writing, composing, drawing, radio, the telephone, CB radio, newspapers, books, television, film, recorded drama and music as well as live drama and music, ad infinitum!

The upshot of all of this as far as the arts are concerned is that individuality and diversity are enhanced to the max, so to speak. Everyone with access to the Web can express their own ideas by means of their personal blogs or "audition" their books, paintings and musical talents without the "people in the middle." There are really no restrictions, then, as would be the case if it were necessary first to please an "agent" of some kind in order to gain an interview with a publisher or producer. There are no filters to pass through. Of course presenting one's self on the Web is no guarantee that the proper people will witness your efforts. But now there is the chance to bypass the "authorities" and speak or otherwise perform directly to the desired audience.

Radio has expanded its content far beyond its initial and traditional programming simply by virtue of newer technology, which frees it from the arbiters of taste, the FCC. Once, rogue/pirate radio stations transmitted from beyond national boundaries to escape governmental control — Mexico being a major case in point — but now they can escape the boundaries of the earth itself. (Sirius and XM Radio started this trend.) This desire to evade control has had many advocates for many, usually political, reasons. As it pertains to rock music, offshore stations in old oil rigs or permanently anchored ships have been the most recognizable means, but moveable and concealable broadcasting from on land has probably been more prevalent. Several films have played around with this playing around: *Born in Flames* (1983) has a feminist and gay rights agenda; *Pump Up the Volume* (1990) focused on just playing alternative music; and *Pirate Radio* (2009) tells a mid-sixties tale about fighting British censorship of rock and roll. The phenomenon has made it into song as well: John Hiatt's "Pirate Radio" and The Blasters' "Border Radio" are two good examples. In all cases, the underlying "message" conveyed by this medium is freedom ... and individuality.

Book publishing on demand (all computerized) is just one prominent example of how the computer and the Web have brought profound changes to the arts. What used to be the sole province of "vanity presses" has made its way into the legitimate writing and selling of books. Publishers are now far more willing to accept for publication a manuscript by a risky unknown writer when the neophyte can prove existing sales from the "self-published" books.

Something very similar is happening in the music production business. As an example of this phenomenon, take the "open source" record labels. Like independent minded publishers of books, these producers use the Internet to publicize, market and distribute their recordings. Calabash Records, for example, founded in 2001, has markets throughout the world and produces music in well over a hundred genres. Amend distributes thousands of albums worldwide and operates on donations. LOCA has a more typical business approach, in that its albums are for sale. Magnitude uses print-on-demand technology much as the print publishers do. In all of these cases, not only does this make older technology more useful, it also strongly encourages artistic freedom — certainly a facet of the overall collection of fundamental revolutionary values.

Video sharing sites (YouTube, Vimeo, MyVideo, etc.) where individual musicians and groups can post their latest creations has even made open source record labels somewhat irrelevant. Although many musicians use these sites primarily for publicity (as do others involved with other art forms), online everyone appears in full equality with every local band freshly emerging from their garage. Equality, in other words, is implicit in the medium.

Getting back to education for a moment, we can also see that something akin to the medieval style of teaching and learning is retrieved by online education. Curricula designed individually according to each person's distinctive needs and interests and guided by instructor/tutors specifically involved with particular students is a "retrieval" of our past. Implicit within this, again, is the enhancement of individuality and diversity.

Actually, no media are ever "lost." They are forever being reborn, remade and re-presented in an enhanced form as the "content" of newer media. Radio, recordings, film and television are still with us and are being remade and re-presented via the Computerization Movement. With the nearly universal appreciation of what the new computerized and "Web-afied" media can do regarding the instrumentation of rock music, it was inevitable that older, non-electrified instruments would be recalled and re-employed in new ways. The orchestra, both in classical and big band configurations, has been used in numerous ways by numerous groups. Specific instruments, such as the piccolo trumpet in The Beatles' "Penny Lane," have frequently been called into service. Ian Anderson's flute made the same kind of dramatic entrée into rock. And The Beach Boys resurrected the Theremin for "Good Vibrations." (It was actually an electro-theremin invented by Bob Whitsell, for caretakers of trivia.) And George Harrison's sitar in "Norwegian Wood" set off an entire "craze."

What Does the Medium Flip Into When Pushed to Extremes?

Here's where Hegel's dialectic may come into play, because this question — on its own — is hardly self-explanatory. Paul Levinson refers to Hegel's "famous tripartite parser" as a "better known tool for assessing human culture and activity," and uses it to explain McLuhan's question:

> The synthesis in effect retrieves the thesis which had been earlier obsolesced by the antithesis; and when the synthesis goes on to serve as the new thesis and generates a new antithesis, it is performing in a manner akin to what the tetrad calls reversal.[6]

While this is helpful, there is a question begged here: Is this medium now "pushed to extremes"? Further, what does "pushing a medium to extremes" mean in the first place? Hegel is no help here. Levinson, too, is a bit confused by this, and in his personal conversations with McLuhan about Hegel's triad versus his own tetrad, he concluded, "There are no magic numbers of components in tools for social analysis." McLuhan, however, came up with a way, he thought, of resolving the three- or four-fold conundrum: music! He compared Hegel's notions to a three-note chord and his own to a more complex four-note chord! Of course, as Levinson pointed out, there are yet more complex chords that use more notes. Are these superior to a McLuhanesque four-chord tool? As interesting as this playful analogizing might be (after all, it concerns music), I think a different approach might be more helpful when it comes to understanding the role of rock music in America's cultural revolution.

One of McLuhan's fundamental points was that all electronic media are "cool" and that the earlier typographical media are "hot." I think we might profitably explore the possibility that in extremis the colder electronic media may "flip" into something rather "hot." Keeping in mind that McLuhan understood these temperature analogies to be on a continuum, it follows that certain elements of hot media may be more tepid than hot and some might even approach cool. Similarly, some cool media may venture toward a bit more heat than others may. Furthermore, and this is a bit of an elaboration on my part, it is possible to conceive of some cool or hot medium "pulsating" irregularly back and forth. No one medium is likely to be at exactly the same temperature as another and no media are likely to maintain a constant temperature. There are no thermostats in human culture! Moreover, I think it's best to understand this "flipping" idea as more of a warning, something to be avoided if the full blessings of a medium are to come to fruition. McLuhan made this somewhat clear when referring to the "flip side," so to speak, of the Global Village. As we expand our reach to eliminate the distances that separate us, "Big Brother" is invited into our lives.

I take this as one way of conceptualizing the various ways our privacy may be invaded by means of computerization and our being progressively "Web-olutionized." McLuhan was right, and the warning should be heeded. Yet there may be other dangers as well from a given medium's tending toward the extremes.

I think the most profitable way to explore the intricacies of this warning is to keep in mind the basic idea that hot media appeal to, or make use of, fewer senses than do cold media, and as such hot media require less involvement than do cold media in order to be effective. With cooler temperatures, and with more senses appealed to, the individual is called upon to organize and actively grasp what is being communicated. The meaning is not presented to a passive audience. Simply put, hot media slam you over the head with their messages and cold media force you to interpret the message for yourself.

If this makes sense, it then becomes necessary to ask what might precipitate such pulsations. What would bring about this kind of shift in temperature? What would "contradict" (to use a Hegelianism) the essence of cool by warming it up? McLuhan's notion of the media "flipping" when "pushed to extremes" provides something to work with — as long as we keep in mind that a medium's approach to extremity is metaphorical; it does not connote the impending death of the medium. OK, so it may work — analogically — to suggest that hot media pushed to extremes will "boil over" while cool media will "freeze." In so doing, hot becomes cold, and cold becomes hot.

To my mind, this "flipping" or "dialectal reversal" is more than evident in house or techno music and actively practiced on the dance club floors of America's cities and in the raves mysteriously scheduled in out-of-the-way warehouses and parking lots on the fringes of these cities. Chicago and Detroit are often cited as places of origin for house and techno respectively, while the rave phenomenon harks back to the United Kingdom of the 1950s and Continental Europe. America followed suit with expanded subcultural and underground versions in the 1980s and 1990s, and thusly it spread elsewhere. The music may seem atavistic to outsiders, since it is loud, up-tempo and heavily percussive, utilizing the latest electronic synthesizers, the prices of which had dropped precipitously during this time. Of course, it could be argued that the DJs at raves and clubs are pushing the turntable to extremes. But I see this being closer to a retrieval of older technology, or an evolution and mutation of such. In any case, the musical roots were in soul, Latin, disco, funk and even jazz, and the dancing was a mixture of punk-pogo slam and undisciplined rhythmic gyrations. Entering a rave was a little like being an explorer coming upon a hitherto unknown exotic civilization during a religious orgiastic rite of passage. The drug of choice was often an entactogenic drug known as Ecstasy, and also as "E," "X," and "XTC." The emotional effects mimicked feelings of empathy, closeness and love — perfect for the overall Dionysian or Bacchanalian atmosphere of celebratory madness. The complex world of contemporary rock music in the 1990s and beyond, in some of its extreme forms, looked a lot like the so-called primitive world, where music was performed for seemingly unending hours on drums and cymbals for the dancing throngs, where participation was accomplished with the rhythmic motions of the body in unison with others, and where little else was needed. Many studies have been done about the rave phenomenon, but one of the most suggestive is the collection of essays in *Rave Culture and Religion,* edited by Graham St. John. I am particularly impressed by the contributors' collectively viewing raves through the various windows of religious phenomena. The four major parts of the study include: Techno Culture Spirituality; Dance, Rapture and Communion; Music: The Techniques of Sound and Ecstasy; and Global Tribes: The Technomadic Counterculture.[7]

Is the medium of the computer or the Web about to "flip" in some similar way? Actually, I think it doesn't make sense to ask the question in this way. It makes far more sense to ask whether specific instances of electronic media expressions are "warming up"—making it unnecessary for audiences to participate. Moreover, since I am dealing with a cultural revolution—expressed and furthered by rock music—where participation is crucial if the revolution is to succeed, it would be worrisome if rock music were tending toward warmer forms of expression.

It would also be worrisome for computerized media to threaten individuality and freedom, as McLuhan's "Big Brother" warning suggests. We are already aware of how the computer can be used by criminals to "steal" a person's identity, and we are also aware of how the government can misuse the technology to invade our personal lives in the service of "national defense." The alleged excesses of the USA PATRIOT Act (2001) and the Homeland Security Act (2002) passed in the aftermath of the 9/11 terrorist attacks, seem to be perfect paradigms of what McLuhan was warning us about. Panic and terror, he surmised, would both support such invasions of privacy and produce it as well, and thus continue further the invasions. It becomes a self-perpetuating beast. The First Amendment generally prohibits direct, overt intrusions by the federal government into the arts, but such intrusions are all too common in the media and in the business world in general. "Broadcast Standards and Practices (BS&P)" is the technical term for "Office of Censorship" in the broadcast media. Stories and anecdotes of censorship and rock music, and I include all subgenres in this category, are legion, and academic studies abound. Just to mention one, because it includes a variety of articles and extends the subject to other nations, *Policing Pop* by Martin Cloonan and Reebee Garofalo does the academic job pretty well. It also considers the how the censorship of rock and roll was affected in the years after 9/11. They note in their Introduction that not only were "Search and Destroy" by Metallica and all songs by Rage Against the Machine banned from the air, so also were Carole King's "I Feel the Earth Move" and—of course—John Lennon's "Imagine."[8] McLuhan's warning is both apt as well as unnecessary. It is obvious that the technology can be and is being used to thwart the development of revolutionary values. Suffice it to say that in a computerized world, we can expect the powers of censorship to expand. In a global village, the defenders of traditional values have the technology too.

As a brief example, Google's business relationship with China was always a mixed blessing for both dissidents and the repressive regime. Google compromised its belief in open access to gain hordes of subscribers by allowing government censorship. Perhaps Google really did believe that a gradualist approach would eventually work. But in early 2010, China's repressive regime managed to hack into Google's information base in order to find information on the dissidents. As a result the arrangement was put in jeopardy.

It makes little sense, however, to talk about rock music as a whole as far as it is "flipping" from cold to hot, but if we look into some of the subgenres, I think I can find a few examples of how to use this approach. What, for example, made Dylan's "Blowin' in the Wind" (1963) a far more effective protest song than the thrash metal group D.R.I.'s (Dirty Rotten Imbeciles) "Stupid, Stupid War" (1987)? It's the lyrics! Dylan's lyrics are far more indirect and subtle, that is, they are involving, whereas "You can't make me kill," sung repeatedly in D.R.I.'s song, leaves little to the imagination. Participation in order to understand the meaning is not necessary. D.R.I. has "flipped" back into a hot, print media screed with their lyrics. But watch out! This is not a metal vs. folk thing. It has to do with the features of the medium. Metallica's "Blackened," although explicit, refers to the "dance of death," playing with metaphors. Country Joe's "Fixin' to Die Rag" refers to not giving a damn what we're fighting for but the next stop is Vietnam where we're all comin' home in a box — is certainly metaphorical, but it's no longer subtle and in a real sense its metaphor of a box becomes literal in the song. We may sing along (as with the bouncing ball in the film *Woodstock*) but we don't need to be involved. Even more explicit is Pink's "Dear Mr. President" (with the Indigo Girls). It's addressed to President George W. Bush and it asks the question of how he can sleep while the rest of us cry. It isn't at all subtle, and consequently we listen but we do not get involved.

Yet it may still be too simplistic to focus on literal lyrics versus metaphorical lyrics. In fact, it just seems wrongheaded. However, I think it does point us in the right direction: toward the lyrics. Here is where things may go awry — not in the type of language used (literal vs. figurative), but in the particular assemblage of nouns, verbs, adjectives, adverbs and so on. Keep in mind that although the lyrics are the message of the medium of rock music, they are also a medium, as well, that comprises words and language. As such, we should look at the words and language alone — as a medium — quite apart from the messages they convey. The medium of language, in other words, may "flip" into something that is dialectically contrary to its nature. It may also "retrieve" something that has obsolesced. McLuhan's worldview was divided into three eras: oral, written and electronic. Language is at the very beginning — pre-technological — yet it exists in all stages and in all technologies. It is the foundation.

To be effective in the written era, language had to be more or less warm, but in the electronic age, language has to be on the cool end of the continuum. This much seems reasonably clear. We also know that cooler use of language engages the listener or reader and necessarily involves the audience. To be effective, the lyrics of rock music must be cool. (I suppose the pun is inescapable.) But what does this really mean? One answer may seem circular at first, but I think it's not: cool, engaging language must be "lyrical"! (I should probably wait for the scoffing to cease before proceeding. After all, it does sound a little like answering the question, "How do you cook soup?" with "Apply heat.") For language to be "lyrical," it has to appeal primarily to the emotions; it has to be rhapsodic, effusive. Metaphorical language can do this, of course, but not necessarily. Literal language is not exactly designed to do this — quite the opposite. Yet it still can on occasion wax lyrical. The lyrical quality of lyrics is not automatic. Hence, it would seem that the lyrical quality of music is something that the writer or lyricist must creatively bring into being. To put it as succinctly as possible, cool, effective and involving lyrics depend on "creative writing"! It makes no difference whether it's country, rock, metal or hip-hop, good writing is good writing, and a good writer has to create it.

If we return to Chapter 2 and Herbert Marcuse, I think we can flesh out how lyrical coolness can meet the criteria of revolutionary art. Marcuse was adamant in maintaining that genuine revolutionary art must, dialectically, participate in the revolutionary movement and yet not succumb to it. It must be immanent within, and yet transcendentally critical of the movement. The loss of either element would spell the doom of its revolutionary character. Using the examples from above, Pink's "Dear Mr. President" is too immanent, too hot to communicate effectively. The same goes for D.R.I.'s "Stupid, Stupid War." On the other hand, Ed McCurdy's "Last Night I Had the Strangest Dream" may have been too transcendent — it was filled with dreams of people singing and dancing when an end is put to war. There was little connection to the revolutionary struggle. (Well, it *was* written in 1950.)

Good, lyrical, creative writing that both transcends and participates in the cultural revolution seems to provide the appropriately cool temperature. Now here's the "flip" that rock musicians need to avoid at the extremes of the computerization movement: too much reliance on the computer and the Internet. Such an extremity would vitiate both transcendence and immanence as well as make genuine lyrical expressions impossible. Just as the enormous availability of information and the ease of contributing to it has resulted in a veritable plethora of "wikis," often with suspect or unreliable content, so also can the creation of original, lyrical material suffer from the easy use of computerized tools of writing. Computerization may in extremis tend to make writing too easy, too artificial and too boilerplate. If we rely too much on the technology to help us say what needs to be said, we wind up not saying anything at all, and we would neither be participating in nor transcendent over the cultural revolution.

Part Three
REVOLUTION AND REVELATION

There's no incompatibility between observing the world and being tuned into an electric, multimedia, multitracked McLuhanite world and enjoying what can be enjoyed about rock & roll. Rock & roll really changed my life ... I really had a revelation.... It seems clear to me that rock & roll is the greatest movement of popular music that's ever existed.
— Susan Sontag

>Revelation, reveals the truth,
>Revelation
>It takes a revolution to make a solution
>Too much confusion
>So much frustration
>I don't want to live in the park
>Can't trust no shadows after dark
>So my friend I wish that you could see
>Like a bird in the tree
>The prisoners must be free
>— Bob Marley & the Wailers

There was something so utterly and disarmingly preposterous about the fiery purges of rock and roll advocated by the fundamentalist Pastors Peters that it is still difficult to appreciate the fact that, in many ways, their fears and anger were and still are fully justified! Ordained by the Jesus People Fellowship of Minneapolis, Minnesota, the brothers Jim, Steve, and Dan, together with their dad LeRoy, comprised the once formidable family ministry of the Zion Christian Life Center in North St. Paul, a family seemingly dedicated to the total eradication of rock music in our lifetime. Recalling some of the religious protests of the fifties, their many campaigns throughout the South and Midwest during 1979 and 1980 led to the roasting of everything from The Beatles and Blondie (which might be expected) to John Denver and the Osmond siblings (which kind of catches a person off guard). For the moment, it would appear that they haven't yet accomplished their overall goal, but should they falter in their resolve, there are others like them lurking in the woodwork to whom their torch can be passed.

Almost thirty years have passed since the Peters boys warned us about the demonic presence in our culture, manifested in rock music. They have long since left center stage, but their torch has indeed been passed, and none other than the pseudo-rock icon Pat Boone is one of those in whose hands we can find that torch still burning brightly. In one of his weekly blogs on *Worldnet Daily* (September 19, 2009), his warning was clear:

In the last two decades ... laws that once provided order and restraint have been tossed out.... As a consequence, crime and immorality rage across the land today. Rank pornography, not just in plain brown wrappers, but in celebrated movies, whole TV channels, best-selling books and

> magazines — and wholesale across the Internet — has been legitimized. Bizarre practices, condemned throughout history, are now promoted as "rights." Powerful forces and legal groups are waging war against all public expressions of Judeo-Christian faith, and demanding that we be "no longer a Christian nation." ... The bottom line: Like it or not, believe it or not, the end times seem to be drawing near. And unless we Christians exercise our freedoms and our faith, collectively, unapologetically and openly, we will most certainly be facing different, though still savage and deadly, lions.

In an earlier (2008) commentary for *Worldnet Daily*, "Mr. Love Letters in the Sand" ruminated about American youth being the primary target of attack amid our current social turmoil:

> It's the campaign in the world of entertainment to absolutely throw off every restraint, abandon every moral guideline, exploit every taboo and be free to portray and present anything human beings are capable of. In prime time and full color and without any regard for the sensibilities of parents or ministers or censors, or anybody else. On TV, in movies, in music even and especially in video games.

The word "preposterous" is given a completely new dimension by the insistence of such crusades that Satan is somehow associated with rock music. Often the allegation is simply that the musicians have been possessed by demons, the devil's minions. (In this case, the performers wouldn't seem to be evil themselves, merely dupes or victims of the Evil One.) At other times, rock musicians are accused specifically of satanic worship, seen as a most unforgivable offense.

All sorts of evidence is enlisted in support of these and related contentions, much of which is highly esoteric, requiring almost as much blind faith in what the data supposedly portend as that needed to convince oneself of the deity's very existence. Some of the more creative efforts at proof include the various perceptions of "backward masking," all of which declare an allegiance to Satan, presumably for the benefit of those who listen to their records in reverse (the most notorious of the obscure examples being found in Led Zeppelin's "Stairway to Heaven," causing the infamous Black Oak Arkansas among others to lay in a few backward tracks — deliberately, I'm sure — as much for the enjoyment of the brothers Peters and their fellow travelers as for the potential publicity value.) Another strange bit of evidence is the photograph on the interior album cover of The Eagles' *Hotel California*, in which a mysterious figure looks down from a balcony in the Beverly Hills Hotel — perhaps as an explanation for the group's ominous warning that people could check out any time they liked, but they could never leave, since the hotel is alleged to be a satanic church. Other "clear" works of Satan include the group KISS allegedly creating their name from an acronym, "Kids in Service to Satan"); the cover of The Alan Parsons Project album *Eve*, which supposedly shows girls with syphilis sores; the perceived ambivalent sexuality of Mick Jagger, David Bowie, Rod Stewart, Elton John, and Boy George; and the non–Christian as well as satanic imagery used by such groups as Blue Öyster Cult, Black Sabbath, Ozzy Osbourne, Styx, Rush, and Mötley Crüe. Of course, some "authorities" trace Satan's influence back to the inception of rock and roll itself. Others find Beelzebub making his debut with the Rolling Stones' "Sympathy for the Devil" (which, ironically, was a forceful plea against all forms of evil and violence) and their album *Their Satanic Majesties Request*.

Aside from these (to be charitable) questionable interpretations, the very idea of Satan makes sense only to believers like the Peters brothers, who share a certain perspective about the nature of reality — a perspective presumably not shared by any of the people or groups just mentioned. In any case, these accusations have resulted in the destruction of many dollars' worth of record jackets and rock paraphernalia; the records themselves cannot be burned, since flaming vinyl gives off toxic fumes (no doubt further evidence of Satan's influence).

This state of affairs is as sad as it is humorous, for beneath this paranoia is a genuine anxiety at the prospect of even the slightest amount of cultural change. Like Gnostics of all ages, this amorphous collection of sectarians — represented here by the Peters boys — has correctly inferred that to alter or modify perfection in any way is necessarily to make it imperfect. For some, perfection is disclosed through reason alone, while for others it comes through revelation; it makes no difference. Change is inherently wrong. This is only a logical point, of course, but if people truly believe that the truth has been granted to them, then any threat to it will inevitably be opposed with all the strength and cunning that can be mustered, and with any and all means available.

The reason for their anger and anxiety is the justifiable conviction that rock and roll is somehow a challenge to traditional religion, especially Christianity (although, in principle, every institutional religion both ancient and contemporary is attacked). It's a challenge coming from a heretical faith, as they see it. Actually, all cultural revolutions are, at their core, religious movements in the sense that they involve a total commitment. As such, cultural revolutions are nothing less than struggles and conflicts at the deepest levels of our consciousness (personal and collective) — religious warfare. It is not that rock music exemplifies an antireligious state of mind, as its naive critics often assert; rather, its vitality and appeal stems from the fact that it represents and proselytizes for an alternative religiousness. This makes it a much more potent threat to the established order than even its most vociferous opponents believe it to be. Here is the very essence of the cultural revolution taking place in America: the rejection of America's religious heritage and its replacement with something contrary. It is not the devil that's behind rock and roll — it's another "god"!

Before getting too carried away with this idea, we'd better pause to consider precisely what's involved with religiousness. Far from being describable in terms of a set of generalized concepts, religion is a certain kind of experience, and the best account of it was done in 1923 by Rudolf Otto in *The Idea of the Holy*.[1] His approach was to focus on the seminal religious consciousness prior to the inevitable attempts to comprehend its components rationally. This meant characterizing the experience as a set of six non-rational feelings, feelings characteristic of every historical manifestation of religion without exception. These feelings are equally characteristic of the rock experience.

The clearest illustration of this might be to suggest how Otto's six components apply to the typical rock concert. Although not typical, the massive rock music festivals need to be considered in this context as well. Originating with Monterey Pop (1967) and Woodstock (1969) — themselves paradigmatic if not mythic — they continued with, among many others, Watkins Glen (1973), the U.S. Festivals (1982 and 1983), Live Aid (1985), the often bizarre Lollapaloozas (from 1991 and scheduled up to 2018) and even the *usually* bizarre Ozzfests (from 1996 through 2010 and possibly beyond depending on Ozzy's mood and mental and physical health — to say nothing of Sharon's health and her ongoing disputes with Iron Maiden). The Altamont Free Concert has to be considered too — not despite, but because of, the dark events (including one murder) surrounding it.

The first of Otto's six components is the feeling of insignificance, which Otto called *creature consciousness*. It happens when people are overwhelmed by the knowledge of their own utter nothingness, when they sense themselves in the presence of something infinite. For Western cultures, this is most often identified as a god, but it need not be so restricted. Otto preferred calling it the *numinous* — that which is experienced as ultimate. As for the rock revolution, the ultimate is perhaps best understood as the experience of our common humanity and our bond with all other elements of creation. For this is the prime source of the alternative set of values: feelings that combine to negate our sense of superiority and self-importance as individuals and as a species, making us aware of a much larger unity in which everything participates harmoniously. (That's the ideal, anyway.) So what concertgoers experience is a depth dimension of human nature not otherwise available to them in such mass numbers. When you see the throngs swaying together to the music, when you hear them singing, chanting and screaming along with and dancing and even crowd-diving to familiar songs, and when at the end you watch them light thousands of matches or lighters in appreciation, it's hard to come to any other conclusion. The feeling of being in a larger unity cannot be more plainly evident in the nearly universal appellation attributed by commentators to the massive crowds in upper New York state in the summer of 1969: "the Woodstock nation." In many ways, the concert and festival are the paradigm experiences which recordings, disc jockeys, films, and television all seek in some way to emulate.

The second is a feeling akin to *awe* or *dread*, which "first begins to stir in the feeling of 'something uncanny,' 'eerie,' or 'weird.'" Being extremely complex, it "may indeed be so overwhelmingly great that it seems to penetrate to the very marrow, making the man's hair bristle and his limbs quake. But it may also steal upon him almost unobserved as the gentlest of agitations, a mere fleeting shadow passing across his mood." The experience is not at all unpleasant, producing, instead, enjoyably chilling sensations, which the typical rock fan expects from a concert and seeks to reproduce through live recordings. Although highly exaggerated by those for whom rock music is considered innately dangerous, the concert and festival experiences do involve an element of risk, especially since rock performers are well known for their physical and emotional exuberance and enthusiasm, often inciting the audience to similar excesses. Usually this doesn't amount to anything resembling actual danger, but that's not the point. What's important is the illusion or imagery of danger in the concert or festival setting—that's what holds the appeal. Besides, genuine tragedies are exceedingly rare, and often the result of events external to the concert, such as the stampede for thousands of unreserved seats at the 1979 Who concert at Cincinnati's Riverfront Stadium, in which eleven people died. The Altamont disaster cannot be so easily attributed to "outside" factors; rather, it seems more accurate to see these events as being akin to the religious excesses seen in impromptu revival meetings, wherein some devotees swoon into fatal frenzies and others fall victim to the venom of faithless serpents.

The feeling of being *overpowered* by something both mysterious and majestic is the third component. When experienced almost to the exclusion of everything else, the result is mystical absorption. It is a *non*-rational experience—not to be confused with one that is *irrational*. The latter is in opposition to reason, while mystical absorption is beyond reason. We need only recall some of the films and photographs taken at Elvis and Beatles concerts to appreciate fully what mystical identification can mean in this context. Obviously, not everyone at a concert succumbs to this extent, but for those who do the experience is nothing short of ecstatic. Others, not able to achieve this degree of identification, tend to resort to artificial means, the point being that the *desire* for absorption is virtually universal among concertgoers and festival attendees. The use of marijuana at concerts and festivals and Ecstasy or MDMA (3,4-Methylenedioxymethamphetamine) at raves, dance clubs and the like are two of the more prevalent forms of illegal artificial means; alcohol is of course legal. All are intended to produce feelings of unity, euphoria and even sensations of love. Of course, they are not necessary for this purpose, yet they are often sufficient.

The fourth component concerns the experience of *energy* or *urgency*, the sensation of being grasped or controlled by a power or force both intimate with and alien to our nature. When this happens at a rock concert or festival, the atmosphere becomes positively electric, charged with an indefinable presence. Often manifested as a surge forward, it is not an attempt to overwhelm the performers but a response to what is felt to be a fervent invitation to participate. A superlative illustration of this was captured on a kinescope taken from a BBC broadcast called *Don't Knock the Rock* (not to be confused with the film of the same name), with Jerry Lee Lewis, Little Richard, the Animals, and a few other lesser-known performers. As Jerry Lee sings "Whole Lotta Shakin' Goin' On," the studio audience gradually but inexorably moves forward toward him, climbs onto the stage and surrounds his piano—all the while Jerry Lee just keeps pumping out the rhythms and singing one chorus after another. He plays as if possessed, and the audience responds in kind; the music seems to have a life of its own. The whole scene is reminiscent of an altar call following a fire-and-brimstone exhortation. Many concerts and festivals have a mosh pit for the more fervent "believers" wherein the truly blessed may engage in crowd surfing or stage diving.

Otto believed, as the fifth component, that the source of this rapturous experience is forever beyond our rational understanding. It is *wholly other* (and the pun on "holy" was probably not intended). Not only is it beyond our powers of comprehension (which might be a mere difference in degree), its reality is entirely different from ours (which is a difference in kind). In the typically religious understanding of the *numinous*, this may seem obvious, but the same is true for any experience of an ultimate, no matter how this-worldly it might appear. Non-ultimate or finite beings cannot possibly comprehend that which is ultimate, in principle, even if the ultimate is humanity itself. The only way to express whatever is experienced as ultimate or infinite is indirectly, through what Otto called "signs," that is, special persons, places, events, and the like. Paul Tillich expanded on this idea in his theory of symbols, and I'll be making extensive use of this theory in the chapters on Elvis and The Beatles. In the meantime, it should be obvious that, as far as events and occurrences are concerned, the concerts at Woodstock and Altamont are signs par excellence. Still today the "Woodstock Nation" is looked upon as the paradigm of the new order. And Altamont is regarded as the warning of what might happen if Woodstock is taken too literally. Both are "signs."

The sixth and final component, *fascination*, creates a paradox, for to the feelings of dread and horror already mentioned is now added this curiously compelling quality. Fascination, for Otto, is the key for understanding the religious consciousness: "These two qualities, the daunting and the fascinating, now combine in a strange harmony of contrasts, and the resultant dual character of the numinous consciousness ... is at once the strangest and most noteworthy phenomenon in the whole history of religion. The demonic-divine object may appear to the mind an object of horror and dread, but at the same time it is no less something that allures with a potent charm." It is precisely this strange harmony of contrasts that ties together the negation of Elvis and the fifties rebels with the affirmation of The Beatles and the new romanticism of the sixties. It also explains how Simon and Garfunkel on the one hand and the Sex Pistols on the other can possibly represent the same thing—to say nothing of Woodstock and Altamont. It also partially explains the presence of circus-like "freak" shows at Lollapalooza festivals and Ozzfests. It's all, in one unfathomable way or another, "rock and roll."

Together, in an insoluble unity, these six components constitute the fundamental religious experience, although, depending on the cultural conditions, some are more likely to be experienced more intensely than others. In every instance, however, there will be some symbolic reference to an ultimate. The symbol is the singularly indispensable facet of the religious encounter, for in no other way can ultimacy be expressed. Christianity has its cross and the person of Jesus; Judaism has its Torah and the Wailing Wall; Islam has Mecca and Muhammad; and nationalistic religions have their flags and leaders. This holds true for the rock experience as well; a symbolic reference will necessarily be present. Obviously, there are many such symbols, some more inclusive, more potent, and more enduring than others. In the entire history of rock from its twin roots in the Black South and the White Appalachians, and thus in the vast sweep of America's cultural revolution, there have been but two.

At this point it is necessary to sketch out the bare bones of Tillich's theory of symbols so as to prepare the way for the analyses to follow, and again there are six characteristics.[2] *One* is that symbols necessarily point to something beyond themselves. *Another* is that they participate in, are intimately involved with, that to which they point. A *third* is their ability to disclose aspects of reality that are not available to us through any empirical or scientific means. Similarly, as the *fourth* characteristic, they can reveal a connection between the ultimate and the depth dimension of our human existence, a connection that just might be an identity. With respect to this depth dimension, Tillich believed that "there are within us dimensions of which we cannot become aware except through symbols, as melodies and rhythms in music." *Fifth*, they cannot be intentionally manufactured or produced as so many contrivances; symbols are natural developments that must emerge from and be accepted by our collective human experiences. Hence, as the *sixth* and *final* characteristic, they grow and die only insofar as they elicit or fail to elicit a response. Supposedly, "dead" symbols may only be dormant and are thus capable of being reawakened; symbols always embody in themselves the power and vitality of their original meaning, and that which has been truly meaningful for people can never really die.

My contention is that a symbolic interpretation is the only complete way to understand the Elvis and Beatles phenomena and explain their continued influence. To be clear about this, to acknowledge their symbolic stature does not in any way require an agreement with what they stand for; nor does it imply anything about their validity as symbols. Tillich's test for validity isn't all that helpful, since applying it is intrinsically subjective, a matter of personal opinion. Nevertheless, the test quite effectively indicates the one prerequisite for validity, that without which a symbol is intrinsically idolatrous: *self-negation*. He wrote, "Every type of faith has the tendency to elevate its concrete symbols to absolute validity. The criterion of the truth of faith, therefore, is that it implies an element of self-negation. That symbol is most adequate which expresses not only the ultimate but also its own lack of ultimacy." Faith, for him, was the attitude of *ultimate concern*, an attitude shared by everyone, differing only in terms of how it's symbolized. Conflicting symbols, then, imply conflicting faiths, and this is by far the most revealing way to understand the cultural unrest in America: as a conflict between incompatible ultimate concerns, each believing itself alone to be valid.

Symbols never appear in isolation, however. "They are united in 'stories of the gods,' which is the meaning of the word 'mythos'—myth." Tillich wrote. He added, "Myths are always present in every act of faith, because the language of faith is the symbol." If taken literally, a myth becomes idolatrous, so here, too, self-criticism is absolutely vital if myths are to point effectively beyond themselves; something in the mythic tales must express self-negation. When considering the numerous accounts about Elvis and The Beatles in particular, the perhaps overwhelming tendencies toward idolatry must not be overlooked. Equally necessary, of course, are careful observations of the extent to which self-negation is present. It is most important to remember, however, that neither idolatry nor self-criticism are qualities intrinsic to the symbol or myth; they are qualities of the perception — their presence is a matter of interpretation. No matter how many data are available, these qualities are always a matter of what the observer supplies to the experience.

To complete this introduction to the "religiousness" of rock, some of the distinctive attributes of mythology ought to be highlighted. In the classic study by Mircea Eliade titled *The Sacred and the Profane*, the religious consciousness is portrayed as regarding every facet of reality (space, time, nature, and humanity itself) as qualitatively different from the way they are experienced by the nonreligious consciousness. This difference, however, is a matter of interpretation; there are no objective measures to determine which is correct. Both perceive the same empirical data, but they see the data as having conflicting meanings. To be meaningful, reality has to be organized and structured in some way, and the religious way of doing this differs from the profane as dramatically as night from day.

Similarly, American mythology is organized and structured according to one ultimate perspective or another. The established order has its perspective, and the revolutionaries have theirs; what's interesting about this conflict is, again, not the data but how the data are given meaning. No one will deny the existence of the personalities, events, artifacts, and history of rock and roll; but a considerable dispute will inevitably arise over what all of this means. Our interest, of course, is in the meaning given by the cultural revolutionaries, and Eliade's description of the structure of myth is of considerable assistance.

Essentially, from the religious-mythological perspective, certain times and places are qualitatively different from all others, for they hark back to The Beginning, the events of which can periodically be recovered and restored through the use of symbols. The entire cosmos, in fact, is understood to reveal the ultimate to those with the proper perspective. The process of human existence from birth to death is also believed to involve a relationship with the ultimate, and the constant human quest is to establish a proper relationship. Only in this way can life have any meaning. The symbolism of various rituals affords humanity the opportunity for achieving a meaningful and worthwhile life. Eliade felt that none of these attributes of the religious consciousness were totally absent in today's profane world; there are vestiges to be found everywhere, and this extends to the ongoing cultural revolution.

In this final section of the book, I'll be utilizing a selection of ideas adapted from the work of Otto, Tillich, and Eliade in order to comprehend the course that the revolution has taken so far. None of the five chapters is intended to be a chronological account; all are conceptual in nature. Nevertheless, they obviously reflect the five major periods of America's revolution and the meaning I believe to be implicit in them. Although the end is still to be written, one thing is certain: the cultural revolution in America has exposed us to a new and disturbing revelation.

9

Elvis and the Negation of the Fifties

Once upon a time, there was no such thing as rock and roll. Oh, there was the music, of course; at least all the necessary ingredients were present in roughly the correct proportions. But it wasn't called rock and roll, and the naming of it as such was a momentous occurrence.

Most people attribute the naming to Cleveland disc jockey Alan Freed, whose observations of White teenagers buying rhythm and blues records in 1950 led to him programming this music on his *Moondog Show*. Although it was called "race music" at the time, Freed tried to avoid the epithet — and, no doubt, the accompanying bad publicity and poor ratings — by adapting some of the music's frequent phraseology as a more apt description. (He did, after all, have a large White audience.) Probably the term originated from "We're Gonna Rock, We're Gonna Roll," a 1947 song by Wild Bill Moore, or the even earlier but stylistically different, "My Daddy Rocks Me with One Steady Roll," recorded by a variety of artists throughout the 1920s.

By 1954, the term still hadn't achieved widespread acceptance, but the impact of the music had surely been noticed. In the July 3 edition of *Cash Box* that very year, Jerry Wexler and Ahmet Ertegun reflected on what they termed "The Latest Trend: R&B Disks Are Going Pop."[1] They suspected that it was only a matter of time before the trend would blossom into a full-fledged craze. As evidence, they cited reports from the South, where high school and college students had begun dancing to rhythm and blues records instead of those by nationally known artists such as Jo Stafford, Eddie Fisher, Perry Como and Patti Page. They also found it significant that, while "hillbilly fans" apparently initiated the trend, they were quickly followed by the more financially influential "bobbysoxers." When disc jockeys saw which way the wind was blowing, they were not only forced to bring R&B records with them to record hops, they were also forced to change the format of their radio programs. Larger audiences and more advertisers were the immediate results.

After tracing how this music had spread throughout the South and into the North, the Midwest and the West Coast, Wexler and Ertegun made a self-consciously futile attempt to define the kind of music that they were talking about. Resorting to an "ostensible" definition (by examples), they listed about a dozen examples, including songs by Lloyd Price, the Clovers, the Drifters, the Crows, Joe Turner, Ruth Brown, Fats Domino and the Chords. Following the Southern "hillbillies" and the "bobbysoxers," they called it "cat" music. It was music with a beat, with infectious catchphrases and with a "message."

It wasn't long before jukebox operators followed suit by putting "cat" records in more and more ostensibly "pop" locations. Record companies responded by having their contracted artists "cover" the new music. In both cases, although Wexler and Ertegun didn't mention it, White kids were beginning to adopt Black music as their own, and the mixture was bound to be volatile. They concluded their observations with the conviction that cat music was now on center stage in the national music scene. Indeed it was. In fact, in the documentary *Make It Funky* (2005), Ertegun makes a point that I've been stressing throughout, namely, that all music today is, at its core, Black music. Moreover, he meant more than merely American music — he meant all music in every corner of the globe. I think he's right.

In the beginning, White teenagers, initially the social outcasts and then later the mainstream middle class, began listening to and buying Black recordings, music that was expressing an almost total disillusionment with American society and its prevailing values. Underneath the danceable rhythms and high spirits was a mixture of indignation and accommodation, resentment and resignation, none of which was lost on the new White audience. What developed was a curious and potentially explosive conflict, a conflict that could only have arisen under circumstances such as these. For the "message" conveyed by this music was in direct contradiction to what virtually every middle-class White had always been taught about the American dream — equality before the law, hard work leading to success, human dignity for everyone, the guarantee of opportunity, an appreciation of individuality, liberty for all, and the pursuit of happiness. These are all potent ideals, and the more they were believed (consciously or unconsciously), the greater the anger and outrage at being confronted with the fact of their denial to all but the powerful and privileged few. White teens in massive numbers were now stricken with a divided consciousness: the ideals they had been taught were being subjected to a complex attack through the music they had come to love. On the one hand, they had to face the fact that, for a significantly large group of Americans, these ideals seemed like they would never be realized; on the other hand, they had to absorb a whole new set of ideals, some of which violated their accepted beliefs. No other group in America could incorporate this internal dilemma in exactly this way, and, as a consequence, it was from them that the explosion emanated.

When Whites started writing and performing this music on their own, not just covering it, subtle new elements were added — a barely suppressed rage and fury at the hypocrisy to which they had been subjected and a fascination with hitherto forbidden attitudes and pleasures. With these driving forces behind the music, genuine rock and roll was born.

Its parents were the rhythm and blues of Black Americans and the hillbilly sounds of White Southern outcasts. Bill Haley put them together with his cover of Sonny Dae's "Rock around the Clock" in 1954, but it took the film *Blackboard Jungle* to catapult the song into national prominence and notoriety and establish it as a lasting phenomenon. Bill Haley, however, with his recently transformed country and western band, The Saddlemen, could in no way exemplify the material they were playing. What was needed was someone who could merge the two musical traditions into something uniquely one, as a direct manifestation of a singular personality. Neither Fats Domino nor Chuck Berry, who were far more talented and had hits that year to boot, could do it either. None of them, their music aside, had the kind of basic and universal appeal that might accomplish such a merger, and because it was to be a merger of Black and White, a truly charismatic personality would be essential.

As myth would have it, Sam Phillips of Sun Records in Memphis, Tennessee, had been on the lookout for just such a person, and with Elvis Aron Presley — a part-time truck driver for the Crown Electric Company hailing originally from Tupelo, Mississippi — he found him. Wexler and Ertegun couldn't have known it, of course, but just three days after their column appeared in print, Elvis was in the studios of the Memphis Recording Service at 706 Union Avenue (a mere stone's throw from the justly famous Beale Street), readying his first single, "That's All Right (Mama)," for release. The rest of the story is too familiar to repeat, but it's worth remembering that none of it would have happened had not Elvis been familiar with Black music as well as White. (He grew up listening to C&W performers like Hank Williams and Jimmy Rogers, pop singers like Dean Martin and Mario Lanza, blues singers like Big Bill Broonzy and Arthur "Big Boy" Crudup, and the R&B sounds of Johnny Ace and Rufus Thomas.)

Because of Elvis's dissipated final years and death, there is a tendency to dwell on the weaknesses associated with his arrested adolescence, his preference for kinky sex, his dependency on a veritable cornucopia of pharmaceuticals, his perverse pleasure in the martial arts, his inability to accept anything but toadyism from his employees and associates, and, of course, his savage abuse of carbohydrates. To concentrate on his flaws, however, would be to miss his monumental significance for contemporary American culture. No doubt quite apart from his conscious intentions, Elvis forced us to confront the repressive sexual morality so characteristic of our Western religious heritage. Further, his very success pointed out the outrageous disparity between the quantity and/or quality of effort on the one hand and the social rewards on the other; there was no correlation whatsoever, no justice at all. He also single-handedly transformed America's color from White to Black. If this last claim, similar to Ahmet Ertegun's, seems a bit extreme, consider for a moment an analogy—the racial designation attributed to the children of mixed parentage: *never* are they designated as White. Such is the power of racism to regard anything non–White as a contaminant. Similarly, the merger of Black and White music was perceived by nearly every antagonist to have been just such a "contamination"; rock and roll, no matter what its actual origin, was deemed to be Black, and everyone knew what this connoted. The premier playing of "That's All Right (Mama)," on WHBQ's blues program, *Red Hot and Blue* (hosted by Dewey Phillips, no relation to Sam), was so well received that Phillips had to play it repeatedly all evening, and was finally compelled to have someone drag Elvis out of a local movie theater for a live interview. A reception like this stunned everyone involved with the making of the recording; they had no idea what to expect. If they had any expectations at all for the recording, they probably bordered more along the lines of being run out of town on a rail after having been unceremoniously dipped in tar and feathers. Elvis was White, but he clearly sounded Black—a very heady brew for the folks at that time.

Dread

Of all the feelings described by Otto, the one most emphatically characteristic of Elvis was the sensation of dread or horror, all the other components of the religious consciousness being colored by this one feeling. Even those of us who were, openly or secretly, his fanatic devotees found him in many ways terrifying. He wasn't anything like anyone we had ever known or even heard about: he dressed differently, he wore his hair differently, he spoke differently, he moved differently and he sure sang differently. He wasn't Black, but somehow he wasn't White either; he was "something else," something to be regarded with extreme caution. If he struck *us* this way, there was no telling the apoplexy suffered by our *parents* because of him.

Today, all of this might seem laughable, but at the time, it was traumatic. Elvis was authentic—no poseur. His alien-ness was genuine, as Greil Marcus observes *in Mystery Train*: "Elvis didn't have to exile himself from his own community in order to justify and make real his use of an outsider's culture ... as a Southerner and White trash to boot, Elvis was already outside." No matter what became of him later, he would always remain something mysteriously other, unapproachable in some vaguely absolute sense. His self-imposed seclusion within the confines of Graceland obviously contributed to this, but even when he toured, his performances were seemingly intended to perpetuate this image. Even the degeneration of his personal life served to distance him from us. Remember, revulsion, too, is an important facet of Otto's concept of demonic dread.

His alien-ness notwithstanding, his attraction for the youth of the nation was overpowering, mystical even. Given that McCarthyism was still a virulent presence in American life, anything as captivating as this was necessarily viewed as a threat. While there were some who alleged he had a direct connection with "the international communist conspiracy," others, along with Frank Sinatra, believed that rock and roll was "the martial music of juvenile delinquents," with Elvis as their general—leading a pack of black-leather-jacketed hooligans bent on the total destruction of life as we know it.

Elvis was part of, if not the founder of, the whole rockabilly movement, the first fruits of the merger of Black and White. In *White Boy Singin' the Blues*, Michael Bane links this movement with the entire history of rock that followed: "It was rockabilly—the music of Sam Phillips and Elvis Presley—that set the tone for rock. Rockabilly, with its balanced exuberance and fury, its tension between blues and country, Black and White, plucked a chord that is still vibrating strongly. It was rockabilly that decreed rock and roll should be more than just fun; that rock was a revolution in lifestyle as well." Ultimately, this is what scared the hell out of everyone, the specter of rebellion, of the outcasts arising and losing their chains, the haunting prospect that everything familiar and secure was about to be overthrown. As it turned out, everyone was right. It is worth remembering exactly what rockabilly was all about, and Bane recaptures its spirit perfectly:

> Rockabilly, at its very bottom, is mean music, sung through clenched teeth by red-eyed men who look as if they've seen the wrong end of too many broken bottles. That's something we've lost sight of today.... It's easy to forget that beneath the insipid lyrics and the simple rhythms, rockabilly tapped a wellspring of revolution. It dipped below the calm surface of the 1950s to the dark smoldering potential of a generation looking for a voice.... With a few decades safely between the music and us, we can manage to overlook the level of violence inherent in it, the shattering of a way of life. Yet the violence walked hand in hand with an overwhelming sense of joy and release. Rockabilly is a statement of identity and a call to battle at the same time.... To the kids around Memphis, rockabilly was a revolution deeper and more profound than anything that would happen in the 1960s.... What happened in Memphis in the days that followed a certain July afternoon in 1954 was that for a second or two, Black and White understood each other completely, on a gut level, and the world rocked.[2]

The pinnacle figure behind all of this was the overpowering presence of Elvis Presley, who embodied the paradox of violence and joy, anger and release, that Bane notices.

Greil Marcus sees the same kind of paradox in Elvis's music, especially in *The Sun Sessions* (his earliest singles, recorded originally by Sun, but bought and released in 1976 by RCA): "What I hear, most of the time, is the affection and respect Elvis felt for the limits and conventions of his family life, of his community, and ultimately of American life, captured in his country sides; and his refusal of those limits, of any limits, played out in his blues. This is a rhythm of acceptance and rebellion, lust and quietude, triviality and distinction."

Coming out of the South was perhaps the only way this revolution could have begun, for it was there alone that race was the singularly most influential, yet wholly unsuppressed, determinant of consciousness; and only in the South was a strain of Puritanism both practiced and violated with equal and unashamed enthusiasm. According to Marcus, "[I]f Elvis's South was filled with Puritans, it was also filled with natural-born hedonists, and the same people were both."[3] So, just as hordes of unregenerate Southern patriots had been impatiently awaiting, lo, these many years, the South did indeed "rise again," but not quite as they had anticipated.

The Man in the Pink Cadillac

Just as Elvis symbolized the initial period of the cultural revolution, the pink Cadillac convertible came to symbolize him, and no one was more aware of it than Elvis himself. Immediately after buying one of his very own, as a measure of his newly achieved status, he adapted the lyrics of a Black blues song by Arthur Gunter, "Baby, Let's Play House," as an expression of his mixed feelings: "You may have a pink Cadillac/But don'cha be nobody's fool." Marcus believes that "the pink Cadillac was at the heart of the contradiction that powered Elvis's early music; a perfect symbol of the glamour of his ambition and the resentments that drove it on ... Elvis sang with a wish for its pleasures and status. Most of all he sang with delight at the power that fame and musical force gave him: power to escape the humiliating obscurity of the life he knew, and the power to sneer at the classy world that was now ready to flatter him."[4] Michael Bane, too, sees the symbolic link between the man and the car. Prior to Elvis, performers were just "good ol' boys," providing a service for which they were duly compensated; they were not yet "personalities." Bane wrote, "The first time Elvis went tooling down the street in his pink Cadillac all that changed. Elvis was more than simply an extension of his audience. He was a figurehead for that audience, a living, breathing symbol of the revolution that all the kids of the 1950s were beginning to feel. He had come from the community ... but he was no longer part of the community and he never would be again."[5] No observer of contemporary American culture, no matter what his or her personal feelings about Elvis might be, can avoid sympathizing with Greil Marcus's conviction that "Elvis Presley is a supreme figure in American life, one whose presence, no matter how banal or predictable, brooks no real comparisons."[6]

All of this is right on the mark, but it only makes sense when Elvis is correctly understood as a symbol, when his status as such is clearly distinguished from him as a flesh-and-blood person. No matter that his goal was to be another entertainer like Dean Martin, that his songs were written by others (Black and White), that he also recorded some of the ickiest glop ever heard, that he eventually became a parody of himself, and that he would always be known in the Black community as "the White boy who stole the blues." Of such things are symbols made.

In Tillich's terms, Elvis Presley pointed to a dimension of sensuality and pleasure hitherto forbidden (if not unknown) to Whites, and by so doing he smashed the barriers separating the races. It was a level of reality in which he himself lived, not very successfully, admittedly, but the important thing in this is how he was perceived. Sam Phillips may have been looking for just such a person, but it's extremely important to recognize the fact that he *found* him; he didn't *create* him. The distinction is crucial, for if the Presley phenomenon was a deliberate creation, then it could be duplicated. Virtually everyone in the business tried, of course, even Phillips himself, and he tried with some of the very best (Carl Perkins, Roy Orbison, Johnny Cash, and Jerry Lee Lewis). All attempts failed. If anything, the Elvis phenomenon resulted from the unconscious strivings of the vast numbers of repressed American youths who had tasted the forbidden fruit of the tree of rhythm and blues.

The key element responsible for its working out like this was Elvis's Whiteness. A revolution of this character could never have come from those already excluded from a genuine entry into American society. It had to come from those invited inside, from those who were self-consciously benefiting from America's class and racial divisions. In other words, the revolution had to come from the immense patriotic and religiously conservative middle class. No other group could feel the contradictions in numbers sufficient to threaten the status quo. Comfortable Whites would never have been disturbed by the complaints of Blacks or even poor Whites; as so often in the past, their rumblings could easily have been dismissed as sour grapes or simply ignorance, if not the pure manifestation of laziness. However, when they heard these same complaints coming from their own children who had begun to identify themselves with the sentiments of the outcasts, something was bound to happen. Imagine the internal contradictions these youths must have felt when they first adopted this strange music as their own; it was expressing emotions and attitudes dangerously at odds with everything they had been taught, and they were buying into it in ever increasing numbers. At the very least, it caused them to question the legitimacy of their position and the position of the outcasts in American society; at the most, it caused them to do something about it.

The primary carrier of this infection was, of course, Elvis, the symbol. Were it not for his unique status, he would never have been able to broach the legal and moral fortress the established order had erected to protect itself. Writing from a White's perspective, Michael Bane is convinced that "the final element necessary to turn rock into something other than just another musical fad was the element of rebellion, and that had to come from the Whites themselves. Chuck Berry could slyly hint at it, and Little Richard ... could even shout it out, but the message wouldn't become real until it came from one of *us*, as opposed to one of *them*.... A fusion had to take place; a White boy had to sing the blues. There had to be an Elvis."[7] Make no mistake about this. Elvis was no mere imitation; he absorbed the music of both Blacks and Whites, but what resulted was something never before heard. According to Marcus, "It is vital to remember that Elvis was the first young Southern White to sing rock 'n' roll, something he copied from no one but made up on the spot; and to know that even though other singers would have come up with a White version of the new Black music acceptable to teenage America, of all that did emerge in Elvis's wake, none sang as powerfully, or with more than a touch of his magic."[8] We could listen to him and admire him because he was White, but he told us about a world of forbidden pleasures, and when we heard about it, like it or not, we would never be the same.

Some say it all came to an end when he acquiesced to the United States Army's apparently desperate need for his services, although this was years before an opposition to the draft would mean anything. Others mark the decline even earlier, with his leaving Sun Records for the seductive entrapments of the corporate world of RCA. It really makes no difference; Elvis the living man ceased to be. Yet, like a well-known predecessor, he rose again to live on in spirit. The tragic hulk of flesh and blood that Elvis eventually became was committed to the ground at Graceland, but the real Elvis, the symbol, has never died. Shortly before his death, John Lennon, in a *Playboy* interview, remembered all those years ago when rock and roll became a way of life for him: "I think it was 'Rock around the

Clock.' I enjoyed Bill Haley, but I wasn't overwhelmed by him. It wasn't until 'Heartbreak Hotel' that I really got into it." And he was still into it in December of 1980. In the same interview Lennon stressed the distinction between Elvis himself and what he stood for: "The early Elvis records live on without Elvis being a beautiful male animal who swung his pelvis ... I didn't see him. I heard the music first. Afterwards I saw that it did come in a package. But you don't need the package. With Elvis, the basic thing, the basic energy, is on the records."[9] So it is, but even more, it's in our consciousness, ready to be reawakened whenever the occasion arises.

The single most important factor hindering his resurrection for many people is the idolatrous regard in which he has always been held. Perhaps it was unavoidable, but his countless worshippers have never been able to distinguish between the transitory and finite Elvis and the Elvis who is eternal and infinite. In all probability, they've never tried. If so, the only thing remaining to them is the sediment of nostalgia, a dead past. Avoiding idolatry is the only possible way for a symbol to live on eternally, and self-negation is the only means to accomplish this, which is Tillich's criterion for validity.

Despite the fact that many of his fans missed or ignored Elvis's self-negation, there are ample illustrations of how he satisfied the criterion. No doubt he was completely unaware of what he was doing, but his awareness is totally irrelevant. As I've tried to stress so often throughout, what matters is how things are perceived, for there is no other reality available to us. For most observers, Elvis's self-negation actually comes closer to self-destruction. The debauchery of his later years seems now as if it were intentionally undertaken to accomplish the necessary self-negation, but the indications were clear even in his prime. Greil Marcus feels that "he was implicitly presenting his new successful self as a target for his own resentments.... Somehow taking both sides, Elvis could show his listeners just how much, and how little, that pink Cadillac was worth: more and less than anyone would have guessed." He adds in a footnote, "When he smashed through the contradictions of his career with such music, we have Elvis at his greatest." Marcus, I think, is one of the most astute of all the practicing Elvisologists, but his analysis was done while Elvis was still alive, before all the postmortem exposés and maudlin retrospectives complicated the possibility of intelligent criticism. He saw an Elvis who "parodied his menace," an Elvis whose quintessential performance was

> an overwhelming outburst of real emotion and power, combined with a fine refusal to take himself with any seriousness at all. Finding that power within himself, and making it real, was part of the liberation he was working out in his music; standing off from the power, with a broad sense of humor and amusement, was another. This was the saving grace of Elvis's ambition, and a necessary counter to it. It allowed him to transcend his success and his public image ... that casual élan would let him see at least part of the way through the unprecedented adulation he received.[10]

Whether or not this attitude lasted with him to the end can never be known, but what is certain is the fact that he felt trapped by what he had become. This is a sure sign that he was aware of the liabilities of being Elvis Presley.

An infamous episode from his "coronation" (his three appearances on *The Ed Sullivan Show*) suggests the presence of self-negation from the very beginning, for anyone who had eyes to see. Only on the third show was he shown from the waist up; for the earlier two, he was merely requested to control his suggestive body movements so as not to offend common decency. During one song performed in the first or second appearance, however, he was so caught up in the music that he apparently forgot his instructions. When he realized his "wiggling" was beyond the pale, he laughed and crossed his legs at the knees as if to conceal his pelvic parts from the invasive scrutiny of the network censors, knowing full well that the audience would scream with delight. At other times, while singing or during a pause, he would feign a snarl or hint at the possibility of an illicit movement — and laugh at himself. The point is that he knew very well what he was doing, and we knew that he knew, and he knew that we knew that he knew. Ed Sullivan didn't know and our parents didn't know, but we didn't care, and he didn't care either, and we and he knew that too. Under these circumstances, the only people who were taking Elvis with ultimate seriousness were those most distant from him, people who tended to identify the flesh and blood person with what he symbolized. As a result, much of the outrage and adulation was misdirected; attention was mistakenly focused on the swiveling hips of someone who died in 1977 (and thereby calling far more attention to them than even the best efforts of Colonel Tom Parker could ever hope to approximate). Those who knew better, fans and enemies alike, were looking at someone whose presence still lingers with us.

Recognition of Elvis's significance hinges directly on his symbolic stature, which Greil Marcus perceptively acknowledges:

> At his best Elvis not only embodies but personalizes so much of what is good about this place: a delight in sex that is sometimes simple, sometimes complex, but always open; a love of roots and a respect for the past; a rejection of the past and a demand for novelty; the kind of racial harmony that for Elvis, a White man, means a profound affinity with the most subtle nuances of Black culture combined with an equally profound understanding of his own Whiteness; a burning desire to get rich and to have fun; a natural affection for big cars, flashy clothes, for the symbols of status that give pleasure both as symbols and on their own terms. Elvis has long since become one of those symbols himself.[11]

Marcus wrote these words in 1974, three years before Elvis died; he revised the book in 1982, five years afterward, and he chose, quite consciously, to retain the present tense. That says it all.

Illud Tempus

In the beginning was the music, and the music was with Elvis, and the music was Elvis. So it began.

The fifties began with a new testament. The promises of the old order were now in the process of being fulfilled by that which was at the same time ending the old order. The Latinization of "That Time" was Eliade's way of stressing the paramount importance of the "Time of Origin," the events of which are always preserved in myth and symbol, making its return and re-actualization an eternal possibility. Michael Bane, too, is sensitive to this dimension of the cultural revolution: "The late 1950s mark the beginning of the rock and roll mythology, the gospel according to rock."[12] And forevermore, this would be the essential spirit to be recaptured, the final measure of authenticity, the time before which there was only darkness upon the face of the nation.

None of this should imply, however, that there were no roots that led up to this moment. Any decent history of American music would dispel that impression immediately. But we are not really dealing with facts of this kind; our attention is on the mythic account, *interpreted* facts organized in such a way as to provide a meaning for whatever data actually exist. And there's quite a bit to work from in this case. By now, of course, many of the musicians' names are legend, but many more are known only to those who've devoted their lives to a study of rock's prehistory. Sadder still is the fact that an unknown number of names are lost for good, no one ever thinking that their many contributions would amount to anything worth noting for future generations. In any case, this music has a past that ought not be forgotten.

From its African roots, which took hold in the South and traveled north along the banks of the Mississippi, to its eventual merger with a variety of old–English traditions hidden away in the hills of Appalachia, rock and roll was played, sung, and performed by countless musicians of varying degrees of talent and skill. Elvis certainly didn't create his distinctive sounds ex nihilo; more accurately, he gave a shape and meaning to the musical traditions he found readily available in the multiracial culture of the South. It was a shape and meaning that the world had never before experienced, something wholly unanticipated.

According to Eliade, "Every myth shows how a reality came into existence, whether it be the total reality, the cosmos, or only a fragment.... To tell how things came into existence is to explain them and at the same time indirectly to answer another question: Why did they come into existence?" A factual account is obviously important, but far more important for our human existence is the meaningfulness of it all, and this is the overriding purpose of myth. Without providing a meaning, a direction, or an overall scheme, a myth could not fulfill its raison d'être; indeed, it would not be myth. Eliade added that "the supreme function of the myth is to 'fix' the paradigmatic models for all rites and all significant human activities," and he listed such activities as eating, sexuality, work, education, economics, and war.[13] In other words, everything.

As for Elvis, in his very being he showed us how it all came about; he was, after all, a White boy singing the blues, and the message wasn't lost on anyone, least of all our parents. Those old enough may recall the now laughable rivalry between Elvis and Pat Boone. Pat covered some of Fats Domino's songs and, for one brief moment, embodied the "clean" (non–Black) side of rock and roll. He was one of the establishment's attempts to co-opt something it could neither appreciate nor understand. He was at that time the only safe alternative to Elvis available to the establishment, and his white bucks and ducks seemed deliberately fashioned to indicate just a bit more than the color of his favorite beverage. Guess whom our parents preferred?

As has happened so often before with the founders of cultural movements, an outcast led the way and became the model for his followers to emulate. If Elvis could walk on what was, for then, the "wild side," then so could we. If Elvis could express uninhibited sexuality, then we'd try it too. If Elvis could regale, to the point of obscenity, in what everyone knew to be wealth and privilege not "earned" through hard work, then our attitudes toward work would be transformed accordingly. Our parents worried about our affecting the outward trappings of the Elvis imagery—a black leather jacket, long sideburns, a DA (duck's ass) haircut, a certain suggestive demeanor of body movement, and a well-practiced, disdainfully cavalier turn of the upper lip. The trappings were important, of course, but the real changes weren't visible; they took place in our consciousness. Even the vast majority who adopted none of the visible signs was irreversibly influenced, and this includes all the "squares" who ostensibly hated everything Elvis stood for. No one escaped. Elvis the symbol told us how it all happened and what it all meant. It took some time for everything to sink in, but once it did, we were never the same.

Through appropriate rituals, the mythic time of origin is infinitely recoverable and the founding events eternally repeatable. According to Eliade, every religious festival ritually makes present a sacred event that originally took place *in illo tempore* (at that time). In this way, the participants in the festival can become contemporaries of the earlier mythic event. In his last years, Elvis himself assumed the role of re-actualizing his mythic past in the highly ritualized setting of his concerts. (The 1968 comeback special on TV is a notable exception in only one respect: it was superlative, a work of genius.) During his typical arena concerts, usually toward the end, he would go through a medley of his early classic hits, attired, as he always was in his later concerts, in what for lack of a better phrase can only be described as an "Elvis suit"—a gold lame, white or black sequined monstrosity—girdled with a wide ornamental belt (designed partially to hold in his girth) and a buckle that could stop an artillery shell; accented with a raised collar at least four inches high; framed with an immense, swooping cape that he would unchain with a ceremonial flourish at an appropriately dramatic moment; and designed to reveal an equally ostentatious shirt that displayed every chest hair he could possibly cultivate. During the medley, one of his sycophants would hand him a continual supply of cheap silky scarves, which he would ritualistically pass around his neck and toss out into the worshipful crowd (overflowing with aging men practically dragging their sideburns over their shoulders, and their plumpish wives sporting their own distinctive bleached beehive coiffures).

A sad and tacky exercise in nostalgia? Perhaps. Yet it was also much more than that, as one of John Lennon's friends found out. "A friend of mine," Lennon reported, "a big Elvis fan, bigger than I was, went to see him.... When he saw him in Vegas, I asked my friend how he was. He said, 'Well, if you sort of half shut your eyes and pretended, it was heaven.'"[14] Ordinary, chronological time doesn't permit this kind of reversal; mythic time, however, demands it. "Religious man," who for Eliade is the only fulfilled human, "feels the need to plunge periodically into this sacred and indestructible time. For him it is sacred time that makes possible the other time, profane duration in which every human life takes it course." It is not, however, "a rejection of the real world and an escape into dream and imagination"; on the contrary, "it is at once thirst for the sacred and nostalgia for being."[15] More than anything else, Elvis's audiences came to reorient themselves to something they felt to be timeless, the source of everything they had come to be. This was no simpleminded journey down memory lane; this was their attempt to get in touch with their existential roots.

Before Elvis, there were rich and vital musical traditions among both Blacks and Whites, but there was no revolution. Before Elvis, there was even something called rock and roll, but there was no revolution. Before Elvis, there was rage and alienation throughout the entire country, barely held in check by a dogmatically repressive and subtly authoritarian regime, yet still there was no revolution. Before Elvis, there were many people who embodied perfectly the tensions that lay just beneath the surface of the supposedly placid fifties, but they were neither symbolic nor actual revolutionaries. Hence, as John Lennon observed on hearing about his death at Graceland, "Before Elvis, there was nobody."

Vignettes of Negation

If Elvis symbolized the negation of the prevailing attitudes towards sex, race, and work, there were countless others who were living the negation. Two groups in particular were the beats and the greasers.

After the Soviet Union's wholly unforeseen triumph in putting the first artificial satellite in orbit around the earth (*Sputnik*), beats came to be known as beatniks, to suggest in the suffix their leftish leanings did not go unnoticed. A more perceptive appraisal came from *On the Road*, Jack Kerouac's literary tone poem on the American hipster. Aside from virtually defining what it meant to be beat, Kerouac and his North Beach associates named an entire generation. Although the beats were few in number, their influence was staggering. Those who didn't emulate them in some way were frightened by them, but no one could ignore them. In one of those paradoxes so incredibly strange that it necessarily escapes a mind attuned only to the rational, the very people who had the most to fear from what the beats stood for were also the very ones to propagate and popularize the beat movement. The established order devoted far more attention to it than would seem to have been warranted— news coverage, editorial lamentations, sociological and psychological analyses, religious outrage, and, most important of all, commercial exploitation.

Many people, including myself, first encountered the beat movement without meeting a single genuine beat. One colleague of mine in high school, for example, affected the style pretty well, and we all went along with his charade, because, well, real beats were hard to come by. On Saturday nights, a group of us would hang out at one of Baltimore's hip "coffeehouses," the Flambeau, and pretend to be hipper than thou, snapping our fingers to the absurdist poetry and minimalist music while sipping expensive and oddly named herb teas and spiced coffees. Last, and certainly least, was Maynard G. Krebs, TV's picture of the lovable, harmless, and slightly touched-in-the-head beatnik, whose weird and unthinkably wild clothing consisted of dungarees and a sweatshirt. Thus, in the strangest of ways, were most of us introduced to the beat movement, at least in style if not in substance. The idea that a counterculture group existed was what was propagated, causing us to wonder what it was all about. And so the movement was spread farther and wider than if the established order had left it well enough alone. What we eventually learned from the beats mirrored precisely the messages we were receiving from rock and roll; the only significant difference was the beats' enjoyment of something called marijuana, and of that, we would learn more later.

Greasers were another matter entirely. They challenged the same values but in a very different way. The beats were essentially peaceful and nonaggressive, almost to the point of isolationism, while the black leather jacket crowd presented the image of violence and terror. Again, this was far more the result of creative publicity than hard, verifiable fact, but the image is what counted. I remember asking my parents for a black leather jacket for Christmas one year; I also remember the consternation that this request caused them, yet they never explained why such an artifact had this effect on them. (My gift turned out to be a rather bulky *brown* leather jacket, which I consigned to my little brother as soon as decency and good taste would permit.) Unlike the beats, who tended to relate to each other in small, amorphous, and ever-shifting groups, the greasers were gang oriented. Everyone needs some kind of support group for the development and protection of personal identity, but a gang gives its members a sense of power as well, which every youth at that time lacked, simply by virtue of youth. Although the greasers were just as small a minority as the beats, their influence might actually have been even more disproportionate; we didn't want to join them, or God knows, even associate with them, but we sure envied them. Marlon Brando and James Dean weren't youth heroes for nothing.

Of the three issues most obviously and intimately involved in the fifties negation, race topped the list. In a very real way, all other facets of the negation were implicit in the toppling of the prevailing attitude toward race relations. What was being negated was the notion that Whiteness was equivalent to goodness, both moral and non-moral, (for example,

"That's mighty White (meaning decent) of you," and "If it's White, it's all right"). This equation had been so ingrained in our culture that it wasn't until Diana Ross and the Supremes that White males could openly acknowledge that Black women could be just as beautiful and desirable as White women. And still today, it remains the case that "innocent until proven guilty" is much more of an unrealized ideal for Blacks than for Whites. Yet this disparity is no longer an openly acceptable part of our culture, as it once was. One of the most interesting illustrations of how this racial equation was negated has to do with Johnny Otis, a White man who consciously chose to live Black and play the blues. Never before was it so clearly apparent that Blackness and Whiteness are the result of social conventions, not physical characteristics (except in minor and unimportant ways). For him to "pass" in the opposite way would have been unthinkable without the destruction of the racist equation, at least for him and all those who accepted and admired his "passing." It's also interesting that this term has virtually ceased being used — by everyone, White or Black. With the inception of rock and roll in the fifties, the destruction began in earnest, an irreversible process that continues to this day.

The second most influential negation concerned sexuality, and again, what was being destroyed was an equation involving goodness: goodness associated with a certain set of sexual mores, notably virginity or abstinence, self-restraint, male dominance, exclusivity, procreation, heterosexuality, all of which were based on the religiously sanctioned monogamous marriage. Sex was unclean, a weakness to be strongly resisted, an understandable drive for men but a craven urge for women; its ultimate (and often singularly) justifiable purpose was to fulfill the divine command to multiply and subdue the earth. Rock and roll's attack on this ideology has been so massive as to be impossible as well as pointless to document. The very term "rock and roll" is sexual in origin, and "dance" is used euphemistically so often that, for all practical purposes, "to dance" is to attack the inherited equation. In the music, sex is portrayed positively, a part of our physical nature to be enjoyed, desirable in and of itself, good for no other reason than that it's pleasurable. Other implications of the attack would have to be worked out in the future (especially the sexist baggage and the sexual orientation luggage), but for the moment, it was sufficient to undermine the rectitude of the traditional standards, replacing the fundamental idea that sex is bad with its opposite. After all, the usual reason given as to why rock and roll was so devilishly corrupting was sex, and those who felt (and still feel) this way were pretty close to the mark. An interesting change has taken place, however, since the attack was first engaged. In 1958, at what seemed to be the pinnacle of his career, Jerry Lee Lewis was ruined because of a sex scandal, having married his cousin, age fourteen (or thirteen, or twelve, depending on the source). The specific charge was incest, but rock and roll was deemed to be the underlying cause. Significantly, this was the last time a sex scandal ruined any rock and roller's career; soon a "sex scandal" had pretty much the opposite effect.

The third and final activity singled out for negation was the complex set of norms commonly referred to as the Protestant work ethic: the idea that effort, skill, and talent are in some mystical way directly proportional to success and rewards; the idea that work itself is desirable as an ultimate value; and the idea that a morally good person would necessarily be hardworking. So again, there is an equation: work is intrinsically good as an end and necessary as a means. Because of the music, however, it was becoming increasingly obvious that work and success were unrelated; not only were the founders of the rock tradition never adequately compensated for their contributions, but luck and aggressive promotion were playing a much larger role than anything else. How else can the likes of Frankie Avalon and

Fabian be explained except through the well-financed campaigns of their manager, Robert Marcucci (about whom the 1980 film *The Idolmaker* was made)? If hard work wasn't very effective, neither was it desirable. If anything, it was a means to an end, but the end was pleasure. The Protestant work ethic was being confronted with nothing less than the gospel of hedonism, an unequal contest if there ever was one.

Often cited as the best biography written about "the king," Jerry Hopkins's *Elvis: A Biography* and its sequel have both been updated and re-released. What's important about this is not so much the information and Hopkins's interpretations — what's important is the acknowledged need for it to be reissued! But it's not surprising if you keep in mind Elvis is nothing less than a symbol.

The negation of the fifties came very close to what some philosophers have termed "negative freedom," the freedom *from* certain interferences and barriers. The removal of these obstacles was the immediate project, but we must never lose sight of the fact that nothing less than freedom and individuality were the ultimate aims. What this meant in positive terms would be spelled out in the sixties, but the sixties could never have happened had the fifties not cleared the way. And so if anyone captured the spirit of this negation, and embodied its threefold attack in his person so perfectly that the very mention of his name can evoke its power still today, that person would have to be — still today — none other than Elvis Presley.

10

The Beatles and the Affirmation of the Sixties

The sixties began with a bang, three of them to be exact, all presumably fired from the sixth-story window of the Texas School Book Depository in Dallas, Texas, at 12:30 P.M. on Friday, November 22, 1963. Thus are we provided with the one infallible criterion for identifying the sixties generation: If it has been indelibly etched into your consciousness where you were when you first heard the news (and if Pearl Harbor is *not* a part of your consciousness in this way), then no matter what your social, political, or cultural allegiances, either then or now, you are a "child of the sixties." Far too much has been made over participation in one or more of the various, highly visible counterculture groups, such as the New Left, the Black militants, the hippies, the Student Nonviolent Coordinating Committee (SNCC), the Congress of Racial Equality (CORE), or any number of others, as the distinguishing measure, when everyone was equally affected and permanently changed by the overwhelming reality of the assassination — not in the same way, of course, but just as thoroughly as the Pearl Harbor generation was by its key event.

It was more than a murder, more even than an assassination; it was the destruction of a dream, the hope that a better world was about to happen. Kennedy brought to our national consciousness the belief that we could appreciate the past without being trapped by it, that there was a promising future just ahead. All we needed to do was to work together and all of our national and international problems would eventually be resolved. America was in for a new day in the sun. There you have it — Camelot.

No matter that John F. Kennedy was perceived far differently than what the facts can support. Even some of the most sympathetic accounts of his presidency point out that his legislative accomplishments were slight and his innovative proposals more often than not the products of other minds. Further, on civil rights, his support was less than wildly enthusiastic, resulting more from political expediency than moral conviction. In foreign policy, the nearly universal opinion is that he redeemed himself for the debacle at the Bay of Pigs with his courage and decisiveness in dealing with Khrushchev in the Cuban missile crisis. This is an opinion derived undiluted and unaltered from a frame of mind structured by the Cold War. His "redemption" only makes sense, as such, to those whose consciousness has been set by the remembrance of Pearl Harbor, those who viewed the war in Vietnam as if it were like our war with the Japanese. Speculation still abounds as to what might have happened in Southeast Asia had Kennedy survived, but this kind of fruitless activity reveals more about the speculators than anything else. What really matters is the meaning John Kennedy had for the American people, not what he did, didn't do, or might have done; his stature as a symbol is what's important.

Looking a bit more deeply into the Camelot mythology, we see that something else was destroyed in Dallas along with the dream of a particular kind of national destiny. It was the unspoken and mostly unconscious assumption that difficult and dramatic changes could be expected to occur in an evolutionary fashion. No radical measures would be required: no fundamental break with the past, no questioning of ultimate values, and certainly no introduction of new and conflicting values. If anything new were necessary, it would be acceptable only insofar as it could be modified and absorbed so as not to threaten the received tradition. This, too, died in Dallas.

The multifaceted consequences of the assassination help partially to explain the magnitude of the shock, disbelief, and outpouring of emotion throughout the nation and the world that followed. Many world leaders followed along behind the funeral cortege. Even Fidel Castro expressed sorrow at the news. More than likely, all of them were experiencing the loss of the unspoken assumption too. We mourned for a shattered future, but also for the peaceful transition that was to take us there. Kennedy had symbolized both, and with his death, we were left with a strange feeling of emptiness, a loss of direction and a failure of confidence. "He was a friend of mine," sang The Byrds, "His killin' had no purpose/No reason or rhyme." Such feelings rang true no matter what worth there might be to the many and varied conspiracy theories. Even more to the point was "He never knew my name/Though I never met him/I knew him just the same." All of us, like The Byrds, felt that we knew him but what we really knew was what he meant to us. Years later, and from a very different rock musical perspective, Lou Reed would still recall "The Day John Kennedy Died" as the death of a dream, even when the dream he sang about bore little resemblance to John Kennedy's. Kennedy spoke to something far deeper within us than our political convictions, and he represented something that would never again be. That's how we felt at the time.

It was only fitting that all television and radio programming ceased normal operations to cover the martyrdom in its entirety. Despite our divergent religious beliefs, political affiliations, ethnic backgrounds, and patriotic sympathies, we all sat, stunned, in front of the television for the duration. All normal activities had come to a complete halt (even cloistered nuns were released from their religious isolation to watch), as the reality of it all began to sink in. And so for a short time, we as a nation were united. We who had at one time playfully asked "Lyndon Who?" were now prepared to entrust to him our destiny. A national consensus such as that experienced by perhaps only one other president, Franklin D. Roosevelt, was his.

But this unity was not to last. Exactly eighty days later, cracks were to appear that would grow ever wider. The process was imperceptible at first, but in retrospect, it was inexorable. For on Sunday, February 9, 1964, America was invaded by the British. To be sure, there were only four of them, but they were carrying ideas and values that were directly at odds with traditional American beliefs, ideas and values that would, for many Americans, fill the void left by the assassination.

When Ed Sullivan's plane was forced to circle London's Heathrow Airport in the middle of the night in order to permit something called The Beatles to land first so that they could be transported safely through thousands of their screaming fans, he decided then and there to sign them for his "really big shew." He didn't care what kind of act they were; if they could draw that kind of crowd at that hour, he wanted them. Thus it was, on that Sunday evening in February, that we sat down in front of our TV sets to watch, as we usually did, *The Ed Sullivan Show*. When it was over, we weren't quite sure what had happened, other than being introduced to a new prefix for the word "mania," but one thing was certain: America had just surrendered to these four British invaders.

Bob Dylan and I (and probably many others as well) have one thing in common: neither of us would admit at the time how much The Beatles had overwhelmed us. Anthony Scaduto reports, in *Bob Dylan: An Intimate Biography*, that Dylan laughed condescendingly along with his friends at how faddish and juvenile their music seemed, suitable only for the listening enjoyment of those still committed to satisfying their oral fixations with a stick of bubble gum: "We were driving through Colorado, we had the radio on and eight of the Top Ten songs were Beatles songs. They were doing things nobody was doing. Their chords were outrageous, and their harmonies made it all valid.... But I kept it to myself that I really dug them. Everybody else thought they were for the teenyboppers, that they were gonna pass right away. But it was obvious to me that they had staying power. I knew they were pointing the direction where music had to go ... in my head, The Beatles were it. In Colorado, I started thinking but it was so far out I couldn't deal with it — eight in the top ten. It seemed to me a definite line was being drawn. This was something that never happened before."[1] I wonder how many of those driving along with him that day were keeping the very same secret, embarrassed or afraid to admit that the times were indeed changing, but perhaps not in the ways they had always anticipated. My guess is that quite a few were keeping it to themselves.

In my own case, I was heavily into the classics, refusing to admit to any interest whatsoever in popular music; not jazz (music for the terminally obscure); certainly not rock and roll (music for the witless); and not even the new folk trend, which was attracting so many refugees from rock who were searching for some way to express a growing uneasiness with American society (music for pseudo intellectuals). This was possibly my own way of distancing myself from an increasingly alien society, although I was hardly aware of it at the time. After returning to college from our extended Thanksgiving break (because of the assassination and funeral), I was in the mood for some serious discussion of the impending crises, especially concerning civil rights. (Lyndon Johnson, after all, was a Southerner.) My ex-roomies offered the best prospects, since our ethical convictions about society were very similar and were leading us to seminary after graduation. Expecting to hear the latest from Joan Baez or Ian and Sylvia emanating from their hi-fi, folkies that they were, I was startled to find them listening intently to top 40 radio, madly switching stations and barely acknowledging my presence.

Then it happened. "Listen to this!" they insisted, turning the volume up higher. They had come across "I Want to Hold Your Hand" somewhere in the middle of the song. It was something I had never heard before — the harmonies, the bass, the volume, that incredible falsetto on "hand" — chills went immediately up my spine. Who is this? I wanted to ask, but didn't. It would have severely compromised my sophisticated detachment, so I feigned disinterest. "Isn't this different?" they asked, obviously excited, and certainly not expecting any disagreement.

"It sounds just like any other rock and roll to me," I lied, with as much haughty condescension as I could muster without offending them too much. I had, of course, already heard about The Beatles from the news, but I had never actually heard them. The music was overwhelming, but I couldn't admit that. It had dredged up those long-forgotten memories of hearing "Rock around the Clock" and "Heartbreak Hotel" for the first time. This time, however, there was an enormous difference: Bill Haley and Elvis Presley had been tearing something down; these guys were building something up; you could hear it in just the first few bars.

It hadn't happened overnight, of course. Ever since The Beginning in 1955, England had been going crazy with hastily formed skiffle bands, one of which was The Quarrymen, out of Liverpool. America had exported the rock revolution to England, and in 1964, England returned it with interest. In the meantime, The Quarrymen had paid their dues in dingy little clubs, playing impossibly long hours in the strip joints along the Reeperbahn in Hamburg, losing two of their original members, adding a new drummer from Rory Storm and the Hurricanes, acquiring a devoted and sensitive manager, and, of course, changing their name.

What was about to happen (in England, America, and throughout much of the Western world) was a change of consciousness: the complete reorganization, reinterpretation, and reevaluation of the perception of reality in accordance with a new and contrary set of ultimate beliefs and values. In his *Invitation to Sociology*, Peter Berger describes this as a conversion experience or (to avoid the religious connotations) the process of "alternation," in which people opt for a system of meaning radically at odds with the one they abandon. Most important, a change like this is comprehensive — everything is altered. Within our consciousness, even the past is "malleable and flexible, constantly changing as our recollection reinterprets and re-explains what has happened." Conversion is thus "an act in which the past is dramatically transformed." Most of the time we undergo such alternations unconsciously and haphazardly, stumbling "like drunkards over the sprawling canvas of our self-conception, throwing a little paint here, erasing some lines there, never really stopping to obtain a view of the likeness we have produced." Berger maintains, however, that "there are some cases where the reinterpretation of the past is part of a deliberate, fully conscious, and intellectually integrated activity. This happens when the reinterpretation of one's biography is one aspect of conversion to a new religion or ideological weltanschauung, that is, a universal meaning system within which one's biography can be located."[2]

Obviously, not everyone had such a conversion experience, an alternation of weltanschauung. Also, when it did happen, it was neither instantaneous nor completely conscious. Nor has the opportunity for its happening ceased. The fifties had shaken the foundations of the established order and had left an entire generation expecting something new. The assassination made it clear that the something new wouldn't be forthcoming from those succeeding Kennedy. The problem wasn't just that there was no longer a charismatic leader who could lead the way; rather, people came to the unsettling realization that the prevailing order was intrinsically incapable of providing anything new. It had given us its best and its brightest (as David Halberstam so aptly put it), but these people were sincerely committed to a set of fundamental values that many of us could no longer unquestioningly accept. Along with everyone else, we were shocked into insensibility by the killing that had neither rhyme nor reason, and we mourned Kennedy's passing and all that he meant. Yet those of us whose consciousness had been troubled by the vision of the man in the pink Cadillac, who had heard the voice crying in the wilderness, were ready and waiting for a new beginning. We had been left with no viable alternative to the established order.

Into this void, straight off of their BOAC jet from London, stepped those four lads with their outrageously long hair. Two days later they ascended the very stage that Elvis had ascended eight years earlier and underwent the same rites of coronation that had confirmed him king. That evening Elvis relinquished his crown and even sent a congratulatory telegram, giving substance to a story so often retold, that Brian Epstein was the only manager to claim his group would be bigger than Elvis — and be right.

Fascination

Just as dread colored every aspect of the Elvis phenomenon, so fascination was the overwhelmingly pervasive quality with regard to The Beatles. Together, these two feelings create the "strange harmony of contrasts" referred to by Rudolf Otto as the key characteristic of the religious experience. Although both Elvis and The Beatles have given expression to the other's primary sensation as well, their one quality has been so dominant that every other element of the religious experience is subsumed within it.

At this point, an extended reference to Otto is necessary if The Beatles' exemplification of fascination is to be fully appreciated. Most often present in traditional religions as a quest for some kind of salvation, the feeling of fascination incorporates the desire and yearning for something ultimate. Throughout history this longing has taken many different and seemingly incompatible forms, but

> in all these forms, outwardly diverse but inwardly akin, it appears as a strange and mighty propulsion towards an ideal good known only to religion and in its nature fundamentally non-rational, which the mind knows of in yearning and presentiment, recognizing it for what it is behind the obscure and inadequate symbols which are its only expression.[3]

At its peak, the feelings associated with fascination account for "the unutterableness of what has been yet genuinely experienced, and how such an experience may pass into blissful excitement, rapture, and exaltation verging often on the bizarre and the abnormal." If these comments are divested of Otto's conviction that only something supernatural (the numinous) can possibly provoke such feelings, Beatlemania becomes intelligible as more than a teenage fad: it becomes apprehensible as the phenomenon of mass conversion.

John Lahr wrote in the December 2, 1981, issue of *The New Republic* that "'Beatlemania' was a misnomer. Beatles fans were not so much hysterical as spellbound. The Beatles' music was a form of sympathetic magic, and The Beatles were local divinities who could change the mood and the look of their times by a song, a style, a word." The Beatles themselves were caught off guard by such adulation and were never comfortable with or fully recovered from the role imposed on them. "At first The Beatles didn't understand either their healing power or their shamanistic role," Lahr continued, citing a remark by John Lennon in support: "It seemed that we were just surrounded by cripples and blind people all the time. And when we would go through the corridors, they would be touching us."[4] The role had its benefits, of course, but there were liabilities as well, and ever since, they have tried to separate themselves from this mixed blessing. Each of them came to know, more than anyone else could possibly know, how much of a burden being a Beatle had become. They reacted by partially accepting and partially rejecting the burden, using their power to accomplish certain goals and using it against themselves as well. They had the power to shape popular consciousness, the greatest power there is, but they were trapped; no matter what they did, they couldn't rid themselves of it. In their earlier days, they had often voiced their mutual commitment to make it "to the top," but they had achieved far more. They had become the long-awaited promise for filling the void.

The darker side of the phenomenon was evident from the beginning. The four musicians embodied Otto's paradox so perfectly that religion is the only appropriate characterization for Beatlemania. Their early Teddy Boy image, though not an expression of their fundamental nature, was nevertheless a genuine manifestation of their anger at having been relegated to working-class oblivion. None of them had shown any promise whatsoever of becoming anything different from all their contemporaries, who were similarly condemned. In a fairly rigid class system, such as that in England, the chances of breaking free without showing exceptional promise are practically nonexistent. Knowing this, as each of them surely did, made for a potentially explosive situation. As more recent events in Britain have revealed, the frustration and anger among working-class youths hasn't abated very much in the intervening years, if at all. It is from this repressive social context that The Beatles' negation had its source — theirs and everyone's who saw their lives leading nowhere, inhibited and determined by a political structure that ignored them (at best). The Beatles, of course, broke free, and in so doing, they gave voice to the hopes of everyone who was left behind. Perhaps this explains why their anger was so often tinged with the brash and carefree playfulness that we so often associate with them.

Both of the early biographies are written, however, from a decade's perspective (*The Beatles* by Hunter Davies and *Shout!* by Philip Norman), as well as the personal recollection written from the same period by their friend, business associate, and manager Peter Brown (*The Love You Make*), tell the tale far more effectively than needs to be done here. All three document the unresolved and barely restrained tension that's so evident in all of the group's finest music. Examples are legion, but a sample from The Beatles' various musical periods would no doubt include the following: "I Saw Her Standing There" from their first American album, *Meet The Beatles* (which opens with what Greil Marcus believes to be Paul shouting "One, Two, Three, Fuck!"); "Run for Your Life" from *Rubber Soul* (which incorporates a line from an old Elvis song — "I'd rather see you dead, little girl, than to be with another man"); "Taxman" (Harrison's scathing indictment of a government that would tax even the pennies on the eyes of a corpse) from *Revolver* (itself an interesting play on words); "Baby, You're a Rich Man" from *Magical Mystery Tour* (satirizing the "beautiful people," including themselves); practically everything on *The Beatles* (popularly known as "The White Album") so egregiously misused by Charles Manson ("The Continuing Story of Bungalow Bill," "Happiness Is a Warm Gun," "Piggies," "Why Don't We Do It in the Road?," "Helter Skelter," and the two versions of "Revolution"— nos. 1 and 9); and even "Her Majesty" from *Abbey Road* (exemplifying at the end of the Beatles' career the class antagonisms that were there at the beginning). Yet there was also something positive in each of these songs, something promising. The quality of affirmation was never far removed from even the darkest and most negative music, for hidden within was the implicit and firm conviction that salvation could be grasped. John Lahr sees this creative paradox in what I, personally, regard as the finest piece of music ever written: "Even the great finale of the Sgt. Pepper album, 'A Day in the Life,' is a collage of two moods, which creates at once the sense of escape and the sense of terror."[5] It is hard to avoid the power produced by the collaboration of fascination and dread, for the power is essentially religious.

The numerous biographies, autobiographies, memoirs, tales-told-from-the-inside and so on published since then note the same paradoxical qualities. One of the more controversial of these is Steven Stark's *Meet the Beatles: A Cultural History of the Band That Shook Youth, Gender, and the World* (2005), wherein the paradoxes of sex and gender internal to the group and their appeal are explored. Stark, in true psychoanalytic fashion (though not a practicing Freudian) finds many of these paradoxes evident in their music. Bob Spitz's massive 992-page tome, *The Beatles: The Biography* (2006) retells all of the dark and light, up and down, ugly and beautiful tales and more. What both of these accounts suggest is that there is a seemingly endless need to understand this collective of, in a phrase so often used, four lads from Liverpool. It's not so surprising, when you think about it: They *are* mythic after all!

The other religious qualities (the sensations of wholly otherness, activity, mystical identification, and creatureliness) are so completely integrated within the paradox dominated by fascination that it would be misleading to isolate them for analysis. Suffice it to say that "A Day in the Life" captures them all in the paradoxical harmony of ultimate tragedy and certain victory. No other song better illustrates the religious import of Beatlemania, and no album symbolizes their numinous qualities more fully, than *Sgt. Pepper's Lonely Hearts Club Band*. With anticipation no doubt magnified by advanced publicity, the album had been eagerly awaited as perhaps no other in the history of recording, either before or since. After having spent nearly seven hundred hours in the studio, The Beatles scheduled it for radio release at midnight, Sunday, June 2, 1967, a week before it would be available in record stores. Many a fan stayed awake that night listening to the endless replaying and the disc jockeys' repeated attempts to get one of The Beatles on the phone for a live interview. Such was its initial impact.

In an essay entitled "Learning from The Beatles," Richard Poirier singles out this one album for especially close analysis, subjecting each and every song to his exegetical scrutiny.[6] His overall conclusion is that "nothing less is being claimed by these songs than that The Beatles exist not merely as a phenomenon of entertainment but as a force of historical consequence.... Listening to the *Sgt. Pepper* album one thinks not simply of the history of popular music but of the history of this century.... The songs emanated from some inwardly felt coherence that awaited a merely explicit design." Peter Berger's "alternation," the present-oriented act of transforming our consciousness of both the past and future in the act of conversion, comes to mind immediately, especially when one considers the collage of historical personalities on the album jacket as an interpretive act. Poirier (who undertakes to examine the meaning of the figure portrayed on the cover of his own book *The Performing Self*) understands the collage to be "a celebration of The Beatles themselves, who can now be placed (and Bob Dylan, too) within that tiny group who have, aside from everything else they've done, infused the imagination of the living with the possibilities of other ways of living, of extraordinary existences, of something beyond 'a day in the life.'" Sensing the power of this album to shape our consciousness with the promise of salvation, another commentator, Langdon Winner, maintains that "the closest Western Civilization has come to unity since the Congress of Vienna in 1815 was the week the *Sgt. Pepper* album was released.... For a brief while the irreparably fragmented consciousness of the West was unified, at least in the minds of the young."[7]

What they revealed to us was a dream, an ideal, and they gave us the promise that it could be realized. The ideal was never portrayed as actual; nor was the actual ever portrayed as ideal. The former would be quixotic, the latter defeatist, and both absurd. No, The Beatles offered a vision of what ought to be as distinct from what is, and in so doing, refashioned the past and future into something entirely new. Greil Marcus, in *Rolling Stone Illustrated History of Rock and Roll*, puts it this way:

> As was so often pointed out in the mid-sixties, the sum of The Beatles was greater than the parts, but the parts were so distinctive and attractive that the group itself could be all things to all people ... this was what had never happened before. And so it began. The past was felt to dissolve, the future was conceivable only as an expansion of the present, and the present was defined absolutely by its expansive novelty.... The Beatles seemed not only to symbolize but to contain it all — to make history by anticipating it.... The Beatles event ... intensified not only in momentum but in magnetism, reaching more and more people with greater and greater mythic and emotional power, for at least four years. The Beatles affected not only the feel but the quality of life — they deepened

it, sharpened it, brightened it, not merely as a factor in the cultural scheme, but as a presence. The Beatles affected not only the quality of life, they affected its worth.[8]

John Lennon was right, of course: The Beatles were more popular than Jesus. Though he was probably unaware of the true import of his controversial observation, which led to record burnings and anti–Beatles demonstrations primarily throughout the American South, he had nevertheless hit the proverbial nail squarely on the head, especially when he added, "I don't know which will go first — rock and roll or Christianity." There it was, for all to hear and contemplate: the competition between two incompatible religious movements, one supernatural and supportive of the status quo and the other immanent and threatening to it. He later apologized for having made these offhand remarks, but he never recanted their meaning. For The Beatles had become far more than just an incredibly successful rock group — they had become the symbols par excellence of America's cultural revolution.

The Lonely Hearts Club

The club has had but four members — additions, replacements, or resignations would be neither possible nor tolerated, its membership being the most exclusive in history. Admission and departure were at one time voluntary, but after the coronation, there was no longer any choice. The members were trapped — the four loneliest people on the face of the earth — for with whom can the gods commune?

In recognition of what they had become, and as perhaps their last desperate attempt to separate themselves from it, they created mythic personae of themselves — Sgt. Pepper's Lonely Hearts Club Band. If so, the attempt was futile; it had exactly the opposite effect. The insertion of what turned out to be yet another symbol between themselves and the multitudes not only preserved but actually enhanced their absolute *mysterium*. The art for both the album and the film *Yellow Submarine* is so reminiscent of the iconography of the Byzantine church that this effect is hardly surprising. The Orthodox traditions within Christianity, of which the Byzantine church is one of the earliest examples, have always avoided exact representational religious art as being too crass and presumptuous for portraying the divine. They've preferred a mosaic styling, which seems to have ensured the art's symbolic nature; for who could believe these odd mosaics are exact replicas of the ultimate? At best, they can only point to it. As a result, the object of worship has been removed almost entirely from the material world, making the artistic intermediary even more necessary as a spiritual bridge.

This might be exactly what orthodoxy has always desired, but not so The Beatles. Their elaborate attempt at demystification, due to the nature of symbols, was bound to be counterproductive. Fanciful though they be, Sgt. Pepper's little troupe serves to remove The Beatles further from us. Yet, in true paradoxical fashion, it also grants us access to them and to what they in turn symbolize.

Any adequate Pepperology must make some mention of the narrative of *Yellow Submarine*, no matter how firmly the tongue must be placed in the cheek, for it contains some interesting clues. Basically, it's a straightforward tale of good versus evil. The ultra-innocent people of Pepperland, whose god is Love, are set upon by the infamous Blue Meanies, who wish to deny to Pepperlanders the "pleasures of food and music and perpetual celebration and colorful beauty" (as it's so coyly expressed by the liner notes). Sgt. Pepper's Lonely

Hearts Club Band is sent to request aid from The Beatles, who of course are only too willing to comply, and together they inevitably prevail.

There is little subtlety or complexity to this message, but then none is intended. Pleasure is affirmed as the ultimate value, but only insofar as it is provided with the moral guidance of love. Yet the implications of this value scheme are nowhere spelled out or even hinted at. Furthermore, the forces of evil are simply characterized as repressive, having no values of their own; they merely oppose the morality of love and pleasure and are thus, by definition, wrong. However, beneath the surface, there is a message of considerable importance being sent, a message of extreme confidence. By the end of the film, the Blue Meanies have been converted to the Pepperlanders' morality, not killed, as might have been the case within the purview of traditional values. The message is clear: Human nature is such that a new way of relating to one another and a new world are possible, all based on the new set of values expressed through and exemplified by Sgt. Pepper's music. This degree of optimism about the human character is a key foundational assumption of anarchism, for only by presupposing supreme confidence in how people would relate to each other without external guidance does anarchism make any sense; and given the assumption, *only* anarchism makes sense. "All You Need Is Love" is another way of putting it. "There's nothing you can do that can't be done.... No one you can save that can't be saved."

Such was their message to the sixties, and at the depths of human existence, it was received. The evidence is in the music, for communication of this kind must occur first at the level of feelings; later it can be expressed at the rational level, after the commitment has already been made. There have been numerous explicit references to Sgt. Pepper in song, but two come to mind as especially revealing of the relationship between The Beatles and the sixties. The first is Al Stewart's "Post World War II Blues" from his 1973 album *Past, Present and Future*, which includes the following lyrics:

> I came up to London when I was nineteen
> With a corduroy jacket and head full of dreams
> In coffee bars I spent my nights
> Reading Allen Ginsberg, talking civil rights.
> On the day Robert Kennedy got shot down
> The world was wearing a deeper frown
> And though I knew that we'd lost a friend
> I always believed we could win in the end.
> Music was the scenery
> Jimi Hendrix played loud and free
> Sergeant Pepper was real to me
> Songs and poems were all you needed...

Sgt. Pepper was real to a lot of people, not because of who they were but because of what it meant.

Another set of lyrics, from "Sgt. Pepper's Band," written by Joan Baez with Lennon's murder fresh in her mind, also highlights the relationship. The chorus goes as follows:

> Now I think I understand
> That it was Sergeant Pepper's Band
> That put the sixties into song
> Where have all the heroes gone?

Heroes, of course, are symbols, and genuine symbols can never die; only people die. What the heroes symbolize lives on after them. So it is with The Beatles.

There is no easy way to explain the complex set of values that they pointed to, and the task is made even more difficult by the fact that some of the values have been for so long ensconced in American tradition that they are regarded as unquestioned truths. I have in mind such verities as freedom, equality, justice, happiness, fraternity, individuality, and community, none of which have been fully realized, and some never even attempted. Much of what The Beatles affirmed had to do with satisfying these ideals, feeling as they did the disparity between the promise and the reality. The Beatles' push towards fulfillment spoke to many of their generation, people who had been raised to believe in these values but whose experiences exposed them to the contradictions (first made evident to them in music). It was their inchoate but decidedly disturbed consciousness that The Beatles tapped into, organized, and expressed, and all they were saying was that the time had come to actualize the values and to do so without any further delay.

But there was a lot more to it. A set of ultimate values is just that — a set. Values are interrelated in a complex unity; a set is not some kind of list, from which some values might be added and others subtracted without affecting the others. On the contrary, the relationship is that of an organic whole that is larger than the sum of its parts. The set of values pointed to by The Beatles includes more than those inherited from the tradition; just as important, it omits some traditional values. The overall result was something entirely new, disclosing a quality of existence not hitherto thought possible — a gestalt that formed the motivation and the goals of the sixties.

Included among the additional values were a pantheistic form of spirituality, anarchism, pacifism, pleasure, individuality, mysticism, sensuality, emotionality, and eccentricity. Eliminated were such values as individualism (not to be confused with individuality), nationalism, militarism, imperialism, and traditional religiousness (especially Western). David Pichaske characterizes the decade as a dialectic between "an angry no" and "a transcendent yes." Although I might disagree with some of his ideas, I think his notion of a dialectical tension is absolutely correct: "It is in this context of denial as affirmation that the decade must be viewed. Only by grasping this yes in the no can the high moral seriousness of sixties protest be understood." And, "The yes of the sixties, very different in almost every particular from the angry no, was just as compelling. Rooted in idealism, this affirmation could overlap and encompass both protest marches and liberal politics.... The sixties yes was a magic yes, a hidden reality that might break out (or through) in any circumstance, extraordinary in its ordinariness, lunacy, spontaneity, freedom, magic."[9] This complex set of values amounted to something logically contrary to the prevailing set. But because of this complexity, the new set, symbolized by The Beatles, made for an extremely difficult target. The established order often found itself taking potshots at values that it, too, affirmed. A more effective counterattack would have to wait for the 1980 election.

Interestingly, because The Beatles were not American they may have been all the more effective as symbols. For the tendency to confuse the symbol with what it points to was necessarily blunted: how could a British rock-and-roll band represent revolutionary values for Americans? The connection just didn't seem to be there. Yet, in some strange way, the four spoke to the deepest part of the American consciousness, and many responded by seeing them as the linkage between their personal selves and their shared ultimate beliefs. In such a situation, idolatry is hard to avoid, and The Beatles phenomenon has had its share — as have all the traditional religions. The kind of idolatry feeding The Beatles' mystique, however, is capable of making a great deal of money for anyone who can replicate it. Attempts to do just this are instructive, since they make perfectly clear the impossibility of deliberately creating a symbol. It didn't work for the Monkees in the sixties, and it didn't work for The Knack in the seventies. While these, along with many others, were *manufactured*, The Beatles *happened*. Since then, the many obvious and deliberate attempts to create a "new Beatles" have largely been abandoned—not that every record producer, manager and musician doesn't hope for a discovery of this kind.

As for satisfying Tillich's criterion for validity—self-negation—The Beatles took the ultimate step: they destroyed themselves. In so doing, they guaranteed immortality for themselves but, more important, they focused attention squarely on what The Beatles have come to mean. John Lennon, in a *Playboy* interview, said, "If The Beatles of the sixties had a message, it was to learn to swim. Period. And once you learn to swim, swim. The people who are hung up on The Beatles and the sixties dream missed the whole point." The message was the thing; as far as he was concerned, The Beatles could be dispensed with. Given his iconoclastic sense of humor, especially as it pertained to The Beatles (from which he was forever trying to separate himself), he no doubt would be amused by William Scott's drawing on the cover of Rhino Records' *Beatlesongs!*, a collection of songs about The Beatles. Standing amid tacky Beatles artifacts strewn about the floor, festooned with John buttons, and holding an autograph book in his fist, is, as George Harrison put it, "the devil's best friend, someone who offended all." (I'm referring to John Lennon's killer, of course.) Yes, this is sick, and it's not of their doing, but it's just this kind of desperate measure they felt to be necessary if they were ever to be freed from the mythology that had trapped them.

Given what they had done, and all their succeeding efforts to preserve their individuality, the numerous calls for a reunion would never have been answered, especially if it would have amounted to a mere nostalgic look backwards. (A creative risk-taking reunion, which looked forward with something new and challenging to say, would have been another matter entirely.) On those occasions when we've been able to avoid the pitfalls of idolatry and think clearly, we've always realized that a reunion (even for a single concert) was not in the cards. And in our exceptionally wise moments, we've even felt it to be an undesirable possibility.

For a long time the four knew that The Beatles were more than just another rock group, and their mixed feelings about what had happened made for some of their most creative work. Much of their creativity manifested their efforts to shatter the various images that imprisoned them. The infamous "butcher block" cover made for the first copies of *Yesterday and Today* is an example. It was their attempt to destroy their prevailing image of being decent, innocent, fun-loving, and harmless. Throughout their career, however, self-parody was their usual tactic, and Richard Poirier finds this to be among their finest qualities, preserving them from the kind of self-deception that might otherwise have been inevitable in their case. I agree. One song comes to mind as an exceptional example: "You Know My Name (Look Up the Number)." Originally released as the B-side of "Let It Be," it makes fun of almost everything, especially themselves.

Nothing worked, however, and destruction of The Beatles became the only possible recourse. Having to be The Beatles finally overwhelmed them. It was all too much. Touring and live concerts had to be halted; after a while, they couldn't even hear themselves play. Their last performance was an impromptu concert on the roof of Apple Studios, captured for the film *Let It Be*. It is worth seeing if only for the sensation it caused.

In the tenth anniversary issue of *Rolling Stone* (December 15, 1977), Jonathan Cott reflected on the "Children of Paradise, the sixties generation," from the perspective of what he termed "the calculating, mean-spirited perspective of the Seventies."[10] Trying to communicate what he had felt so strongly, he wrote, "We forget that the Sixties impulse to bring us back to where we once belonged was almost single-handedly delineated and symbolized by one rock group from Liverpool." The reader can almost feel him straining for the appropriate analogy: "The group's four members came to be seen and thought of symbolically — like the Four Evangelists or the Four Elements. And in an elementary sense, each of The Beatles — in the way each became defined by his face, voice, and songs — took on an archetypal role: Paul, sweet and sensitive; John, sly and skeptical; George, mysterious and mystical; Ringo, childish but commonsensical — like Sancho Panza." It makes no difference how many people agree with him, or even whether the observations are at all accurate; what matters is the fact that thousands, nay millions, of others have made similar attempts at capsule summaries. Even Brian Epstein was reputed to have offered his own characterizations. The point is that, as individuals and a group, The Beatles reached a generation that was looking for a new set of values to replace those found no longer meaningful. Cott saw them as the perfect archetype of wholeness, musically expressed in "the merging of their singing voices at the conclusion of 'Happiness Is a Warm Gun,'" which for him was "one of the inimitable moments in rock history." Maybe wholeness is the key; they certainly pointed to it as an ideal and to the best of their abilities, they tried to live the ideal. "They presented themselves to us," Cott continued, "as members of a little tribe which provided an example of how each of us could become part of the necklace of Shiva in which every diamond reflects every other and is itself reflected." He ended his comments with the acknowledgment that all was not sweetness and light, but "The values of the Sixties — non-grasping, non-authoritarian, non-invasive — still make sense to me."

How and why these values can still make sense to people requires a three-part response. First, it has to do with what Tillich called the dormancy of all valid symbols — valid ones can never really die. They can be reawakened whenever the time is ripe. Second, such reawakenings are, according to Eliade, one of the inherent possibilities of mythic time, partially explaining what Tillich had in mind. Third, however, it has to do with the times being ripe, and ripe they became.

The Beatles Forever!

This now-famous slogan seems to promise much more than it can possibly deliver, but this is so only if we lose sight of the basis for a genuine immortality and, instead, substitute a superficial dredging up of nostalgic remembrances. We can never go back, as the pain of nostalgia so clearly implies, just as we can never recapture our youth. In fact, the irreversible process of aging is a decent analogy for understanding how the continuing presence of The Beatles can possibly make any sense. Cott has no use for those "who take the flickering simulacra of the television tube to be reality," who either narrow-mindedly debunk or unreasonably glorify the period. He also pointedly answers those who accuse sixties people of wanting to live in the past: "When we were told that we could only get to heaven if we became like little children, we were not supposed to infer that we should remain children forever."[11] Nor should we infer that our childhood should be forgotten, if this were even possible. Coming to maturity means, among other things, accepting our past and learning from it. For all of us there are certain events, persons, and places that we shall remember all our lives, because they have given meaning to our lives. These are best understood as personal symbols, and though we inevitably change, they are not likely to lose their importance for us unless we radically alter our identities in the act of conversion or alternation (for then we abandon them and adopt different personal symbols).

Those who have maintained their personal and social identities as "children of the sixties" can legitimately retain The Beatles' symbol-ology as long as it enables them to look ahead to the future with a particular set of values for guidance. If The Beatles are merely something to look back to, if they evoke only memories, then their symbolic function has been lost—if it ever truly existed. They would then function only as idols, false symbols, and would be dangerously stultifying. My guess, however, is that for literally millions of people, the dream goes on. The future that The Beatles once pointed to still lies ahead and the symbolic lens through which we once saw it is still clear.

John Lahr concludes his piece on remembering The Beatles for *The New Republic* by stressing the fact that, though the times have changed, The Beatles endure: "Then, as now, the songs ventilated life with their articulate energy. Familiarity has robbed the music of its astonishment, but the songs still have the power to tap ancient longings.... The Beatles' music makes joy; and that joy, once felt, is never easily forgotten."[12] These ancient longings are for what The Beatles pointed to, not them, and examples of attempts to re-actualize and regenerate their mythic power are legion. According to Eliade, "religious man assumes a humanity that has a trans-human, transcendent model. He does not consider himself to be *truly man* except in so far as he imitates the gods, the culture heroes, or the mythic ancestors."[13] In this way The Beatles can continue with us as a living presence, fueling the fires that have been smoldering ever since the sixties came to an end.

Imitation is more than the sincerest form of flattery; it is the essence of "worship"— intended as such or not. Consider the following random illustrations:

1. Not too long ago a radio station in Texas dropped its top 40 format so as to program Beatles music twenty-four hours a day. This is a tad extreme, but it's similar to the special Beatles programs that virtually cover the dial on particular anniversaries. Furthermore, there continue to be regularly scheduled (usually weekly) programs devoted to Beatles music and events.

2. For a few months beginning in July 1983, Abbey Road Studios was opened for guided tours while undergoing some refurbishing. Throngs of people waited their turn outside, in what seemed like never-ending lines.

3. The popular stage show Beatlemania, which grew out of and has in turn spawned numerous smaller and lesser-known versions of the same thing, seems always to be playing somewhere. I once saw a rather good performance (one of the smaller and lesser-known versions) at an obscure shopping mall in Manassas, Virginia. With no advance publicity whatsoever, the mall became increasingly choked with startled suburbanites who immediately interrupted their shopping to watch. Seeing the costumed performers was visibly unnerving for quite a few of us. Since then I've seen a few excellent and some not-so-excellent "tribute" bands in the darkened booths of casinos in Laughlin, Nevada (seemingly the "tribute" band capital of the world) and in Las Vegas.

4. The furor once caused by Klaatu, a mid–1970s rock group, whose emulation of The Beatles' sound, coupled with its refusal to be identified by name or visage, once stimulated some of the best rumor-mongering since the Paul-is-dead controversy. Were they really The Beatles? Like The Beatles, Klaatu was under contract to Capitol Records, raising suspicions of an eminently successful hype. The group went from obscurity to instant fame on just the vague glimmer of a hoped-for unlikelihood.

5. The film *I Wanna Hold Your Hand*, which re-creates the moment of The Beatles' coronation on *The Ed Sullivan Show*, was a surprising critical success, due in large part to its focusing not on the singers but on their fanatical worshippers. Most interesting is the fact that every one of the characteristics of religion described by Eliade is clearly evident in the film, with fascination predominating.

6. The TV special *All You Need Is Cash*, starring the Rutles, is the kind of parody that can be done only by those who fully understand what The Beatles were all about. Not only were Monty Python and *Saturday Night Live* people associated with it at all levels of production, but Paul Simon, Mick Jagger, and George Harrison made cameo appearances as well.

7. One of the more subtle imitations derives from an obscure remark one of the four made in response to a question as to how the group got its name. The reply was something to the effect that "it's just a name. It could have been anything. We could have called ourselves 'the Shoes.'" This was a flagrant lie, of course, as any fan of Buddy Holly and the Crickets could tell you. Nevertheless, as you check out some of the vintage LPs at your local classic record store, you'll notice one group with the unlikely name "the Shoes."

8. Among the French, rock and roll is still known as "yeah-yeah" music. In 2000, an indie rock band from New York took the name the Yeah Yeah Yeahs — meaning "Whatever..." in the local vernacular but inevitably establishing a link to their past.

9. *Rolling Stone*'s February 16, 1984, issue was devoted entirely to the twentieth anniversary of The Beatles' conquest of America and the world. One article describes the new generation of Beatles fans.

10. Perhaps the illustration with the greatest significance is the one most likely to be overlooked. Because of the influence of television shows like *Sesame Street*, and because of the many sixties people teaching in the elementary school classroom, and because the children of today are the descendants of sixties people, the very young are being introduced to Beatles music as earlier generations were introduced to nursery rhymes. This is still the case today; the countless tee shirts made for young children confirm it.

11. In August and September, 2009, VH1 did a complete Beatles retrospective, including a showing of the multi-disk *Anthology*.

12. Consider the countless garage bands created in the image of the Beatles beginning with their earliest exposures to the public. None of them really lasted very long, but that's not the point. Submitted for your approval: Der letzte Schrei ("The Last Cry"— a German expression for "the coolest of the cool"), a German garage band. In 1965, four guitar-playing and one mandolin-playing German Mädchen decided to form their own "beat-music" band that covered not only The Beatles but also The Rolling Stones, John Lee Hooker and other American blues artists. They did a few gigs in some local taverns and dissolved a year later to go their separate ways, never to meet again. Yet Gisela Erma today includes a collection of eight photos of her group on Facebook as part of her bio — it's her life story, after all.

13. Finally, there is a seemingly never-ending supply of books about The Beatles in print. Two notable works are *Remembering The Beatles* by Steven Charles and John Tobler, released in 2008, and Robert Hilburn's *Cornflakes with John Lennon*, released in 2008. Although comprising his reminiscences about a variety of rockers, including Michael Jack-

son, Bono, Bruce Springsteen and Bob Dylan, the book is named after who Hilburn regards, perhaps unconsciously, as the seminal figure of our time.

> No single rock 'n' roll diet works for everyone. We all have different musical DNA, and we all follow different musical paths. Yet there is a unifying quality about rock 'n' roll that helps instill confidence and hope in millions of fans at times in their lives when little else makes sense.
> What linked Elvis Presley ... and the Beatles was the old-fashioned American notion that each individual can make a difference.... Rock 'n' roll is the promise of a better day, and the best artists spread that message with an almost missionary zeal. I've always believed in that liberating message, which is probably why I respond to most artists who fight to keep the promise alive.[14]

Hilburn observes in these few remarks the twin values of freedom and individuality that makes rock music the revolutionary force that I believe it to be.

It is important to keep in mind the fact that such examples of "Beatleography" can be found from shortly after their appearance on *The Ed Sullivan Show* until the present. In other words, the imitative and re-actualizing processes have been continuous. The implicit reason has been to capture some of the energy and magic that propelled The Beatles from nowhere to the zenith of popular culture and beyond. More than just an attempt to capitalize on their success or mere nostalgia, this drive is motivated by a yearning for wholeness, meaningfulness, and the indefinable ultimate. Much as the people attending later Elvis concerts were doing so for more than simple nostalgia, so too the many recollections and imitations of The Beatles have been more than rock necrophilia. With appropriate apologies for altering Eliade's thought beyond what he intended, he did nevertheless provide an insightful perspective from which we can comprehend all of this: "It is easy to understand why the memory of that marvelous time haunted religious man, why he periodically sought to return to it. In *Illud tempore,* the gods had displayed their greatest powers. The *cosmogony* is the supreme divine manifestation, the paradigmatic act of strength, superabundance, and creativity. Religious man thirsts for the real. By every means at his disposal, he seeks to reside at the very source of primordial reality, when the world was in *statu nascendi*."[15] If Elvis symbolizes the mythology of The Beginning, The Beatles symbolize the mythology of The New Beginning. Hence, together, the fifties and the sixties give shape, direction, motivation, and meaning to America's cultural revolution.

The most direct and obvious form of imitation, in music, is the practice of covering. The Beatles have perhaps been covered more often than any other rock group, and possibly more than any other composer or team of composers in history. To be sure, the results have been mixed. "I Call Your Name" by The Mamas and the Papas is one of the best, but nothing can salvage Barry Gibb's rendition of "The Long and Winding Road" (from the equally bad "cover film," *Sgt. Pepper's Lonely Hearts Club Band*, in which the practice of covering reaches a new low). Equally interesting is the apparent refusal to cover any Beatles music at all by those who do not find the practice offensive otherwise. For it is precisely this kind of reluctance that can most perfectly acknowledge The Beatles as symbols. Not only is idolatry avoided and concentration focused on what they pointed to, but practically every quality of feeling described by Otto is involved. Symbols need not be loved, and in many ways, it is best that they not be loved, since their purpose is to point beyond themselves.

No one, of course, was less in love with The Beatles than the person who said, "Fuckin' big bastards, that's what The Beatles were"; who sang, "I don't believe in Beatles"; and who, in the same song, added,

> The dream is over
> What can I say?
> The dream is over
> Yesterday
> I was the dreamweaver
> But now I'm reborn
> I was the walrus
> But now I'm John

Au contraire, by forcing us to look beyond a transitory group of four individual musicians, John Lennon helped preserve the myth and pass it along to all future generations. Because of them, we too can return to and live in *illud tempus*.

Vignettes of Affirmation

The affirmation of a new set of values symbolized by The Beatles was a living reality for a wide variety of Americans in the sixties, wider than the media and the analysts would have us believe. Collectively, they exemplified the positive dimension of freedom, the liberty to accomplish certain goals both personal and social. Accomplishment, however, should not be understood to be the sole criterion of success. If this measure were used to evaluate the sixties, everything attempted would no doubt be seen as an unqualified failure: absolutely none of the revolution's ultimate values were actualized to any meaningful extent. This criterion might be useful in some instances, but not for the sixties; a stage prior to actualization had to be reached first.

A more appropriate, more revealing, and certainly more accurate approach would be to use a different and more realistic criterion. Given that the prevailing values had become solidly entrenched in American culture, and given that the fifties had been able only to dislodge the unthinking obedience to these values for a relatively small number of people (primarily powerless youths), it would be the height of absurdity to expect the prevailing order to be overturned and a new and conflicting set of values introduced within a few short years. If nothing else, inertia would prevent this from happening, to say nothing of the inevitable opposition. The most that could be expected would be for the new set of values to be recognized throughout American society as *capable* of being realized. In other words, to have them accepted as a genuine possibility, not merely for intellectual contemplation but for actual realization, is a much better measure of success. And from this standpoint, the sixties were overwhelmingly successful.

The most visible, yet essentially amorphous, of the groups manifesting these new values were Black Americans, the New Left, and the hippies. In each case, there was a musical expression that reflected, as well as shaped, the group's consciousness — defining the group as much as anything could.

The activities of Black Americans throughout the sixties were obviously an outgrowth of the Civil Rights movement of the fifties, but something new was added: the implications of the earlier goal of equality were forcefully expressed. More than the acquisition of parity in the social and political marketplace, equality means the establishment of an identity respected by one self and others; in a word, *pride*. This, in turn, depended on one's group being considered worthy of *respect*.

If the rock and roll of the fifties was characterized by a merger of Black and White, the sixties saw the gradual reintroduction of separation. This time, however, the separation was undertaken as a positive act, as a way to preserve and perpetuate Black identity. In the decades to follow, ethnic (as well as other forms of) "diversity" would assume a prominent place in the pantheon of revolutionary values. First evident in the different path taken by Motown recording artists under the direction of Berry Gordy, Jr. (the Supremes, the Four Tops, the Temptations, Smokey Robinson and the Miracles, Martha Reeves and the Vandellas, Marvin Gaye, and Stevie Wonder, among others), it matured as soul in the mid- to late sixties. Sixties soul is best personified by James Brown's "Say It Loud — I'm Black and I'm Proud," Otis Redding's "Respect," and Aretha Franklin's album *Young, Gifted and Black* (to say nothing of her classic cover of "Respect," which Otis Redding said he liked even better than his original recording). Whites listened to and could even identify with the earlier Motown sounds, but soul was different; it set Black Americans apart as a distinct and not entirely comprehensible entity. While it had never been the case that Whites were given access to Black consciousness, now Whites became aware of how little they actually knew about "these others." For the first time, Whites were made conscious of not holding all the cards; more important, Black Americans knew it too.

The implications of the Black Pride and Black Power movements of the sixties extended much further than anyone could know at the time. The freedom and necessity for the expression of group pride isn't limited in principle to a specific race or any other identifiable characteristic. If full equality is contingent on group pride and respect, as the necessary foundation for individual self-worth, as it most assuredly is, then full equality would be demanded by other groups as well: women, gays, assorted ethnic groups, and the aged, among others.

Growing out of an opposition to militarism, the war in Vietnam, and a perceived failure of true democracy in the United States, the amorphous New Left was a loose alliance of many student movements throughout the country, which had their beginning with the struggles for free speech and relevance in education. Some semblance of unity was brought to this varied assemblage by their collective vision of a new American society, represented by the Port Huron Statement of 1962.

"Participatory Democracy" was a key slogan bandied about by all these varied groups, but its meaning, surprisingly enough, remained consistent: political decisions can only properly be made with everyone's equal and effective participation; unilateral decisions imposed from above are necessarily immoral and must be opposed no matter what they might be. The process of decision making is just as important as the decision itself. Implicit within this deceptively traditional idea is the unequivocal rejection of the principle of majority rule (or popular sovereignty), the notion that political obligation is defined by the will of the majority. The people in the New Left knew, as everyone knows, that mere numbers have never been a sufficient moral criterion; they just simply collapsed the distinction between moral and political decision making, using the former to judge the latter in every instance.

The founders of American constitutional democracy relied on a balance between majority preference as expressed through the legislature and the limitations imposed by universal, natural rights protected by the courts. Majority will and human rights were to be equal bases of political obligation, with the naive hope that a conflict between them would never arise, there being no way to resolve the potential dilemma peacefully and rationally. (A rereading of Federalist No. 51 might be in order here.) The founders were convinced that the composition of majorities (or "factions") would constantly be shifting and that there was general agreement that certain rights were inalienable. It was assumed that individual preferences were based solely on self-interest and that rights had to be protected because of this; hence the necessity for some authority over individuals.

The New Left gave preeminence to the authority of rights and hoped that universal participation would mitigate the unpleasantness of occasionally going against the majority. On the other hand, the majority could be expected to recognize the superiority of human rights over individual preferences. In fact, their preferences weren't expected to violate the rights of others. The vicissitudes of opinion were more the result of a society that structurally encouraged self-seeking than of anything innate to humanity. The belief that such a society could be achieved and actually function was based on the fundamental assumption that moral truths are either innate or the inevitable consequence of people living together freely. This assumption also explains their opposition to the war in Vietnam. With few major exceptions, the New Left was not a pacifist movement; rather, it advocated selective opposition based on the individual's conscience. The obvious implication was that the individual's moral authority superseded that of the government, in this and every instance. In other words, anarchism: there being no legitimate authority whatsoever over the individual, a government is neither necessary nor proper — it has no legitimate existence.

None of this was well delineated by the New Left, either for itself or for those on the outside. But for those who had ears to hear, it was all there in the music. Anarchism and its underlying assumptions were implicit in much of the protest music of the time, but the focus of this music was usually on specific events, persons, policies, and the like. A more subtle and consequently more effective form of music occurred with the merging of folk and rock, called, for lack of anything better, "folk rock." Dylan, the Byrds, Simon and Garfunkel, as well as numerous others made it as clear as it could be that we don't need this (or any) government to tell us how to get along with each other. Dylan's "Maggie's Farm," The Byrds' "Wasn't Born to Follow," and Simon and Garfunkel's "Big Bright Green Pleasure Machine" demonstrate how effectively political values can be expressed in this manner.

As far as the hippies of the sixties were concerned, a brief glance backwards would provide some needed perspective. This aspect of the sixties is often regarded as transient phenomenon, an anomaly never before encountered among civilized people and one not likely to be repeated. Exactly the opposite is the case: no matter what their guise and no matter what they might be called, there have always been counterculture groups in society, and there always will be. In the April 1978 edition of *Head* magazine, Bruce Eisner discusses "the hippie revolution" in "Looking Back at Sgt. Pepper." During the course of his essay, he has occasion to mention briefly the history of such movements. Long before the beats of the fifties, he says, there were

> the agnostic [sic — he probably meant the Gnostic] Christian sects in the Greco-Roman world of the second century, the "cult of pure love" of the twelfth-century Troubadours, the Brethren of the Free Spirit of fourteenth-century England, as well as the pre–Raphaelite Brotherhood headed by the Rosettis which existed in England in the late 1800s and evolved into the Aesthetic Movement, the Dadaist Movement with its absurd style, initiated by the Frenchman Gautier at the turn of the 20th century, and the Bohemians of the twenties. All of these displayed aspects of the style which would later be adopted by the hippies.[16]

The hippie style included communal living, "free" sex (that is, sex uninhibited by conventional morality, never licentious — the moral guidelines were simply different), mind-altering drugs (especially marijuana and LSD), a fascination with all things Oriental, the free expression of the unique and valuable personality, an emphasis on emotions and feelings, and individuality. This last value — the notion that infinite worth resides in and every one of us—should not be confused with *individualism*, which values oneself *above* all others. Many things are implied by this style of life, not the least of which is the assumption that humans are *not* by nature self-seeking but rather social and cooperative. This supports the assumption of the New Left and further opposes the psychological egoism of America's founding fathers. Another implication is the notion that the emotional dimension of the person is just as important as the rational and ought to assume its rightful place in our lives (freeing us from the tyranny of reason so long a part of Western civilization). More than providing psychological health, emotional liberation makes us aware of reality in a different way. Drugs assisted in this process and were thus used for more than recreational purposes. The Oriental interest supported not only a nascent movement toward an appreciation of the environment and its life-forms but also the conviction that everything in reality is intrinsically related in an overall unity. Most of all there was a genuine sense of the possible, including peace, love, and understanding.

Musically, hippies listened to anything that might complement or enhance whatever state of mind they happened to inhabit. Obviously, this included the psychedelic music recorded and performed by The Jefferson Airplane, The Grateful Dead, The Doors, Jimi Hendrix, and Janis Joplin, but classic Black blues and pure folk were just as much a part of the scene. Given such a promising market, all sorts of rock musicians did their best to produce something psychedelic. Even the Rolling Stones made an attempt with "We Love You" and "Dandelion," and if a heavy blues rock band was converted, there's no telling how far the impact extended.

Many people identified with Black Americans, the New Left (soon to dissolve), and the hippies (soon to devolve into mere costumed mimicry) in one way or another and were perhaps even more influential for not having joined in any explicit way. Being on the outside, so to speak, they were in a unique position to see the commonality underlying all of them. What they saw was the harmony and mutual support provided by the affirmation of freedom, equality, human rights, and individuality. They were also better able to see the ramifications of these values, how they were interrelated and the difficulties in bringing them into existence. Although it was certain that the affirmation of this new set of values did not require membership in one or another of these groups, it was equally certain that some kind of action was called for. And such action could, and did, take many forms. Actions of this non-affiliated assemblage are most often overlooked in retrospectives of the sixties, but when their role is properly appreciated, the necessary conclusion is that the adoption of the new set of values was much more extensive than is commonly believed.

Though they never again performed together, The Beatles are of such enormous cultural significance that anything said about them is necessarily an understatement. For some people they were the chief indication, if not the chief cause, of an irreversible decline in Western civilization. For others, they were nothing less than the pure distillate of all that is hopeful within humanity's many and varied cultures, and an all-too-brief glimpse of a better world. Regardless of how they were evaluated, they could not be ignored, and as long as the dream lives in the consciousness of a single person, they will not be ignored in the years to come.

Perhaps, as Chuck Berry once proclaimed, Beethoven has indeed rolled over and given Tchaikowsky the news. But the news is mixed. What seemed so easy and so imminent in the sixties is now viewed with greater realism, but with no less hope. Realization of the dream is by no means impossible, but "it don't come easy." As with all cultural revolutions, success will depend on having symbols to point the way and provide the motivation—symbols that have passed the test of self-negation.

11

Dormancy and the Re-creation of the Interim

With the Paris cease-fire agreement on January 28, 1973, ending America's involvement in Vietnam, and Nixon's ignominious resignation on August 9, 1974, the sixties came to an end. There were no special news bulletins announcing the fact over radio and television, no celebrations, no offers to join hands again, no peace, no love and no understanding — only exhaustion. The capitulation of Saigon in April 1975, being completely anticipated by virtually everyone, occasioned only relief that the last shards of the tragedy had at last fallen to the ground.

America's cultural revolution had entered a six-year hiatus, coinciding almost exactly with the presidencies of Gerald Ford and Jimmy Carter. Such pauses are not uncommon, for it is the nature of cultural revolutions to engage every facet of a culture, and a culture can only endure so much internal tension before some kind of collapse becomes inevitable. Usually, however, neither the revolutionaries nor the old order has crushed the opposition by this point; hence, the conflict will necessarily be rejoined.

During this brief interim from 1974 to 1980, the revolutionary symbols became dormant, creating the impression for many people that the struggle had ended in failure. Meanwhile, the established symbols remained in place, encouraging a strengthening and rejuvenation of the old order so recently threatened. This, too, is typical of cultural revolutions, and in a very real sense, revolutions are "won" or "lost" during this period. The outcome depends on whether the revolutionaries can revive themselves sufficiently so as to challenge again the rejuvenated establishment. Although a renewed struggle is as certain as can be, the outcome is most certainly not. Nothing is promised by history. There are no guarantees, no assured results, no predetermined destinies. The future is a creature of the present, not the reverse. In situations like this, those in authority and control hold almost all the cards. The very weight of tradition, the nearly universal fear of change, the psychological need for stability, and the simple but powerful force of inertia all combine to make the revolutionaries' task even more difficult than it was at the outset. No longer do they have the element of surprise and the intrigue of something new on their side; now they must fall back on the intrinsic appeal of the new set of values they have proposed, relying on this alone to garner support and carry them through to victory. A culture will discover during this period whether the adherence to the new set of values was merely a passing fancy or a commitment likely to endure and perhaps even prevail. In short, the revolution must be re-created if it is to continue with any real hope for success.

Recreation/re-creation is one of those wonderfully ambiguous words that allow us to play around with a variety of meanings, all of which enhance each other. Depending on which pronunciation pops into mind first, diversion, refreshment, and entertainment may seem to capture its fundamental meaning; but restoration, renewal, reformation, and rededication are facets of it as well. I intend all of these meanings. Together they describe the essential character of the revolution during the Interim.

Others see this period quite differently. Peter N. Carroll, for example, in his book *It Seemed Like Nothing Happened: The Tragedy and the Promise of America in the 1970s*, sees the decade from 1970 to 1979 as one of decline from the pinnacle of the activist sixties. He concentrates on what was preserved from the initial period of the cultural revolution, not noticing its further developments. His perspective is hardly unusual, and it is mirrored in the many critical observations about the music of the time. In an article from the *Washington Post*, June 10, 1979, titled "Is Rock Dead or Just Beat?" the author, Brad Chase, laments that "Many second-generation rock fans (those who went steady to 'The Beatles,' 'I Should Have Known Better,' and became serious with 'Abbey Road') feel the boredom of the 'Me' decade has eclipsed the spirit that once intoxicated the music and its audience in the '60s." Both of these pessimistic appraisals overlook the likelihood of a pause in such cultural struggles and, more important, the re-creative function it serves.

The process of re-creation is complex, however, for it relates directly to the achievement of self-identity and the desire for self-actualization. Re-creation, in other words, entails self-creation. Jean-Paul Sartre and Abraham Maslow provide some vital clues as to how the restorative and regenerative processes of re-creation occur. A combination of their ideas can help us understand what happened to the revolution during the latter part of the 1970s until the election of Reagan.

According to Sartre, true self-identity can be realized only through the "look" of others, which creates an awareness of the self as an object for others. This awareness makes it possible for the self to "look," in turn, at others and thus know itself as a knowing subject with an identity of its own. "The way to interiority," he wrote in *Being and Nothingness*, "passes through the other person." In his novel *The Reprieve*, one of the characters rejects Descartes' famous dictum "I think, therefore I am" for the more cogent "I am seen, therefore I am." The point is that we can become conscious of ourselves as genuine individual subjects only if others first take notice of us as objects. Having achieved self-consciousness, we may then cast our gaze onto others as a free act of our own. Unfortunately, the inevitable consequences of this process are separation from others and an uneasy conflict with them.

Maslow, on the other hand, would regard this stage as merely the penultimate one in a process of human fulfillment — a goal Sartre would see as forever beyond our grasp. Self-actualization, the ability to realize our potential in cooperation with others, was for Maslow the ultimate itself, the goal for which all of us are striving. Yet in order to reach this goal, we must pass through and satisfy the demands of four other stages. The resultant model is what has come to be known as Maslow's "hierarchy of needs." At the first level physiological needs must be met: food, clothing, shelter, and the like. Next are safety needs: assurances that all the more fundamental needs will be met in the future. The social needs for interaction and friendship are at the third level. The fourth, penultimate stage concerns everything Sartre described and more: on the one hand there is the need for self-esteem (self-respect, self-confidence, and competence) and on the other is the need for status (recognition, appreciation, and respect). Only after all these needs have been reasonably satisfied is it possible to entertain the possibility of self-actualization, the realization of our own uniquely personal goals in a harmonious collaboration with others. Given the almost infinite variations in individual circumstances, some are bound to feel a given set of needs more directly than others do, but the strongest motivations will always be to achieve the next higher stage, the one just beyond the level currently enjoyed. In other words, until identity has been accomplished, self-fulfillment can't even be contemplated.

Maslow only intended this to be a rough approximation of human motivation, as a heuristic typology; the actual course of human development can never be as neat and orderly as this scheme might imply. Further, he had only individuals in mind; he was a psychologist, not a sociologist. Nevertheless, with a bit of social psychology under our collective belts, and with his same qualifications preventing us from making too much of it, this hierarchy can serve just as well as a device to explain group behavior.

Combining the conceptual highlights from Sartre and Maslow, we can get an insight into the re-creative efforts of several important groups during the Interim, some voicing their claims for identity and fulfillment for the first time, others renewing or preserving the claims they had already made. For the remainder of this chapter, I plan to concentrate on how their struggles were reflected in and encouraged by the music, noting along the way how the dialectical attitudes of negation and affirmation were preserved in America's post-sixties culture.

Black Americans

Emerging out of the move toward independence evidenced first by Motown and then by soul, Black music in the Interim continued by achieving an almost complete separation from the various White traditions, becoming an object for their gaze. Few Whites were even vaguely familiar with the newer Black musicians, and fewer still could appreciate their music. The music was definably different, defiantly different, and most certainly non–White. This much was apparent.

Perhaps more than anyone else, George Clinton personified this development. As the major creative force behind Parliament/Funkadelic (one group recording under different names for different companies), he was instrumental in funk's emergence as a significant musical and cultural force in the 1970s. One of the marvels of his wizardry is Funkadelic's *One Nation Under a Groove*, a 1978 album that embodies both negation and affirmation in an almost perfect balance. The former comes across with undisguised passion in the impossible-to-pronounce "Promentalshitbackwashpsychosisenemasquad (The Doo Doo Chasers)." He describes the world as a toilet, albeit toll-free, and our mouths spouting mental diarrhea a mile a minute. And yet selfishness stems, paradoxically, from our constipated thinking. His imagery — "me-burgers" with "i-sauce" — are hysterical and unparalleled as portrayals of negation. On the other hand, the title song, "One Nation Under a Groove," clearly affirms a greater, all-inclusive unity as the fundamental human goal.

The theme is continued by "Groovallegiance," in which everyone, regardless of color, is encouraged to join "the funk" which can make us all free. The very next song is an allegorical reference to the alienation between and among the races, primarily Black and White. The theme, evident in the title, is that it can be overcome: "Who Says a Funk Band Can't Play Rock?" The music types are used metaphorically, of course. Still, the rejection of a history of racism is an overwhelming presence on the album. In the cartoon collage on the inside cover, for example, a Klansman is portrayed as trying to steal the "funk." Nevertheless, Clinton is conscious of the separation's achievement; self-identity has been accomplished on Black terms, and a reunion, without destroying the valid differences, is being urged. In other words, Black self-actualization has now become a real possibility.

Another funk group with the same essential message is Kool and the Gang: "Funky Stuff" (1973), "Jungle Boogie" (1974), and "Spirit of the Boogie" (1975). Notice in these titles that an interesting reversal has taken place: whereas in the past any reference to the "jungle," especially in connection with doing the "boogie," would be an embarrassment or an insult, now it's affirmed with pride. Other funk performers from this period include Con-Funk-Shun, the Bar-Kays, and Rick James.

Although not funk strictly speaking, but close enough to defy any other description, Johnny Guitar Watson has also made the blend of affirmation and negation into a fine art. It is impossible to listen to his late 1970s albums without feeling a mixture of anger and joy coming through the music. Further, on many of his album covers he is pictured in the guise of a well-to-do pimp, surrounded by several dazzling women, Black *and* White. On his 1977 album *A Real Mother for Ya*, the back cover adds a shot of him with his mother. The paradox so evident in this imagery is just as clear in his music.

Lest the impression be created that funk exhausted Black musical styling during this period and that little else indicated the separatist tactic for achieving respect and fulfillment, several other groups ought to be mentioned. The Brothers Johnson, Rufus (featuring Chaka Khan), and War employed a variety of musical styling as expressions of the struggle, and all did so with considerable effectiveness. The meaning of "Free Yourself, Be Yourself" on the Brothers Johnson album *Right on Time* (1977) couldn't be more obvious. *Ask Rufus*, from the same year, has one of the most hauntingly beautiful instrumentals I've ever heard, "Slow Screw against the Wall," using nothing but strings followed by an eighteen-second explosion of funk, "A Flat Fry"— a subtle but forceful message that racial harmony is possible. War bridged the sixties and the Interim with such depressing songs as "The World Is a Ghetto" (1972) and "Slippin' into Darkness" (1972), but they followed with the more upbeat "Why Can't We Be Friends?" (1975) and "Summer" (1976). But despite their highly appealing combination of soul, funk, and Latin rhythms, few Whites found them more than marginally accessible. War was the most accessible of these groups. Then there was and still is Stevie Wonder, whose adopted surname is one of the true understatements in rock. As far as I know, he is one of the few performers whose career has spanned every period of the cultural revolution. He was discovered in 1961, and his first album (*Little Stevie Wonder: The Twelve Year Old Genius*) was released in 1963. The now-classic *Innervisions* (1973) includes a savage indictment of American society in "Living for the City," but it also has the highly optimistic "Visions." The latter expresses the idea that all men somehow feel truly free, free at last, but wonders [no pun intended] whether this is just a vision in our minds.

His last albums of the Interim were *Songs in the Key of Life* (1976), a complex mixture that both negated traditional values and affirmed revolutionary values, and *Journey through the Secret Life of Plants* (1979), as enigmatic an album as there is in popular music. I wouldn't venture even a tentative hypothesis toward classifying Stevie Wonder's music, but I have no hesitation in assessing it to be among the finest and most culturally significant ever written. In the years since, his music has continued to reflect and provide direction for Black Americans and, increasingly, White Americans as well. Both *Conversation Peace* (1995) and *Say It with Love* (2005) say as much with their titles as with their included songs.

Obviously, this sketch can in no way cover the enormous diversity of Black popular music during these six years, but it's not intended to do so. My purpose has been to suggest the meaning of what was happening, nothing more and certainly nothing less. (One glaring omission from this list, disco, will be addressed in the following section.)

Finally, although I've concentrated on Black music exclusively, symbolically, at least, the Black struggle for identity and fulfillment has represented all oppressed racial minorities: Chicanos, Native Americans, and Asians among them. In a later section, concerning Americans with Third World ties, this same notion will come up again.

Homosexuals

Homosexuals, bisexuals and transsexuals (basically everyone whose sexual orientation diverges from "the narrow") have had perhaps the most difficult time of all achieving self-identity to say nothing of self-actualization. During the Interim, however, they came out of their metaphorical closets as never before, forcing the rest of society to look at them, acknowledge their presence, and accept them on their own terms (to like them or to agree with them is, of course, another matter entirely, and is not at all implied by Maslow's hierarchy). Their greatest visibility came initially in the resurgent dance clubs, the discotheques found in almost every large American city, although, certainly, not everyone attracted to these clubs was gay. Disco had (and still has) its own intrinsic appeal, especially (originally) in the dismal wreckage of Vietnam and Watergate. Nevertheless, it was in the discotheque that some semblance of recognition and respect seemed possible, where costume, performance, style, and showiness were not only expected but vital. "Coming out" could thus become part of the show, and the club could be a place where gays and straights could mingle with equality. On the dance floor, all things seemed possible.

At first, the music played in these clubs was a combination of soul, funk, Caribbean, and the slick Philadelphia sounds of artists like Barry White—overwhelmingly Black, in other words. Some say the trend began in 1973 with "Soul Makossa" by Manu Dibango, an African who was living in Paris. In any case, it rapidly picked up with music specifically intended for the disco audience. Among the avalanche that followed were "Rock Your Baby" by George McCrae, "Rock the Boat" by the Hues Corporation, "TSOP (The Sound of Philadelphia)" by MFSB, and "Love's Theme" by Love Unlimited Orchestra, all in 1974. The next year the songs included "That's the Way (I Like It)" by KC and the Sunshine Band, "Fly Robin Fly" by Silver Convention and "The Hustle" by Van McCoy. In 1976, there was "Love to Love You Baby" by Donna Summer, "More, More, More" by the Andrea True Connection, "Tangerine" by the Salsoul Orchestra, "Turn the Beat Around" by Vicki Sue Robinson, "I Love Music" by the O'Jays, "You Sexy Thing" by Hot Chocolate, "Play That Funky Music (White boy)" by Wild Cherry, and "Love Machine" by the Miracles. The year 1977 was perhaps the zenith of the phenomenon, capped off by the film *Saturday Night Fever*, which included many disco classics by the Bee Gees, "Disco Inferno" by the Trammps, "If I Can't Have You" by Yvonne Elliman, and "More Than a Woman" by Tavares. Also that year were "Brick House" by the Commodores, "Dancing Queen" by ABBA, "Whispering/Cherchez La Femme" by Dr. Buzzard's Original Savannah Band, and "Keep It Comin' Love" by KC and the Sunshine Band. "Boogie Oogie Oogie" by A Taste of Honey, "I Love the Night Life" by Alicia Bridges, "Jack and Jill" by Raydio, and "Le Freak" by Chic were released in 1978. The gay presence was finally acknowledged openly by the popularity of the Village People, whose thinly veiled celebrations and spoofs of the homosexual lifestyle (in which they allegedly participated) were contained in songs such as "Macho Man" (1978) and "YMCA" (1979).

In 1979, as the craze was winding down, "Pop Muzik" by M, "Rapper's Delight" by the Sugarhill Gang, and "I Wanna Be Your Lover" by Prince pointed to something new again. With "Pop Muzik," disco and punk were showing signs of merging; with "Rapper's Delight," Black music was developing a new social consciousness; and with "I Wanna Be Your Lover," Black musicians were renewing their appeal to Whites. All these tendencies would be reinforced in the near future.

As with any fad, disco made a juicy target for parody. Rick Dees and His Cast of Idiots had a number one hit in 1976 with the novelty song "Disco Duck," but toward the end, the parodies became more hostile. Frank Zappa's 1978 *Sheik Yerbouti*, for example, was filled with venom. One of its songs made it big on the charts: "Dancin' Fool."

As the antagonists gained in passion and numbers, involving many of those formerly indifferent to the phenomenon, critics and disc jockeys joined the fray, perhaps sensing fatal weaknesses in their enemy. And there were many targets. By the end of 1978, 40 percent of Billboard's "Hot 100" were disco albums, as were eight of the top ten singles. One year later, however, disc jockeys were breaking these very same records on air, record companies were shifting their emphasis back to a more traditional variety of rock, anti-disco rallies were being held across the country, and performers were blowing up disco records at their concerts. Aptly dubbed "anti-discomania" by the media, it culminated in the rather nasty "Do Ya Think I'm Disco," recorded by Steve Dahl, then a rock disc jockey on Chicago's WLUP, a parody of Rod Stewart's "Do Ya Think I'm Sexy":

> My shirt is open, I never use the buttons.
> Though I look hip, I work for E.F. Hutton.
> Do ya think I'm disco,
> Cause I spend so much time blowdrying out my hair.

Most radio stations, however, simply decided to follow the movement back to rock without antagonism, feeling that it was either not necessary or not in keeping with the sixties' ideal of freedom of choice and expression. In any case, by the end of 1979, disco had run its course, and so had America's respite from the revolutionary conflict.

No doubt there is a variety of explanations for its demise, but they are likely to fall into one of two radically different categories — one morally acceptable, the other not. For many people, disco (and its sophisticated dance styling) was just another kind of rock and roll; some of it was good and some of it was bad, pleasing to some, offensive to others. The problem was not so much the music but the media's insistence on programming it over practically everything else, smothering the dial. It was all too much. Their rejection of disco was merely the desire to hear something different for a change.

There were others, however, whose rejection of disco was morally suspect, for theirs was a rejection not so much of the music as of the people involved with it. It was too Black, too gay, too pretentious and upwardly mobile, and not socially or politically aware. Now we might all agree that social and political awareness is a good thing. And we might also agree that nothing's really wrong with being upwardly mobile, so long as the path upward isn't littered with the bodies of those serving as stepping stones for a privileged few, and so long as the path is wide enough to accommodate all who wish to travel it. But an opposition to the battle for equality, identity, and fulfillment for anyone is another matter entirely. This ought not be tolerated, so the cultural revolutionaries' feelings went.

Disco might not have lasted as long as its aficionados may have hoped as 1980 dawned, but it did help establish the gay presence in American society as visible and significant. No longer could gays be ignored. Because of this, they have come to symbolize the plight of all social outcasts: if those at the very nadir of social acceptability can achieve some degree of respect, should anyone be left out?

Reports of its demise, however, were — as Mark Twain would have it — greatly exaggerated. Initiated, perhaps, by house music, its close cousin techno and reinforced by the DJ phenomenon of "turntablistic" mixology," a genuine resurgence of disco began in the last years of the 1980s and continues to the present. Such artists as Gloria Estefan ("Get On Your Feet"), Cher ("Strong Enough"), and Paula Abdul ("Vibeology") pointed the way, with Janet Jackson ("R&B Junkie"), Madonna ("Hung Up") and Bananarama ("Look on the Floor"). The overwhelming presence of women artists can't be avoided, and this too implies something about gender and sex-orientation equality — especially since many performers play around with androgynous imagery. Madonna comes to mind immediately and, more recently, Lady Gaga (her name allegedly inspired by Queen's song "Radio Ga Ga").

There was another movement in rock during the Interim, with some superficial similarities to disco, but far darker, far more involved with the negation of traditional values and far more abusive of heavier drugs. Largely British, it nevertheless had a major impact on its former colonies. Often called glam or glitter, it was born in the early seventies with Marc Bolan and T. Rex's *Electric Warrior*, it quickly picked up David Bowie, Gary Glitter and Slade. Mott the Hoople's *All the Young Dudes*, the title song written by and the album produced by Bowie, is emblematic of the movement and its connection with the gay community: It's the story of Billy who dresses like a queen, but he's on a real mean team. He can love, but he never got off with his father's fascination with The Beatles and the Stones. That "revolution stuff" was a drag ... too many snags.

Already there is a clear reference to a new generation that rejects the revolutionary course of their fathers. Yet, paradoxically, they were carrying forth with the revolution, digging it deeper into the values of the traditional culture, their protestations to the contrary notwithstanding. Lou Reed, Iggy Pop, the New York Dolls, themselves young dudes, carried the news to America. It was submerged in a sea of punk, reggae, and new wave to the casual observer but, like early styles of rock, it has never died.

The impact that all of this flux in music has had on American culture continues, although with less notice. After all, the mix of glam and disco succeeded admirably in inviting assorted social outcasts into full participation in American social and political life. Punk spoke to radically disaffected youth, and reggae yearned for a harmonious ideal community of one and all. Full equality, however, remained and still remains a goal to be achieved politically. The paradigmatic issue on which success or failure is measured in the minds of many, however, is equality in marriage between heterosexuals and homosexuals and all persons in between, so to speak. A few states have haltingly approved gay marriage proposals, but there have often been as many steps backward as forward. Nevertheless, overall, movement is in one direction — toward freedom and individuality. Many believe that when those least respected in society are granted full admission, so also with the others.

Women

Women have always been involved in rock music, but unlike in the earlier blues tradition and some of its offshoots, they've rarely been able to assume creative control. In those rare instances when they have, moreover, they have not been expected to express the hard edge and toughness of rock, as evidenced best by the singular exception of Janis Joplin. In the Interim, this tendency began to change.

The justly famous "girl groups" of the sixties such as the Supremes and the Teddy Bears were produced by men, Berry Gordy and Phil Spector, respectively. Folk rock had Joan Baez, of course, along with Mary Travers, Judy Collins, and Janis Ian, but there was precious little hard rock in this crowd. Female lead singers (for male-dominated groups) occasionally received a great deal of attention (Grace Slick of the Jefferson Airplane/Starship being the major example), but this doesn't do much to counter the indictment. Moving into the 1970s, Carole King, Joni Mitchell, and Carly Simon achieved considerable artistic independence but, just as before, not in hard rock. Even less effective in countering the restrictive stereotypes were the otherwise excellent feminist singer/songwriters such as Laura Nyro and Holly Near.

Given that the recording industry was male to the core, it is no wonder that sexist stereotypes, male fantasies, and, occasionally, misogyny found expression in rock music. Most notorious, perhaps, were some of the adolescent songs by the Rolling Stones ("Honky Tonk Women," "Under My Thumb" and "Stupid Girl," for example) and some of the imagery in Bob Dylan's work ("Just Like a Woman," "Lay, Lady, Lay," and "Rainy Day Women #12 & 35"). But the Rolling Stones and Dylan were hardly alone.

Aside from the instances of genuine pathology, much of this misogyny is directly attributable to a patriarchal culture. If changes were to come, the orientation of the larger culture itself would have to be replaced with one that was nonsexist. There is some evidence that this began to occur even before the Interim, since the values affirmed by the sixties challenged patriarchy at its roots (the Western religious tradition) and espoused universal equality. The fact that a nonsexist culture wasn't actualized doesn't deny what was intended or even impending. The greatest accomplishment of the sixties was to set the process in motion for the eventual accomplishment of its goals, and a nonsexist society was one of its major implications. To illustrate, on what many regard as Dylan's best album, *Highway 61 Revisited*, released in 1965, "It Takes a Lot to Laugh, It Takes a Train to Cry" he croons to his lover (in his Dylanesque way) that he wants to be her lover and not her boss. Seven years later, Helen Reddy's enormously popular "I Am Woman" showed how extensively the feminist implications of the sixties had infiltrated the popular consciousness. Times had already begun to change.

The height of the ERA movement was reached during the Interim at the same time that women finally broke into the hard side of rock, equaling in excitement, intensity, and volume anything males had ever done. Their numbers were still small, but the walls of male exclusivity had been breached; in the years to come, women hard rockers would pour through as never before. Black women had begun making some progress with disco and, to a small degree, funk; soon, however, White women were involved with the more raucous styles of rock.

Patti Smith, in my opinion one of the most creative and influential rockers of all times, male or female, deserves special attention. Her style, performance, melody, and lyrics capture everything of the essence of rock. On her 1978 album, *Easter*, a classic of the genre, is the absolutely devastating "Rock and Roll Nigger." No one can listen to this without sensing every facet of the cultural revolution with such immediacy that neutrality about it is impossible. ("Nigger" is used to describe anyone outside of society — she specifically names Jimi Hendrix, Jesus Christ and "grandma" as examples.)

Suzi Quatro's album with the revealing title *Your Mama Won't Like Me* (1975), includes a song called "New Day Woman" with the lines "God gave us freedom/You know he gave me my Rock and Roll/Come on and join me now." But far more important is her entire demeanor as a performer: she rocks with the best of them. The same is true of Ann and

Nancy Wilson of Heart; it's their overall style more than anything else that admits them to those areas hitherto restricted to males. So also with Pat Benatar and Joan Jett (the latter first as one of the Runaways and then the lead singer of the Blackhearts); both have exhibited the kind of aggressive, overt sexuality formerly regarded as the exclusive province of men. Finally, it's important to note about all of them that they started young, and remained active as long as their male contemporaries.

Also worth mentioning are Rickie Lee Jones, Chrissie Hynde (of the Pretenders), Donna Summer, and Diana Ross. Although not all of them are acknowledged as singers of hard rock, their status as independent, self-directed women makes them important examples of what developed during the Interim. By the end of the 70s, Siouxsie Sioux (the singer of Siouxsie and the Banshees), Debbie Harry (the lead singer of Blondie) and the Misfits (later to become the Go-Go's) were starting to make it big. Interestingly, all three groups emerged from punk and not from mainstream rock and roll.

At first glance, the primary musical style of these active and determined women who began breaking into the inner sanctum of hard rock suggests more negation than affirmation, yet the fact that *women* were performing it made all the difference. Their very presence was the message. As an illustration of the dialectics of historical change, negation of the patriarchal order in rock music had become an affirmation as the role of women began to undergo a dramatic shift.

Despite their numerical majority, women had always been ignored by a male-dominated society, but by the end of the Interim, this was no longer the case. Further, their essentially subservient role in the cultural revolution was also coming to an end. No longer could they be ignored, and in this, they have come to symbolize all the "others" ignored by society, the helpless and those without any power or voice. The very old, the very young, and the handicapped come to mind immediately as being totally at the mercy of those in power, much as women have been. All those who listened to this new music could hear the changes that were taking place and were bound to be affected.

As the revolution moved into its next phase, the women's movement would assume a position of fundamental importance. It is no exaggeration to say that the success or failure of the revolution will increasingly depend on the support given to it by the women's movement, and the clues will be found in the role of women in rock and roll.

Southerners

Ever since the Civil War, the old Confederacy has not been regarded by the rest of the nation as completely deserving of trust and equality, and certainly not respect. (The mistrust has existed in reverse as well, of course.) The ostensible reason was the continued evidence of racism in the South. Although there was just as much evidence for racism everywhere else (the superficial differences between the two regions notwithstanding), the defeated rebel states have borne the brunt of the accusation. After the war and its aftermath in the period of "Reconstruction" and prior to Jimmy Carter, only three southerners had sat in the White House: Andrew Johnson, Lyndon Johnson, and Woodrow Wilson.

The first two came to the office through assassination; and Wilson purged himself of his regional blemish by moving north, presiding over Princeton University and governing the state of New Jersey. (He was born in Virginia, the son of minister with southern sympathies.) With Carter's election, however, a genuine down-home southerner was in the nation's highest office. At long last, the national divisiveness brought about by slavery seemed to be coming to an end, with the defeated Confederacy finally being accorded some degree of respectability.

This movement toward a new southern self-identity and a more acceptable ideal for self-actualization actually began in Memphis, in 1954, along with the cultural revolution itself. But at that time, it was only the social outcasts who were representing the new South. During the Interim, a much larger contingent of southerners joined in, expressing their independence in their own unique musical way. Carter's election was one of the manifestations of this new sentiment; but even more important, the revolution gained the participation and allegiance of a body of people who had, in many ways, come to symbolize the opposition to the revolution.

No doubt, only a comparatively small number of southerners were converted to the new faith, yet the defections were significant enough to cause alarm among more traditional southerners, all of which is evident in the music. Country and western music by this time had come to represent the established values so solidly that any deviation from the straight and narrow could not possibly go unnoticed. The "outlaw" deviation was so severe that Michael Bane subtitled his book on the movement, *The Outlaws*, with the phrase *Revolution in Country Music*. He was right, but the outlaw revolution concerned more than music; it was part of the larger cultural revolution that had been in progress throughout the rest of the country for at least twenty years. What the "outlaws" brought to it, however, was a much-needed revival of the attitude of negation.

It began with Hank Williams, whose career and life ended tragically in 1953. Williams' influence on country music has been so overpowering that everything since his death has in one way or another been an attempt either to emulate him or to reject him. Elvis, in effect, forced the choice — one way or the other. Country had neither heart nor mind for the rebelliousness of rockabilly, so the softer, pop-oriented "Nashville sound" seemed to be the only available alternative. Abandoning the youth audience to rock and roll, Nashville sought the older and more traditional generation as its audience. Yet the legacy of Hank Williams wouldn't die. His fatalism and sense of the tragic were preserved in the C&W sounds of Nashville, while his hedonism and hell raising were to emerge in the early 1970s as the music of the outlaws from Austin.

In 1972, Waylon Jennings recorded a song written by Lee Clayton called "Ladies Love Outlaws," which soon became the virtual anthem of the movement. "Outlaw" described perfectly the sentiments and the consciousness of the new southern youth, those who couldn't identify with either their parents and their values or the images of hippies, New Left revolutionaries, or counterculture freaks coming from the North. Yet because these southern youths held freedom, pleasure, and sensuality as ultimate values, they found themselves allied with the cultural revolution, if not squarely within the fold. It was only a matter of time, however, before they would self-consciously reject the traditional set of values and join up. And join they did, but in their own way and on their own terms. Thus it was that Willie Nelson, perhaps the symbolic leader of the movement, held the first of many Fourth of July "picnics" in Austin, Texas, with an almost exclusive emphasis on this new southern music. Soon Waylon Jennings would team up with Willie to produce one of the most durable duos in any kind of music.

Without any pretense whatsoever of attempting an all-inclusive historical survey of the major outlaw recordings, I do want to suggest some of the breadth and depth of the movement as well as indicate some of its crossovers to rock. In 1973, shortly after it began,

Lynyrd Skynyrd (mockingly named after a high school gym teacher who abhorred long hair—which the band sported to a man), quite independently, released the electrifying "Free Bird," illustrating that southern rock (not just the "W" of C&W) had an outlaw sensibility too. In addition, the song became a personal anthem for those in all geographical regions who felt a lack of freedom in their lives. (In 2009, it would find its way to number 3 of *Guitar World*'s list of top 100 guitar solos of all times.) Jerry Jeff Walker's recording of Ray W. Hubbard's "Up against the Wall Red Neck Mother" seemed to be a direct rejection of the revolution (including as it does the line "Jes' kickin' hippies' asses and raisin' hell"), but raising hell is certainly not within the traditional value scheme. Paradoxically, this song, too, became kind of an anthem for hippies, albeit with tongue in cheek. On the other hand, a more favorable attitude toward hippies was expressed in Charlie Daniels' "Uneasy Rider" (and in the following year with the Charlie Daniels Band's "Long Haired Country Boy"). "Ramblin' Man" by the Allman Brothers Band, celebrating freedom of a different kind, was another classic crossover from rock and is now a legend.

By 1974, the New Riders of the Purple Sage had entered the outlaw camp. Their "Instant Armadillo Blues" includes a direct reference to the outlaws' unofficial headquarters in Austin—a defunct National Guard armory called the Armadillo World Headquarters, used also for numerous outlaw concerts. Also, an important new southern rock anthem was released: Lynyrd Skynyrd's "Sweet Home Alabama," an unabashed celebration and defense of Southern culture—in the rock idiom. It became an instant crossover classic.

Country rock, a softer rock style of outlaw music, was in full swing by 1975. Willie Nelson's *Red Headed Stranger* topped the country charts and forced Nashville to sit up and take notice of what was happening. The Nitty Gritty Dirt Band, Pure Prairie League, and the Eagles all released albums this year as well. Meanwhile, Commander Cody and His Lost Planet Airmen were keeping the southern boogie tradition alive. Outlaw music had become so broad by this time that it had spawned variations without losing its defining center.

The year following, this variety was fully evident in albums such as these: Poco's *Rose of Cimarron*, ZZ Top's *Tejas* (with such wonderful tunes as "Arrested for Driving While Blind"), the classic Eagles album *Hotel California* (as much pure rock as outlaw—and more than a hint of reggae!), and Bobby Bare's *Winner and Other Losers*. Bare's collection significantly includes a parody of southern "born-again" Christianity in "Drop Kick Me, Jesus (through the Goalposts of Life)." Also, Moe Bandy did "Barstool Mountain," the meaning of which is obvious, reflecting the ambiguity of drink in the southern consciousness—it being a sin yet a form of salvation). And finally, another outlaw anthem was released, "Willie, Waylon and Me," by David Allan Coe. His lyrics tie together the outlaw movement with the sixties as no other song has ever done, and they deserve to be at least partially cited:

> They say The Beatles were just the beginning of everything
> music could be.
> Just like The Stones, I was rollin' along,
> Like a ship lost out on the sea.
> And Joplin would die for the future,
> And Dylan would write poetry,
> And in Texas the talk turned to Outlaws
> Like Willie, Waylon and me.
>
> Well, they say Texas music's in the make
> And we've been makin' music that is free.

> Doin' one night stands,
> Playin' with our bands,
> Willie, Waylon and me.

By this time the American consciousness was being inundated by outlaw music as well as disco, an uneasy juxtaposition if there ever was one.

In 1977, outlaw music achieved enormous popularity with Jerry Reed's "Eastbound and Down," which was the theme for the film *Smokey the Bandit*, and Johnny Paycheck's "Take This Job and Shove It." Together, they illustrate the outlaw's fundamental attitude toward established authorities. Emmylou Harris made it to the top with her *Luxury Liner*, crossing over the other way from Nashville to Austin with a cover of Chuck Berry's "(You Never Can Tell) C'est La Vie." Jimmy Buffett also hit with *Changes in Latitudes, Changes in Attitudes*, with the hedonistic "Margaritaville" making him rich, famous and important. (Soon thereafter, *Rolling Stone* did an interview with him, confirming his status as a popular artist.)

As if to consciously stress the diversity within the outlaw movement and thus further increase its presence nationwide, the Marshall Tucker Band had a major hit in 1977, with "Heard It in a Love Song." Townes Van Zandt, writer for many others, released an album of his own in 1978 (*Flying Shoes*); and Willie Nelson, one of the legends of the movement, had another hit ("Whiskey River"). All illustrated the fact that outlaw music has a mellow side as well.

The son of another legend, Hank Williams, Jr., working hard to maintain his own identity, released "Family Tradition," "Whiskey Bent and Hell Bound," and "Women I've Never Had" all in 1979. Bobby Bare's "Numbers" this year deserves special attention, since it's one of the few clear indications that outlaws were beginning to sense the new role of women in American society. Although one of the finest songs in the C&W genre about gender equality, it was by no means the first — not by a long shot. Tompall Glaser, one of the outlaws' founding members, released "The Streets of Baltimore" way back in 1967. Because it told the story of a country girl leaving her husband and going off to the big city to make a living in a rather unsavory profession, he had a lot of trouble getting it recorded and played. Even "Gentle on My Mind," produced by Glaser, encountered the same difficulties (sex outside marriage being its theme).

There are numerous others with an outlaw consciousness who ought to be discussed were there time and space enough: Dr. Hook, Rita Coolidge, Jessi Colter, Johnny Cash, and Jerry Lee Lewis, to name a few. But the above list should be sufficient to show that the South during the Interim had begun to associate with the larger cultural revolution, reinvigorating its sense of negation while giving southern youth a renewed feeling for their own identity, with their self-fulfillment becoming a live possibility as a result. Again, all of these rumblings had at their core the ideals of freedom and individuality.

Latinos

Latin rock had its beginnings with "Donna" (1958) and "La Bamba" (1959) by Ritchie Valens. A few years later, Cannibal & the Headhunters did "Land of 1000 Dances" (1965), and Los Bravos had a hit in 1966 called "Black Is Black" (the non–Western orientation of the last mentioned song is clear, despite the group's having a German lead singer). About the same time (1965), Sam the Sham (Domingo Samudio) and the Pharaohs began racking up hits with "Wooly Bully." And with these groups, the viability of Chicanos in rock and thus in the cultural revolution was established. Although never in danger of making it to the top, El Chicano kept the Latin presence alive in the mid–1970s (*Cinco* in 1974, for example). But the biggest Latin performer by far has been Carlos Santana, whose *Abraxas* (1970) has become a rock classic.

So it's clear that Chicano rock has been around as long as rock itself, but for decades it existed, barely noticeable, within the larger context. Although there were two major dimensions to their contributions — one based in the same ocean of blues and country as other rockers and the other having its roots in the larger and more varied Latin American cultures — hardly anyone gave either one much thought. In fact, were this distinction pointed out to the young cultural revolutionaries of the fifties, it would no doubt have been met with blank stares. The Chicano community and the other Latino communities were just not significant enough to attract attention ... yet. But Chicanos knew. So did all the other Latinos. And soon, all Americans would finally notice, especially when their votes began to count.

It all began during the interim. Now, we can look back and appreciate the two flavors. Those arising from blues and country included Ritchie Valens, Sunny and the Sunglows ("Talk to Me"), The Sir Douglas Quintet, Thee Midniters (not to be confused with Hank Ballard's group), Los Lobos, Malo, War, Tierra, El Chicano and Cannibal and the Headhunters, The Champs ("Tequila!"), Sam the Sham and the Pharaohs and Question Mark & the Mysterians ("96 Tears"). Most non–Latino and non–Chicano people knew these groups and their music very well, but many assumed that they were Black groups. This includes many very well-known musicians like Tower of Power. The giant of this genre, however, Carlos Santana, was far too much to be captured in any one category from the very beginning.

More recently, although the invisibility of Chicano and Latino rock has continued to a certain extent, it is not so much because these artists are unnoticed. It's more because there is now a veritable plethora of cultural influences on rock, and the earlier simplistic categories seem somewhat beside the point. The Chicanos and Latinos are here — get used to it! This might have been a slogan adapted for their usage at one time. But it's really no longer necessary. The overt presence of various contemporary forms and styles of rock does not begin and end with the tragic Selena Quintanilla-Pérez. She was not a solitary phenomenon. Consider the punk variant in Chicano rock: Los Illegals, The Brat, The Plugz and the Cruzados. This trend would continue much later with Rage Against the Machine, Los Lonely Boys and others. Ozomatli and Quetzal would later fuse multiple musical styles into something generally referred to as "alternative."

Perhaps it should be emphasized that in Mexico itself a semi-indigenous rock and roll cultural revolution has taken place. In 1968, a student massacre occurred in Mexico City, consequence of a rising middle class opposed to the authoritarian regime of PRI (the Mexican political party that ruled the country for more than 70 years). One result was a Mexican "Woodstock": the Festival Avandaro in 1971. It demonstrated that music could be a means of protesting against the established order and a means of revolutionary change. One of Mexico's preeminent groups, Mana, who began in the early 1980s in Guadalajara, personify Mexican rock history in many ways. After achieving critical and popular success in their home country and in the United States in the 1990s, they set up a monster tour that took them to 17 countries with over 250 performances. Emulating their name (derived from the Polynesian term for positive energy) they've focused world attention on programs needed to attack hunger and heal the environment. Overriding everything is their commitment to peace, justice, liberation and an end to persecution. In short — they rock!

The Third World

My interest here concerns the achievement of respect and the hope for self-actualization as they relate to the various Third World communities in America. The music during the Interim that both reflected and encouraged this process was the independently revolutionary music from Jamaica: reggae. Interestingly enough, some of its roots can be traced back to America in that reggae evolved out of ska and rock steady, the former influenced by rhythm and blues programs broadcast from Miami and New Orleans in the fifties and the latter by soul in the sixties. Jamaican musicians, perhaps sensing the drive for liberation contained within this music, concocted an amalgam uniquely suited to their own cultural setting. Ska, possibly deriving its name from the sound produced by strumming a guitar, quickly spread to England, where there was a large West Indian population. America first felt its impact with "My Boy Lollipop," in 1964, by Millie Small. Soul introduced a more upbeat, guitar-oriented sound into Jamaican music, but the resulting rock steady was to evolve still further. With the addition of a slower, more complex syncopation and an aggressive, albeit esoteric, political/religious ideology, the transition to what we now know as reggae was virtually complete. In 1968, the Maytals released "Do the Reggay," and a year later Desmond Dekker had the first American reggae hit with "Israelites."

Except for Toots and the Maytals (who have espoused a kind of revivalist Christianity) and Jimmy Cliff (a Black Muslim), most of the reggae artists (Bob Marley and the Wailers and Peter Tosh being the most notable) have been advocates of Rastafarianism. Emphasizing Black Pride, a strong anti-colonialism, and a belief that Haile Selassie (the late emperor of Ethiopia, whose common name was "Ras Tafari") is the incarnation of God, Rastafarianism symbolizes the plight of all Third World peoples who have been exploited by the primarily White colonial powers of the West. The downtrodden, represented lyrically as "Trenchtown" (Kingston's poverty-stricken ghetto), are thus portrayed as engaged in a struggle of cosmological proportions with the forces of evil (represented by "Babylon"). The wearing of dreadlocks, the open and defiant smoking of ganja, and, of course, reggae music itself are some of the outward manifestations of this revolutionary affirmation. The 1972 film *The Harder They Come*, starring Jimmy Cliff, metaphorically portrays this struggle and has since become a cult classic. The next year, a song written by Bob Marley for Johnny Nash, "Stir It Up," became a hit; yet another dimension of America's cultural revolution was well on its way.

Soon, British and American groups began to incorporate the reggae sound into their own music and thus publicize the Rastafarian movement even further. In 1972, reggae-inspired music included Johnny Nash's "I Can See Clearly," Paul Simon's "Mother and Child Reunion," and the Staple Singers' "I'll Take You There." Led Zeppelin's "D'yer Mak'er" from *Houses of the Holy* followed in 1973 along with Paul Simon's *There Goes Rhymin' Simon* (especially "Take Me to the Mardi Gras"). The trend continued the next year with Eric Clapton's cover of Bob Marley's "I Shot the Sheriff" and Stevie Wonder's "Boogie on Reggae Woman." In the following two years, War released "Why Can't We Be Friends?" and the Eagles did "Hotel California." Curiously, neither of these two latter songs has been generally recognized as reggae inspired, which they most certainly are. In the following years, with the emergence of punk and new wave, reggae became a fully expected component in contemporary rock (the Clash, the Police, and Elvis Costello, for example).

Most reggae, of course, came directly from Jamaica: Bob Marley and the Wailers, Toots and the Maytals, Peter Tosh, Jimmy Cliff, and many others less widely known, such as George Dekker, the Peacemakers, Scotty and Lorna Bennett, Rudie Mowatt, Third World, the Heptones, Arthur Lewis, Augustus Pablo, Desi Young, and Burning Spear. By the 1980s, many record stores had added a separate section for reggae, indicating the extent of its increasing popularity.

In any consideration of Third World music in the United States, the work of Joan Armatrading has to be recognized. Although British by residence, she was born in the West Indies, and her music and consciousness reflect this mixed heritage. Her first album was recorded in 1973, and by her third in 1976, she had become a major artist. Perhaps because of her eclecticism, which makes her music impossible to categorize, Americans have not been overwhelmingly enthusiastic in their purchases. Yet the critics have regarded her as something of a phenomenon. "Love and Affection," for example, from her 1976 album, is paradigmatic of the eclecticism and quality of her music. The albums that have followed have been every bit as good and just as weak in sales. Nevertheless, her presence in American rock ensures not only that the Third World's struggle will have visibility, but that so also will the struggle of women.

Other cultural groups have occasionally been active in rock but not in significant numbers. Link Wray in the fifties was one of the two Native American performers to become successful in the business. Redbone (not Leon) was the other—the only rock band led by Native Americans—with a 1974 hit, "Come and Get Your Love." African groups would have to wait until the 1980s for credible representation, and Asians are still waiting. Yet largely due to the impact of reggae, all of them have been included in the revolution.

The New Youth

Youth is the only group whose struggle for identity, respect, and fulfillment is their defining feature; for them, the struggle is permanent in principle but, of course, can never be accomplished. The very essence of youth is the struggle itself—its defining quality; in other words, maturity, an end to youth, is necessary for these goals are to be accomplished. This being the case, they, perhaps better than any other group, can provide us with the best possible report on the state of the cultural revolution. If American youth continue to express and respond to the negation of the fifties and the affirmation of the sixties, then the revolution lives. But if they've come to express their struggle in different terms, seeking for example the values of the rejuvenated established order, then the cause is lost. The success of any revolution depends on passing its cause on to the succeeding generation, a process that is by no means automatic, especially if some gains have been made. Even paltry gains may tempt some to believe that the struggle has been won. In such a case, these youth would experience of the conditions that precipitated the revolution in the first place to lesser degree, and thus the need to continue would not felt as strongly — if it were felt at all. The perennial problem for all cultural revolutions, then, is the maintenance and continuity of a revolutionary consciousness.

Two major criteria measure progress in achieving this objective. One has to do with the instigation of a revolutionary sentiment unique to the new generation; a mere imitation of their parents' consciousness would not only be transparently artificial, it would never last. A genuine revolutionary consciousness has to be a manifestation of the people who feel it; it can't be imposed from without. It has to be a new expression of the revolutionary values. The second criterion might seem difficult, if not impossible, to accomplish in light of the first. There must be a clear linkage with the historical roots of the revolution in the new consciousness of the young. In this case, the fifties and sixties have to be accepted as a living presence in their own lives. In my opinion, they have been, but suggesting how this is so will entail a list of staggering and controversial proportions.

There were quite a few musical styles within rock during the Interim, some almost exclusively negative, others primarily affirmative, and still others expressing a mixture. Except as otherwise noted, all of the following achieved prominence during these six years, and together they should convey an accurate impression of what the new youth were listening to, and more important, what it all meant.

Most evident in heavy metal has been the attitude of negation, with its emphasis on the images of death, satanism, sexual aberration, dismemberment, and the grotesque. In the years 1967 to 1969, heavy metal became an authentic trend with album releases by Blue Cheer, Iron Butterfly, Deep Purple, Steppenwolf, The Velvet Underground, Led Zeppelin, The MC5, Black Pearl, The Stooges, and Grand Funk Railroad. Since then, the theatrical excesses and the decibels have increased to the point where the old banana-in-the-ear joke needs to be updated. ("Pardon me, sir, but are you listening to heavy metal?"/"I'm sorry, you'll have to speak louder; I'm listening to heavy metal.") Some of the more prominent of the genre have included Ted Nugent, Ozzy Osbourne, Van Halen, Black Sabbath, Blue Oyster Cult, Aerosmith, AC/DC, Kiss, Thin Lizzy, Cheap Trick, Queen, Styx, Boston, Kansas and one of my personal favorites of this period, Judas Priest.

My characterization should not be construed to imply in any way that heavy metal is either undesirable or qualitatively inferior; neither is the case. Negation is absolutely necessary for any change to occur, and the genre has, surprisingly enough, produced some rather interesting insights into the human condition: "(Don't Fear) the Reaper" by Blue Oyster Cult (1976) and "Dust in the Wind" by Kansas (1977) are among the best of them. Interesting also is the Judas Priest cover of Joan Baez's "Diamonds and Rust" on their third album, *Sin after Sin* (1977). This, in a sense, touches base with their musical predecessors Moreover, the very volume of heavy metal has a unifying effect on its listeners; the differences that tend to divide people are almost literally blown away. As with many other musical stylings, allegiance to this kind of music has resulted in a clearly definable and continuing subculture among the youth; it began in the Interim, and its significance has not abated.

Another almost entirely negative point of view is punk, which began to emerge during the latter part of the 1970s, but has roots reaching back to the fifties and sixties. Its origins were in some of the wilder rockabilly performers, such as Gene Vincent, Charlie Feathers, Eddie Cochran, and of course Elvis Presley. Screamin' Jay Hawkins, especially with his "I Put a Spell on You," added a Black basis to the style as well. The path continued through the Hamburg period of The Beatles and the very early Rolling Stones. Youthful unemployment, the economic hardship of the lower classes amid upper-class affluence, a conservative music industry, an even more conservative political establishment, and a curious but aberrant version of traditional Christianity (the "born again" movement) all combined to set the stage for a massive, seemingly nihilistic outrage from those at the bottom of society. But there were many others who in some way could identify with them. Dr. Feelgood, the Ramones, Blondie, and *The Rocky Horror Picture Show* were some of the earliest manifestations of

American punk. The British quickly followed with the Sex Pistols and the Clash, among others. Almost immediately we were hearing from the likes of the Dictators, the Weirdos, the Zeroes, the B-52's, the Fabulous Poodles, 999, and Richard Hell and the Voidoids. Since 1980, the punk subculture not only continued but expanded, in partial response, no doubt, to the election of a new symbol for the rejuvenated establishment.

Closely associated with punk was the revival of rockabilly (neo-rockabilly for lack of a better designation) as much a British as an American development. Dave Edmunds and his frequent cohort, Nick Lowe, were major proponents of the genre, later teaming up formally as Rockpile. Robert Gordon (sometimes in collaboration with Link Wray), the Stray Cats, and Billy Hancock and the Tennessee Rockets have been among the purists in the revival; while Tom Petty and the Heartbreakers and Southside Johnny and the Asbury Jukes have opted for a more modified styling. Even many of the punk and new wave groups have incorporated a few rockabilly songs in their repertoire. It is hard to avoid the conclusion in all of this that the negation of the fifties has been *intentionally* adopted as a response to a growing perception of the contemporary world. Another essentially negative style has been maintained in blues rock. In 1974, this was evident in albums by the Rolling Stones (*It's Only Rock and Roll*), Little Feat (*Feats Don't Fail Me Now*), and Van Morrison (*Veedon Fleece*). ZZ Top's *Fandango* and Bob Seger's *Beautiful Loser* came out a year later. Then followed Rod Stewart's *A Night on the Town* (including the sensitive "Killing of Georgie," which portrayed the murder of a homosexual) and albums by Steve Miller, the Blues Brothers, George Thorogood and the Destroyers, Delbert McClinton, and Van Morrison. In 1976, the Rolling Stones released their highly controversial *Black and Blue* album, the issue being misogyny. Although a blues styling might suggest a far greater Black representation, the overwhelming majority of musicians in this category are White. This genre of rock, however, essentially uses blues; it's not part of the blues tradition. Besides, Black music was then in the process of establishing its independence with something new.

The last primarily negative style has been variously identified as art rock, glitter rock, glam or simply avant-garde rock. Highly experimental and usually eclectic, involving non-rock ingredients, it has not always been accessible for the mass audience. Avant-garde, however, is necessarily a relativistic description, for what may appear to be so in one period may be considered the norm in another. In any case, the Interim had a veritable wealth of such artists. Among them were Lou Reed, David Bowie, Brian Eno, Alice Cooper, and Frank Zappa, and groups such as Roxy Music, Pink Floyd, Jethro Tull, and the Tubes. Although questing for an innovative way to express the alternative set of values, the focus of art rock was an antagonism to the resiliency of the old values so deeply embedded in the American consciousness.

As the obverse of punk, new wave has been imbued with a large dose of the affirmative attitude, espousing values virtually identical to those of the sixties. Elvis Costello's *Armed Forces*, in addition to opposing militarism, includes a song called "(What's So Funny 'Bout) Peace, Love and Understanding" (1978), and the Talking Heads *Talking Heads: '77* contains the satirical "Don't Worry about the Government" (1977). Both are implicitly anarchistic. Others emerging during the Interim include the Police, Ian Gomm, the Cars, Dire Straits, Blondie (after their punk incarnation), and even the savage Warren Zevon.

Much of the rock music early in the Interim is not easily classifiable, and perhaps for this reason alone, it's worthwhile having a sample. Albums released in 1974 include those by Jackson Browne (*Late for the Sky*), Eric Clapton (*461 Ocean Boulevard*), Linda Ronstadt (*Heart Like a Wheel*), Supertramp (*Crime of the Century*), and ABBA (*Waterloo*). The following year there were albums by Bruce Springsteen (*Born to Run*), Earth, Wind and Fire (*Gratitude*), Fleetwood Mac (*Fleetwood Mac*) and Carole King (*Really Rosie*). Releases of 1976 included albums by Joni Mitchell (*Hejira*), Daryl Hall and John Oates (*Bigger Than Both of Us*), Jeff Beck (*Wired*), Diana Ross (*Diana Ross*), the Eagles (*Hotel California*), Marvin Gaye (*I Want You*), and the phenomenal live album by Peter Frampton (*Frampton Comes Alive*). By 1977, most of the major releases were beginning to fall into one of the categories already mentioned in this chapter. My guess as to why this was the case concerns my admittedly biased observation that the previously mentioned categories are definable as negation or affirmation, while the albums here mentioned are not. As the 1970s came to a close, it became increasingly difficult to produce rock music with neither orientation; neutrality was coming to an end.

The fifties were kept alive by Elvis himself, among others, until his death in 1977, and maybe even more so thereafter. Although much of his later work was of extremely low quality, there were always glimmers of his greatness: "Burning Love" (1972), "T-R-O-U-B-L-E" (1975), "Hurt" (1976), and "Moody Blue," "Way Down," and "My Way" (all in 1977). When the historic *Sun Sessions* album was released in 1976, making his first, revolutionary recordings generally available for the first time, Elvis and the fifties were ensured as a continuing reality in the consciousness of American youth. The 1973 film *American Graffiti* and the TV imitation, *Happy Days* (debuted 1974), had already prepared the way, but Elvis was the real thing. Also real, in a different sort of way, were John Lennon's two Interim albums: *Walls and Bridges* (1974) and *Rock 'n' Roll* (1975), consisting exclusively of covers of fifties songs.

The sixties never came close to dying; many if not most of the major sixties performers were still producing new and significant music. Not only was their work enormously popular, it was critically acclaimed as well.

The folk tradition lived on in the music of Al Stewart, Joni Mitchell, James Taylor, Carly Simon, Gordon Lightfoot, Randy Newman, and John Stewart. All had been active to some extent in the sixties, but their major successes came during the Interim. Paul Simon, however, had major successes in both periods, even teaming up for one new song with Art Garfunkel in 1975, "My Little Town." It was different with some others. Judy Collins had one major hit in 1978, "Send in the Clowns," but produced little else. Joan Baez began reasserting herself toward the end of the Interim with *Honest Lullaby* in 1979, as did Peter, Paul and Mary in their *Reunion* album in 1978. The latter included the song "Sweet Survivor," which concerned maintaining the dream throughout the 1970s. As in the sixties, this newer and revived folk music was overwhelmingly affirmative of the new values.

A more complex set of emotions and attitudes accompanied the rock-oriented music of sixties survivors. By this time, The Beatles had gone their separate ways, but they still provided momentum and guidance to the revolution. Despite the 1974 *Walls and Bridges*, John Lennon settled into a self-imposed semi-reclusive life, thereby adding to the *mysterium* of The Beatles' Paul McCartney, meanwhile, became increasingly prolific; but, like Lennon, he too was trying to separate himself from a past which had by now assumed mythic proportions. His tactic was a new group, Wings, and a new low profile. To the extent that they succeeded, in the process they also solidified the symbolic stature of The Beatles for the future. In 1977, The Beatles' first (and only) official concert recording was released, *The Beatles at the Hollywood Bowl*, followed two years later by their earliest live recordings ever (at the Star Club in Hamburg in 1962). The enormous efforts taken to restore these crude tapes illustrate perfectly the regard in which The Beatles had come to be held.

Other sixties musicians were active as well: Dylan, with *Planet Waves* and *Before the Flood* (both in 1974), *Blood on the Tracks* and *Desire* (both in 1975), *Hard Rain* (1976), *Street Legal* (1978), and *Slow Train Coming* (1979); the Rolling Stones, with *It's Only Rock 'n' Roll* (1974) and *Some Girls* (1978); the Grateful Dead, with *Terrapin Station* (1977) and *Shakedown Street* (1978); the Who, with *Odds and Sods* (1974), *Who by Numbers* (1975), and *Who Are You* (1978); the Beach Boys, with *M.I.U. Album* (1978) and *L.A. (Light Album)* (1979); the Kinks, with *Soap Opera* and *Schoolboys in Disgrace* (both in 1975), *Sleepwalker* (1977), *Misfits* (1978) and *Low Budget* (1979); Crosby, Stills, and Nash, with *CSN* (1977); Led Zeppelin, with *Physical Graffiti* (1975), *Presence* (1976) and *In through the Out Door* (1979); Elton John, with *Caribou* (1974), *Rock of the Westies* (1975), *Blue Moves* (1976), and *A Single Man* (1978); Jefferson Starship, née Airplane, with *Dragon Fly* (1974), *Red Octopus* (1975), *Spitfire* (1976), *Earth* (1978), and *Freedom at Point Zero* (1979); and the Moody Blues, with *Octave* (1978). While many of these groups might have manifested negation during the sixties, their close identification with the period resulted in their becoming, paradoxically, vehicles of affirmation, so powerful was the mythic stature of the sixties by then.

The Death of Rock?

By 1979, many observers wondered if the age of rock had run its course. Left unsaid, but clearly implied, was the larger claim that the cultural revolution, if in fact there had ever been one, had ended in shambles. Other observers were convinced that after the sixties nothing of worth happened, and contained within was the very same implication: the revolution was over.

Nothing, however, could be further from the truth. Even the briefest of surveys will show that the conflict of fundamental values continued within the course of historical events. Domestically, the "incident" at Three Mile Island fed the fires of the anti-nuke movement and expanded its focus. The increasing scarcity of natural resources (the energy crisis being the most dramatic illustration) led to a growing environmentalist movement, while other economic crises were manifested in the surprisingly effective "housewives' meat boycott." Internationally, both the Iranian kidnappings and the capture of the *Mayagüez* prompted a nearly universal outrage among all Americans. Yet the differences in how Carter and Ford handled these two crises occasioned a split response. Although generally ineffective, Carter's emphasis on a respect for universal human rights was regarded positively by those associated with the revolutionary sentiment. Ford's approach, however, was a narrow-minded display of nationalistic macho, and it was not regarded favorably. Both presidents, however, were parodied on *Saturday Night Live*. While Chevy Chase's impression of Ford was unrelentingly merciless, Dan Aykroyd's version of Carter was much more sympathetic. The difference was not accidental.

Looking back on this period from the vantage of the present, there is reason for confidence in the continuation of the revolution. Many individuals have departed the scene, but others have taken their place. Some of the most significant groups disbanded, but they had blazed a trail for others to follow. The social issues assumed a different configuration, but the underlying problems and conflicts have remained. Throughout it all, the music — and the revolution — endured.

12

The Counter-Reaction and Defense

All revolutions, no matter what their focus or nature may be or how they may be described (cultural, religious, political, social, sexual, etc.), face some kind of counter-reaction from the institutions they seek to supplant. Consider for a moment the three main faith communities of the West. When the Hebrew leader, Moses, sought to introduce a fundamental change in the religious thinking and behavior of his followers, many of them rebelled and forcefully opposed his edicts. When the new Christian movement emerged in the dawn of the Common Era, its proponents faced strong reactions from fellow Jews and the Jewish religious authorities. And when Mohammed proclaimed a new order for the world, he had legions of opponents angrily confronting him and religious warfare ensued.

It has been no different with America's cultural revolution. During the period from the election of Ronald Reagan as president of the United States to the election of Barack Obama to the very same office, the counter-revolutionaries mounted a massive attack on the values and ideas that were struggling to replace their own. And, as with all revolutions of any color and stripe, the revolutionaries mounted a sturdy defense. In this chapter, we'll look at this defense and see how it played out, so to speak, musically.

Like all revolutionary movements in the process of growth and development, however, before defending themselves from without, they must first deal with the inevitable conflicts internal to the movement itself, conflicts that necessarily arise with the passage of time — generational conflicts. The true danger for most revolutions does not come from the established order — the real danger comes from the younger [succeeding] generations. The Soviet revolution failed, for example, not so much from threats from the Western powers, but from its younger generations failing to incorporate the original revolutionary fervor and its values into their consciousness. (And this, I think, had more than a little to do with the infiltration of rock music and its values behind the Iron Curtain.)

Somehow, for a revolution to continue and successfully defend itself from the established order, the past has to be incorporated into the present in such a way that the focus remains primarily on the future. If there is to be any hope of success, the integrity of both the old and the newer generations that follow must be protected and appreciated. If not, the internal tensions, which are otherwise vital as the source of creativity and change, will degenerate into self-destruction. This kind of danger is all the more acute when it's realized that the past and future are simply two different dimensions of the present; they co-exist in our consciousness, as remembrances and anticipations. The conflict, in other words, is necessarily internal and inevitable, and as such, it characterizes the consciousness of all participants in the revolution. So the defense against the attacks of the established order is essentially a struggle from within; or, to use the metaphorical words of another—"a house divided against itself cannot stand." (A citation here should not be necessary!)

In this chapter, I'm going to suggest the shape of this conflict as it occurred during the period from Reagan to Obama and indicate some of its central features. Although the existing evidence allows for only tentative conclusions, it seems to me that the revolutionary generation during this time achieved considerable success in establishing a harmonious balance between the demands of past and future, while allowing for the continued existence of creative tensions. In so doing, whether they realized it or not, they were deeply involved in the difficult process of re-actualizing the attitudes of negation and affirmation in their own distinctive way. Hence, the new generation emerged from this period alive and well, and the revolutionary consciousness was living still in the hearts and minds of those who were making and listening to the rock music.

A Generation in Tension

Without conflict, change is impossible; but without a satisfactory resolution, the changes will not last. It is the overriding task of every generation of revolutionaries to resolve the potentially destructive conflicts bequeathed to them, while encouraging the healthy tensions. In order to appreciate the extent to which this has already happened, we first need to have a rough approximation of the kind of conflicts that confronted them.

Analyses of the present are usually notoriously misleading and are therefore subject to radical revisions, if not outright abandonment, with the acquisition of greater perspective. Even after a few decades, such analyses are basically self-interpretations. How we understand things is necessarily colored by the fact that historical events achieve meaning only as we, individually, give them meaning. They are not "self-interpreting"—they are interpreted by the self. This not the same kind of understanding we seek for the physical world around us. Rather, we are supplying a meaning to events, not finding a meaning that's already there. We can never be sure that all the biases and distortions have been removed in this process, and there is nothing that can give us this assurance. On the other hand, what we're interested in is not a so-called objective and neutral account but the self-appraisal itself. So we need not fear the intrusion of opinions and assumptions that inevitably color the description. It is precisely these qualities that give us an insight into the character and the people of an age. Those assessing the character of a given time have, from within that time, their own set of ultimate values and are therefore a part of what they are assessing. Perhaps it's a bit of an oversimplification, but it's not so much *what* these observers see as *how* they see it that's of interest. Their interpretations, in other words, are themselves cultural artifacts worthy of investigation. The music of the time will yield the most direct access to the consciousness of the period, but those otherwise intimately involved with the generation under consideration can offer us valuable insights as well. After all, they all hear the same sounds.

The first and most exhaustive analysis was a seven-part series done by Dan Morgan for the *Washington Post* (December 27, 1981–January 2, 1982) entitled "Coming of Age in the '80s." His basic conclusion was that the present generation is internally divided between its allegiance to many of the ideals of the sixties and its acknowledgment of the practical demands of the present. In many ways, his characterization of this early part of the Counter-Reaction seems quite valid throughout this entire period and into the present. It may very well be a fundamental feature of America's cultural revolution (or, indeed, any kind of revolution) as it continues into the future. So this analysis deserves further attention.

On the one hand Morgan noted that persons then coming of age were concerned to make the dream of peace, freedom, equality, and justice for all come true, many even suspecting that the sixties rebels had sold out to the establishment. Individual fulfillment was one of their fundamental goals, and it took shape in the quest for a meaningful job as well as the search for an all-inclusive spiritual reality. While many returned to the religion of their parents, others associated with some of the non–Western traditions, and a well-publicized few sought the security of a cult. On many social issues (including race, sex, and drugs) they were generally liberal; however, there were also issues on which they were divided sharply (abortion, capital punishment, nuclear energy, pacifism, and America's proper role in the world among them). Mostly, they were patriotic, yet it was patriotism minus an excessive nationalism; they had a pride in what our country stands for, if not always for what it has done. Underlying all of this was a fundamental idealism and a concern for others as well as themselves.

On the other hand, for Morgan, rampant inflation, increasing scarcity, and the ever-present threat of war and ultimate destruction combined to produce something akin to an obsession with personal security and practicality. This should not be confused with simple greed or egoism, as is so often done. Rather, it was the completely understandable result of this generation's fear for what the future had to offer. Despite having grown up during the 1970s, they uncompromisingly rejected any association with what some referred to as the "Me Decade," being suspicious that the appellation actually had no referent whatsoever. From their perspective, they saw themselves confronted by a crazy world, which had forced them to concentrate their attention on practical concerns to the exclusion of almost everything else. To them, this was not selfishness at all; it was being realistic.

To reiterate, Morgan's portrayal seems to be an entirely appropriate understanding of America's cultural revolution as it continues into the future, and Maslow's notions may further clarify it. The dilemma portrayed by Morgan amounts to a conflict between Maslow's second and fifth stages, the need for security and the need for self-fulfillment. For reasons that are perhaps obvious, the assurances of previous generations that their basic survival needs would be met had not been successfully transmitted to their *descendant*s — unsurprising, given the present state of the nation and the world at that time. This was actually true for both defenders and challengers of traditional values. The loss of these assurances struck all of them as patently unfair, and they wanted to know why it happened and who was responsible. They felt cheated. Because of this, the revolutionaries distrusted all authorities and even hated some. These authorities included parents, politicians, the government and, above all, school (Pink Floyd's *The Wall* became something of an anthem for revolutionaries, while a growing "home-schooling" movement served the interests of many traditionalists). Curiously, however, both often deferred to the very authorities they distrusted in their quest for security. They tended to respond differently, however, to the rising amount of personal freedoms. Almost universally, those sympathetic to revolutionary values exhibited difficulties in handling the freedoms they had inherited from their revolutionary predecessors, and as a result, they tended to reject the very guidance they felt they needed. The traditionalists, on the other hand, responded by tending to reject or deny the legitimacy of these freedoms.

If Maslow is correct, the struggle for security will have to succeed before anyone can properly engage in a quest for self-actualization. But the satisfaction of this prior set of needs is predicated on knowing why these assurances have been denied. More and more the revolutionaries were coming to believe that the rejuvenated establishment was to blame. As this suspicion grew into a firm conviction, the renewal of the revolutionary conflict was rejoined in earnest. The traditionalists, of course, already assigned responsibility for this to those advocating the overthrow of traditional values. Each blamed the other.

Mother Jones, an antiestablishment magazine with an "Old Left" slant, devoted an entire issue (September/October 1983) to the rising political consciousness of women and their potentiality for wielding enormous political power. While there are many blocs of Americans whose voting behavior has traditionally not been commensurate with their populations, women were becoming increasingly convinced that the rejuvenated establishment was responsible for their present situation, since it saw itself as the protector of the traditional set of values, which were heavily sexist. (The election of Barack Obama did not alter this fundamentally, since his successful bid for the presidency stifled the competing bid by then–Senator Hillary Clinton.) Although *Mother Jones* didn't dwell on it at the time, the result of women's rising political consciousness was an increasing conflict between those wishing to preserve the traditional relationship between the genders (supported by a patriarchal culture) and those who wished to destroy it as repressive. More important than the conflicts engendered by this issue between men and women were the conflicts engendered among women themselves. For, as I've already mentioned, the fate of the cultural revolution in many ways depends on the fate of the feminist movement. And this movement itself has never been solidly unified. More simply, as the women go, so goes the revolution.

Ellen Goodman pointed out yet another conflict experienced within the revolutionary generation in the period of Counter-Reaction—a conflict internal to their parents and as valid today as it was then. In a July 1983 article in *Ms.* magazine, "The Turmoil of Teenage Sexuality: Parents' Mixed Signals," she discussed the extraordinary tensions created by parents who have adopted the ideals of sexual liberation and gender equality from the sixties, but who, for many psychological and sociological reasons, try to prevent their children from putting them into practice. Inevitably, they must face accusations of cowardice or, worse, hypocrisy, followed by the loss of affection and respect. Since the new sexual ideals generally had been accepted as morally desirable by both parents and children, there was no real possibility of rescinding them; the only real alternative was for parents to support and guide their children in their sexual explorations. Most parents, however, were fighting against two major obstacles: one was their traditional upbringing or vestiges thereof, and the other was a barely suppressed envy for a freedom they never had or never utilized. Their adolescent children, on the other hand, were rarely capable of empathizing with their parents' plight; even rarer were moments of recognition and appreciation of the fact that their opportunities existed only because of their parents' ideals.

It is important to realize that this is not the typical parent-child conflict, for it doesn't derive from their differing levels of maturity. The conflict Ellen Goodman is describing could occur between any two age groups (although the involvement of adolescents certainly complicates the issue). It is at essence a conflict between the espousal of values and their implementation. Further, because it involves sexuality, it is especially dramatic and visible. Difficult and painful as it must inevitably be to resolve such conflicts, a resolution must be attained if the revolution is to have a chance of success. Sexuality and its place in morally proper behavior is a live and disturbing issue among the revolutionaries as well as between them and the traditionalists. In many ways, the more complex problem exists among the former; the traditionalists do not face the internal conflict between ideals and practice.

One of the most provocative observations at the time was spelled out in a "Point of View" column in *The Chronicle of Higher Education* (November 4, 1981). In his guest editorial, H. Bruce Franklin wrote that teaching about Vietnam was even more subversive then than it was in the sixties, because students were learning that the causes of our involvement were not unique — not a one-time thing, never to be repeated. The lesson was that it could happen again, and the analogies Franklin drew between Vietnam and El Salvador were neither excessive nor subtle. (Two controversial wars in Iraq and another in Afghanistan since then make Franklin's case even stronger.) Although Franklin was writing about his own moment in time, it nevertheless serves to link the sixties with the present. The issues of the war then and the wars now are essentially the same. The bond thus created is doubly solid insofar as the music of these periods is inextricably linked as well.

Another journalist, Aaron Latham, was interviewed on the *Today* show (July 23, 1983) about the status of the sixties generation. He felt that they were still active. They had come to recognize, however, that the process of change is far slower and much more complex than they had at one time believed. With this accommodation to reality, they had entered the various institutions and professions that they once regarded with scorn. Yet they found ways to do so with their values reasonably intact, making change from within a real possibility for the first time. (Latham didn't mention it, but these same people had by this time become parents and grandparents, with all that this implies about continuing the revolution.) It's worth noting that recognition of the length of time involved with revolutionary change was a major achievement. Cultural revolutionaries who have followed and have incorporated this notion into their thinking owe a debt of gratitude to these revolutionaries who lived through the Counter-Reaction, discovered this truth and passed it on.

Looking at observations of American youth as the Counter-Reaction progressed into the 1990s, we are talking about the so-called Generation X, described as those born from the mid–1960s through the mid–1970s. The term itself was popularized by Douglas Coupland's 1991 novel, *Generation X: Tales for an Accelerated Culture*. Coupland has always been a bit ambiguous as to how he came up with the title. Sometimes he attributed it to Billy Idol's punk band of the same name and at other times to Paul Fussell's sociological study *Class*. Coupland said, "In his final chapter, Fussell named an 'X' category of people who wanted to hop off the merry-go-round of status, money, and social climbing that so often frames modern existence."[1] Coupland is Canadian by birth, so his observations from a distance, as it were, in this novel had the ring of truth. Recall for a moment Sartre's notion of "the look." In a 1991 interview with Mark Muro of the *Boston Globe*, Coupland said, "I just want to show society what people born after 1960 think about things.... We're sick of stupid labels, we're sick of being marginalized in lousy jobs, and we're tired of hearing about ourselves from others."[2] In this novel, he titled one of his chapters "Quit Recycling the Past" as if to reinforce this notion. One of his major themes throughout was to depict the antagonism the so-called X-ers felt for the baby boomers in particular. This rejection of the past (the revolutionary heritage) is the kind of internal tension that can destroy a revolution; it is far more insidious than attacks from the traditional order.

As the 1990s proceeded, so also did the somewhat questionable practice of classifying each new generation according to the change of digits in the tens column. As I've contended earlier, this kind of numerology reveals no intrinsic meaning concerning the change of generations; rather, it's the appearance of significantly meaningful events that define generational boundaries. Closely following Generation X according to many observers, "Generation Y" arrived. Their assessments came just as quickly, and the prevailing agreement about this new collective was no agreement whatsoever — including whether or not this nomenclature was even sensible. Alternative labels, such as "The Trophy Generation" and "The Millennial Generation," were close competitors for the honor. More significant perhaps was the absence of agreement on how to characterize this new crop of youth except in the most general and obvious ways. They conclude that persons born from the late seventies to the late eighties, for example, have been deeply and profoundly affected by the explosion of communication technology — hardly a startling revelation. However, the consequences of this massive infusion of new technology into American culture were then and continued to be startling. The computerization of virtually everything coupled with the impact of the Internet has enabled the creation of new social arrangements extending not only throughout the nation but also throughout the world. Among other things, the effects include the following:

- New ways to find and develop intimate relationships via a plethora of dating services (all tailored to one's specific proclivities)
- Live computer gaming via numerous online services across vast distances and national boundaries
- Instant messaging via applications created by AOL Yahoo, MSN and others
- Continuous communication via cell phone texting, Twitter and its clones
- Sending homemade videos via YouTube and its clones for the world to witness
- The presentation of self in everyday life (to resurrect the title of Erving Goffman's seminal sociological analysis of 1959) via social sites such as Facebook, MySpace, and LinkedIn
- Exchanging music via the various fee based services on the Web (all created in the wake of the demise of Napster's free and later decreed illegal service).

All of this, and more, meant something significant about this new generation and its inheritance of the revolution.

Though they may not have been aware of doing so, this generation was wiser, more realistic and more determined than their immediate predecessors (the radicals and countercultural devotees of the sixties) in achieving their goals. In the midst of his bleak look backward in American history from the perspective of the economic disasters of 2009, Kurt Andersen offered a few optimistic sentiments while opining in *Time Magazine* on his book *Reset: How This Crisis Can Restore Our Values and Renew America*:

> The postwar generation was the first to refuse to grow up, but Gen-X and the rest have followed in their footsteps. And the selfish, heedless, if-it-feels-good-do-it approach enshrined by young boomers subsequently enabled the risk-taking, party-hearty paradigm that has governed so much of American life, economically and otherwise, for the last quarter century. Now in the twilight of their hegemony, with this crisis and the necessary reshaping of America, the boomers have their last best shot at helping to straighten out the mess they helped make.[3]

It's interesting that a turn has been taken toward the one generally recognized philosophical orientation specifically attributed to America: Pragmatism. Despite its focus on what works as the determinant of value and truth according to many of its critics, the idea of destroying racism, militarism, ignorance and so on because they "don't work" doesn't seem so bad. With the election of Barack Obama in 2008, this American creed, if you will, was wedded to all of the possibilities implicit in the new technology. His campaign was the most efficiently computerized of anything of its kind. Perhaps this is what gave Kurt Andersen such optimism, albeit tempered by the recognition that no matter how idealist people may be, they are still "people."

In terms of two of the fundamental values of the cultural revolution, freedom and individuality, think briefly about how rock music's message has been affected by the revolution in technology. The disbursement of music over the Internet, either for free or relatively cheaply, has allowed each person to become his or her own program director. One need not be limited to the mass-produced recordings created by others or radio programs dedicated to a particular genre. Each of us can "produce" whatever music we wish according to our individual tastes. Further, the Internet has, in effect, erased a whole set of artificial boundaries — those that divide nations, peoples, music, languages and cultures. No wonder the dictatorial regimes in China and Cuba, for example, try to restrict their populations from free access to the Web.

Finally, I'd like to venture a few personal observations about the "generations" that emerged during counter-reactionary period. As a high school student during the fifties, a university student during the sixties, and a university professor from the 1970s to 2009, I've had the opportunity to observe closely the changing of the generations. (As with all observations of this nature, mine are entirely subjective, biased by my own values and limited by my perspectives.) On the negative side, the younger generations exhibit an incredible naiveté and ignorance about virtually everything, two unfortunate characteristics that feed on each other. They tend to manifest themselves in such ways as a simplistic patriotism, an even more simplistic religiousness, a lack of critical thinking, and a new form of illiteracy. (Although they have the ability to read and write, rarely do they exercise this ability unless required to do so.) On the positive side, they tend to develop a complex mixture of idealism and pragmatism that the sixties only dreamed about and the fifties couldn't even imagine. They see no intrinsic tension between working in a highly complex and structured "traditionalized" society on the one hand and affirming their individuality on the other — even if this occasionally requires breaking the drug laws. In other words, they see no incompatibility between freedom and structure. All generations, of course, embody negative and positive features; the problem is how to decrease the former and encourage the latter.

As I listened to rock music from its origin through the Counter-Reaction, however, I found some basis for confidence. The angry negation of the fifties and the optimistic affirmation of the sixties were reawakened, giving substance to the positives while calling into question the negatives. As my first and only witness, I call upon the music.

The Reawakening of Negation

One of the most fascinating and revealing manifestations of the consciousness of musicians is, not the lyrics of the songs they write, but rather the names they've intentionally adopted for their groups. Individuals, of course, have adopted stage names, but group names may be more significant. Invariably, they disclose something about the group's overall ideological orientation, whether expressed in straightforward or ironic fashion. Occasionally, the meaning of the name will be obscure or arcane, esoteric to all but a devoted few; more often, it will be reasonably clear and unambiguous. In what follows, I've tried to include only those names with comparatively obvious meanings. Interestingly, the overwhelming majority of groups that became active in the Counter-Reaction period have adopted names that express the attitude of negation. Perhaps this was to be expected, since the traditional values were being reasserted — some would say with a vengeance. The first order of business, then, was to oppose them.

The 1980s

Negation pure and simple is the meaning evident in names such as Anti, the Anti-Nowhere League (suggesting the negation of negation), the F.U.'s (the Fuck You's), Richard Hell and the Voidoids, Mood of Defiance, N.O.T.A. (None of the Above), Suicidal Tendencies, T.S.O.L. (True Sounds of Liberty), Void, and, perhaps the best-known, X. "Anti Social," written by a French rock group (Trust) and covered by Anthrax in 1988, is particularly interesting for the variety of features packed into it. It also appeared on an album curiously named *State of Euphoria*. Other groups had a more specific form of negation in mind, such as governmental institutions or the state, obviously suggesting anarchism: Black Flag, the Dictators, Gang Green, Falling Idols, Government Issue, Kilroy and the Anarchists, Law and Order, Manson Youth, MDC (Millions of Dead Cops), My Rules, New Order, No Authority, 100 Flowers (from a speech and policy directive of Mao Tse Tung, as his name was then spelled), Rank and File, the Red Brigade, Red Rockers, Social Distortion, S.S. Decontrol, the System, the Vandals, and Vox Populi. Similarly, there were many groups whose names imply an antiwar theme: Agent Orange, the Clash, Electric Peace, Gang of Four, Ground Zero, Die Kreuzen, Modern Warfare, the New Marines, Spandau Ballet, War Zone, and White Flag.

Negation of a more social nature was directed against religion (mainly Western and Roman Catholic) by groups such as Bad Religion, Battalion of Saints, Catholic Girls, Christ Child, Christian Death, Christian Lunch, Crucifix, the Damned, Doo Doo Church, Last Rites, Lords of the New Church, Moslem Birth, 999 (the "mark of the beast" inverted), Sisters of Mercy, the Stepmothers, the Nuns, and Shattered Faith. Protestantism and Catholicism are symbolic targets; all religions are implicitly being rejected by these groups. Traditional sexuality and the morality that supports it were also attacked: the Buzzcocks, Naughty Women, the Sex Pistols, Sham 69, the Slits, Sin, Sin 34, Violent Femmes, and X Offenders. Continuing with negation of a social nature, some of the most amusing names concerned the middle class and all its trappings: Barbie and the Kens, the Jones (despite this probably being their real name), Jerry's Kids, the Microwaves, the Middle Class, Suburban Adventure, Suburban Blight, the Suburban Lawns, the Suburbs, Television, and the Young Home Buyers. The status and condition of youth at that time yielded names for still other groups: the Adolescents, Dead Youth, the Misfits, Musical Youth, Wasted Youth, Youth Brigade, and Youth Gone Mad. Even the technological bent of contemporary society was negated, especially insofar as it had a dangerous tendency toward dehumanization: Channel 3, Devo, Essential Logic, Four out of Five Doctors, Modern Industry, and Saccharine Trust.

Sometimes these new musical groups chose to express not so much their ideological stance as their relationship with a particular part of the past. Since negation was emphasized by the fifties, the references to this period were especially interesting. At least three have Elvis in mind: Elvis Costello and the Attractions, the Elvises, and Kid Creole and the Coconuts. (Actually, any group that adopted a name in the form "The ___ and the ___" had the fifties in mind.) There's more: The German group Matchbox takes its name from a song by Carl Perkins, and many groups use the term "cat"—all having reference to the wild rockabilly (or "cat") music of the period, of which Carl Perkins was a prime example. Hence, there were the Alley Cats, the Pole Cats, the Rockats and the Stray Cats. Some groups had a specific historical event in mind (the Red Scare, the Payolas, and the Body Snatchers); while others sought to evoke the mood of the fifties with names such as the Beatnik Flies, the Chesterfield Kings, Switchblade, and Klark Kent.

The new music included far too many songs evidencing negation to catalog here, but I do want to cite one category of songs that had recently emerged—songs about Vietnam (implying, as they often do, an antiwar message). Robert Hilburn noted in his column for the *Los Angeles Times* (October 3, 1982) that "pop music was a haven in the '60s for antiwar expression,"—and he mentioned The Beatles, Dylan, and Joan Baez, among others— "but musicians were mostly silent during the '70s about the emotional scars left by the nation's Vietnam involvement. They've only recently begun to reopen this delicate wound."[4] His examples, however, were the Charlie Daniels Band's "Still in Saigon," Stevie Wonder's "Front Line," and Billy Joel's "Goodnight Saigon." All of these are excellent examples, no question. But Hilburn apparently missed the same trend in the new music (Warren Zevon's "Roland the Headless Thompson Gunner" and the Dead Kennedys' "Holiday in Cambodia," for example). Don Henley's "Them and Us" and Randy Newman's "Song for the Dead" should have been included as well. All of them were stark portrayals of the horrors of war, both the fighting itself and its aftermath. In the years to come, we will find more songs of this kind and more about Vietnam in particular.

In this connection, we shouldn't overlook the direct involvement of musicians in protest activity. The MUSE concerts held in Madison Square Garden (September 19–24, 1979) were especially significant. Sponsored by Musicians United for Safe Energy, these concerts left no doubt of their antiwar sentiments. The performers represented a wide variety of musical styles, including folk rock (Crosby, Stills, and Nash), jazz fusion (Gil Scott-Heron), blues rock (Bruce Springsteen), and funk (Chaka Khan). This, and the ethnic mix, foreshadowed the racial mergers to occur a few years later.

It was also increasingly clear that, among the new musicians at least, Reagan was now seen as the primary symbol of the revitalized established order, illustrating clearly the antagonism between the traditional values and those expressed in the new music. The antagonism was not very subtle either. The cover of the October 30 issue of *1981*, an alternative newspaper published in Washington, D.C., was satirically emblazoned with a cropped photo of Reagan taken from one of his patriotic World War II movies. He is shown bedecked in uniform, with a serious and determined expression, sporting a red mohawk (courtesy of *No* magazine, a punk fanzine from Los Angeles). *Flip Side*, another punk publication, reported in its issue number 37 (no date) that the winner of its annual poll for Asshole of the Year (1982) was none other than our president. Other interesting data include an anti–Reagan album entitled *Let Them Eat Jellybeans,* a savage satire of Reaganomics called, simply enough, "Poverty" by Relentless Cookout, and a group that has deigned to name itself *Jodie Foster's Army.* (In case the connection of this latter group to Reagan is obscure, recall that John Hinckley's assassination attempt on Reagan was influenced by his belief that this would attract the erotic attention of Jodie Foster—simply because of the character she played in the movie *Taxi Driver.)* The conclusion is obvious: Ronald Reagan had become the bête noire of the cultural revolution.

Also worth noting is the fact that high school groupings (not gangs) largely defined themselves in terms of their preferred music. Hence, punk, new wave, mod, and reggae all refer to social groups as well as musical styles; while head bangers (or heshers) and preppies have their music allegiances as well, heavy metal and top 40 respectively. Very often the musical tastes of these groups overlap, making identification somewhat difficult for all but the participants, but clothing, hair, and language are other indicators that help set them apart. Despite their mutual antagonisms, many of which stem from the fact of their youth alone, they are nevertheless in remarkable agreement concerning the various facets of negation (even many preppies are highly critical of the traditional values). Given their overt musical affiliations, these groups are best understood as direct manifestations of the revolutionary attitude of negation, much as were the various youth groupings of the fifties.

As a final slice of negativity, it should be recorded by someone that a wide variety of Americans were present at the August 1983 ceremony honoring the placement of a new star in Hollywood Boulevard's "Walk of Fame." It reportedly attracted a larger crowd than all previous ceremonies of this kind. The subject of interest was the Three Stooges: Larry, Moe and Curly, a trio of shifting personnel throughout their tenure. Although they were on the surface a slapstick comedy trio (celebrated in the novelty hit "The Curly Shuffle" by Jump in the Saddle), their comedy was the dark view of anarchism personified. But their destruction was not random; it was directed to the established order. Dare I add — their medium was itself their message?

The 1990s

Continuing with the "name game," negation was prominent in the 1990s and expressed in ways similar to the 1980s. Now, however, there was a much stronger presence of rap and hip-hop. Anger and disdain were perhaps even more clearly expressed than in the previous decade, and the targets were often clearer as well. Again, a reminder is necessary: The names are here being considered for their role as a *medium*, and as with all media, there is a message conveyed by the medium itself— apart for their messages (their music).

A veritable assault by verbs, nouns and adjectives is obvious in Smashing Pumpkins, the Beastie Boys, Nine Inch Nails, Rage Against the Machine, The Notorious B.I.G., Guns N' Roses, Public Enemy, My Bloody Valentine, Marilyn Manson, Outkast, Nick Cave & the Bad Seeds, Megadeth, Garbage, Bad Religion, and Type O Negative. Sometimes a general target is specified, as with Faith No More, Jane's Addiction, Manic Street Preachers, Foo Fighters, Our Lady Peace, The Presidents of the United States, Damn Yankees, Skid Row and Alice in Chains. Usually, the target is intentionally vague, and the result is the expression of anger itself, as with the Butthole Surfers, Arrested Development, Slayer, 10,000 Maniacs, Extreme, Rancid and the Screaming Trees.

As far as genre goes, the 1990s saw the emergence of grunge and hip-hop. Genre labels are also names — and as such, media to probe for their meanings. "Grunge" seems almost self-explanatory, suggesting dirt, filth and waste, but this is too simplistic. Those are not the qualities expressed in the music. Yes, "grunge" suggests negation, but the negation of what, you may wonder. Nirvana personifies this genre in the minds of most observers, and their phenomenal hit song, "Smells Like Teen Spirit" (1991) personifies the negation offered by grunge. Although seemingly complicated by the fact that the lyrics express contradictions, such as "I'm worse at what I do best" and nonsense phrases, such as "I feel stupid and contagious," an interpretation of the lyrics is kind of beside the point. Kurt Cobain, is not really expressing anything *in* the lyrics — he's expressing something *by* the lyrics: meaninglessness and absurdity. Kurt Cobain was an existentialist but, unlike Camus, who rejected suicide as the rejection of freedom (the very "essence" of what it means to be human), Cobain succumbed to the absurdity instead of accepting it.

The true origins of the genre label "hip hop" may never be known, but some things are clear: Its roots are exclusively in African American culture. It passed through the disco era and made its first widely acknowledged recorded appearance with Sugarhill Gang's version of a rap written by Nile Rogers, "Rapper's Delight" (1979); it has spread throughout the world; and it has as its major progeny "gangsta rap" and the rivalry between East Coasters and West Coasters. There is no possible way to comprehend the lyrics of "Rapper's Delight," other than to say they express a sense of freedom and abandon through breaking and dancing in the midst of poverty and desolation. And there is no way to comprehend the anger of gangsta rap in either of its coastal variations other than as the expression of the denial of freedom. Snoop Doggy Dogg, from the West Coast, in "What's My Name?" (1992) expressed his anger at a society that has no place for him after prison, but as with grunge, it was not so much *what* was expressed but *how* it was expressed. The profane and misogynistic language led to banning the original version from the air. In the East, the Wu-Tang Clan's second album, *Wu-Tang Forever* (1997) had a rap called "A Better Tomorrow" which expressed this sentiment in the lyrics. Yet the focus was on all the things that should *not* be done to get there. In a darkly wry twist of logic, the wrong ways out of poverty and desolation were negated.

The 2000s

Most of the groups of the nineties in the idioms of metal, punk, hip-hop and grunge kept on a-comin' at the turn of the 21st century. After ten years, *Time* magazine, on its December 7, 2009, cover, proclaimed this first decade to be "The Decade from Hell." Maybe it was. It began with 9/11 and ended with a monstrous financial and economic crash throughout America. Rock and roll was still focused primarily on negating the traditional values of American culture. Negation was sprinkled throughout the first decade in its music and was not as much evident in group names as in song titles. Consider these examples: "Boulevard of Broken Dreams" (Green Day), "Gold Digger" (Kanye West), "No One's Gonna Love You" (Band of Horses), "Bombs Over Baghdad" (Outkast), "Sometimes You Can't Make It on Your Own" (U2), "They Died for Beauty" (Ilya), "Rehab" (Amy Winehouse), "I Don't Love You" (My Chemical Romance), "Darko" (Booka Shade), "All Good Naysayers, Speak Up!" (Sufjan Stevens), "Politik" (Coldplay), "Dare" (Gorillaz), "Say My Name" (Destiny's Child), "Move Along" (All American Rejects), "Seven Nation Army" (White Stripes) and even "Toxic" by Britney Spears.

While anger at the traditional set of values was expressed throughout rock music, it's worthwhile to explore the music of one person in particular who came to prominence during this period: Marshall Bruce Mathers III — better known as "Eminem," by far the best-selling musician of the 2000s. You can read all about his numerous rap and hip-hop music and film awards elsewhere, and you can get all of the personal information you want from the tabloids. What I'm interested in is what he *meant* during this time in terms of negating the traditional scheme of values. To do so, It is absolutely essential to keep in mind the methodology he employed in his various albums; losing sight of this can only lead to fundamental misunderstandings.

In his first album, *The Slim Shady LP*, he adopts the "Slim Shady" persona to voice despicable ideas and to perform acts of unspeakable violence — all expressed with the most profane and obscene language possible. Is all of this intentionally objectionable? Of course it is! And that's the point — no one can listen to Slim Shady and not be repelled by his actions and words and, overall, by Slim Shady himself. (Even those who took to emulating Eminem's persona knew it was repellent; that was why they did it.) Now whether or not Eminem realized what he was doing is beside the point, but what he accomplished was to paint a brutal picture of a person created by a dead and ugly society. The result was for listeners to see the flaws of the traditional set of values that spawned Slim Shady. My own view is that he knew fully what he was doing, and he did it very well. He took the idiom of rap and "made it his own"—as the much overused saying goes. Less widely known is his other major persona, Ken Kaniff, who appears on all of Eminem's albums. He is used to attack savagely the critics of Eminem's music and life. But "he," too, is a product of the traditional society, and while we scorn him, we do not necessarily scorn him for who he *is* (being homosexual for example)—we scorn him for what he *does or might do* (pedophilia, for example).

Don't think I'm portraying an artist who manufactures "others" to represent the evils in society while he somehow remains above it all. Far from it! In good dialectical fashion, Eminem's personae are no other than Eminem himself. *He* is the product of the society he is castigating—and he as much as admits it from the beginning. On his first album, in "Guilty Conscience" he and Dr. Dre portray the devil and an angel trying to influence a succession of people to do evil or good. He is the devil behind the devil in Slim Shady. It's not so much that Eminem uses the medium of Slim Shady to send a message; rather, it's Eminem, the medium, who is the message.

Finally, I do need to say a few special words about "metal"—in all of its raucous configurations and embodiments, first emerging in the mid–1980s. Nothing, it seems, says negation like bashing and thrashing. One of the most accurate summations every made about the role of metal, was captured in the (masterful, I must say) documentary, *Metal: A Headbanger's Journey* (2005), directed by Sam Dunn, a Canadian anthropologist who is himself one of more fanatic of the breed. Not only does he deal with the overall history of metal and its complex variations (accompanied by a massive flow chart of the subgenres as he sees them), he introduces the audience to both a musicological analysis of the genre and a variety of central figures. Musicologically speaking, he explores metal's characteristic use of the so-called devil's note or interval (actually it's a chord) and cites illustrations of its use in classical music, jazz, the theme for *The Simpsons*, as well as in other forms of rock music. Among the highly enlightening interviews with performers and various hangers-on, one was with Thomas Baptiste Morello, the lead guitarist for Rage against the Machine. When asked about the essence of metal, Morello responded with this: It's all about "negation of the world as it's handed to you." There it is—as succinctly put as anyone could want it. Yet in good dialectical fashion, there is implicit in every negation something affirmed. This is true of even the darkest of metallurgists. In a December 4, 2009, radio interview with Carlota on KOMP 92.3 Las Vegas, James Hetfield, lead singer of Metallica, wistfully confessed that the greatest gift he has ever been given is the freedom to practice his art—"metallurgy" at its hardest and finest. Further, ask any metal-head you want about the basic value expressed by the genre and you'll pretty much get the same answer: freedom. Note further that this appeal to the essence of metal, in effect, bypasses any reference to specific genre or subgenre. The "essence" and not the "accidents" is what is important. Sam Dunn's amazing flow chart of metal, with its intricate, colorized lines linking over 20 boxes, each containing a few sample artists, is somewhat beside the point. No doubt, even further subclassifications are possible, a fact that would (in good dialectical fashion) contradict the whole effort. For example, would some of the "Swedish death metal" groups actually fit better in a new "Laplandian" subgenre? James Hetfield had it right. Freedom is the thing— for metal and for rock music as a whole.

The Reawakening of Affirmation

Focusing on the sixties will be unavoidable in this section, since affirmation was that decade's predominant attitude. Even though negation was the watchword during the initial stages of the Counter-Reaction, logically, negation can have no meaning without at in implicit affirmation of something else. A word of caution, however: I'm not at all interested in a simple, backward-looking nostalgia. It's a sentiment that has its rightful place, but not here. Rather, I'm interested in the attempts that were made to recover the affirmation of the sixties so as to provide their generation with the proper impetus and direction for the future. The difference might be subtle, but it's still important.

I see at least three major facets to this reawakening of affirmation: one concerns the sixties survivors themselves (and it's interesting how often they used term "survivor" to refer to themselves), a second concerns the new musicians, and the third concerns the Re-actualization of certain key values.

Sixties Survivors

After the election year of 1980, many of the musicians from the sixties who had, for one reason or another, ceased performing re-entered the music scene. Some did so as individuals, while others re-formed with their original groups.

Of first importance was John Lennon. Himself the foremost symbol of the most symbolic group of all time, he further ensured by his respite from "playing the game" that, when and if he emerged, he would be noticed. He was. His and Yoko Ono's album *Double Fantasy* (1980) was an incredibly forceful affirmation of the direction the revolution must take in the future—namely, like Lennon himself, it must undergo the difficult and often painful process of self-examination so that it might achieve a maturity consistent with its ultimate values. Quite apart from Lennon's murder, committed shortly after its release, the album has come to be regarded as one of his best efforts. It signaled a new beginning for the revolution and a new role for himself within it.

Public anguish over the loss of his potential was registered far and wide, and the yearly memorials held on December 8 throughout the world make certain that the loss will not be forgotten. As more time passes, however, I would expect that the focus of these occasions will increasingly be on his dreams for the future and not so much on the past. The final Lennon/Ono album, *Milk and Honey,* which they almost completed before his death, turned out to be an apt finale. The anguish, however, will always remain, and so it should.

Ellen Goodman expressed the tragedy for us all in her syndicated column written just after hearing the news:

> The Lennon I'll miss isn't the brilliant Beatle of the sixties with his hair "rebelliously" grown below his ears. That John Lennon exists on my records. The man I'll miss is the one I just met again, the man of the eighties, moving in new ways, making new sounds. Five bullets wiped out this father, husband, musician—human work in progress...
>
> The new record he made with his wife, Yoko Ono, *Double Fantasy,* was the work of a survivor. "You have to give thanks to God or whatever is up there (for) the fact that we all survived—survived Vietnam or Watergate, the tremendous upheaval of the whole world," he said in an ironic prelude to his death...
>
> In a way he was talking to and for his own generation. "I'm saying, 'Here I am now, how are you? How's your relationship going? Did you get through it all? Wasn't the Seventies a drag, you know? Well, here we are, let's make the Eighties great because it's up to us to make what we can of it.'"

You can't kill what a man has already done. You can only kill what might have come next. The antique John Lennon had already been preserved. Dammit, it's the promise that's gone.[5]

The three remaining Beatles obviously felt Lennon's loss in a unique and personal way. Yet, as public figures as well as musicians, they inevitably revealed their grief to us, and did so in such a way as to preserve his legacy and the legacy of what The Beatles had come to mean. Harrison's "All Those Years Ago," McCartney's "Here Today," and Ringo's album cover of *Stop and Smell the Roses* (showing him weeping while holding three remaining roses), together, have created the reunion so many had sought for so long.

Also of considerable significance was the Simon and Garfunkel reunion, initiated at their free concert in Central Park in September 1981. In an interview with *Rolling Stone* immediately following the concert, which attracted over a half million people, Simon remarked that there were really only two big reunions possible from the sixties. "And now," he said, visibly expressing his emotion, "one of them can't happen. And I think they probably would have done it too — eventually." Since then, Simon and Garfunkel have toured together and individually in Europe, Asia, and the United States.

Peter, Paul and Mary also reunited and toured the country in 1978, releasing a new album aptly titled *Reunion*. They also appeared at the twentieth anniversary of the Civil Rights march on Washington (August 27, 1983), just as they had in 1963. Peter Yarrow in 2004 looked back on their career as musicians and political activists and commented, "At the beginning of America's cultural revolution, I personally believed that Folk Music would play a significant role in it."[6] He never wavered from this belief, despite the fact that this genre ceased being on the cutting edge of the revolution. It was, after all, at the beginning, and its role was indeed, as he said — significant. Mary's death in 2009 put an end to the trio's recording and performing career, which lasted through 2008. Others attempting the comeback trail included The Animals, Chad and Jeremy, The Everly Brothers, The Hollies and (with a revised membership) The Mamas and the Papas. Only the Everlys, however, retained vocal and performing qualities equal to, if not in some ways, better than in their heyday.

Many other sixties musicians never "retired" in the first place and simply remained active, with greater or lesser degrees of success. Among the most successful was a collage of Brits: The Rolling Stones (their *Shine a Light* concert in 2007 was one of their best ever), The Who, Pink Floyd and to lesser degree The Kinks. (It's probably not unusual, but I personally know of several three-generation-concert-goers who've now seen Stones concerts in their times of youth.) Not only did they all continue to produce quality material, they developed an enormous following among the current generation. The Stones and Pink Floyd continued more successfully into the Re-Actualization period than did the others, most especially Mick and the boys. The Beach Boys came up a bit short on new material at this time, but their popularity at concerts seemed to hold. The death of Dennis Wilson in 1983 did not affect this adversely. They played to over a million people on July 4 in Philadelphia and another million later that day at the Washington monument. Carl Wilson died in 1998, signaling the end for the troubled group, yet the remaining "boys" reunited on the top of the Capital Records Building in Hollywood to celebrate the 40th anniversary of their masterpiece, *Pet Sounds*. (Their rooftop performance deliberately evoked memories of The Beatles' last live performance, in 1969 on a rooftop of Abbey Studios in London.)

A few Motown groups also remained active, a few with their original members intact (as with the Four Tops) and others with a succession of replacements (as with The Temptations). Some of the major solo artists, such as Stevie Wonder, are of course still active as of this writing (as was Marvin Gaye until his death in 1984). Moreover, many former lead singers became soloists — Diana Ross, Eddie Kendricks, and Smokey Robinson, for example. Michael Jackson, of course, was a phenomenon and continued to be active until his death in 2009, despite his rather unusual lifestyle and controversial predilections. As for soul, James Brown (until his death in 2006) and Aretha Franklin, among many others, appeared occasionally, but distinctively Black music had begun to emerge as something entirely new and different during the Interim. These differences have continued to grow and develop and have had an enormous impact on American music.

Those sixties musicians who were able to accommodate to newer forms and adjust their message to a different time were quite successful; others were relegated to the inferior and degrading status of playing nothing but "oldies but goodies," which is where many persons and groups both Black and White found themselves. Concerts comprising oldies were and continue to be fun and nostalgic, but they offer nothing new, no challenges for the future.

Reunions and re-entries are more often than not very difficult, but to regain contemporary significance these musicians had to re-actualize their capacity to make *significant* music as well. To be sure, this is always incredibly difficult, especially for those in danger of becoming trapped in their own mythology, so it's surprising how many pulled it off. My interest, however, is in a particular kind of music they made, music intended as a commentary on their times — specifically, the transition from the sixties, through the Interim, into the Counter-Reaction and beyond to the Re-actualization.

John Lennon's "(Just Like) Starting Over," on *Double Fantasy* is a fitting beginning for this list, since his purpose was to comment not only on his relationship with Yoko but also on the status of the cultural revolution itself. "Hard Times Are Over," a song by Yoko from the same album, contains a similar double message. McCartney's 1982 album, *Tug of War*, is one of his best, and many critics think it exceeds all his previous solo output by far. It not only includes his personal remembrance of John, "Here Today," it also expresses his pessimism about the prospects for economic recovery given the political structure of the time ("The Pound Is Sinking"). There is also his hope for a genuine improvement in racial relationships (the overly saccharine "Ebony and Ivory" sung with Stevie Wonder), his homage to the fifties ("Get It," sung with Carl Perkins) and his vision of freedom ("Wanderlust"). There was no simple nostalgia among any of these songs.

Returning to Simon and Garfunkel, they did more than merely reunite for a series of concerts. One of Paul Simon's newer songs at that time had to do with the senseless deaths of Johnny Ace (an R&B singer from the fifties), John Kennedy, and John Lennon: "The Late Great Johnny Ace." Even more significant was his addition of a new stanza to "The Boxer":

> Now the years are rolling by me
> They are rocking evenly
> I am older than I once was
> Younger than I'll be
> That's not unusual
> No it isn't strange
> After changes upon changes
> We are more or less the same...

The times may change, in other words, but the human condition remains the same.

Just before Simon and Garfunkel's 1983 tour of the United States, Simon was asked why he thought there was such an overwhelmingly positive response to their reunion. His answer implied that the reawakening of affirmation had become a widespread need: "I feel we've been living in just brutalizing times and any time you come across any public figure or figures that represent the opposite, they become very important." His words of over thirty years ago couldn't be more current.

Continuing in this vein, though Peter, Paul and Mary's *Reunion* was released in 1978, it included one song in particular, "Sweet Survivor," which could almost be an anthem for sixties survivors:

> You have asked me why the days fly by so quickly
> And why each one feels no different from the last
> And you say that you are fearful for the future
> And you have grown suspicious of the past.
>
> And you wonder if the dreams we shared together
> Have abandoned us or we abandoned them
> And you cast about and try to find new meaning
> So that you can feel that closeness once again
>
> Carry on my sweet survivor
> Carry on my lonely friend
> Don't give up on the dream
> Don't you let it end
>
> Carry on my sweet survivor
> Though you know that something's gone
> For everything that matters
> Carry on
>
> You remember when you felt each person mattered
> When we all had to care or all was lost
> But now you see believers turned to cynics
> And you wonder was the struggle worth the cost
>
> Then you see someone too young to know the difference
> And the veil of isolation in their eyes
> And inside you know you've got to leave them something
> Or the hope for something better slowly dies
>
> Carry on my sweet survivor
> You've carried it so long
> So it may come again
> Carry on

It would be hard to imagine a more insightful portrayal of the consciousness of the revolutionaries just prior to Reagan's election and the consequent period of Re-actualization. (Peter Yarrow also thought so, for after seeing what I was writing about in this book, he graciously granted me permission to use the entire song free of charge.)

Joan Baez's *Honest Lullaby* was also released before the election, in 1979, and as with Peter, Paul and Mary, her reflections and sentiments still ring true. The chorus of the title song goes: "And I look around and I wonder/How the years and I survived/I had a mother who sang to me/An honest lullaby." The clear implication is that it's now time to pick up where we left off. Actually, Joan Baez herself has never stinted in her dedication to the causes of peace, freedom, and justice throughout the world (through her organization, Humanitas International). Despite the fact that she has had difficulty recording some of her more relevant songs ("Sergeant Pepper's Band" and "Children of the Eighties" among them), she continues to be an extremely credible activist. What makes it work is her dedication, and the fact that it has endured is evident to everyone. I came across an interesting curiosity in doing my research for this book, which underlines her staying power. Judas Priest covered her 1975 song, "Diamonds and Rust," two years later in good heavy metallic fashion and they have performed it regularly ever since. Baez also recorded it live with Mary Chapin Carpenter in 1995, and she has performed it often in a variety of concerts through 2009. What makes it interesting (aside from the always jarring juxtaposition of metal meeting folk) is the enigmatic protagonist of lyrics — Bob Dylan or her war-protester husband at the time, David Harris? Either way, the song links the sixties to the present and future.

I'm not really sure whether Crosby, Stills, and Nash reunited, or whether they were ever a group to begin with. In any case, their 1982 album, *Daylight Again* (a title that says something in itself), includes their feelings about the times in "Wasted on the Way." Written by Graham Nash, who, for a while, returned to the Hollies, it has such lines as: "Oh when you were young/Did you question all the answers/Did you envy all the dancers/Who had all the nerve" and "So much time to make up (So much love to make up)/Everywhere you turn/Time we have wasted on the way."

Regarding the Hollies for a moment, their album at the time included a cover of the Supremes "Stop! In the Name of Love." What's interesting about it is the video they made to accompany it: "stopping" referred to warfare and all the militaristic and nationalistic posturing associated with it. Pink Floyd's *The Final Cut*, Neil Young's *Reactor*, Elton John's *Jump Up* (which has his remembrance of John Lennon, "Empty Garden") and The Kinks' *Give the People What They Want* are all oriented around similar antiwar and antiviolence themes.

Some more recent survivors have expressed other facets of America's cultural malaise. Bruce Springsteen's *Nebraska* explores the effects of loneliness and the loss of hope. Don Henley's *I Can't Stand Still* is a painful reminder that society has failed us ("Johnny Can't Read") and has unfeelingly invaded our lives ("Dirty Laundry"). Bob Seger's *The Distance* focuses on the people most injured by the then current economic disasters. And Billy Joel's *Nylon Curtain* includes a little bit of all of the above and adds his elegy to the men and women who spent their youth and lives in the misadventure in Southeast Asia, "Goodnight Saigon."

Last, but certainly not least, is the strange case of Robert Zimmerman from Hibbing, Minnesota — strange, because "survivor" seems inapt when it comes to him. It's hard to see how in any way he was "put upon" which would necessitate a struggle to survive. He recorded his first studio album, *Bob Dylan*, in 1962, receiving modest acclaim, but followed quickly with *The Freewheelin' Bob Dylan* a year later — to worldwide acclaim. Thereafter, he has put out a combination of studio, live and compilation albums almost yearly, and the acclaim has never ceased. On one of his most recent albums, as of the writing of this update in 2009, *Together Through Life,* he collaborated with Robert Hunter (The Grateful Dead), David Hidalgo (Los Lobos) and Mike Campbell (Tom Petty and the Heartbreakers). Aside from original songs, it covers "Why Can't We Be Friends" (War), "Too Many Parties and Too Many Pals" (Hank Williams), "You've Got a Friend" (Carole King), "My Friends" (Howlin' Wolf), "Howdy Neighbor" (Porter Wagoner), and others. In other words, he recapitulates the entire history of rock music, and thus the cultural revolution, from its beginnings. (I'm using the term "recapitulate" metaphorically from biology in that he appears to repeat the evolutionary stages of a species during its embryonic development. Or, to be more scientific, it's the view that ontogeny recapitulates phylogeny.) The album debuted at number one on Billboard's Top 200, in the U.K. and in various other countries throughout the world. No, he's no "survivor" in the strict sense of the word within the revolutionary process; in many ways, he *is* the revolutionary process.

It's worth mentioning that *Saturday Night Live*'s 34th season finale (May 16, 2009) concluded with cast members doing a seriocomic rendition of "Goodnight Saigon" sung by Will Ferrell and backed by members of Green Day. The "comic" element was the punch line that Ferrell's elegy to his "duty" in "the Big Nam" amounted to a vacation trip during the summer of 2008. The "serio" element was the plaintive yet grim, dead-on somber mood of his singing. The medium here was indeed the message. Not to be overlooked during this episode, Green Day performed "Know Your Enemy," which wonders whether we really do know our enemy, and "21 Guns," which asks the question whether we know what's worth fighting for. There you go—negation and affirmation in the twin nutshells of these two songs. The sixties survived in more ways than in the persons of the survivors. It survived in the music.

New Musicians

When we look at the names that some of the musicians of the Counter-Reaction period gave their groups, their perhaps unintentional recovery of the sixties and what it affirmed becomes immediately obvious—this even if their names seem otherwise negative. They include Catch 22, The Dead Kennedys, Megadeth (evocative of nuclear war), The Insect Surfers, Kent State, The B-52s, The Police, The Pranksters, The Rutles (an homage to/parody of the Beatles), Dire Straits, The Shoes, The Surf Punks, and the ambiguously named U2 (spy plane? unemployment form? "you too"?). Despite the hostility evident in some of them, it was not directed against the sixties; it was directed against those who would preserve the past at the expense of the present. U2 in particular manifested a sixties-like antiwar/antiviolence message in songs such as "I Will Follow" and "Sunday Bloody Sunday." So also did Big Country and R.E.M., although their names hardly suggested it. Nevertheless, it was clear that the past, including its outrages, had to be preserved in the present's consciousness if genuine progress was to be made. Some individual musicians called forth the past in their adopted names. Elvis Costello is only perhaps the most obvious example. Many of these groups continued to be active throughout the period, and others came on board as well.

Album sales figures also indicate a look both backward and toward the future. For the first half of the 2000s, the top-selling album was a Beatles repackaging, *One [1]*. It was closely followed by Linkin Park's *Hybrid Theory*, and an eclectic list: Norah Jones, Usher, Shakira, Britney Spears, two Eminem albums, Avril Lavigne, Evanesence, another by Linkin Park, and *NSYNC. There is actually a much wider representation of musical forms in the top 100 albums than might first appear, since groups such as The Black Eyed Peas have men and women members as well as representation from a variety of racial and ethnic groups. Plus, many groups such as Linkin Park have incorporated metal musical forms with rap and punk.

What does all of this affirm? Certainly, diversity is evident but so also is individuality. It has become by this time extremely difficult if not outright artificial to utilize the old labels to classify the type of music a group plays as well as the group itself. The traditional genre categories, in other words, have pretty much lost their usefulness. For example, in the 2005 documentary film *Metal: A Headbanger's Journey*, the director, Sam Dunn, uses a complex flow chart to illustrate the origins and diversity of metal music, and in so doing (in good dialectical fashion) unintentionally shows the entire effort to be pointless. He uses over twenty categories (one populated by only four members) and includes such question-begging grouping as "Early Punk" and "Grunge." One is devoted exclusively to "Swedish Death Metal" and another to "Norwegian Black Metal." My suspicion that another "metallurgist" may well arrive at a totally different scheme is confirmed by Wikipedia's list of thirty categories, including one called "Folk Metal"—all of which have subcategories! Chad Bower on the Q and A website *About.com* sees the complexity this way: "At the beginning there was just traditional heavy metal. Shortly after it evolved and splintered into many different styles and subgenres.... As time has gone on, there are literally hundreds of subgenres."[7] The point is that as attempts are made to accurately depict these categories, they necessarily devolve into nonsense. Without questioning the notion of similarities among groups or deriding the attempt to identify them, the fact remains that each metal group is unique unto itself. The differences among them (their individuality!) just might be more significant than the similarities. (Sociologists, among other social scientists, have long since realized this and have regarded such categorizations as worthwhile heuristically, not objectively.) This is also true for not only the genre of metal rock but also all genres of rock. (Just try categorizing the British all-girl-singer-all Black-backup-band-and-dancers group Girls Aloud. You'd wind up needing to utilize practically all of the existing genres, and that would make the point.) Then there's the "experimental-metal-indie-folk-art-rock band" mewithoutYou that sings of suicide, Eastern and Western religion, love and war. Putting it as simply as possible, individuality is an intrinsic component of diversity.

There were some interesting references to the past in the lyrics as well. Philip Lynott (formerly of Thin Lizzy) revealed his personal bond with the fifties in "King's Call," a song about how Elvis's death affected him. His personal evocation of the memory of Elvis functions as an apt paradigm for how it affected many musicians of the time. Lynott also wrote "Talk in 79," about how transitory he thought the new wave was likely to be. This suggested, by implication, that no new symbols were to be expected from the present; the basic symbols already exist. The Ramones' "Do You Remember Rock 'n' Roll Radio?" recalls, among others, Ed Sullivan, Alan Freed, Murray the K, T. Rex, Jerry Lee Lewis, and John Lennon. They sing about the end of the seventies and the end of the century and include the plea "We need changes we need it fast/Before rock's just a part of the past/'Cause lately it all sounds the same to me." This call for the revival was necessarily directed to those who were "living in the past," since the Ramones clearly were not doing so; rather, they exemplified the present. A genuine revival had to gather its force and direction from its roots, but the present had to make use of it.

An even stronger call for a revival, based on an affirmation of the sixties, came in Blondie's "English Boys":

> When I was 17
> I saw a magazine
> It had those English Boys
> who had long hair
>
> When I was on my own
> they moved into my town
> and I just called em up
> and they'd be there

> In 1969
> I had a lousy time
> I listened to the songs
> read letters sent from Nam
>
> Now peace and love were gone
> the tired soldiers home
> Ideal society
> gunned down the 70s
>
> Does it feel the same to you?
> Why do you act the way you do?
> Pack it up or pack it in
> There's no excuse
>
> Could the hands of time reverse
> Would we wake or take the ride
> And again speak with one voice
>
> We knew each other well
> Although we never met
> Messages passed to tell
> Equal respect...

It takes little imagination to recognize that the "English Boys" being referred to are those "four lads from Liverpool."

Affirmation was also evident in some of the rather unexpected musical developments. Most curious was the apparent synthesis between punk and country evident in groups such as The Alarm, Blood on the Saddle, Jason and the Scorchers, Lone Justice, Rank and File, and the all-female group The Screamin' Sirens. Equally interesting was the development of a viable Latino rock, as with The Brat, The Cruzados, Los Illegals, Los Lobos, and Tierra. A neo-psychedelic genre (a.k.a. the paisley underground) also began to emerge with groups such as the Bangles, The Long Ryders, Rain Parade and The Three O'Clock. Then, of course, there were groups whose music defies description, as is perhaps evident in their very names: Tupelo Chain Sex and the Fibonaccis (derivative of a 13th-century Italian mathematician), Wall of Voodoo and perhaps the most enduring, Oingo Boingo. All of them were genuinely new, and this in itself was affirmative.

There are no doubt many songs from this period that illustrate where rock came from, what it was doing and where it was going. "Hey Ya!" by Outkast (2004), for me, says it as well as any individual or group can. It's not simply their lyrics and the fact that they are an interesting duo of African Americans with an infectious hip-hop style; it's all of that and more — it's the *gestalt*. The whole is larger than the parts. They're named "outkast" and they're obviously not. They're not even a group. Their music is a mix of power pop, funk, electronic, hip-hop, soul and tuba-flavored-kazoo-ishness with beat-box and tin-can rhythms. (Their style is more often than not characterized as "experimental.") It's "freedom" epitomized or "musicalized" by two guys from a small town in Georgia — André "André 3000" Benjamin and Antwan "Big Boi" Patton. Together they personify not only genuine freedom but also genuine individuality. They've taken from the past, digested it, and with at least six Grammys and about thirty million albums sold, they indicate where the cultural revolution in heading.

The White Stripes say it too. Their 2003 "Seven Nation Army," a punky-bluesy minimalistically produced single not only won all sorts of awards but in its bleak tension-filled lyrics celebrates what free individuals can accomplish. Much like Outkast, Meg White and

Jack White in their very persons are iconoclastic of standard rock fare. They "look" as normal as anyone's next-door neighbors on their way to church in rural Kansas. In reality they're from the streets of Detroit and when they married, he took her surname — deliberately countering one seemingly small traditional value, but suggesting that a lot more were to be dispatched. They often claimed to be brother and sister for reasons never clearly disclosed, but wound up calling it quits just as they were on the verge of making it big. Nevertheless, they — as The White Stripes — continued to play on as free individuals.

Oh, there's more ... lots more — many so well known that we might tend to overlook them: Kylie Minogue's 2001 "Can't Get You Out of My Head" (one of the most hypnotic dance popsicles you'll ever suck on), "Cherry Blossom Girl" by Air in 2004 (so surrealistically mellow and insinuatingly sensual you'll do anything for her or him or anyone over and over), R. Kelly's 2003 "Ignition" (a smooth, simple love rap) and in 2007 Panda Bear's "Bros" (Beach Boys meets Moody Blues and swizzles electric gin). What do all of these have in common? Nothing! That's the point! Freedom, diversity and individuality ruled.

Covers

Covering the music from the past was another form of affirmation, even when the originals were from some period other than the sixties. When covering someone else's music for reasons other than pure profit (as was done in the early fifties), the act is necessarily an acknowledgment and acceptance of the past as well an incorporation of it into the present. It's the recognition that any movement into the future cannot be successfully accomplished until the present has achieved its self-identity, and this is contingent on the present generation having accepted its origins.

The table that follows lists a few sample covers from this period. Though a much more extensive compilation is certainly possible, I think this clearly conveys the idea that this generation knew where it came from and where it was going. Note: I've included a few songs in the list where "sampling" was done (utilizing a small portion of another song in the main song) as well as complete covers of songs; I thought they were significant enough to warrant mention.

Covers During the Counter-Reaction

Title	Original and Date	Cover
"Fever"	Little Willie John '56	The Cramps '80
"Blue Suede Shoes"	Carl Perkins '56	Toy Dolls '82
"Breathless"	Jerry Lee Lewis '58	X '83
"Rockin' Robin"	Bobby Day '58	Nine below Zero '81
"Johnny B. Goode"	Chuck Berry '58	Peter Tosh '97
"Poison Ivy"	The Coasters '59	The Avengers '80
"Hey Little Girs"	Dee Clark '59	Microwave Dave & the Nukes '06
"Doggin' Around"	Jackie Wilson '60	Klique '83
"Theme from Psycho"	Soundtrack '60	The Fibonaccis '83
"Money"	Barrett Strong '60	The Flying Lizards '79
"Stand by Me"	Ben E. King '61	Seal '08
"This Train (Conductor Wore Black)"	Peter, Paul & Mary '62	Rank and File '82 and Strange Bird '04
"Something's Got a Hold on Me"	Etta James '62	David Lindley '90
"He's a Rebel"	Crystals '62	The Morning Benders '08

Title	Original and Date	Cover
"Heat Wave"	Martha & the Vandellas '63	The Jam '80
"Louie Louie"	The Kingsmen '63	Black Flag '81
"Ring of Fire"	Johnny Cash '63	Wall of Voodoo '82 and Social Distortion '90
"Pipeline"	The Chantays '63	Agent Orange '81
"Wipe Out"	The Surfaris '63	Toy Dolls '84 and Phish '98 and Smashing Pumpkins '08
"You Really Got Me"	The Kinks '64	Oingo Boingo '81 and Metallica '09
"Needles and Pins"	The Searchers '64	Tom Petty '86
"Glad All Over"	The Dave Clark Five '64	Bon Jovi '07
"Viva Las Vegas"	Elvis Presley '64	The Dead Kennedys '80
"Oh, Pretty Woman"	Roy Orbison '64	Van Halen '82
"Land of 1,000 Dances"	Cannibal & the Headhunters '65	Die Toten Hosen '89
"Midnight Hour"	Wilson Pickett '65	Guy Sebastian '07
"I'm Down"	The Beatles '65	Kentucky Headhunters '06
"Satisfaction"	The Rolling Stones '65	Cat Power '08
"Dirty Water"	The Standells '65	The Inmates '81 and Aerosmith '06
"Kick Out the Jams"	MC5 '69	Rage Against the Machine '00
"19th Nervous Breakdown"	The Rolling Stones '66	Jarvis '08
"Time Won't Let Me"	The Outsiders '66	Psychedelic Jukebox '03
"Sloop John B."	The Beach Boys '66	Simple Minds '09
"Tomorrow Never Knows"	The Beatles '66	Oasis '08
"Under My Thumb"	The Rolling Stones '66	INXS '94
"I Fought the Law"	The Bobby Fuller Four '66	The Clash '78
"Somebody to Love"	The Jefferson Airplane '67	Angry Samoans '86
"Higher and Higher"	Jackie Wilson '67	Jimmy Cliff '84
"Getting Better"	The Beatles '67	Public Enemy '90
"Little Bit o' Soul"	Music Explosion '67	The Ramones '83
"Mr. Soul"	Buffalo Springfield '67	Rush '04
"Purple Haze"	Jimi Hendrix '67	The Fibonaccis '84 and Buena Vista Social Club '07
"I Had Too Much to Dream"	The Electric Prunes '67	Webb Wilder '09
"Helter Skelter"	The Beatles '68	Aerosmith '91
"Dear Prudence"	The Beatles '68	Siouxsie & the Banshees '83
"Revolution"	The Beatles '68	Stone Temple Pilots '01
"Mony, Mony"	Tommy James & the Shondells '68	Billy Idol '87
"Spooky"	The Classics IV	R.E.M. '93
"Everyday People"	Sly & the Family Stone '69	Joan Jett & the Blackhearts '83 and Pearl Jam '95
"Gimme Shelter"	The Rolling Stones '69	Sisters of Mercy '83
"Na Na Hey Hey Kiss Him Goodbye"	Steam '69	Jay-Z '09
"Pinball Wizard"	The Who '69	Flaming Lips '08
"American Woman"	Guess Who '70	Lenny Kravitz '98
"Tears of a Clown"	Smokey Robinson & the Miracles '70	Eve '07
"Truckin'"	The Grateful Dead '70	The Pop-O-Pies '84

12. The Counter-Reaction and Defense

Title	Original and Date	Cover
"Who'll Stop the Rain"	Creedence Clearwater Revival '70	Bruce Springsteen '93
"Battle of Evermore"	Led Zeppelin '71	Heart '03
"Riders on the Storm"	The Doors '71	Snoop Dogg '94
"Jealous Guy"	John Lennon '71	Roxy Music '81 and Lou Reed '01
"Thank You for Talkin' to Me Africa"	Sly & the Family 8tone '71	Soundgarden and Janet Jackson '89
"Ziggy Stardust"	David Bowie '72	Bauhaus '82
"Drift Away"	Doby Gray '73	Uncle Kracker '03
"Forever Young"	Bob Dylan '74	will.i.am '09
"Jolene"	Dolly Parton '74	White Stripes '04
"Havana Affair"	Ramones '76	Red Hot Chili Peppers '03
"Live for Today"	Grass Roots 67	Lords of the New Church '83
"My Way"	Frank Sinatra '70 and Elvis Presey '77	Nina Hagen '80
"Dancing in the Moonlight"	Thin Lizzy '77	Smashing Pumpkins '93
"Another Brick in the Wall"	Pink Floyd '79	KoЯn '04
"Comfortably Numb"	Pink Floyd '79	Sissors Sistors '04
"Abracadabra"	Steve Miller Band '82	Sugar Ray '99
"Thriller"	Michael Jackson '82	Lightspeed Champion '08

Key Values

Among the values reaffirmed and reinforced were those concerned with the expansion of freedom, an appreciation of diversity, interracial respect, a variety of feminist ideas, and the primacy of the human individual over the artificiality of national boundaries. In many ways, the ultimate success of the cultural revolution depends on how the conflicts associated with these values are eventually resolved.

As virtually everyone knows, Black and White music underwent a dramatic separation during the Interim, both reflecting and encouraging a similar separation throughout American society. This was in some very important ways beneficial, in that it enabled Black Americans to achieve the kind of self-identity that was impossible to acquire while at the same time seeking the goal of integration. Too often "integration" meant "becoming White." The response was in a sense to "become more Black." After self-identity was largely accomplished, a continuation of this kind of separatism (by choice or by force) would have been unjust. (It had already worked a financial hardship on Black artists, and the media only haltingly began to correct the imbalance in programming that reinforced the inferior status of Black artists.) The evidence suggests, however, that a merger was even then beginning to take place, this time, however, on the basis of mutual respect and equality.

Black musicians began to play the kind of rock and roll usually associated with Whites. Among the best representatives of this trend were the Bus Boys. Not only did they produce some of the finest rock music of the time, they were quite self-aware about what they are doing. "Johnny Soul'd Out" says it perfectly: "Johnny was known as the King of Soul/He was a brother had it under control," and "James Brown was his cousin/Little Richard was his friend." Then they continue, "I saw him do the jerk/I saw him do the twist/The next thing I know/He was acting like this." The chorus follows with "Johnny soul'd out, I tell you Johnny soul'd out/He's into rock and roll and he's given up the rhythm and blues."

The phrase "soul'd out" is, of course, a pun! It could mean "sold out" (a negative notion) or literally something akin to "rocked out" (a positive notion). Of course "rocking out" was what they were doing. Their debut album, *Minimum Wage Rock and Roll*, had two other songs that added a little bite to this theme. In "KKK" they intimated that being an American should allow them access to every nook and cranny of society, entrée to the Klan as well as rock and roll! And while the point of "Respect" might be obvious, it included the proclamation "If you don't like rock 'n' roll music/You can kiss my ass," a message intended for everyone, Black as well as White.

Prince's "Black Album" (with no official title), released in 1987, self-consciously mirrored the Beatles' "White Album." His *1999* and *Around the World in a Day* (with a cover reminiscent of The Beatles' *Sgt. Pepper*) included many if not most songs in an ostensibly White style. Michael Jackson's 1984 *Thriller* did the same. It included a duet with Paul McCartney on "The Girl Is Mine," and "Beat It" with Eddie Van Halen on guitar. On his 1991 *Dangerous,* he had a hit single, "Black or White," which was clearly a rocking dance number about racial harmony and the rejection of racism. The album reveals a hint or two from The Beatles, and Slash from Guns N' Roses played guitar on the album. From 1989 on, Lenny Kravitz has been doing hard rock with a touch of soul, winning a massive, diversified audience and critical appeal in the process. There is no better example of this than his 1998 hit "Fly Away."

Other Black performers doing White rock included Irene Cara, Junior, the Pointer Sisters, Terry Scott (whose debut album was sent to program directors in a blank jacket to disguise his race), and Donna Summer. As the media began to open their minds and doors to this possibility, the way was paved for still more crossovers. After all, to paraphrase Funkadelic, there's no reason why a funk band can't play rock and roll.

To paraphrase George Clinton's Parliament-Funkadelic even further, there's no reason why a rock band can't play funk, and several were beginning to do it. One of the earliest was M, with its 1979 hit "Pop Muzik," which many perceived as a blend of disco and new wave. Actually, this assessment wasn't too far off the mark, since funk comprised much of the disco sound at the time, while new wave was mostly White. The blend could be heard as the 1980s developed, in Blondie's "Rapture," David Bowie's "Cat People" and "Let's Dance," the Clash's "Rock the Casbah," Haircut One Hundred's "Love Plus One," Pete Shelley's "Homosapien," the Thompson Twins' "In the Name of Love," and many others. Ex–Sex Pistol John Lydon (a.k.a. Johnny Rotten), in his new group Public Image Ltd. (PiL), "foreshadowed much of the current punk/disco merger by extending the moody, highly textured aural-cinema tradition of bands like the Velvet Underground," according to Robert Hilburn in the *Los Angeles Times* (June 5, 1983). Hilburn also remarked that "far from the annoyingly repetitious and vacuous records associated with the disco fever of the late '70s, today's dance music benefits from a healthy blend of early disco energy and wry, new-wave spirit."[8] One of the finest, yet generally unknown, examples of this blend was an album by the Was brothers (David and Don) called *Was (Not Was)* (1981), especially on "Out Come the Freaks" and "Carry Me Back to Old Morocco." Their adopted surname might imply the past, but their music definitely pointed to the future. Their album *Born to Laugh at Tornadoes* (1983) bore this out.

It followed, of course, that if Blacks and Whites began playing each other's style of music, the chances were pretty good it was because each found something they liked in the other's music. Changing radio formats, diversification of video programming, and the then new twelve-inch discs all seemed to reflect this growing mutuality of interest. Whites found that they could identify with the music of artists like Grandmaster Flash, Gloria Gaynor, Eddy Grant, Michael Jackson, Rick James, Prince, Donna Summer, and Stevie Wonder. Blacks, on the other hand, had always been familiar with White music, since fewer than three hundred of the more than eight thousand radio stations in this country had a Black-oriented format. One record promoter, Randy Cunningham, felt that the divisions between Blacks and Whites were breaking down: "The club jocks are helping to bring cultures together. They realize people are interested in dancing to good music, not just 'White' music or 'Black' music. Radio is starting to pick up on what's happening out there, and we should see some changes on that level, too." It should be emphasized that this mutual interest was not in music modified to appeal to the others' tastes (as happened in the fifties); on the contrary, interest was in the original music itself. Their differing styles were finally being appreciated for their differences. Diversity, in other words, was accepted as a primary value. Another form of this appreciation is exemplified by joint performances, as with the frequent collaboration between 2002 and 2004 of Linkin Park (White, hard rock) and Jay-Z (Black, hip-hop).

As if to underscore this merger, the twentieth anniversary of the March on Washington (August 27, 1983) had a considerably larger White participation than in 1963, bringing it closer to equality. Significantly, the march's theme was not integration as it had been twenty years earlier, but peace, freedom, justice, and economic security for all. Differing racial cultures were no longer being seen as an obstacle to harmony but rather as a prerequisite.

Some may have wondered at that time if before too long there would come an end to the odious divisions implied by the three and sometimes four music charts (pop, R&B, C&W, disco). Because of the overwhelming similarities between the pop and R&B charts in the fifties, *Billboard* (and others) discontinued the latter for a short period, only to revive it with the emergence of soul. However, the elimination of the distinctions isn't what I foresee; nor do I think it would be desirable. Partly due to newer kinds of media and technology that would appear in the late 1990s, I anticipate a large diversity of musical styles becoming increasingly appealing to and being enjoyed by an ever larger number of people. The result might be one chart with many styles represented. Or, more likely, it will be several charts but they all will be understood to be part of a larger whole. Much will depend on how radio programming goes; the temptation will be to program assiduously along genre lines thus reinforcing the differences and the isolation of the various cultural groups from one another. However, even this may not be fatal to incorporating genuine diversity into American culture, as long as the differences are respected. Ultimately, however, I expect the major "awards" shows, such as the Grammys, the American Music Awards, MTV Awards and the Video Music Awards, to hold the key. (The medium is the message!) So far, they have continued to incorporate all forms of music equally — although not without the inevitable disputes within, for example, in 2009 when Kanye West stormed onto the VMA stage during Taylor Swift's acknowledgment speech and proceeded to proclaim that Beyoncé was more deserving of the award for best female vocalist. The *Crossroads* series on the Country Music Television channel has often featured interesting juxtapositions of artists, including Taylor Swift and Def Leppard. No doubt, in the near future, we'll see Taylor and Kanye together again, under more congenial circumstances. Such is rock and roll!

The influence of feminist values on the American consciousness continued to grow, despite the failure of the Equal Rights Amendment in 1982. As mentioned in the previous chapter, women had begun to take an increasingly active role in those areas of rock hitherto regarded as the sole province of males. Among those I've already mentioned are Debbie

Harry, Joan Jett, Grace Jones, Diana Ross, and Donna Summer. Others now included Laurie Anderson, the Bangles, the Belle Stars, Kate Bush, the Flirts, the Go-Go's, Lisa Hartman, Cyndi Lauper, the Leather Angels, Lene Lovich, Lydia Lunch, Madonna, the Roches, Tin Angel, Vanity 6, and The Waitresses. Among this diverse listing was an anomaly, The Waitresses. Although only two of the group's six members were women, the group's overall message was nevertheless an advocacy of full and complete gender equality. Best known for the satirical "I Know What Boys Like," the group's debut album, *Wasn't Tomorrow Wonderful* (1982), also includes "No Guilt." This song portrays a woman's gradual struggle from dependency on a man to full independence: "I've done a lot since you've been gone" and "I'm sorry but I don't feel awful/It wasn't the end of the world/I'm sorry I can't be helpless." In a similar vein, Grace Jones's "Nipple to the Bottle" has a line stressing that she will neither give in to male pressures nor feel guilty about her independence. As a final indication of how things were proceeding, the Leather Angels, from Southern California, became one of the first heavy-metal bands comprised entirely of women — studs, chains, leather and all. They continued where The Runaways (Joan Jett's group) left off.

Since then, bands with women, all or mostly women bands, individual women performers in every conceivable genre have emerged. The Bangles, whose "heyday" was in the 1980s, reformed in 1999 to do a spot in *Austin Powers: The Spy Who Shagged Me* and then continued on to tour. The Go-Go's had pretty much the same history. More significant, I think is the fact that these two groups proved that women in rock were no mere novelty. Vixen (hard rock), Hole (with Courtney Love fronting several males, though the band has included numerous women. Hole has moved beyond their punkish origin to other styles), Queencore (who play everything), the Pandoras (psychedelic paisley) and others could rock with the best regardless of gender. Individual women singers of recent vintage (with or without backing band), of course, have become commonplace. Aside from the heavyweights like Madonna, Janet Jackson, Chrissie Hynde, Annie Lennox, Debbie Harry, Stevie Nicks, k.d. lang, Patti LaBelle, Cher, Sheryl Crow, Melissa Etheridge, Alanis Morissette, Tracy Chapman, Sade and the like, there are numerous others waiting to take their place. Nico, for example, Ani DiFranco, Erykah Badu, Kim Deal, Kim Gordon and Tina Weymouth are a second, or perhaps third, generation of gender benders. A recent article in the *Los Angeles Times* (February 7, 2010) devoted a cover story to the punkish Mika Miko's celebratory dissolution. The point of the article, however, was that four more bands of women (Best Coast, Dum Dum Girls, Nite Jewel and Pearl Harbor) are ready to rise up and take their place. Without too much exaggeration, I think, this battle for equality is over.

The next time around, if there were to be another attempt to pass ERA, it certainly won't fall prey to the sentiments expressed in Charlene's reactionary "I've Never Been to Me." If there is to be a next time, the victorious sentiment would most likely be that expressed in Donna Summer's "She Works Hard for the Money." The ERA may never pass, but then again, but I suspect it might no longer be deemed necessary.

A concern for individuals over national allegiances should not be confused with "internationalism," which still regards the existence of the nation-state as justified and beyond question. Genuine individuality, on the other hand, considers the nation to be an artificial construct and "nationalism" a dangerous threat to the possibility of self-actualization and the sooner it's abolished the better. Hence, "non-nationalism" would be a more accurate way to describe what's implied by individuality. It's not so much that "nations" should be abolished; rather, it's the ultimate faith given to a nation that's the problem — "'nationalism," which in its extreme form is "fascism" (a perspective captured so well by the phrase, "my country, right or wrong"). Rejecting fascism should never be confused with a failure to appreciate one's own nationality (or "exceptionalism"). Increasingly, at rock festivals around the world, members of the audience can often be seen waving their own national flags. (Waving the Confederate "Stars and Bars" at hard rock or heavy metal concerts raises other issues, but suffice it to say here, that fascism is not being celebrated.) The value structure of revolutionaries is the idea that individuals should be given primacy, before nations.

Also prominent in the value structure is an antagonism to organized and authoritarian religiosity. With groups naming themselves "Blind Faith," "Faith No More" and "Bad Religion"; with songs such as "Losing My Religion" by R.E.M., "Jesus" by The Feederz, and "Jesus of Suburbia" Green Day; with the "satanic" affectations of old-style heavy metal and nu-metal groups; and with the deliberately excessive profanity in hardcore punk and hip-hop, you could easily (and too hastily) conclude that all forms of spirituality are and have been forever cast out by rock and roll. Not so. It's the kind of religion that demands total mental and physical acquiescence from everyone as the sole bearer of absolute truth: This is the target of rock. It's the kind of hubristic pomposity that still outlaws atheism in seven American states and the kind of dictatorial religion that declares homosexuality to be a capital offense (as Uganda has attempted to do). This is the "religion" defamed by rock. Too easily is George Harrison forgotten, to say nothing of the rock bands attempting to create a form of religious rock (Halo, Lost and Found, Amos and Skillet, for example) and the numerous rock performers who are spiritual in their own private lives. Yet, all attempts to resurrect (pun intended) the *traditional* religiousness within the rock medium are doomed. The medium is contrary to their message.

The increasing popularity among Americans of rock music from around the world was a manifestation of this still relatively inchoate sentiment of non-nationalism. I don't include music from the rest of the English-speaking world in this survey (especially Britain), since ours and theirs have been so closely intertwined from the beginning of the cultural revolution. It would be impossible, and pointless, to attempt an isolation of their music at this point in order to ascertain its impact on us.

Rock music from continental Europe is another matter. When Americans heard rock music performed by people whose native language was other than English, the impression was unavoidable. Something unified all individuals and all cultures, something deeper and more profound than the nationalistic peculiarities that tend to drive us apart. Those Americans most closely associated with the revolution were coming to discover that people from vastly different cultures all have certain fundamental values in common, values very similar if not identical to those of the cultural revolutionaries. Once this was recognized, nationalistic conflicts began to be revealed as artificially induced and thus intolerable.

Idealistic? No doubt. But if the medium of music is in any way its message, this may be an accurate assessment of future developments into the Re-actualization period. In any case, music was, during this time, expressing this ideal far more effectively than any discursive ideology could ever hope to do. A small sample from the import bins included bands from Austria (Falco), France (Dun), Germany (Nena, Peter Schilling, the Scorpions, Spliff, and Die Toten Hosen), Holland (Taco and Vasmak), Italy (Il Volo), and Sweden (Von Zamla). Some of the German groups have, perhaps more than some of the others, expressed anti-nuclear and antiwar sentiments, for example, Nena's "99 Luftballoons" and Peter Schilling's "Major Tom (Coming Home)." This should not be surprising given that the parents of this generation of Germans may have been involved with the Third Reich in one way or another. They knew, learning from their parents' horrific experiences, that "war was not the answer."

One European group that most of us are unlikely to have heard was, surprisingly, a group from the Soviet Union called Time Machine. In a nation so paranoid and defensive that it could be suspicious of, and thus shoot down, an unarmed, civilian passenger plane—Korean Air flight 007 on September 1, 1983—killing well over two hundred people with no apparent remorse, it comes as something of a shock that the authorities would permit a rock-and-roll band to exist, much less allow it to perform. According to the *Washington Post* (April 17, 1982), Time Machine was selected as the most popular ensemble of 1982 by the Young communist League. Unsurprisingly, a few weeks later, these same musicians were denounced by the government as un–Russian, unmusical, and given to the expression of dangerous ideas. It was felt that, along with blue jeans, sweatshirts, and beards, popular music was responsible for spreading degenerate Western influences throughout the Soviet Union. Some of Time Machine's disturbing lyrics were the following (unfortunately, the song title is not available):

> I do not believe in promises and will not do so in the future/There is no point in believing in promises any longer.
>
> Tell me, why are you happy?/Wait, look back, and see how the fallen leaves decay/How a crow circles where once a garden bloomed.
>
> You have to wear masks, wear masks/Because only under the mask can you remain yourself.
>
> I am calm only for the fact that now nobody can deceive you/And you are now prepared to do things for yourself.
>
> One sunny day when millions of young men died/With song on their lips.

No wonder the Soviets were in trouble. Could it be that this presaged the Re-actualization of the authentic Russian revolution? We only hoped for this at the time, but barely nine years later, the USSR collapsed. Its sudden and entirely surprising demise has been assessed and analyzed and pontificated upon ever since. Depending on the ideological framework from which the pontificating derived, the final cause (to use an Aristotelian term) was the Soviet state's flawed economy, its size and ethnic composition, its corrupt political leaders, its militarization at the expense of the populace and even the policies of Ronald Reagan—in particular, the former cowboy actor's protestation in Berlin, "Mr. Gorbachev, tear down this wall!"

I prefer to think that the Soviet government itself—or many of its former officials—had the best explanation of all: it was the fault of those bearded, long-haired, sweatshirt-and-jeans-wearing rock and rollers! If so, the genuine "Russian revolution" was, in effect, caused by America's cultural revolution through the medium of rock and roll. (Thank you very much!) I'm hardly alone in making this observation. Paul McCartney's 2003 concerts in Red Square and St. Petersburg's Palace Square not only elicited an overwhelmingly enormous and enthusiastic response from the massive audiences but also elicited from some of the musically inclined fans the observation that it was The Beatles' "gentle intervention" through their music that helped bring down the entire Soviet system. The Soviet youth envied the kind of freedom and creativity that the Beatles represented that was not only discouraged in the old order but was forbidden. But they listened anyway ... and the walls came tumbling down. Tellingly, in the St. Petersburg installment of McCartney's visit (his first ever, by the way, to territory formerly known by various "SSR" suffixes) one fan held up an enormous sign saying, "Thank You!"

I'm sure almost everyone on the planet is well familiar with the 1962 two-minute black and white film documenting a performance in Liverpool's Cavern Club by a then unknown and unrecorded rock and roll band. It was made by Leslie Woodhead, who would go on to make documentary films in the USSR throughout the sixties, and in the process would discover the enormous impact this band had had on Russian youth and their consequent disaffection with the status quo in the Soviet system. All of this is the substance of his remarkable 2009 documentary, *How the Beatles Rocked the Kremlin,* done for WNET.ORG (a PBS affiliate). The conclusion he arrived at is articulated with fervor in the film by one of the leading sociologists and rock critics in today's non–Soviet Russia, Artemy Troitsky (It's tempting, eisegetically of course, to find some connection between his last name and the all-too-similar last name of Leon Trotsky. Both, after all, were zealous opponents of Stalinism.) It's worth quoting him from the film:

> In the big bad West they've had whole huge institutions which spent millions of dollars for undermining the Soviet system. And I'm sure that the impact of all those stupid Cold War institutions has been much, much smaller than the impact of The Beatles. The Beatles, Paul and John, George and Ringo, have done more for the fall of Communism than any other Western institution.[9]

A genre indigenously called "shakes" music, was invented by Russian youth during the sixties. Innumerable bands formed to emulate The Beatles. One, mentioned above, was Time Machine, and in this documentary film, the band's founding member, Andrei Makarevich, makes the same point. Aquarium was a Leningrad band from the same period; it, too, had roots in Beatles music. Michael Apted's documentary *The Long Way Home* (1989), followed the band's leader, Boris Grebenshchikov, "from East to West and back again." But these bands are merely representative of thousands of others and millions of devotees. Literally, millions of young Russians instantly found a symbol that served to focus their disillusionment with the Soviet system and at the same time point to something new — freedom. The song "The Yeah Yeah Virus," popular in Russia and used in the film — performed by a contemporary expatriate band headed by Yury Pelyushonok — proclaims, "We were building Communism, but The Beatles butted in." One of Russia's most recognizable TV commentators, Vladimir Pozner, concurs; for him The Beatles first destroyed the fear that held the Soviet Union together and then its underlying beliefs. Even Putin's deputy prime minister Sergei Ivanov explained how the Beatles helped him learn English and showed him another way of life.

Timothy Ryback's 1990 film *Rock around the Bloc* expanded the claim by looking at rock music in the entirety of eastern Europe as well as the Soviet state. His contentions concerned the introduction of both individuality and personal freedom as primary values, values that were antithetical to Stalin's and Lenin's version of Marxism. The result, as he says, was revolutionary: "In a very real sense, the triumph of rock and roll in Eastern Europe and the Soviet Union has been the realization of a democratic process. Three generations of Soviet-bloc youths have compelled governments to accept outgrowth of Western capitalism. In the course of thirty years, rock bands have stormed every bastion of official resistance and forced party and government to accept rock-and-roll music as part of life in the Marxist-Leninist state." And in so doing, it was their undoing.[10]

Along with the increasing popularity of reggae among Blacks as well as Whites in America, Americans were also beginning to respond favorably to some of the rock music produced in several African cultures. There are at least five anthologies worth listening to in order to get an excellent sample of what was happening: *Assalam Aleikoum Africa* (West Africa), *Rhythm of Resistance* (South Africa), *Sound d'Afrique* (Central Africa), *Soweto* (South Africa), and *Viva Zimbabwe!* (East Africa). Albums by individual performers include King

Sunny Adé's *Juju Music* (Nigeria), Juluka's *Scatterlings of Africa* (South Africa), Fela Anikulapo Kuti's *Black President* (South Africa) and Prince Nico Mbarga and Rocafil Jazz's *Sweet Mother* and *Free Education* (Nigeria). Africa, of course, is one of those areas where injustice existed (and still does) in paradigmatic dimensions, so good and evil were and are not so difficult to distinguish for the American cultural revolutionaries. Hence, the music was likely to have a great deal of popular appeal, especially the music from South Africa. Apartheid officially ended, an agonizing process that took place from 1990 to 1994, and the seeds of its dissolution were present in the ideas and feelings so forcefully expressed in African music. Again, America's cultural revolution was at work—through its music.

Underscoring rock's growing cognizance of the worldwide implications of the cultural revolution and the ultimate meaninglessness of nations were the 1980 Concerts for the People of Kampuchea. Sponsored by Paul McCartney, they involved an interesting variety of groups. Aside from McCartney himself, there were The Clash (punk), Elvis Costello (new wave), the Pretenders (new wave), Queen (heavy art metal), Rockpile (neo-rockabilly), The Specials (mod/ska) and the Who (classic mod). The clear implication of this breadth was universal scorn for nationalism and ethnocentrism. Then there was the Live Aid concert, held jointly in Philadelphia and London on July 13, 1985, in order to help feed millions of drought-stricken Ethiopians. It brought together an even larger assemblage of performers, representing styles from the fifties to the present. Other countries participated through live and taped media: Australia, Austria, Japan, and the Soviet Union. The message was clear: national boundaries are not only less important than the people they enclose, but they are in fact obstacles. The message was not merely *in* the music, it *was* the music.

The more Americans were to incorporate this diversity of music into their consciousness, the sooner the Re-actualization of the revolution would be accomplished.

An Assessment of the Counter-Reaction and Defense

Several things seem clear from my perspective. From 1980 until 2009, the struggle between revolutionary values and traditional values proceeded apace. The revolution effectively met the counter-attack and fended off disaster.

Even more important, the revolutionaries successfully dealt with their own internal struggles and emerged from the chastening more humble in their expectations and more realistic in their hopes.

The values associated with individuality and freedom were more clearly and more forcefully articulated than ever before.

Above all there was a general recognition that if the cultural revolution were to succeed, it would not result in some kind of utopia. This term, after all, literally derives from the Greek words for "nowhere." Hence, a clear distinction could then be made, albeit unconsciously for some, between themselves and their 19th-century socialist and Christian predecessors. This movement was not going to devolve into separatist sects, atavistic Puritanism or naïve perfectionism. It would deal with bettering the human condition, with dreams but not illusions. But these dreams would be big, complex and revolutionary dreams.

As someone once said about the process, when you talk about revolution, you can count me out ... in.

13

The Re-actualization and Rebirth

This chapter, and thus the book, must necessarily remain unfinished, for the denouement of America's cultural revolution has yet to be played out. Although it is obviously true that the future cannot be predicted with any degree of certainty, it is nevertheless the case that some reasonably accurate speculation is possible. Based on an analysis and interpretation of the music that emerged during the Interim and the music of the Counter-Reaction that carried forward both the negation of the fifties and the affirmation of sixties, plus the recent beginnings of the Re-actualization, several observations can be ventured without too great a risk of exhibiting naïveté and harboring utopian dreams.

It seems virtually certain, for example, that a continued renewal of the conflict between the old order and the cultural revolutionaries can be anticipated. Neither side has slackened its devotion to the set of values it holds most dear; on the contrary, there is every indication that a rededication has taken place on both sides. Pat Buchanan's speech to the 1992 GOP convention ought to dispel any thoughts to the contrary. Cable television, operating 24 hours, has become a major battlefield for this conflict. The zealous advocates for traditional values, and some even less palatable, have found a home, it would seem, on the Fox Network and in the person of Sarah Palin. Spokespersons for the revolutionary set of values are more likely to be found on MSNBC. Moreover, every election, presidential and off-year, embodies the conflict in one way or another — with the candidates as well as the issue proposals. No, the conflict is not going to go away.

Less certain but still highly probable, the revolutionaries will continue to rejuvenate themselves just as much as the old order has been able to do. Many of the original participants from the fifties and sixties who are still with us have recovered from their exhaustion while a new generation has arisen to join them. Members of the latter have developed their own unique identity along with maintaining a strong connection with their revolutionary heritage. Together, they are re-engaging the old order with a renewed and revitalized energy. While not specifically a goal of the revolutionary process, the election of Barack Obama in 2008, has given renewed hope to those who feel a fundamental change of ultimate values can be accomplished. (The "Yes We Can" slogan of the Obama campaign is vague enough that virtually anyone can use it and ascribe a particular meaning to it.)

A third observation that can be made with reasonable confidence is that women have opened up a new dimension within the movement, making clear the implicit link between feminism and the larger cultural revolution. Because of the so-called gender gap (separating women from Reagan) and the fact that women comprise a majority of the population, this new dimension is potentially the most powerful force available for the cause, and more and more people are coming to recognize this, on both sides of the conflict. This is not intended to suggest that all women are feminists or that all feminists buy into the same set of values as cultural revolutionaries. Rather, the existence of feminism itself is the force to be reckoned with — regardless of the specific issues involved. They are the medium for advocating "choice," for example, in their very being — not only regarding the legal status of abortion.

Similarly, the full equality of homosexual men and women in American society is now and will remain an accepted element within the larger revolutionary agenda. The struggle to achieve the right to marry for gay and lesbian couples is obvious locus for the continued conflict. There is optimism, however, in the wide support for dumping the insulting and degrading "don't ask, don't tell" edict that has been guiding the military since the Clinton administration. Besides, with such a suggestively titled group as the Scissor Sisters (which includes both men and women) with roots in glam and disco as well as having an international appeal, a new age seems to be developing. No one really cares to ask or tell anything about them or other performers who affect a flamboyant style such as Lady Gaga — people just like to see them perform, without caring a whit about their style of life. The ideal, in other words, is for homosexuality to become completely irrelevant, and it's becoming more and more the case.

Often smiled at as being frivolous, infantile, counterproductive or even illegitimate as an issue, similar legal struggles to legalize certain drugs (or at the very least, to decriminalize laws prohibiting marijuana use) will continued to be a battleground. Perhaps because of its medical usage (now legal in some states), the legalization of marijuana is gradually gaining acceptance. When fully understood, the free use of recreational drugs bases its underlying appeal on John Stuart Mill's "Harm Principle," and this makes this a necessary component of the struggle. Other major issues surrounding war, universal health care and America's place in the world will continue to be contentious between traditionalists and revolutionaries as well as among themselves.

Finally, it seems obvious that the revolutionary symbols and their attendant attitudes of negation and affirmation have been awakened from dormancy, supplying the revival of the revolution with its direction and strength

If it makes sense to characterize cultural revolutions as essentially religious movements, then we have a context in which this process of re-actualization can be understood. According to Eliade, "Sacred time is indefinitely recoverable, indefinitely repeatable." By participating in the re-creation, it is possible for anyone at any time to become "contemporary with *illud tempus*" (the time and events of the beginning). He was quick to stress, however, that this "is not merely the commemoration of a mythical (and hence religious) event; it *re-actualizes* the event."[1] Eliade was not alone. Kierkegaard made a similar claim in *Philosophical Fragments*. Accordingly, whenever an absolute commitment is at issue, a faith commitment in other words, "There is not and never can be a disciple at second hand; for the believer ... does not see through the eyes of another ... he sees only what every believer sees — with the eyes of Faith."[2] All generations are alike in this sense; all are contemporaries. It makes no difference when such a commitment is made — all those who share in it are, by definition, contemporaries.

So let's take a look at the major symbols of both negation and affirmation, to see how they are now "reborn" for the contemporary "believers." In the introduction to Part Three, I briefly introduced Paul Tillich's notions about symbols. It's time now for a bit of a refresher: First of all, Tillich reminds us that genuine symbols must point beyond themselves — to something ultimate. Second, symbols do this only as long as they elicit a response. Third, there is a constant tendency for every faith to elevate its symbols to the stature of ultimacy (the very essence of idolatry). Finally, and most important, a genuine symbol will include within itself an element of *self-negation*—it must clearly express its own lack of ultimacy.

The Re-actualization of Negation

"He has risen!" No, not that other guy ... Elvis! Elvis never really "left the building" in the first place, and I'm not referring to the series of so-called Elvis sightings shortly after his physical demise. (This is not, however, a phenomenon to be ignored.) Actually, I'm not even really referring to Elvis Aaron Presley, the one-time truck driver. I'm talking about the "Elvis" of myth. For in the last analysis, *this* is the "Elvis" that matters.

His life as a virtual prisoner of his image and his degeneration into the abuse of drugs as well as his friends and family are all too familiar. There seems little doubt that this particular symbol exhibits a sufficient amount of self-negation. In fact, that fact that he probably saw himself as the mythic ultimate of rock and roll is itself a self-negation—albeit one of which he was no doubt unaware.

There are innumerable instances and examples that could be cited to illustrate how his mythic persona has been adopted and adapted in the American culture of today. Elvis symbology knows no bounds. All of them, collectively as well as individually, are important as indicators of the rebirth of negation. There are those that might seem reactionary—as in *Elvis Meets Nixon*, a docudrama of Elvis's 1970 meeting with Nixon wherein he volunteers his services to the C.I.A. Others might seem frivolous—the "Elvis" who marries couples at the Chapel of Love in Las Vegas. Some examples are patently obvious: The very person of Elvis Costello comes to mind. As a musician, he plays and sings a bluesy-rockabilly form of rock and roll, reminiscent of both the fifties and sixties. Other instances may seem just plain odd, as with the devotion of the former prime minister of Japan, Junichiro Koizumi, who dresses as Elvis, has recorded a CD of his favorite Elvis songs and made a pilgrimage to Graceland in 2006 (with George W. Bush). Still others may seem enigmatic, as with Andy Kaufman's offbeat impersonation of Elvis on *Saturday Night Live* (and duplicated in the biopic about Kaufman by the equally enigmatic Jim Carrey). Again, it's not what happens with the presentation of Elvis ... it's the presentation itself. It may be better to refer to all of them, literally, as *"re-presentations."* For that's what's really going on—Elvis is being continually and constantly "re-born."

One cinematic instance of Elvis, by Harvey Keitel, deserves special mention. In *Finding Graceland* (1998), Keitel portrays "the King" as never having died in the first place. He just needed to take a break from the frenzied, drug-addled life he had fallen into, and he's now on his way back home. On the way, he performs as a savior figure to those he encounters as if pre-ordained to do so. After reaching Graceland in the midst of a massive remembrance of Elvis on his birthday, "the King" slowly ambles among the crowd to the strains of Marc Cohn's elegiac "Walking in Memphis." They, of course, see him as just another Elvis impersonator. "Remember the King!" is the injunction he delivers to all of them, and they cheer in response. At the end of the film, we are deliberately left not quite sure whether he is a deluded soul or the real thing.

Another cinematic portrayal with a similar theme is *Bubba Ho-Tep* (2002). After switching places with an Elvis imitator, Bruce Campbell's rendition finds himself in a creepy nursing home in Texas, where he was placed after an accident. As he ages through the years, he laments having missed his opportunity to switch back, but as fortune would have it, another chance situation arises allowing him to assume the role. Together with Ossie Davis, portraying J.F.K. (sequestered and "colorized" by the C.I.A.) who never quite recovered from the assassination attempt, they battle ancient, revivified mummies who apparently require for their survival the ingestion of human brains extracted from living oldsters resident at the home. Elvis, again, lives to save the day.

Now, from the ridiculous (and I mean that in a good way) to the sublime, a 2007 video shows LeAnn Rimes in prison along with her fellow inmates singing and dancing to a country-blues-rock tune, "Nothin' Better to Do." You can almost see Spider Murphy on the tenor sax and Little Joe on the slide trombone playing "Jailhouse Rock." LeAnn Rimes, too, is re-presenting Elvis. Finally, in many ways the most sublime and grandiloquent of all, Cirque du Soleil premiered its permanent *Viva Elvis!* extravaganza in Las Vegas in 2010. (It makes a fitting pair with their already successful tribute to The Beatles in *LOVE*.)

It's really not at all important what content has been given to his many and varied incarnations; it's the manifestations themselves that are important. The sheer massiveness of the "Elvis factor" is the medium that carries the news of negation. No matter when, where, how or in what guise "he" may appear, Elvis's attack against the traditional set of values has been re-actualized. Thusly were we all enjoined, whether we realized it or not, to "Remember the King!"

The Re-actualization of Affirmation

The Beatles have clearly functioned as the symbols for the ideals of America's cultural revolution, and have just as clearly been mistaken as the ultimate by many if not most of their followers. What else was Beatlemania, if not a pure expression of idolatry? The use of the terms "teen idol," "screen idol" and the like is no accident. So for The Beatles to pass the test of legitimacy as symbols, it's worth considering whether self-negation is an essential component of "Beatle-dom."

It certainly seems to be the case when we look at how they reflected back on their years as Beatles. Self-negation requires, at a minimum, the rejection of an identity with the ultimate, and without exception, they separated themselves personally from "Beatle-ness." John performed and recorded several provocative albums with Yoko Ono at his side for several years. After taking a hiatus for a few years, he returned to recording in 1980 only to be murdered. During the early part of his solo career, he even disparaged the idea of Beatle worship in his song "God" (mentioned in Chapter 10), when he sang "I don't believe in Beatles" and added "Once I was the walrus; now I am John." Paul went on to perform alone and later with a new group, Wings, for more years than he did with The Beatles. He allegedly said in answer to John's question, "You're one of *them*, aren't you?" (in the film *The Two of Us*) "I used to be." Fiction or not, his comment accurately depicted McCartney's passage away from The Beatles. George began recording on his own shortly after the breakup and put out his famous triple album, suggestively titled *All Things Must Pass*, including a song of the same name. Inspired by his Buddhist inclinations, it expressed his sentiments about his new ventures. Ringo, after lending his drumming to the other three on various occasions, eventually formed a touring group of assorted and varying rockers (his All Starr Band) and has consistently and successfully performed for over three decades. Reflecting on The Beatles, he put it as clearly and as succinctly as possible: "It's not our personalities; it's the music."[3] Although all four of the ex–Beatles acted in furtherance of revolutionary ideals, none of them made any pretense of being paragons of revolutionary (or any other kind) of virtue. On the contrary, they evinced all of the strengths and weaknesses of every other human being, and made no protestations to the contrary. Clearly all four of them made a clean break from The Beatles, and refused to equate their identities with their former personae a much as possible.

What about "The Beatles" still eliciting a response? George Martin, producer of most of the Beatles music, commented, "Each generation as they grow up finds The Beatles for themselves."[4] So have they? In many ways, this criterion is so obviously met that it may be an apt example of missing the trees for the forest — the reverse of getting caught up in details and not seeing the big picture. There is such an overwhelming supply of exemplification about the continuing influence of The Beatles that some of the interesting details may be missed. The "devil" may, in some sense, be in the details. Or, to put it differently, some details may illustrate the big picture far better than looking at the whole thing.

Let's just forget about this for a moment and focus on a few of the otherwise suppressed, yet interesting details. As if to give substance to George Martin's comment in the 2008 film *Nick and Norah's Infinite Playlist*, the main character is struggling to make it with his still drummer-less band. Aside from searching for love and a suitable name for their group of mixed straights and gays, they find guidance for everything in the simplicity of The Beatles' "I Want to Hold Your Hand." They had it all figured out, was their mutual observation. On another note, The Beatles' innovations in music have been incorporated into their successors' in so many overt and subtle ways that it would entail a lifelong project to catalog them. Chord structures and key transitions alone would comprise a chapter or two, and there are already compendiums devoted to the analyses of their lyrics. Their political and social activities and experiments have filled tabloids as well as more respected publications from the beginning. A list of tribute bands and reenactors alone would take more time than it would be worth. (A Canadian group, Klaatu, was often rumored to be The Beatles, due to the facts that they sounded Beatlesque and were anonymous.) Their influence on hair and clothing styles is of course so well-known as to be boring. Literally thousands of persons and groups have recorded covers of at least one Beatles song. Hundreds of films, stage plays and TV shows have paid homage to them in various ways. They've also made an appearance somewhat indirectly in video games (*EarthBound*, *Worms and Reinforcements United*, *Curse of Enchantia* and *Guitar Hero 3*, for example). But on September 9, 2009, Harmonix Music Systems released the video game *The Beatles: Rock Band*, devoted entirely to the fab four. (Now almost anyone can become "Beatle-ized.") Finally, an oddity that may, in its very inexplicability, make the case: On the front page of the December 19 edition of the *Los Angeles Times*, just below the top banner, was a pictorial montage advertising a feature article within titled "The Decade in Review." Among all the persons you'd expect to see from 2000 to 2009, were (you guessed it) a picture of John and Paul (circa 1964). It seemed as if some need were felt to acknowledge the continuing influence of the group's two major songwriters into the new century. Of course, Mark Lapidos's *Fest for Beatles Fans* has been going strong since 1974, when he sought for and received permission and encouragement from all four of the lads to carry on.

A final detail is more subtle, but some subtleties dialectically achieve enormity in, dare I say, subtle ways. A song written by John Lennon on and off during 1979 and 1980, called

"Real Love," was resurrected in 1996 for The Beatles *Anthology II* compilation. The three remaining Beatles at the time reworked the song (combining it with another Lennon composition, "Real Life") and performed it "together," as they had earlier with "Free as a Bird"—making it the last semi-genuine Beatles song. Now this is interesting in itself, but what achieves "enormity" is the fact that Regina Ilyinichna Spektor, a Russian-born pianist/songwriter, covered it at the 2007 Lollapalooza Festival in Chicago. She is often placed in the "micro-genre" of anti-folk music, which is characterized by the musicians making sport of the mega-seriousness associated with the sixties folksters. Further, she acquired her taste for Beatles music from her father, a professor of music in the Soviet Union, who smuggled the recordings from eastern Europe back in (to) the USSR. (This harks back to the documentary film I referred to earlier, *How the Beatles Rocked the Kremlin*.) Perhaps "enormity" is hyperbolic; nevertheless, it aptly illustrates the lust for freedom felt everywhere as well as its actualization in some of the most unlikely places, and (a few cynics might add) thus giving hope to Americans.

That The Beatles have been influential is too obvious to belabor, but a few specifics might prove interesting. I have in mind two instances, both of which burst onto the scene about the same time: *LOVE* (the show by Cirque du Soleil that debuted in 2006) and *Across the Universe* (the 2007 film directed by Julie Taymor). The two are surprisingly similar, although a full analysis of that idea will have to remain for another time.

LOVE involved a complex collaboration among the surviving members of The Beatles and the representatives of Lennon and Harrison, plus original producer George Martin, the Cirque du Soleil people, and the Mirage Hotel in Las Vegas. The music for the show was reorchestrated, remixed, remastered and rearranged in a variety of ways so that it fit the surrealistic storyline and acrobatics. Throngs have seen it since its opening and more will see it in the future. The music and storyline, however, are not as significant as the collaborative effort itself and its venue in the sin and entertainment capital of the world (as the Vegas people would have it). The music in *Across the Universe* was similarly repurposed and the story similarly surrealistic. As with *LOVE*, the characters and story were liberally adapted from The Beatles' lives and their songs. In addition, as with *LOVE*, we can gather the film's significance by looking at the complex media of presentation and the collaborative effort that went into its making.

Although there are obvious and important differences between a live and a filmed presentation, the iconic nature of these two accomplishments, and this particular time, diminishes their significance. The Counter-Reaction was gradually ending and new social and political forces were coming to the fore—a multifarious process that would culminate in the election of the first African American president. Also happening was a slow acceptance of same-sex marriage, an incremental movement toward a rational policy on drug use, an even more incremental diminution of irrational religiosity and serious questioning of issues surrounding war and heath care. Lying beneath all of this was a begrudging recognition of the implications of freedom and genuine diversity. Yes, The Beatles symbolized all of this, regardless of their degree of awareness of the fact. Nevertheless, through the re-actualization of the symbolic nature of the Beatles and of their music, these processes are in the process of proofing. Whatever dormancy they have experienced, they have most assuredly reawakened. The aptness of phrase so often used by so many during their "tenure in office" as the unofficial leaders of popular and music culture of the sixties seems as valid now as then: "The Beatles Forever!"

A Vignette of Both Affirmation and Negation

I've mentioned earlier that the person known originally as "Robert Zimmerman" can be seen as personifying all aspects of the cultural revolution, including both its negation and its affirmation. A complete explanation and analysis of this will have to be done at some other time; it's simply far too broad a topic. Nevertheless, consider the film *I'm Not There* (2007): The whole point of the film is to suggest that his various public personae throughout the years have represented a multifarious dimensionality incapable of being expressed by one individual. Indeed, just as "Dylan" is his adopted name (a practice he has used throughout his career on various albums—"Jack Frost" on *Together Through Life*, for example), so also in this film is he is portrayed by five different actors, including one 11-year-old African American boy and one actress. Interestingly, the name "Bob Dylan" only appears once, during the opening credits. As I mentioned earlier regarding his *Together Through Life* album, Zimmerman in many ways recapitulates the entire cultural revolution. That can be said of this film in ways too many to mention here. But suffice it to say, the negation of the fifties flames up in Cate Blanchett's version of Dylan singing "(Ain't Gonna Work on) Maggie's Farm No More" at a New England folk festival. It also shows up on the guitar case carried by Marcus Carl Franklin's Dylan (the young boy) as a paean to Woody Guthrie: "This machine kills fascists." And the affirmation of the sixties glares forth in a jam session with Franklin playing with the real Richie Havens (evoking visions of Woodstock). It's even more pointed when Blanchett's Dylan frolics with "The Beatles" in a scene reprising *A Hard Day's Night*. It's all there—the "no" and the "yes" of the revolution—the "Blowing in the Wind" and the "Times They are a-Changin'." It has all been repackaged, recapitulated, represented and re-actualized for us today.

2009 and Beyond

In this final chapter, I've been discussing trends and only trends. Before departing the scene, however, I'd like to offer a few minor tidbits to accompany these speculations about the re-actualization of both negation and affirmation involved in the cultural revolution.

One thing is certain: the traditionalists have not "given up the ghost." They live on and defend ever more arduously their values. As this book goes to press, there are numerous persons and organizations still very active in their quest to stop the changes taking place in American culture. Nevertheless, there are also the ever more arduous expressions of revolutionary values. Perhaps most important of all, the sexual and gender relationships among the newer revolutionary generations are beginning to show a degree of equality and mutuality unheard of in the past. Moreover, the political powers that be are beginning to listen. After all, these newer revolutionaries actually vote. The oppressive weight of religious zealotry is being progressively questioned by a wider variety of people. Sanity in dealing with drug abuse is on the rise. There is a rising recognition that science and not superstition must guide us in dealing with the environment. Health care for all is now generally recognized as desirable. Freedom in sexual and marital relationships is being progressively accepted if still not recognized in law.

To be sure, these are only small movements forward, and it's hard to tell what it will ultimately come of it. Yet sometimes the smallest things reveal the most. And what these tidbits of movement reveal is that the major trends discussed throughout this chapter are indeed under way. Movement forward is a fact. The ultimate outcome is, of course, unpredictable. However, whatever it is, we shall hear it first in the music — the music we have for so long called rock 'n' roll.

"A Concluding Unscientific Postscript"

Devotees of Danish pastries and philosophers (well, maybe just the latter) will recognize from whom the above title has been purloined. Suffice it to say that the originator of that line, going by the provocative pseudonym Johannes Climacas (a.k.a. Søren Kierkegaard), had the intent of inquiring into the subjectivity of truth and the truth of subjectivity, and he linked the subjective affirmation of truth to the act of faith, or commitment. Acquiring genuine knowledge requires the inquisitor to be immersed in the historical situation, not stand apart and outside of it. This necessarily involves accepting uncertainty as inevitable, and paradoxically, the firmer the commitment, the greater the uncertainty.

With the observations of Johannes Climacas in mind, let me venture a few concluding truths about America's cultural revolution and its co-conspirator, rock and roll music. First, one thing is fairly obvious. Chances are, to echo the immortal lyrics written by Robert Allen and sung by Johnny Mathis to the music penned by Al Stillman, this will be the only update to the book originally titled *You Say You Want a Revolution: Rock Music in American Culture*. Time is the adversary, of course, and as The Guess Who put it, I'm "on my way to better things." This being so, it's still possible to ask if there are any likely conclusions we can anticipate regarding the success of this so-called Cultural Revolution? After all, as I have maintained throughout, this revolution has been underway since the mid-fifties of the previous century! I should be able to say *something* reasonably definitive about its results, should I not?

Aside from the obvious — and trivial — caveat that my consideration of this phenomenon is subjective (but hopefully not biased), I want to answer this question with the strongest possible negative, "No!" And I want to follow this up with an equally strong positive evaluation of this negation, "Good!" Such assessments of the results of a cultural revolution are neither possible nor desirable. All such attempts to assess the successes and/or failures of this or any cultural revolution are not only doomed to failure, they are, in essence, misguided and utterly pointless. The drivel that might result from such an effort of this kind should be and would be attacked from all sides as patently absurd. Consider the following uncontestable facts:

First, historical (and perhaps "historic" is the better alternative) movements, no matter where or when they may have taken place, have no empirically identifiable beginnings or endings. When, for example, did the Renaissance, the Reformation or the Enlightenment begin — and end? The same could be asked about the "post-modernist" movement in art. How about religious movements such as Christianity, Islam and Buddhism? Wilfred Cantwell Smith in his excellent and provocative *The Meaning and End of Religion* argues persuasively that these names of religions are inherently illegitimate and misleading.[5] The same could easily be said for the names given to historical movement in general and cultural revolutions in particular, albeit for slightly different reasons than Smith would cite. Even movements apparently so identifiable as to have specific names, as the Chinese Cultural Revolution of 1980–1987 under Mao Zedong, the Civil Rights movement in the United States, the anti-apartheid movement in South Africa, and the Philippine People Power Revolution of 1986, beg the question. In every case, the alleged beginning and ending points are symbolic events — not intended to be taken literally. In other words, they are interpretive — such crucial events are *assigned* the meanings of "beginnings" and "endings"; the meanings are not empirically discovered.

Second, the assessment of such movements in terms of their success or failure presupposes some set of unproblematic criteria by which these assignments can be made. Clearly, such criteria do not exist. Of course, we can always make an assessment in terms of a particular movement's stated objectives if they are in fact stated. Yet in every case, the movement's goals were far more than achieving a few clear-cut objectives. For example:

- Was apartheid ended? Yes, but there was much more at issue than this. The movement involved the transformation of a whole society — and culture.
- Was segregation ended? Yes, but, again, much more was — and is — at issue.
- What about the People Power Revolution in the Philippines? Here the objectives were initially very clear: to remove the Marcos imperium from power. But the revolution was about more than this, and it goes on today.
- When we ask if Christianity or the Enlightenment were successful, the question doesn't even seem to make sense.

Largely, the inability to assess the success or failure of a movement is because they are constantly evolving processes. The best we can do, then, is to decide whether a movement is moving more or less in the desired direction, and even this is necessarily a subjective undertaking — telling us more about the person doing the assessment than the movement itself.

Third, and perhaps most important, the only possible way to make a final assessment of movements such as cultural revolutions would seem to be to do so long after any glimmer of life has left them. Hence, we might comfortably conclude that Pharaoh Akhenaten's (Amenhotep IV, 1364–1347 B.C.E.) attempt to introduce a monotheistic cult of the Sun God into ancient Egypt has failed. Similarly, we can be confident that Alexander of Macedon (a.k.a. "the Great") succeeded in his attempt to introduce Greek culture throughout the ancient world. Other than that, the best that we can do is simply conclude that a given process is moving in a desirable or an undesirable direction, as the case may be.

As far as I can tell, what America's cultural revolutionaries want to do is to change the world. And In words that deserve a constant rehearing, if you say you want a revolution, you know that you can count me out ... *in*. Ambivalence and ambiguity are unavoidable when it comes to cultural change. We may not know all of the right paths to take — or all the wrong ones either — but we surely can notice what's happening along the way and make adjustments as necessary. To do this, all we may need is love, a mindfulness of the goal and the ability to *imagine*.

Epilogue: The Shape of Things to Come

> The introduction of novel fashions in music is a thing to beware of as endangering the whole of society, whose most important conventions are unsettled by any revolution in that quarter.
>
> — Plato

> Something is happening here but you don't know what it is, Do you, Mister Jones.
>
> — Bob Dylan

California: A Microcosm of the Dialectic

When people become caught in the throes of confusion and exasperation, tossing up their hands and crying out to whatever gods remain to hear them, "What next?!" it should be of some comfort to them that, no matter what it is, it will happen first in California. Californians, of course, go stumbling merrily on their way, blithely unaware of their tendencies to participate in whatever is new — simply because it's new.

Obviously, there's no way to verify or falsify this simplistic belief, but there are many times when I sure feel like it's true. Apparently, I'm not alone, for Theodore H. White, in *America in Search of Itself*, makes a similar observation about this strangest of all the fifty states:

> California lay at the sunset rim of the westering impulse, where Americans came to set themselves free from whatever past bothered them back East. To be free meant not simply political freedom. California had always stood for that — indeed, the very first Republican national candidate, in 1856, had been a Californian, John C. Frémont, demanding free soil. Liberation in California in more recent times meant the freeing of behavior from custom, of the individual from the family, of men from neckties, of women from aprons. It meant a freedom of life styles which would eventually, sweep east to undermine older American life styles — a freedom of sex from marriage, of mating from social conventions, of voters from party affiliations, of Blacks from the White power structure, and later, for Third World emigrants, a liberation from awe at the world of the White man. The piston push behind California's rise to national eminence was ... demographic, for ... those who came from afar were divorcing themselves from old values.[1]

More than a geographical region, California is a state of mind, a condition of consciousness — a place of refuge from the past and openness to the future, with freedom its defining essence. It may not be that everything happens in California first. But it might very well be true that whatever is currently happening is more clearly revealed in California and the California experience. This makes more sense.

The reason why California can function in this capacity follows from the fact that the tensions present everywhere throughout America are more emphasized here, its freedoms far more blatant. In any case, California has been blessed and cursed with virtually every paradox imaginable. Physically, the state is an incomparable paradise as well as a veritable pit of desolation, the two often existing nearly side by side. It is a haven for both preservationists and developers, and the distinction between them isn't always very clear. Its political makeup is an impossible blend of moderation and extremism, with the two ends of the political spectrum frequently merging, making the moderates seem equally extreme. The conflicts between young and old, rich and poor, Black and White, men and women, straights and gays, hippies and bikers, upper and lower classes, and so on are both more destructive and more creative than anywhere else in the world. The most incompatible religious and antireligious sentiments exist here in relative harmony, in the midst of some of the most rabid apathy imaginable. The state's support for education is rivaled only by its seeming insensitivity to those students who wish most to take advantage of it. Its laws allow for an unheard-of degree of freedom in personal matters, yet at the same time they exhibit the kind of moral oppression that threatens to obliterate the very possibility of meaningful personal action. And the most "laid back" of Californians are often the very same people who are "living in the fast lane." Tensions like these give California its highly visible energy and vitality. Nothing in this state is stable, after all, including the ground, so movement and change would seem to be the inevitable consequences of succumbing to this state of mind.

America's cultural revolution is thus more evident in California than anywhere else, revealed dramatically in its conflicts and in its attempted resolutions. One example may illustrate the point clearly: In the span of years between 2007 and 2009, a proposition to recognize the right of gays and lesbians to marry was passed, was overturned, was appealed, then lost and now is being readied again. Because of this kind of rambunctiousness, it's worth taking a final look at the revolution by narrowing our focus to the Golden State in an effort to understand present situation. In keeping with the basic thesis, of course, I believe the best way to appreciate the California experience is to see it through the lens of rock music indigenous to California.

There are really two aspects to look for in this or any revolution: its internal dynamics (in this case revealed by the conflicts intrinsic to California) and its relationship with the established order (revealed by California's encounters with the outside world). The former might help disclose what it means for the very same people to have elected Ronald Reagan, Jerry Brown and Arnold Schwarzenegger governor. It might help us understand the meaning behind all those predictable jokes about California. (For example, someone must have tilted the East Coast up, because everything loose fell into California. And, Q: Why is California like granola? A: Because it's filled with fruits and nuts.) Somehow, the unsettled electoral process and the jokes all relate to the underlying values of the California experience, and these values link it to the cultural revolution, establishing an analogous relationship between the two (or so it seems). As long as this approach isn't pushed too far or understood to be a literal identity, an exploration of California through its rock music just might provide a few interesting insights as to where we are and where we might be headed as a culture.

As a theoretical context for this analogy, I've found that a Hegelian structure helps to explain the internal dynamics and a Thomas Kuhnian structure the external relationship.

The Internal Dynamics

Hegel offers a way to understand the process of historical change. It's not the only way, of course, and it's certainly not the clearest. But for the purpose at hand, it has three distinct advantages. First, change is portrayed as the very nature of reality; it's not something accidental or induced from the outside. Second, change is oriented toward a particular goal—freedom; every stage of the process brings it closer. Third, the process occurs in our consciousness and then necessarily manifests itself in concrete historical events.

In his lectures, collected in *The Philosophy of History*, Hegel said, "universal history shows the development of the consciousness of Freedom on the part of Spirit, and of the consequent realization of that Freedom. This development implies a gradation—a series of increasingly adequate expressions or manifestations of Freedom, which ... it successively transcends.[2] The dynamics of this process result from the continuous conflict between "being" and "nothing," which produces "becoming." Every stage of this process is characterized by explosive interplay. Although Hegel certainly believed this triad to be the actual, fundamental component of reality, I intend it only as a metaphorical way of understanding historical change. Another important caveat: Hegel's concept of "freedom" was, in essence, metaphysical (pardon the redundancy), while I have a more social and political concept in mind.

Being

The thing to keep in mind about pure being is its undetermined immediacy, the fact that there are no differentiating features either within it or between itself and the outside, pure "is-ness" with no *particular* knowledge about it possible. "It is pure un-determinateness and emptiness."

Perhaps the purest, undifferentiated representation of California's revolutionary consciousness occurs in the music of the Beach Boys, specifically in the third part of "California Saga," a trilogy written by Mike Love and Al Jardine. Titled simply "California," the song so perfectly expresses the state's geography, climate, history, idealism, and freedom that nothing else about California is granted any reality at all. It captures the listener's attention so totally that, for its duration, no other place can possibly exist: California is all there is. The power, however, is in more than the lyrics; the music by itself has the same effect. Together the impact is simply overwhelming; nothing other than the singers' image of California is permitted to enter the listener's consciousness. Upon reflection, of course, this image is recognized for what it is: empty of all the specificity that would give it genuine reality.

Other musicians from California of a more recent vintage say the same thing using different styles of rock. With a decidedly upbeat rap/hip-hop style, for example, Beck in "Where It's At," from his highly acclaimed 1996 album, *Odelay*, uses a confusion of Beat-like images ("Shine your shoes with your microphone blues/Hirsutes with your parachute flutes") to portray the kind of purity devoid of specificity. The rhythms and a variety of instruments play against the lyrics to create a unity of "California-ness"—albeit a vastly different vision from that of the Beach Boys.

Nothing

Similarly, pure nothingness has no determinateness with respect to itself or to anything else. It is the complete and total absence of "is-ness," the negation of being. Its reality in our consciousness is not simply "no thought," but the "thought of nothing." In other words, for Hegel it makes sense to speak of the reality of nothingness.

Given that the Beach Boys and Beck portray the pure, undifferentiated fullness of California's revolutionary consciousness, the complete and pure negation of this image is best represented by the Doors (especially Jim Morrison). Everything the Beach Boys are, the Doors are not; everything the Beach Boys advocate, the Doors reject. A more perfect opposition would be difficult if not impossible to find. In "L.A. Woman," the city (which metaphorically represents the state) is personified as a whore whose hair is burning and whose wanderings are confined to freeways, midnight alleys, and topless bars. The imagery is as dominated by the dark as the Beach Boys' imagery is by the light; neither gives any promise of ending. Further, there are no references to geography, climate, history, idealism, or freedom in "L.A. Woman." On the contrary, we are confronted with the unmistakable indications of destruction, disease, disaster, and disillusionment. As with the Beach Boys, however, the overwhelming purity of the Doors' portrayal is expressed in their music as well as in their lyrics. The Doors' use of a double flatted minor key contrasts so sharply with the simple minor along with a major key used by the Beach Boys that there is no way to escape the Doors' undifferentiated mood of negation. Their vision of the California experience is as bleak as the Beach Boys' vision is positive, and as a result, it, too, is necessarily devoid of the content that would give it genuine reality.

A polar opposite to Beck's upbeat rap about California is Tupac Shakur's "To Live and Die in L.A." On his final album *The Don Killuminati: The 7 Day Theory* and performing as Makaveli, a pseudonym adapted from his fascination with Machiavelli, he chants about the City of Angels and being in constant danger, for in South Central L.A., you "can't get no stranger." It's pure bleakness. Any specificity there might be in the lyrics is lost beneath the negativity.

Becoming

Insofar as reality is concerned, pure being and pure nothing have the same characteristics; so neither alone can accurately portray the truth about reality. For Hegel, what is truth is neither being nor nothing, but rather that each immediately disappears in its opposite. Their truth is thus this movement of the immediate disappearance of one in the other: becoming. But everything real contains both.

Neither the Beach Boys and Beck nor The Doors and Tupac can truthfully represent the actual revolutionary consciousness of California, since their portrayals of the positive and negative elements within this experience are pure abstractions. Reality is always a mixture of the positive and the negative and the various processes occasioned by the mixture. So it is with the California experience.

"Hotel California" by The Eagles expresses both the mixture and the resulting processes more clearly than perhaps any other song written about California; nevertheless, there are a few more recent attempts that come rather close. As for The Eagles, The "hotel" is obviously a metaphorical reference to California and the state of mind that accompanies it. After checking in for the night, a traveler comes to the realization that this (California) could be Heaven or Hell; it turns out to be both. While on the one hand it's a lovely place, on the other it's a prison of our own making—where the dancers seek both to remember and to forget. Inevitably, the resulting conflict dislodges the visitor from any possible static complacency; some kind of movement must occur. Escape to where they were before is not possible. The hotel is programmed only to receive guests. Checking out is a mere illusion, because once here in California a person can never leave. Any movement backward or elsewhere is ruled out. The California experience can invade the consciousness so completely that forward motion is the only conceivable movement. So it is also with the cultural revolution; once involved in it, other alternatives cease to have any power or meaning.

Musically, The Eagles have created a song that suggests a combination of major and minor harmonics. Even more important, however, is their subtle use of reggae rhythms as an expression of the paradoxes so often encountered in this state. For while Jamaica couldn't be farther away from California and still be within the scope of American culture, the revolutionary sentiments of reggae are right at home. Overall, the song is a remarkable combination of seemingly opposite tendencies, and anyone lured into its seductive melodies is bound to come away changed.

An apt rival to "Hotel California" just might be the far darker "Californication" on a 1999 album of the same name by the Red Hot Chili Peppers. Although melodic, it is in a doubled minor key and conveys the seductive trap of Hollywood — a metaphorical reference to California. They call it the edge of the world and all of Western civilization. They sing about destruction leading to a very rough road but also leading to creation, and earthquakes (orgasms) being a good vibration "to a girl's guitar." They capture the paradox of California perfectly.

Revolution

If, as Hegel suggested, reality always comprises a mixture of being and nothingness (the positive and negative), and if the tension between them is the fundamental source of change (becoming), then it would seem that the greater the tension the greater the processes of change. Furthermore, if the conflicts are as severe throughout the rest of the country as they seem to be within the state of California, then the kind of movement that's under way can *only* be characterized as revolutionary. The energy being released by the dynamics internal to this situation is too great to be described in any other way.

The External Relationship

Thomas Kuhn's justly famous book *The Structure of Scientific Revolutions* has stimulated thought in so many diverse fields that it would be a shame not to use some of his ideas to help examine cultural revolutions as well. Actually, quite a few others have already delved into this area, as evidenced by a book of essays devoted to the application of Kuhn's thought (*Paradigms and Revolutions*, edited by Gary Gutting). Especially interesting is the way Kuhn's conceptual scheme lends itself to an analysis of the relationship between any given revolution and the established order. In this regard, the following four themes seem particularly appropriate.

Paradigms and Normalcy

"Paradigm" is unquestionably the key concept of Kuhn's theory, and the issue of its clarity has provided the grist for an apparently endless flow of scholarly articles, including Kuhn's reply to several of the more serious criticisms. Without getting bogged down in this debate, a paradigm is essentially a perceptual model which is comprised of basic assumptions about the world, procedural norms for understanding it, criteria for assessing truth and falseness, beliefs about the meaningfulness of reality, the ultimate values implicit in any investigation of its nature and a language designed to express all of this (the Ptolemaic, Copernican and Einsteinian views of the universe, for example). Usually, many people share the commitment to a particular constellation of beliefs captured (often loosely) by a given paradigm; otherwise, it would be of little interest and receive even less attention. When those sharing it hold power, the paradigm assumes the status of normalcy — and, consequently, becomes the unquestioned truth. Rarely do the inevitable anomalies unaccounted for within a given model occasion more than passing notice. Eventually, however, a new paradigm arises which can successfully explain the anomalies better than the prevailing scheme, but since the new paradigm is necessarily incommensurable with the old one, a conflict results. Notice that the location of this conflict is in the human consciousness, and while it may manifest itself in physical violence, this is not inevitable. Fundamentally, the conflict is between incompatible ideas, and the battleground is within the mind. Since the two paradigms entail two different (but usually overlapping) languages, communication between their respective proponents is exceptionally difficult, not the least because this difficulty is not often recognized and/or appreciated.

An amusing but still deadly serious illustration of such a confrontation occurred in 1983, when Secretary of the Interior James Watt refused to allow the Beach Boys to perform their traditional Fourth of July concert on the grounds of the Washington Monument. He alleged that the Beach Boys (and rock music in general) attract the wrong kind of people. Given Watt's state of consciousness, however, his attitude and decision made perfect sense. They were completely consistent with the paradigm he held to be unquestionably true. (By the way, to illustrate the fact that life is a bit more complex and not nearly as neat as any conceptual scheme might suggest, the Reagans, like many others, were upset with Watt's decision, even though they certainly shared the same paradigmatic perspective.) Fans of the Beach Boys and rock music were not only angered but also bemused by Watt's action, since the Beach Boys were not even close to being as outrageous as some contemporary rock groups; they weren't like the Circle Jerks or the Dead Kennedys, after all. Rock fans' incredulity derived from their having a vastly different perspective on reality than did Watt; neither party was really capable of understanding the attitude of the other.

Paradigm Shifts and Revolutions

Essentially, a revolution occurs with the replacement of the established (normal) paradigm by another: an alternation of worldviews. Such replacements occur suddenly and all at once, in the sense that an evolutionary transition from one to the other is not empirically or even logically possible; the paradigms themselves prohibit this. A more appropriate analogy, one which Kuhn himself uses, is a conversion experience: one paradigm must be completely abandoned in order for another to be accepted. In other words, a total reorientation takes place. The resistance to this kind of change is enormous, and it may take quite a while for the shift to be completed. As the process is under way, the personal and societal crises can achieve considerable intensity and become enormously distressing. the status quo makes every attempt to shore up its defenses, and this usually involves some form of repression. Anomalies between the accepted order and things that do not fit in are either ignored or forced uncomfortably into the existing patterns of thought; alien paradigms are simply given no official recognition and are discouraged in every possible way. What this amounts to is a Counter-Reaction, launched by those most threatened by the new paradigm.

A shift of paradigm is revealed by the Mamas and the Papas' "Twelve Thirty (Young Girls Are Coming to the Canyon)," a song that traces their own conversion experience when moving to California: "I used to live in New York City/Everything there was dark and dirty." Then follows:

> At first so strange to feel so friendly
> To say good morning and really mean it
> To feel these changes happening in me
> But not to notice 'till I feel it

Their entire worldview had undergone a change, and to call it a revolution of consciousness is not an exaggeration. Other transplants to California have described their feelings in a similar way: Joni Mitchell (from Canada) in "California," the group America (from England, Florida, and Texas) in "Ventura Highway" and "California Revisited" and the Starland Vocal Band (from the East Coast) in "California Day" among them.

Shifting away from one paradigm to another — or perhaps to no replacement paradigm whatsoever — is an equally momentous shift, especially when the paradigm is so overpowering and engaging.

The Presidents of the United States of America, a group originally from Oregon, in 1994 recorded an amazingly ironic tribute to California called, "Fuck California." They refer to the beauty of the mountains, the cities, Interstate 5, the clarity of the air that "makes them drunk," and the sunset in Santa Cruz that lifts you up "even though you're depressed." All the while the chorus raps the title epithet. Yes, they too experienced a conversion experience, even though it was — perhaps — unpleasant ... yet beautiful. Their paradoxical stance says "California Dreamin'" and nightmare all over it.

Kid Rock's 2001 "Cowboy" is not only ironic but raunchy as well. Aside from referencing the movie industry's effect on young ladies' desire for artificially enhanced mammaries, he calls to mind a variety of other musicians, persons and films, as in rapping that he's not "straight outta of Compton" but straight outta the trailer. Nevertheless, he "rocks like Amadeus," wants to find Heidi Fleiss and chill like Larry Flynt. All this, because he wants to be a cowboy "spendin' all my time at Hollywood and Vine." This too illustrates the seduction of California and Mr. Rock succumbing to it as well.

The Dead Kennedys in 1980 worried about the fascism they saw as implicit in the state's seductive allure in "California Über Alles." Belinda Carlisle in her 2004 "California" wrestles with what was to her the emblematic death of River Phoenix in Hollywood, and sings that it took a lot for her to walk away from L.A. Weezer, however, in "California" (c. 2004) has the protagonist sing about wanting someone to join him, so to speak. He's all alone and needs her "here in Santa Monica" where "the Blue Bus" can take them everywhere.

Regardless of how a person assesses the worth of the "California Experience," its presence is overwhelming — much like Rudolph Otto's description of experiencing the Holy — or, as Jello Biafra of the Dead Kennedys might prefer to put it, *Das Heilige*.

Knowledge and Authority

Kuhn recognizes that revolutions of consciousness are often indistinguishable from ordinary, normal day-to-day events. For this reason, he devotes an entire chapter to an analysis of their invisibility. The principal reason for this problem has to do with the fact that all knowledge is dependent on the prevailing paradigm. Hence, what is taught throughout society is restricted by the status quo; the institutions that educate the young (schools, families, churches, media, governments, etc.) purvey a notion of truth that derives from the official paradigm, and this alone. It is not so much that other paradigmatic ideas are deliberately and consciously excluded (although this certainly happens); more often, these other ideas are not even entertained in thought. Thinking about something new isn't possible within the prevailing system. The meaning of truth and its criteria are thus based on a fundamental commitment to a particular worldview; whatever doesn't fit the pattern is ignored and/or disvalued.

The controversies surrounding The Byrds' rendition of Dylan's "Mr. Tambourine Man," The Association's "Along Comes Mary," Creedence Clearwater Revival's "Proud Mary," and the Jefferson Airplane's "White Rabbit" illustrate how far apart the perceptions based on different paradigms can be. It is not a question of whether or not these particular songs refer to drugs (which they do); it's a question of how drugs are regarded or valued that's important. In *The Story of Rock*, Carl Belz sees such thinly disguised drug references fundamentally as an expression of an alternative lifestyle: "Those who knew the jargon used it to distinguish themselves from those who did not. It became a method whereby young people defined their personal world and excluded adults from it."[3] Although Belz sees the conflict primarily in generational terms, he's essentially correct. These songs, and others like them, place a different truth-value on the use of drugs (and, as I've noted earlier, a clear differentiation is made among various drugs concerning their desirability).

Similar examples could be cited regarding sexuality, the war in Vietnam, the military, the government, and virtually everything else at issue between the revolutionaries and the established order. None of these issues is capable of empirical or logical resolution, for they have to do with ultimate values. A resolution could only occur if one side were to convert to the other's worldview, and even this would not obviate the personal struggles involved with a revolutionary transition, for this is precisely what's entailed by a conversion.

The seemingly eternal debate over abortion rights is a case in point. (Pardon the following excursus into the terminally arcane.) At its very roots, the conflict stems from two contrary worldviews. One accepts the legitimate role of metaphysics in understanding reality and the other rejects its legitimacy. Most disputants, however, are rarely aware of this fundamental division, so their "debates" go nowhere. It's actually an unresolved dispute from earlier cultural revolutions: the Renaissance (from the 14th through the 16th centuries of the Common Era) and the Enlightenment (18th century). Putting it as simply as possible, some people "believe" in the "reality" of "essences" or "substances" while others believe these things are merely "names" we give to common characteristics (realism vs. nominalism). The former asserts that there really is such a thing as "human nature," which comes into being at the moment of conception. The latter asserts that "human nature" is what we "name" common human qualities that gradually emerge in a continuous process. So, to use the phrase "to kill a fetus is to kill a human" is meaningful to one group but not to the other. What can resolve this? The answer is simple: *nothing!* Only a wholesale conversion of one side to the other will end the conflict. The two sides are, in effect, speaking different languages.

Relativity and Justification

The implication that would seem to follow from this is that truth is logically dependent on the acceptance of a given paradigm. Since there are no external and objective criteria (based on a meta paradigm, perhaps) on which to base an assessment of competing paradigms, truth must necessarily be relative. Kuhn, however, is reluctant to follow his ideas this far; he feels that some kind of pragmatic judgment is possible. It is useful, in other words, both to preserve the existing paradigm for as long as possible as well as to encourage the development of new paradigms. Yet this is hardly a sufficient substitute for the idea of absolute truth: pragmatism must either accept epistemological relativism or concede that it presupposes certain absolutes as a matter of faith. Kuhn, in fact, seems to acknowledge that science, in some ways, is clearly distinguishable "from every other creative pursuit except theology." For both, the final appeal is always to some kind of authority — not truth. Actually, the only social system consistent with the unfettered pursuit of truth is anarchy, for the pursuit of truth and an appeal to any kind or degree of authority are utterly incompatible.

How, then, is it possible to assess the comparative truth claims of the cultural revolution and the established order if truth can only be decided from within each paradigm? Is the answer no more than a matter of taste? Like Kuhn and virtually everyone else, I am uncomfortable with this solution, yet there doesn't seem to be any way to settle the issue without begging the question (for choosing among competing justifications involves an infinite regress).

The only way out of this impasse, it seems to me, is neither logical nor empirical. Rather it is the act of commitment itself, a Kierkegaardian "leap of faith." That to which a commitment is made is secondary to the act itself. It doesn't "prove" anything, of course, but a genuine leap of faith certainly *authenticates* the commitment as having as much validity as any similar commitment. This, I think, is about the most we can say about justifying one paradigm against another.

Commitments like this can be shown in a variety of ways, but surely one way is for people actually to live the life they propose as desirable for all. As far as California rock music is concerned, examples abound, but as a paradigm of commitment, we need look no farther than the Grateful Dead. Not only did they choose to live communally in "the Haight" (before its discovery by *Time* magazine), they embodied virtually every other trait of hippiedom, including giving many free concerts. Their performances were literal manifestations of the "trips" they frequently took, "trips" for which they were occasionally busted. Some might conclude that they were unable to separate themselves from the worldview they revealed in their music, but this would be to denigrate their choice without any reason other than distaste for it. The Dead were certainly not the only ones to have made a commitment to this degree, nor is hippie life the only possible form that such a commitment can take. Another exemplar, with virtually nothing in common with the Grateful Dead other than sharing their revolutionary values, has been Randy Newman. More than anything else, his commitment is manifested in the risks he takes in his music. In *Mystery Train*, Greil Marcus sees him this way: "Laconic, funny, grim, and solitary, Randy Newman is a ... man who does not like what he sees but is wildly attracted to it anyway, a man who keeps his sanity by rendering contradictions other people struggle to avoid.... His real task is to make his burden ours."[4] With the success of "Short People" (and his earlier but less successful "Sail Away"), he partially accomplished his aim. Listening to him assume the role of a bigot and a racist, we cannot ignore what he is portraying. For his portrayal is no mere parody or satire; he really does assume the role! In so doing he risks exposing his most cherished values to the grossest of misunderstandings — having others believe he actually is advocating what he so ardently opposes. He fools around with America's most sorely tender wounds and forces the listener either to stick the knife in deeper or to pull it out forever.

Similar examples come to mind in the rap/hip-hop communities, wherein the performers in many ways *must* be committed participants in order to maintain their audience. Not only does this open them to savage and often baseless critiques from without, it also frequently places them in physical danger from within. "Gangsta" rappers like Snoop Dogg and Ice T (often cited as the progenitors of this subgenre) are not alone in this, but they can certainly serve as emblematic of the relationship between a performer and the lifestyle embodied in the music he or she performs. Spike Lee's 2000 film *Bamboozled* mercilessly satirizes their genre (and a lot more) as being little more than a throwback to blackface minstrel shows. (This time, in a hilariously genuine Spike Lee twist, the Black actors all wear blackface!) The risks coming from without are amply illustrated by the murder of Tupac Shakur in Las Vegas on September 7, 1996, and by the murder of Biggie Smalls (Notorious B.I.G.) on March 9, 1997, in Los Angeles. The East Coast vs. West Coast feud (of which these murders were a product) shows what can happen when no distance is maintained between the medium and the message. (A loss of transcendence.) Sacrificing one's life in this way may stem from an ultimate commitment, but it does nothing to establish truth.

No commitment, no matter how strong or sincere, can establish the truth of a paradigm and the set of fundamental values that's implied by it. Nevertheless, by putting a commitment on the line, its authenticity can be established, and no more can be asked of anyone.

The State of California and Rock Itself

Some of the comments made about rock and roll in *Rolling Stone*'s tenth anniversary issue (1977) are remarkably similar to the kind of commentary that is appropriate to the state of California today.

Chet Flippo maintained that rock and roll has always meant more than music: "There are books and movies and people and events and attitudes that matter more to a rock and roll way of life than do many records that are labeled rock and roll. Jack Kerouac was rock and roll; Bobby Rydell was not. Tom Robbins is rock and roll; Andy Gibb is not. *Star Wars* is rock and roll; *A Star Is Born* is not."[5] To continue his list, Nelson Mandela is rock and roll; F.W. Botha is not (despite their unlikely reconciliation). Willie Nelson is rock and roll; Lee Ann Womack is not. David Letterman is rock and roll; Jay Leno is not. Barack Obama is rock and roll; George W. Bush is not. Anthony Bourdain is rock and roll; Martha Stewart is not. Spider-Man is rock and roll; Superman is not. Harriet Tubman is rock and roll; Condoleezza Rice is not. Thomas Paine is rock and roll; Alexander Hamilton is not. And California is rock and roll; Alabama is not.

Jon Landau wrote, "Elvis Presley's rock and roll was a frontal assault on fifties America. It was a unique expression of people trying to transcend the traditional social and emotional limits of their lives ... sixties rock transformed Presley's unconscious impulses into a self-conscious rebellion.... The fifties rebels without a cause became the sixties rebels *with* a cause — and a vengeance." But it was a vengeance with a purpose too. "Great rock not only defines what is, but suggests what might be."[6] These remarks are reminiscent of those made by Theodore H. White, cited earlier, a fact worth pointing out, since Landau wasn't thinking about California and White wasn't thinking about rock and roll. (At least I don't think so.)

The late Ralph Gleason, one of the founders of *Rolling Stone*, always believed in music's ability to change our lives. He wrote that rock and roll "plays a role unlike anything in history, yes, even including religion.... As societal glue, as educational system, as emotional, mind expanding experience and a view-realignment mechanism, music is now in the process of changing the ways in which things are seen. In the process it is changing ways in which this generation will relate to everything and, in the ultimate, it will change the nature of our society." Gleason's optimism might seem a bit naive today, but only insofar as he expected the change to happen quickly. Despite this, he had a grasp on the essential truth about rock and roll: It "is the new educational system for reform and the medium for revolution. Its importance is impossible to overemphasize."[7] As it is with the state of rock music and the cultural revolution, so it is with the state of California: what begins on the West Coast will eventually travel throughout the nation, a prospect which some regard with hope and others with trepidation. Both feelings are no doubt correct.

For those of you who say that you want a revolution, it should be carefully noted that all of us want in our own way to change the world. Some speak of evolution. Most of us, after all, are rightly ambivalent about destruction. Nevertheless, there is good reason for confidence, quite apart from those with alleged plans offering us a solution (and requesting a contribution). More often than not, their solutions merely yield an increase in hatreds, which we can do well without. The basic strategy must always be to change people's consciousness first — not constitutions and institutions. Further, a successful revolution must emerge out of and speak directly to the culture that's involved; the revolutions from elsewhere can never be imported. No one will listen. (I presume this paraphrase is recognizable!?)

Regardless of whether or not America's cultural revolution succeeds or fails, America will never be the same again. The changes already begun are irreversible. The process of negation set in motion by Elvis and all that he represented is still alive, as is the process of affirmation instigated by The Beatles. Neither Elvis nor The Beatles have survived the years. However, in a larger sense, they're still with us whenever we turn on the radio. They're in every song you hear, every rock-and-roll record you play, no matter what the style, no matter who the artist. Were it not for Elvis Presley and The Beatles, the music of today and the revolution would not exist. And were it not for rock and roll, we would not be able to look at America today and *imagine*.

Chapter Notes

Preface

1. Richard Koenigsberg, http://www.amazon.com/You-Say-Want-Revolution-American/dp/0759306109/ref=sr_1_4?ie=UTF8&s=books&qid=1224093235&sr=8-4 (December 20, 2009).
2. Tom Carson, "From Revolution to Institution: The Politics of Rock." *You Say You Want a Revolution: Rock Music in American Culture* by Robert G. Pielke (Chicago: Nelson-Hall, 1986); "Rebel Rock: The Politics of Popular Music by John Street (Blackwell)." *Los Angeles Times Book Review*. August 31, 1986, 1.

Introduction

1. Pat Buchanan, Republican National Convention, 1992. http://www.youtube.com/watch?v=iO5_1ps5CAc.

Part One

1. John Blacking, *How Musical Is Man?* (Seattle: University of Washington Press, 1973), 25, 53, 58, 104, 115–16, 191.
2. Susanne Langer, *Philosophy in a New Key* (New York: Mentor Books, 1948), 191.
3. David Pichaske, *A Generation in Motion* (New York: Schirmer Books, 1979), xix.

Chapter 2

1. Herbert Marcuse, *Counter-Revolution and Revolt* (Boston, MA: Beacon Press, 1972), 79–82, 87, 93, 99–100, 116.
2. William Barrett, *Irrational Man* (Garden City, NY: Anchor Books, 1958), 41–49, 56, 64–65.

Chapter 3

1. Kristol, William. "2009: Could Have Been Worse." *The Weekly Standard*, January 4–January 11, 2010, Vol. 15, No. 16.

Part Two

1. Marshall McLuhan, *Understanding Media* (New York: Mentor Books, 1964), x, 21, 30–32, 63, 71, 224, 243, 266–67.

Chapter 4

1. McLuhan, *Understanding Media*, 261–68.
2. Ibid., 266–67.

Chapter 5

1. McLuhan, *Understanding Media*, 247.
2. Robert Hilburn, "The 12-Inch Record on a Hot Roll," *Los Angeles Times*, February 13, 1983, 66–68.

Chapter 7

1. McLuhan, *Understanding Media*, 61, 273–76, 278, 282, 288.
2. Ibid., 292.
3. Ibid., 272, 275, 294, 297, 300.

Chapter 8

1. Evelyn Joyce Black, "Faculty Support for Distance Education in a Conventional University," University of British Columbia (http://hdl.handle.net/2429/3166). Accessed December 29, 2009.
2. Margaret S. Elliott and Kenneth L. Kraemer (eds.), *Computerization Movements and Technology Diffusion from Mainframes to Ubiquitous Computing*. (Medford, NJ: Information Today, 2008).
3. Ibid., xvi.
4. Paul Levinson, *The Digital McLuhan* (New York: Routledge, 1999), 191–95.
5. Marshall McLuhan, *The Gutenberg Galaxy* (New York: Mentor Books, 1969), 32.
6. Levinson, 192.
7. Graham St. John, *Rave Culture and Religion* (London: Routledge, 2004), 8.
8. Martin Cloonan and Reebee Garofalo. *Policing Pop* (Philadelphia: Temple University Press, 2003), 1.

Part Three

1. Rudolf Otto, *The Idea of the Holy*, trans. by John Harvey (New York: Oxford University Press, 1958), 10–31, 143.
2. Paul Tillich, *Dynamics of Faith* (New York: Harper Torchbooks, 1957), 43, 48, 90.

Chapter 9

1. Jerry Wexler and Ahmet Ertegun, "The Latest Trends: R&B Disks Are Going Pop," *Cash Box*, July 3, 1954, 56.
2. Michael Bane, *White Boy Singin' the Blues* (New York: Penguin Books, 1982), 119–21.
3. Greil Marcus, *Mystery Train*, rev. ed. (New York: E.P. Dutton, 1982), 155, 173.
4. Ibid., 190.
5. Bane, *White Boy Singin' the Blues*, 129.
6. Marcus, *Mystery Train*, 141.
7. Bane, *White Boy Singin' the Blues*, 101.
8. Marcus, *Mystery Train*, 166.
9. G.B. Golson, ed., *Playboy Interviews with John Lennon and Yoko Ono,* conducted by David Sheff (New York: Playboy Press, 1981), 48, 108–09.
10. Marcus, *Mystery Train*, 191–92.
11. Ibid., 208.
12. Bane, *White Boy Singin' the Blues*, 129.
13. Mircea Eliade, *The Sacred and the Profane*, trans. by Willard Track (New York: Harper & Row, 1961), 97, 98.
14. Golson, *Playboy Interviews*, 71–72.
15. Eliade, *The Sacred and the Profane*, 88–89, 94.

Chapter 10

1. Quoted by Greil Marcus, "The Beatles," in *Rolling Stone Illustrated History of Rock and Roll* ed. by Jim Miller (New York: Rolling Stone Press, 1976), 174.
2. Peter L. Berger, *Invitation to Sociology* (Garden City, NY: Anchor Books, 1963), 54, 57, 61, 62.
3. Otto, *Idea of the Holy*, 36.
4. John Lahr, "The Beatles Considered," *The New Republic*, December 2, 1981, 22–23.
5. Ibid., 23.
6. Richard Poirier, *The Performing Self* (New York: Oxford University Press, 1971), 137, 139.
7. Quoted by Marcus, "Beatles," *Rolling Stone Illustrated History of Rock and Roll*, 176.
8. Ibid.
9. Pichaske, *A Generation in Motion*, 92, 93.

10. Jonathan Cott, "Children of Paradise," *Rolling Stone*, December 15, 1977, 37, 41, 43.
11. Ibid., 43.
12. Lahr, "The Beatles. Considered," 23.
13. Eliade, *The Sacred and the Profane*, 99–100.
14. Hilburn, *Corn Flakes with John Lennon* (New York: Rodale, 2009), 6.
15. Ibid., 80.
16. Bruce Eisner, "The Hippie Revolution: Looking Back at Sgt. Pepper," *Head*, April 1978, 37.

Chapter 12

1. Doug Copeland, "Generation X," *Vista* (1989), 1. http://joeclark.org/dossiers/GenerationX.pdf.
2. Mark Muro, "Baby Busters Resent Life in Boomers' Debris," *The Boston Globe*, November 10, 1991.
3. Kurt Andersen, "Boomers: Older and Maybe, Finally, Wiser," *Time*, August 5, 2009.
4. Robert Hilburn, "Pop Breaks Vietnam Silence," *Los Angeles Times*, October 3, 1983, 1.
5. Ellen Goodman, *At Large* (New York: Summit Books, 1981), 204, 205.
6. *Peter, Paul, and Mary: Carry It On: A Musical Legacy*. DVD. Rhino, 2004.
7. Chad Bower, "What Is Heavy Metal? History: Description of Heavy Metal Genres." About.com. (http://heavymetal.about.com/od/heavymetal101/a/101_history.htm). December 9, 2009.
8. Robert Hilburn, "John Lydon: Fed Up with Pop Anarchy," *Los Angeles Times*, April 17, 1982, A23.
9. Leslie Woodhead, director, *How the Beatles Rocked the Kremlin*. Blakeway Productions for WNET. ORG, 2009.
10. Timothy W. Ryback, *Rock Around the Bloc: A History of Rock Music in Eastern Europe and the Soviet Union* (New York: Oxford University Press, 1990).

Chapter 13

1. Eliade, *The Sacred and the Profane*, 68–69, 78, 80–81.
2. Søren Kierkegaard, *Philosophical Fragments*, 2d ed., trans. by H. Hong (Princeton, NJ: Princeton University Press, 1962), 128.
3. Ringo Starr, *All Together Now: A Documentary Film* (Apple Corps & Cirque du Soleil, 2008).
4. George Martin, ibid.
5. Wilfred Cantwell Smith, *The Meaning and End of Religion* (New York: Macmillan, 1962), 16.

Epilogue

1. Theodore H. White, *America in Search of Itself* (New York: Harper and Row, 1982), 64.
2. Georg Wilhelm Friedrich Hegel, *The Philosophy of History*, trans. by J. Sibree (New York: Dover, 1956), 63.
3. Carl Belz, *The Story of Rock*, 2d ed. (New York: Harper and Row, 1972), 171.
4. Marcus, *Mystery Train*, 136.
5. Chet Flippo, "A Style Is Born," *Rolling Stone*, December 15, 1977, 21.
6. Jon Landau, "Rock Ages," *Rolling Stone*, December 15, 1977, 33.
7. Ralph J. Gleason, "What We Are and What We Ain't," *Rolling Stone*, December 15, 1977, 27.

Bibliography

American Culture

Andersen, Kurt. *Reset: How This Crisis Can Restore Our Values and Renew America.* New York: Random House, 2009.
Carroll, Peter N. *It Seemed Like Nothing Happened: The Tragedy and the Promise of America in the 1970s.* New York: Holt, Rinehart and Winston, 1983.
Dickstein, Morris. *Gates of Eden: American Culture in the Sixties.* New York: Basic Books, 1977.
Goodman, Ellen. *At Large.* New York: Summit Books, 1981.
Halberstam, David. *The Best and the Brightest.* Greenwich, CT: Fawcett, 1973.
Holman, Sona, and Lillian Friedman. *How to Lie about Your Age.* New York: Collier Books, 1979.
Medved, Michael, and David Wallechinsky. *What Really Happened to the Class of '65?* New York: Ballantine Books, 1976.
Moment, Gairdner, and Otto Kraushaar, eds. *Utopias: The American Experience.* Metuchen, NJ: Scarecrow Press, 1980.
Obst, Lynda R., ed. *The Sixties.* New York: Rolling Stone Press, 1977.
Pichaske, David. *A Generation in Motion: Popular Music and Culture in the Sixties.* New York: Schirmer Books, 1979.
Reich, Charles. *The Greening of America.* New York: Random House, 1970.
Roszak, Theodore. *The Making of a Counter Culture.* Garden City, NY: Doubleday, Anchor Books, 1969.
Tapia, Andrés. *The Inclusion Paradox: The Obama Era and the Transformation of Global Diversity.* Lincolnshire, IL: Hewitt Associates, 2009.
White, Theodore H. *America in Search of Itself.* New York: Harper and Row, 1982.
Wills, Garry. *Nixon Agonistes.* New York: Mentor Books, 1971.
Wofford, Harris. *Of Kennedys and Kings: Making Sense of the Sixties.* New York: Farrar, Straus and Giroux, 1980.

Media

Black, Evelyn Joyce. "Faculty Support for Distance Education in a Conventional University," University of British Columbia (http://hdl.handle.net/2429/3166). Accessed December 29, 2009.
Cloonan, Martin, and Reebee Garafalo. *Policing Pop.* Philadelphia: Temple University Press, 2003.
Dexter, Dave. *Playback.* New York: Billboard Publications, 1976.
Ehrenstein, David, and Bill Reed. *Rock on Film.* New York: Delilah Books, 1982.
Elliott, Margaret S., and Kenneth L. Kraemer, eds. *Computerization Movements and Technology Diffusion from Mainframes to Ubiquitous Computing.* Medford, NJ: Information Today, 2008.
Levinson, Paul. *The Digital McLuhan.* New York: Routledge, 1999.
McLuhan, Marshall. *The Global Village.* New York: Oxford, 1989.
_____. *The Gutenberg Galaxy.* New York: Mentor Books, 1969.
_____. *Understanding Media.* New York: Mentor Books, 1964.
McLuhan, Marshall, and Eric McLuhan. *Laws of Media: The New Science.* Toronto: University of Toronto Press, 1988.

Newcomb, Horace. *TV: The Most Popular Art*. Garden City, NY: Anchor Books, 1974.
Norback, Craig T., and Peter G., eds. *TV Guide Almanac*. New York: Ballantine Books, 1980.
Sklar, Robert. *Movie-Made America: A Cultural History of American Movies*. New York: Vintage Books, 1975.
Tebbel, John. *Media in America*. New York: Mentor Books, 1976.
Whetmore, Edward. *Mediamerica*. 2d ed. Belmont, CA: Wadsworth, 1982.

Philosophy

Arendt, Hannah. *On Revolution*. New York: Penguin Books, 1965.
Barrett, William. *Irrational Man*. Garden City, NY: Anchor Books, 1962.
Berger, Peter L. *Invitation to Sociology*. Garden City, NY: Anchor Books, 1963.
Blacking, John. *How Musical Is Man?* Seattle: University of Washington Press, 1973.
Brinton, Crane. *Anatomy of Revolution*. New York: Vintage Books, 1965.
Eliade, Mircea. *The Sacred and the Profane*. Trans. Willard Track. New York: Harper and Row, 1961.
Freud, Sigmund. *Civilization and Its Discontents*. New York: W. W. Norton, 1962.
Gutting, Gary, ed. *Paradigms and Revolutions*. Notre Dame, IN: University of Notre Dame Press, 1980.
Hegel, G.W.F. *The Philosophy of History*. Trans. J. Sibree. New York: Dover, 1956.
_____. *Selections*. Edited by J. Loewenberg. New York: Scribner's, 1957.
Kaufmann, Walter. *Hegel: A Reinterpretation*. Garden City, NY: Anchor Books, 1966.
Kierkegaard, Søren. *Philosophical Fragments*. 2d ed. Trans. H. Hong. Princeton, NJ: Princeton University Press, 1962.
Kuhn, Thomas. *The Structure of Scientific Revolutions*. 2d ed. Chicago: University of Chicago Press, 1970.
Langer, Susanne. *Philosophy in a New Key*. New York: Mentor Books, 1948.
Marcuse, Herbert. *The Aesthetic Dimension*. Boston: Beacon Press, 1978.
_____. *Counter-Revolution and Revolt*. Boston: Beacon Press, 1972.
_____. *An Essay on Liberation*. Boston: Beacon Press, 1969.
Maslow, Abraham. *Motivation and Personality*. New York: Harper and Row, 1954.
Otto, Rudolf. *The Idea of the Holy*. Trans. John Harvey. New York: Oxford University Press, 1958.
Poirier, Richard. *The Performing Self*. New York: Oxford University Press, 1971.
Sartre, Jean-Paul. *Being and Nothingness*. New York: Pocket Books, 1966.
Smith, Wilfred Cantwell. *The Meaning and End of Religion*. New York: Macmillan, 1962.
Sontag, Susan. *Styles of Radical Will*. New York: Farrar, Straus and Giroux, 1966.
Tillich, Paul. *Dynamics of Faith*. New York: Harper, 1958.
Tucker, Robert. *The Marxian Revolutionary Idea*. New York: W. W. Norton, 1969.

Rock Music

Bane, Michael. *The Outlaws: Revolution in Country Music*. Garden City, NY: Dolphin Books, 1978.
_____. *White Boy Singin' the Blues*. New York: Penguin Books, 1982.
The Beatles. *Beatles Lyrics*. Introduction by Richard Brautigan. New York: Dell, 1975.
Belz, Carl. *The Story of Rock*. 2d ed. New York: Harper Colophon Books, 1972.
Blackford, Andy. *Disco Dancing Tonight*. London: Octopus Books, 1979.
Brown, Philip, and Steven Gaines. *The Love You Make: An Insider's Story of The Beatles*. New York: McGraw-Hill, 1983.
Burt, Robert, and Patsy North. *West Coast Story*. Secaucus, NJ: Chartwell Books, 1977.
Charles, Steven, and John Tobler. *Remembering The Beatles*. Rock Retrospectives. New York: Penguin, 2008.
Cohn, Nik *Pop from the Beginning: A Wop Bop a Loo Bop a Lop Bam Boom*. London: Paladin, 1972.
Davies, Hunter. *The Beatles*. Rev. ed. New York: McGraw-Hill, 1978.
Denisoff, R. *Sing a Song of Social Significance*. Bowling Green, OH: Bowling Green University Press, 1972.
Eisen, Jonathan, ed. *The Age of Rock: Sounds of the American Cultural Revolution*. New York: Vintage Books, 1969.
Fong-Torres, Ben, ed. *What's That Sound?* Garden City, NY: Anchor Books, 1976.

Golson, G. Barry, ed. *Playboy Interviews with John Lennon and Yoko Ono*. Conducted by David Sheff. New York: Playboy Press, 1981.
Guralnick, Peter. *Feel Like Going Home: Portraits in Blues and Rock Roll*. New York: Vintage Books, 1981.
Herman, Gary. *Rock 'n' Roll Babylon*. New York: Perigee Books, 1982.
Hilburn, Robert. *Corn Flakes with John Lennon*. New York: Rodale, 2009.
Hopkins, Jerry. *Elvis: A Biography*. New York: Plexus, 2007.
_____. *Elvis: The Biography*. New York: Plexus, 2007.
_____. *Rock Story*. New York: Signet Books, 1970.
Jahn, Mike. *The Story of Rock*. New York: Quadrangle, 1973.
Marcus, Greil. *Mystery Train: Images of America in Rock 'n' Roll Music*. Rev. ed. New York: E.P. Dutton, 1982.
McCabe, Peter, and Robert D. Schonfeld. *Apple to the Core*. New York: Pocket Books, 1972.
Miller, Jim, ed. *Rolling Stone Illustrated History of Rock and Roll*. New York: Rolling Stone Press, 1976.
Norman, Phillip. *Shout! The Beatles in Their Generation*. New York: Fireside Books, 1981.
Preiss, Byron. *The Beach Boys*. New York: Ballantine Books, 1979.
Roxon, Lillian. *Rock Encyclopedia*. New York: Workman, 1969.
Ryback, Timothy W. *Rock around the Bloc: A History of Rock Music in Eastern Europe and the Soviet Union*. New York: Oxford University Press, 1990.
St. John, Graham, ed. *Rave Culture and Religion*. London: Routledge, 2004.
Scaduto, Anthony. *Bob Dylan: An Intimate Biography*. New York: Grosset and Dunlap, 1971.
Shaw, Arnold. *Dictionary of American Pop/Rock*. New York: Schirmer Books, 1982.
_____. *The Rock Revolution*. New York: Crowell-Collier Press, 1969.
Spitz, Bob. *The Beatles: The Biography*. New York: Back Bay Books, 2006.
Stambler, Irwin. *Encyclopedia of Pop, Rock and Soul*. New York: St. Martin's Press, 1977.
Stark, Steven. *Meet the Beatles: A Cultural History of the Band That Shook Youth, Gender, and the World*. New York: HarperCollins, 2005.
Stein, Kevin, and Dave Marsh. *Book of Rock Lists*. New York: Rolling Stone Press, 1981.
Woodhead, Leslie, dir. *How the Beatles Rocked the Kremlin*. Film. Blakeway Productions for wnet.org, 2009.
Young, Jean, and Michael Lang. *Woodstock Festival Remembered*. New York: Ballantine Books, 1979.

Index

"A Flat [A♭] Fry" 177
Abbey Road 36, 160, 167, 175
Abraxas 186
AC/DC 56, 127, 189
The Adventures of Buckaroo Banzai 103
The Adventures of Ozzie and Harriet 113
"Ain't That a Shame" 16, 69
Album-oriented rock (AOR) 73, 82, 90
Alice's Restaurant 95
All in the Family 37
"All Shook Up" 9
"All Those Years Ago" 206
"All You Need Is Cash" 168
"All You Need Is Love" 124, 163
"Almost Grown" 75
Almost Summer 97
"Along Comes Mary" 239
Altamont (festival) 36, 41, 137–139
AM radio 73
America in Search of Itself 232
American Bandstand 30, 31, 44, 107
American Graffiti 37, 92, 191; see also *More American Graffiti*
American Idol 20, 53, 108, 112
American Pop 99
"Anarchy in the UK" 99
Animal House 76
Armatrading, Joan 38, 188
Armed Forces 39, 190
Around the World in a Day 43, 216
"Arrested for Driving While Blind" 184
Art rock 19, 53, 190, 211; *see also* avant-garde
Ask Rufus 177
Assalam Aleikoum Africa 221
Atomic Cafe 41
Austin City Limits 54, 109
Avant-garde rock 78, 190

The B-52's 190, 210
Baby Boom 24, 197
Baby It's You 99
"Baby Let's Play House" 146
"Baby You're a Rich Man" 160
Backward masking 136
BAD 44
Badu Erykah 51, 56, 218
Baez, Joan 31, 32, 76, 157, 163, 181, 189, 191, 201, 208–209
"Ballad of the Green Berets" 35
Bane, Michael 145–147, 149, 183
The Bangles 42, 44, 212, 218
"Barstool Mountain" 184
"Be Bop A-Lula" 30
Beach Party 94
The Beastie Boys 44, 54, 202
Beat generation 59
"Beat It"
Beat Street 100
Beatnik 118, 151–152
Beatlemania (stage show) 167
The Beatles 6, 13, 16, 19, 20, 33–41, 45, 49, 52, 55, 71, 76, 88, 95–96, 99, 108–111, 113–114, 117, 124, 128, 130, 135, 138–140, 175, 180, 184, 189, 191, 201, 206, 210, 216, 220–221, 242; and the affirmation of the sixties 155–173; and the re-actualization of affirmation 126–129
The Beatles *see* The White Album
The Beatles at the Hollywood Bowl 191
Beatlesongs! 165
Beautiful Loser 190
Beck 49, 234–234
Before the Flood 192
Benatar, Pat 182
Berry, Chuck 8, 13, 19, 29, 31, 71, 75, 107, 118, 143, 147, 173, 185
"Bette Davis Eyes" 40
"Big Bright Green Pleasure Machine" 172

The Big Chill 42
"Big Train from Memphis" 43
Bigger Than Both of Us 191
Bikini Beach 94
"Billie Jean" 42, 79
Birth of the Beatles (TV film) 110
Black and Blue 190
The Black Crowes 50
"Black Is Black" 185
Black Music Magazine 108
Black power 34, 35, 78, 171
Black President (album) 222
Black Sabbath 76, 136, 189
The Blackboard Jungle 29, 93, 102
The Blasters 40, 42, 129
Blondie 39, 60, 135, 182, 189–190, 211, 216
Blood on the Tracks 192
Blow Up 95
"Blowin' in the Wind" 16, 33, 132
Blue Moves 192
Bob Dylan: An Intimate Biography 157
Bon Jovi 44, 45, 55, 214
"Boogie at Midnight" 25
"Boogie on Reggae Woman" 38, 187
"Boogie Oogie Oogie" 178
The Book of Rock Lists 71
Boone, Pat 14, 61, 69, 71, 135, 150
Born in the U.S.A. 42–43
Born to Laugh at Tornadoes 216
Born to Run 191
Bowie, David 39, 49–50, 60, 136, 180, 190, 215, 216
"The Boxer" 207
Boyz II Men 49
The Brady Bunch 114
The Breakfast Club 56, 100
Breakin' 100
"Brick House" 178
Bridge Over Troubled Water 36
Brooks, Garth 46

249

Brown, James 34, 45, 60, 171, 207, 215
Brown v. Board of Education 27
Buchanan, Pat 8, 223
"Burning Love" 191
The Bus Boys 40, 85, 215
Bush, George H.W. 46
Bush, George W., Jr. 52, 53
Bye-Bye Birdie 31, 94

"California" 238
"California Day" 238
"California Revisited" 238
"California Saga" 234
"Can't Buy Me Love" 33
"Can't Get You Out of My Head" 53, 213
Can't Stop the Music 97
Car Wash 38, 97
Carey, Mariah 48, 49, 54, 61
Caribou 192
"Carry Me Back to Old Morocco" 216
Carter, Jimmy 38, 39, 116, 174, 182
Cat music 84, 142, 143, 200
"Cat People" 216
Cavaliere, Felix 15
Centerfield 43
Changes in Latitudes Changes in Attitudes 185
Chase, Brad 175
Cher (Cherilyn Sarkisian) 96, 109, 111, 180, 218
"Cherry Pink and Apple Blossom White" 81
Chess Records 27, 84
"Chicken Shack Boogie" 25
"Children of the Eighties" 209
"The Chipmunk Song" 71
Cinco 186
Cirque du Soleil 127, 226, 228
Clark, Dick 30, 32, 61, 107
The Clash 40, 41, 60, 79, 119, 128, 188, 190, 200, 214, 216, 222
Claudine (film) 95
"Clean Cut Kid" 43
Clinton, George 176, 216
Clinton, William J. (Bill) 46, 52
"Coal Miner's Daughter" 16
The Coca Cola Kid 100
Coe, David Allan 184
Combat Rock 41
"Coming into Los Angeles" 76
Concert for Bangladesh 37
"The Continuing Story of Bungalow Bill" 160
Controversy 40, 45, 74
"Controversy" 77
Cop Rock 46, 115

CORE (Congress of Racial Equality) 155
Cott, Jonathan 165
Country and western (C&W) 16, 17, 27, 38, 59, 62, 88, 109, 143, 144, 183–185, 217
Country-punk 42, 60
Covering 28, 29, 77, 112, 143, 169, 213
"Cracklin' Rose" 76
"Crazy Man Crazy" 27
Crime of the Century 190
"Crying in the Chapel" 27
CSN (Crosby Stills and Nash [& often] Young) 36, 60, 192
The Cure 44
"The Curly Shuffle" 202

Daddy-O 94
Dance Fever 108
"Dance with Me Henry" 28
"Dancin' Fool" 179
"Dancing Queen" 178
"Dandelion" 173
Darkness on the Edge of Town 39
The Dave Matthews Band 57
"A Day in the Life" 160–161
"The Day John Kennedy Died" 156
Daylight Again 209
The Dead Kennedys 43, 201, 210, 214, 237, 238
"Deadman's Curve" 110
Dean, Buddy 107
The Decline of Western Civilization 41
Def Jam Records 44, 86
Desire 192
Dire Straits 39, 190, 210
"Dirty Laundry" 209
"Disco Duck" 17, 179
"Disco Inferno" 178
The Distance 209
The Dixie Chicks 55
"Do the Reggay" 187
"Do Ya Think I'm Disco" 179
"Do You Remember Rock and Roll Radio?" (Ramones) 63
"Do You Want to Dance?" 75
Dr. Buzzard's Original "Savannah" Band 38, 178
Dr. Dre 47, 49, 126, 204
"Dominique" 71
Don Kirshner's Rock Concert 109
"Donna" (Richie Valens) 185
"(Don't Fear) The Reaper" 189
Don't Knock the Rock (BBC TV concert) 139
Don't Knock the Rock (film) 30, 93, 94

"Don't Let the Stars Get in Your Eyes" 68
"Don't Worry About the Government" 190
Doo wop 16, 60
The Doors 35, 173, 215, 235
Double Fantasy 40, 205, 207
Dragon Fly 192
"Drinkin' Wine Spo-De-O-Dee" 25
"Dropkick Me, Jesus" 184
"Dust in the Wind" 189
"D'yer Mak'er" 187
Dylan, Bob (Robert Zimmerman) 6, 13, 16, 32, 34, 35, 37, 42, 43, 45, 46, 51, 55, 60, 76–77, 105, 113, 119, 127, 128, 132, 157, 161, 169, 172, 181, 184, 192, 201, 209, 215, 229, 232, 239

Earth 192
Earth, Wind & Fire 191
East of Eden 29
"Eastbound and Down" 185
Easter (album) 39, 181
Easy Rider 36, 95
"Ebony and Ivory" 207
Ecstasy (MDMA) 131, 138
The Ed Sullivan Show 24, 29, 33, 63, 108–109, 148–149, 156, 168–169, 211
Eddie and the Cruisers 99
"Eight Miles High" 76
Eisenhower, Dwight David 26, 30
Eisner, Bruce 172
El Camino Collage 121
"Eleanor Rigby" 16, 19
Eliade, Mircea 141, 149, 150–151, 166–169, 224
Elvis (film) 110
Eminem (Marshall Bruce Mathers III) 51–60, 78, 119, 203–204, 210
"Empty Garden" 209
End of the Century 40
"English Boys" 211–212
Epstein, Brian 35, 158, 166
ERA (Equal Rights Amendment) 37, 217, 218
The Ernie Kovacs Show 115
Ertegun, Ahmet 142–144
Eve (album) 136
"Everybody's Somebody's Fool" 71
Excitable Boy 39

FaceBook 56, 125, 168, 198
Fame (film) 99, 103
Fame (TV show) 115

Index

"Family Tradition" 185
Fandango 190
Feats Don't Fail Me Now 190
Feminism 33, 223–224
Ferraro, Geraldine 42
The Final Cut 42, 209
"Fingertips-Pt. II" 71
Five Summer Stories 95
"5–10–15, Hours" 26
Flashdance 99
Fleetwood Mac 191
Flippo, Chet 241
Flo Rida 56
"Fly Robin Fly" 178
Flying Shoes 185
Footloose 42, 99
Ford, Gerald 37, 117, 174, 192
461, Ocean Boulevard 190
Frampton Comes Alive 191
Franklin, H. Bruce 197
"Free Bird" 184
Free Education 222
Free Yourself Be Yourself 177
Freed, Alan 26, 30, 32, 34, 60, 63, 68–69, 72, 84, 110, 142, 211
Freedom at Point Zero 192
Friday Night Videos 108
Fridays 98, 115, 117
"Friend of the Devil" 76
"Front Line" 201
"Fuck California" 238
Fudd, Elmer 120
"Funky Stuff" 177

Gates of Eden: American Culture in the Sixties 6
A Generation in Motion 9
Generation X 197
"Gentle on My Mind" 185
George Mason University 1–2
"Get a Job" 16, 75
"Get It" 207
Ginsberg, Allen 28, 50, 163
The Girl Can't Help It (film) 30, 93–94
"The Girl Is Mine" 216
"Girls Just Want to Have Fun" 77
Girl's Town 94
Give the People What They Want 209
Glastonbury 53, 55
Global Village 64, 123–125, 130, 132
The Go-Gos 41, 60, 89, 182, 218
Go Johnny Go 94
"God" (song) 226
"God Save the Queen" 58, 99
"Good Lovin'" 27

"Good Rockin' Tonite" 25, 75
Good Times (film) 96
Goodman, Ellen 196, 205
"Goodnight Irene" 25
"Goodnight Saigon" 41, 201, 209–210
Gorbachev, Mikhail 46, 220
The Graduate 35, 95–96, 101
The Grateful Dead 35, 60, 76, 173, 192, 209, 214, 240
Gratitude 191
Greasers 151–152
The Great Rock and Roll Swindle 99
Green Day 55, 203, 210, 219
The Greening of America 6, 36
"Groovallegiance" 176
Guitar Hero (computer game) 227
Guns N' Roses 44, 46, 202, 216
Gutenberg Galaxy 63, 65, 123

Haley, Bill 26–27, 29, 46, 60, 94, 120, 143, 148, 157
"Happiness Is a Warm Gun" 160, 166
Happy Days 114, 191
A Hard Day's Night (film) 95–96 99–100, 113, 129
"A Hard Rain's A-Gonna Fall" 76
"Hard Times Are Over" 207
The Harder They Come (film) 95–96, 187
"Have Mercy Baby" 26
Having a Wild Weekend 96
"He Was a Friend of Mine" 156
Head (film) 96
"Heard It in a Love Song" 185
Heart 60, 182, 215
Heart Like a Wheel 190
"The Heart of Rock and Roll (Is Still Beating)" 42–43
"Heartbreak Hotel" 148, 157
Hearts and Bones 42
Heavy metal 35, 42–43, 45, 60, 127, 189, 201, 209, 211, 218–219
Heavy Metal (film) 99
Heavy Traffic 95
Hegel, Georg W. F. 6, 124, 130–131, 233–236
Hejira 191
Help! (film) 95, 113
"Helter Skelter" 160, 214
Hendrix (film) 111
Hendrix, Jimi 6, 35–36, 55, 60, 163, 173, 181, 214
"Her Majesty" 160
Heraclitus 77

"Here Comes the Turning of the Tide" 42
"Here Today" 41, 206–207
The Heroes of Rock and Roll (film) 110
"Heroin" 74
"He's a Rebel" 71, 213
High School Confidential 94
Hilburn, Robert 85–86, 168–169, 201, 216
Holland, Jools see *Later with Jools Holland*
Hollywood a Go Go 109
"Homosapien" 216
Honest Lullaby 191, 208
"The Honeydripper" 23
Honky Chateau 37
Honky Tonk 16
"Honky Tonk Women" 181
"Horizontal Bop" 17
Hot Rod Gang 94
Hotel California 136, 184, 191
"Hotel California" 188, 235–236
Hotter Than July 40
Houses of the Holy 187
"(How Much Is That) Doggie in the Window?" 68
How Musical Is Man? 9
How the Beatles Rocked the Kremlin 221, 228
Hullabaloo 63, 109
"Hurt" (song) 191
"The Hustle" 178
Hynde, Chrissie 182, 218

"I Am Woman" 181
"I Call Your Name" 169
I Can't Stand Still 209
"I Dig Rock and Roll Music" 75
"I Hear You Knocking" 69
"I Know What Boys Like" 218
"I Love L.A." 42
"I Love Music" 178
"I Love the Night Life" 178
"I Saw Her Standing There" 160
"I Shot the Sheriff" 38, 187
"I Should Have Known Better" 175
"I Think I'm Going to Kill Myself" 37
"I Wanna Be Your Lover" 178–179
I Wanna Hold Your Hand (film) 168
I Want You 191
"I Will Follow" 210
"I Will Follow Him" 71
The Idea of the Holy 137
The Idolmaker 154
"If I Can't Have You" 178

"I'll Take You There" 187
"(I'm a) Sweet Transvestite" 98
I'm Not There 102, 127, 129
Imagine 37
"Imagine" 7, 119, 123, 132
In Concert 109
"In My Room" 19
"In the Name of Love" (Thompson Twins) 216
In Through the Out Door 192
The Indigo Girls 60, 127–128, 133
Infidels 42
Innervisions 177
"Instant Armadillo Blues" 184
Invitation to Sociology 158
Irrational Man 21, 42, 66, 138
"Israelites" 187
It Seemed Like Nothing Happened 175
"It Takes a Lot to Laugh, It Takes a Train to Cry" 181
It's Only Rock and Roll 190
"I've Never Been to Me" 218

"Jack and Jill" 178
Jackson, Jesse 42
Jackson, Michael 41–42, 44–48, 54, 56, 79, 108, 207, 215–217
"Jailhouse Rock" 226
Jailhouse Rock (film) 30, 93
Jefferson, Thomas 5
Jennings, Waylon 183–185
Jett, Joan 60, 100, 182, 214, 218
Joanie Loves Chachi 114
"Johnny Angel" 71
"Johnny B. Goode" 8, 213
"Johnny Can't Read" 209
"Johnny Soul'd Out" 215–216
Johnson, Lyndon B. 33, 156–157, 182
Journey through the Secret Life of Plants 177
Judas Priest 46, 189, 209
Juju Music 222
Jump Up 209
"Jungle Boogie" 177
"Just Like a Woman" 181
"(Just Like) Starting Over" 207

"Kansas City" 71
"Keep It Comin' Love" 178
Kennedy, John Fitzgerald 31–33, 41, 51, 56, 155–156, 158, 163, 207
"Kick Out the Jams" 74, 214
Kid Rock 51, 238
Kierkegaard, Søren 9, 224, 230, 240
"Killing of Georgie" 190

King, Martin Luther, Jr. 28, 33, 35, 41
King, Rodney 46–47
King Creole (film) 94
"King's Call" 211
Kings of the Wild Frontier 40
The Kinsey Reports 24, 26
"KKK" 216
"Ko Ko Mo" 69
Koenigsberg, Richard 2
KROQ 54, 78
Kuhn, Thomas 233, 236–238, 240

L.A. (Light Album) 192
"La Bamba" 185
"L.A. Woman" 235
"Ladies Love Outlaws" 183
Lady Gaga 56, 60, 180, 224
Lahr, John 159–160, 167
"Land of a 1000 Dances" 185
Landau, Jon 241
Late for the Sky 190
"The Late Great Johnny Ace" 144, 207
Later with Jools Holland 109–110
Latham, Aaron 197
Laugh-In 35, 115–116
Laverne and Shirley 114
Lavigne, Avril 53, 61, 210
"Lawdy Miss Clawdy" 26, 68
"Lay Lady Lay" 181
"Le Freak" 178
Led Zeppelin
Lennon, John 7, 37, 40–41, 49, 60, 111, 119, 123, 132, 147, 151, 159, 162, 165, 168, 170, 191, 205–207, 209, 211, 215, 227
Let It Be (film) 165
Let Them Eat Jellybeans 201
"Let's Dance" 216
"Let's Go Get Stoned" 76
Lewis, Jerry Lee 16, 30–31, 60, 71, 94, 107, 139, 147, 153, 185, 211, 213
Life Is a Song Worth Singing 39
Like a Virgin 43
"Like a Virgin" 45, 108
"Lisbon Antiqua" 81
Little Stevie Wonder: The Twelve Year Old Genius 177
Live Aid (concerts) 43, 124, 137, 222
"Living for the City" 177
The Lloyd Thaxton Show 107
"Loco-Motion" 71
"Lola" 75
Lollapalooza 46, 54, 137, 139, 228
London Calling 40

"The Long and Winding Road" 169
"Long Gone" 16, 25
"Long Haired Country Boy" 184
Looking for Mr. Goodbar 97
Los Lobos 42, 186, 209, 212
Los Lonely Boys 186
"Louie Louie" 76, 214
"Love and Affection" 188
"Love Machine" 178
"Love Plus One" 216
"Love to Love You Baby" 178
The Love You Make 160
"Love's Theme" 178
Loving You 93
Low Budget 192
"Lucy in the Sky with Diamonds" 77
Lutheran Theological Seminary Gettysburg 120
Luxury Liner 185

"Macho Man" 178
Madonna 43, 45, 46, 50, 52, 55, 108, 126, 180, 218
"Maggie's Farm" 172, 229
Magic Christian 95
Magical Mystery Tour (album) 160
Mahogany 97
"Major Tom (Coming Home)" 219
The Making of a Counter Culture 6
Mana 186
Mandela, Nelson 45–47, 241
Marcus, Greil 145–146, 148–149, 160–161, 240
Marcuse, Herbert 17–21, 59, 133
"Margaritaville" 185
marijuana 76, 101, 116–117, 138, 152, 172, 224
Marley, Bob 38, 40, 51, 60, 135, 187–188
Maslow, Abraham 175–176, 178, 195
McCarthyism 25, 145
McCartney, Paul 36, 38, 40–41, 50, 51, 53, 60, 78, 111, 191, 206–207, 216, 220, 222, 226
McLuhan, Marshall 63–66, 69, 70, 72–74, 80–83, 86, 92, 102–106, 115–116, 118–119, 122–125, 130–133, 135
The Meaning and End of Religion 126, 230
Meet the Beatles (album) 88, 160
Mercury, Freddy 46–47, 124, 127
Metal: A Headbanger's Journey 127, 204, 211

Index

Metallica 46, 52, 56, 126, 128, 132, 204, 214
"Middle of the Night" 26
Midnight Special 109
Milk and Honey 205
Mill, John Stuart 224
Minimum Wage Rock and Roll 40, 216
Minogue, Kylie 53, 213
Misfits (album) 192
Misfits (group) 182, 200
M.I.U. Album 192
"Money Honey" 27, 69, 75
The Monkees 35, 45, 50, 60, 96, 111, 113–114, 165
Monty Python 168
"Moody Blue" 191
The Moody Blues 70, 202, 213
"Moody River" 71
More American Graffiti 103
"More More More" 178
"More Than a Woman" 178
Morgan, Dan 194
"Mother and Child Reunion" 187
"Mother-in-Law" 71
Mother Jones 196
Motown Records 86
MTV 46, 108, 110, 217
Muscle Beach Party 94
Music Magazine 108
"My Boy Lollipop" 187
"My Daddy Rocks Me with One Steady Roll" 142
"My Generation" 75
"My Hometown" 43
"My Little Town" 191
"My Way" 99, 191, 215, 230
MySpace 125, 198
Mystery Train (Book) 145, 240

Napster 51, 52, 126, 198
Nebraska 34, 41, 209
Nelson, Willie 183–185, 241
"New Day Woman" 181
New Left 19, 118, 155, 170–173, 183
New Sensations 42
Newcomb, Horace 116
Newman, Randy 38–39, 42, 60, 191, 201, 240
A Night on the Town 190
"99, Luftballoons" 219
"Nipple to the Bottle" 218
Nirvana 46–48, 202
Nixon, Richard M. 26, 28, 30–31, 35, 37–40, 95, 101, 116–117, 174, 225
No Doubt 53, 67, 70–71, 73, 75, 77, 217, 219
"No Guilt" 21, 218

"No More Doggin'" 26
No Nukes (concert) 39
"No Particular Place to Go" 19
"No Surrender" 43
"Numbers" 185
N.W.A. 45
Nylon Curtain 41, 209

Obama, Barack 8, 56, 193–194, 196, 198, 223, 241
O'Conner, Sinéad 46–47
Octave 192
Odds and Sods 192
Of Kennedys and Kings: Making Sense of the Sixties 6
"Oh My Papa" 68
"Oldie But Goodie" 109
On the Road 29, 152
One Nation Under a Groove 39, 176
"One of a Kind (Love Affair)" 37
One-Trick Pony 99
Osbourne, Ozzy 45–46, 136–137
Otis, Johnny 153
Otto, Rudolf 238
"Out Come the Freaks" 216
OutKast 53, 60, 202, 203, 212
The Outlaws: Revolution in Country Music see Bane, Michael

Palladia TV 110
Parallel Lines 39
Parker, (Colonel) Tom 35, 149
The Partridge Family 114
Past Present and Future 163
Payola hearings 12, 31–32, 70–73, 200
Pearl Jam 46, 60, 214
Performance (film) 95
Peter, Paul and Mary 32, 75, 191, 206, 208
Philosophical Fragments 224
Philosophy in a New Key 9
The Philosophy of History see Hegel
Physical Graffiti 192
"Piggies" 160
Pink (P!nk) 60, 127, 128, 133
Pink Floyd the Wall 39, 42, 60, 88, 118, 190, 195, 206, 209, 215
Planet Waves 192
Plato 232
Play It Cool 94
"Play That Funky Music (White Boy)" 178
"Please Please Me" 33
Poirier, Richard 161, 165

"Poison Ivy" 75, 213
"Pop Muzik" 178–179, 216
"The Pound Is Sinking" 207
"Poverty" (song) 201
Presence 192
Presley, Elvis 9, 13, 60, 157, 169, 189, 214, 241–242; and the negation of the fifties 142–154
Prince 39, 42–44, 47, 49, 51, 60, 74, 77, 79, 100, 110, 178, 216, 217
The Prince's Trust All-Star Rock Concert 49, 110
Private Dancer 43
"Promentalshitbackwashpsychosisenemasq (The Doo Doo Chasers)" 176
"Proud Mary" 239
Public Enemy 44, 45, 202, 214
Purple Rain 100
"The Pusher" 76

Quatro, Suzi 181
Queen 180, 189, 222

Race music 24, 25, 60, 68, 142
Radio On 99
Rage Against the Machine 52, 56, 132, 186, 202, 204, 214
"Rainy Day Women #12, & 35" 181
"Ramblin' Man" 184
The Ramones 38–40, 49, 63, 98, 118, 189, 211, 214, 215
"Rapper's Delight" 178–78, 203
"Rapture" 216
Rave Culture and Religion 131
Reactor 209
Reagan, Ronald 7–8, 40, 54, 98, 193, 201, 220, 233
Really Rosie 191
Rebel Without a Cause 29, 93
Reckless 43
"Red Car" 22
Red Headed Stranger 184
Red Hot Chili Peppers 46, 53, 215, 236
Red Octopus 192
R.E.M. 44, 210, 214, 219
Repo Man 103
"Respect" (Aretha Franklin) 171
"Respect" (Bus Boys) 216
"Respect" (Otis Redding) 171
Return of the Secaucus Seven 98
Reunion 191
"Revolution" (The Beatles) 20, 76, 160, 214
"Revolution" (Bob Marley) 135
Revolver 34, 54, 160
Rhino Records 91, 165
Rhythm of Resistance 221

Index

Right on Time 177
Rimes, Lee Ann 226
"Rip It Up" 94
"Rock and Roll Roll Nigger" 181
Rock Around the Bloc 221
Rock Around the Clock (film) 30, 93
"Rock Around the Clock" (song) 29, 81, 118, 143, 157
Rock Encyclopedia 29
"Rock Me All Night Long" 26
Rock 'n' Roll (album) 191
"Rock 'n' Roll Baby" 37
"Rock 'n' Roll Tonight" 109
Rock of the Westies 192
Rock on Film 96
The Rock Story (book) 82
"Rock the Boat" 178
"Rock the Casbah" 216
"Rock This Joint" 26
"Rock Your Baby" 38, 178
"Rocket 88" 26
The Rocky Horror Picture Show 98, 103, 189
"Roland the Headless Thompson Gunner" 201
Rolling Stone Magazine 78, 161, 165, 168, 173, 185, 206, 241
The Rolling Stones 16, 34, 35, 37, 42, 55, 60, 74, 76, 98, 136, 168, 173, 181, 189, 190, 192, 206, 214
"Ronnie Talk to Russia Before It's Too Late" 40
Roots 38
The Rose (film) 97
"Rose of Cimarron" 184
"Roses Are Red" 71
Ross, Diana 33, 153, 182, 191, 2047, 218
Rubber Soul 160
Run D.M.C. 44, 85
"Run for Your Life" 160
"Runaround Sue"
"Runaway" 71
The Runaways 127, 182, 218

The Sacred and the Profane 141
"Sail Away" 240
St. Elmo's Fire 100
"Sam Stone" 76
SANE 30
Santana, Carlos 51, 52, 60, 186
Sartre, Jean-Paul 175–176, 197
satellite radio 78, 126
Saturday Night Fever (film) 39, 97, 108, 178
Saturday Night Live 38, 47, 98, 115–117, 168, 192, 210, 225
"Save the Last Dance for Me" 71

"Say It Loud — I'm Black and I'm Proud" 34, 171
"Say Say Say" 78
Scatterlings of Africa 222
"School Days" 118
Schoolboys in Disgrace 192
"School's Out" 118
SCTV 116–117
Seaside Swingers 96
Seconds of Pleasure 40
Seeger, Pete 25–26, 109
Selena (Selena Quintanilla-Pérez) 48, 186
"Send in the Clowns" 191
"Sex" 77
The Sex Pistols 38, 58, 60, 99, 139, 190, 200
"Sgt. Pepper's Band" (song) 163
Sgt. Pepper's Lonely Hearts Club Band (album) 35, 161–162, 169
Sgt. Pepper's Lonely Hearts Club Band (film) 97
Shake Rattle and Rock 93, 111
Shake Rattle and Roll: An American Love Story 110
"Shake Your Boogie" 24
Shakedown Street 192
Shakur, Tupac 46, 48–49, 79, 128, 235, 241
"Sh-Boom" 12, 27, 68–69
"She Loves You" 33
"She Works Hard for the Money" 218
Sheik Yerbouti 179
Shindig 63, 109
"Short People" 240
Shout! (book) 160
Showtime at the Apollo 112
Simon, Paul 42, 99, 117, 168, 187, 191, 207
Simon and Garfunkel 12, 16, 19, 34, 36, 54, 123, 139, 172, 206–208
"Sincerely" 27
Single Man 192
"Sixty Minute Man" 7, 17, 26, 68
Skiffle 29, 158
Sleepwalker 192
The Slim Shady 51, 78, 203–204
"Slippin' into Darkness" 177
"Slow Screw Against the Wall" 177
Slow Train Coming 192
Smalls, Biggie (The Notorious B.I.G) 79, 241
Smith, Patti 39, 60, 117, 181
Smith, William Cantwell *see The Meaning and End of Religion*

Smokey and the Bandit 185
The Smothers Brothers Comedy Hour 35, 36, 109
SNCC 155
Snoop Dogg 203, 215, 241
Soap Opera 192
Solid Gold 108
Some Girls 192
"Song for the Dead" 201
Songs in the Key of Life 177
The Sonny and Cher Comedy Hour 96, 109, 111
Sontag, Susan 54, 135
"Soul Makossa" 37, 178
Soul Train 60, 107
Sound d'Afrique 221
"Sounds of Silence" 12, 16, 19
Soweto 221
The Spice Girls 49–50
"Spirit of the Boogie" 177
Spitfire 192
Spock, Benjamin 24, 50
Springsteen, Bruce 37, 39, 41–43, 53, 60, 122, 169, 191, 201, 209, 215
Square Pegs 115
"Stagger Lee" 71
"Stairway to Heaven" 136
A Star Is Born 97, 241
Star Struck 99
"Stars and Stripes of Corruption" 43
Stefani, Gwen 55
The Steve Allen Show 52, 54, 108
Stewart, Al 163
"Still in Saigon" 201
"Stir It Up" 37, 187
Stop and Smell the Roses 206
"Stop in the Name of Love" 209
The Story of Rock 239
Street Legal 192
"Streets of Baltimore" 185
The Structure of Scientific Revolutions 236
"Stupid Girl" 181
"Summer" 177
"Summer of '69" 43
Sun Records 143, 147
Sun Sessions (album) 38, 145, 191
"Sunday Bloody Sunday" 210
Surfin' USA 88
"Sweet Home Alabama" 184
Sweet Mother 222
"Sweet Survivor" 191, 208
"Sweet Virginia" 74
"Sympathy for the Devil" 76, 136

"Take Good Care of My Baby" 71

Index

"Take Me to the Mardi Gras" 187
"Take This Job and Shove It" 185
"Talk in 79" 211
Talk Show 89
Talking Heads 38, 39, 42, 60, 190
"Tangerine" 178
"Taxman" 160
Tea Baggers 57
Tea Party 2; *see also* Tea Baggers
Tejas 184
Terrapin Station 192
Thank God It's Friday 97
"Thank You Falettinme Be Mice Elf Again" 76
"That's All Right (Mama)" 144
"That's the Way (I Like It)" 178
Their Satanic Majesties Request 136
"Them and Us" 201
"Theme from a Summer Place" 71
There Goes Rhymin' Simon 187
Theremin 130
This Is Elvis 41
This Is Spinal Tap 100
Thriller 41, 79, 216
"Thriller" 108, 215
Tillich, Paul 139–141, 146, 148, 165–166, 224
Timberlake, Justin 53
Time Machine 220–221
Times Square 97
Tommy 97
The Tonight Show 54, 116
Top 40, radio 60, 62, 157
"T-R-O-U-B-L-E" 191
Trouble in Paradise 42
TSOP (The Sound of Philadelphia) 38, 178
Tug of War 41, 207
"Turn the Beat Around" 178
"Tutti Frutti" 14, 16
TV: The Most Popular Art see Newcomb, Horace
"Tweedle Dee" 27, 50, 69
"Twelve-Thirty (Young Girls Are Coming to the Canyon)" 238
"Twist and Shout" 33
"Twist Around the Clock" 94
Twitter and Twittering 124, 198
The Two of Us 38, 11, 226
Two Virgins 20

U-2 44, 46, 48, 55, 60
"Under My Thumb" 181, 214
Undercover 42
Understanding Media 63, 105

"Uneasy Rider" 184
"Up Against the Wall Red Neck Mother" 184
Uprising 40
Vacation 41
"Vaya Con Dios" 68
Veedon Fleece 190
"Ventura Highway" 238
"Venus" 31, 71
Victory 79
Vietnam 27, 28, 30–39, 41, 43, 95, 109, 133, 155, 171–172, 174, 178, 197, 201, 205, 239
"Visions" 177
Viva Zimbabwe! 221

"Waist Deep in the Big Muddy" 109
The Waitresses 21, 41, 60, 115, 218
"Walk on the Wild Side" 75
The Wall 39, 99, 118, 195, 215
"The Wall" (Higgins) 43
Walls and Bridges 191
"Wanderlust"
Was (Not Was) 216
"Wasn't Born to Follow" 172
Wasn't Tomorrow Wonderful 218
"Wasted on the Way" 41, 209
Waterloo 190
"Way Down" 191
"We Don't Need Another Hero" 43
"We Love You" 173
"We're Gonna Rock We're Gonna Roll" 24, 142
West, Kanye 55, 203, 217
"West Coast Blues" (Blind Blake) 15
Wexler, Jerry 142–143
"(What's So Funny 'Bout) Peace Love and Understanding" 20, 190
"Where Is the Love" 38
Where the Boys Are 94
"Whiskey Bent and Hell Bound" 185
"Whiskey River" 185
"Whispering/Cherchez La Femme" 178
White, Theodore H. 232, 241
The White Album (The Beatles) 20, 35, 76, 160, 216
White Boy Singin' the Blues 145
"The White Buffalo" 81
"White Rabbit" 239
The White Stripes 53, 60, 203, 212–213, 215
The Who 19, 35, 49, 75–76, 98, 192, 204, 206, 214, 222, 227

Who Are You 192
Who by Numbers 192
"Who Says a Funk Band Can't Play Rock?" 176
"Whole Lotta Shakin' Goin' On" 16, 139
"Why Can't We Be Friends?" 177, 187, 209
"Why Don't We Do It in the Road?" 160
Wild in the Country 94
The Wild One 27, 93
Williams, Hank 144, 183, 185, 209
"Willie Waylon and Me" 184–185
Winehouse, Amy 56, 203
Winner and Other Losers 184
Wired 191
"Witchy Woman" 76
"With God on Our Side" 76
The Wiz 97
WKRP in Cincinnati 53, 72, 114–115
"Women I've Never Had" 185
Wonder, Stevie 38, 40, 60, 71, 171, 177, 187, 201, 207, 217
"Won't Get Fooled Again" 19, 76
Woodstock (festival) 36–37, 39, 45, 51, 137–139; and the Mexican "Woodstock" 186
Woodstock (film) 92, 133
"Wooly Bully" 186
"Work with Me Annie" 28
"The World Is a Ghetto" 177
"World War II Blues" 163

X (the band) 42
Xanadu 97

"Yakety Yak" 75
Yancey, Jimmy 25
"The Yellow Rose of Texas" 81
Yellow Submarine 95, 162
Yesterday and Today 165
"YMCA" 178
"You Can Get It If You Really Want It" 37
"You Know My Name (Look Up the Number)" 165
"(You Never Can Tell) C'est La Vie" 185
"You Sexy Thing" 178
Young Gifted and Black 171
Your Mama Won't Like Me 181
YouTube 125, 129, 198

Zabriskie Point 95
Zappa, Frank 21, 47, 60, 179, 190
Zenyatta Mondatta 40

www.ingramcontent.com/pod-product-compliance
Lightning Source LLC
Chambersburg PA
CBHW060259240426
43661CB00060B/2832